William Sanders Oury

William Sanders Oury

A Tucson contemporary of Bill's in the 1880's
once asked: "Mr. Oury, why don't you write
a history of Arizona?" Bill's rejoinder:
"Because I am too damned busy *making* it."

History-Maker of the Southwest

CORNELIUS C. SMITH, JR.
pen and ink sketches by the author

THE UNIVERSITY OF ARIZONA PRESS
Tucson, Arizona

About the Author . . .

CORNELIUS COLE SMITH, JR., has harvested this
book from one of the branches of his own family
tree. He is the great grandson of the central character, William Sanders Oury. Born at Fort Huachuca, the author grew up on tales of the Army and
the West in frontier times. He now devotes all his
time to writing and painting, with his work on Western historical subjects appearing frequently in such
publications as *Frontier Times, Desert* magazine,
Arizona Highways, and *Montana, The Magazine of
Western History.*

As an artist, Cornelius Smith has had one-man
shows of his painting and sculpture in leading Western galleries. Several of his Arizona watercolors
became part of the U.S. State Department world-
wide touring exhibition of regional American art.

A graduate of the University of Southern California, the author earned his M.A. and Ph.D.
degrees at Claremont Graduate School. He was a
Marine colonel in World War II and was serving
as Marine Officer of the Day in the Navy Yard at
Pearl Harbor on December 7, 1941.

For My Father

Foreword

IT IS A RARE OCCASION when the author of a Southwestern frontier story happens to be eminently qualified as a professional historian while claiming direct kinship with the principals involved. Cornelius Cole Smith — historian, artist, collector, and great-grandson of William S. Oury — has been exposed to the nineteenth-century West and its development in a unique manner that prepares him remarkably well to write a definitive and entertaining history of his brave and adventurous forebear, William S. Oury. His father, Colonel Cornelius C. Smith, decorated with the Congressional Medal of Honor, had an active and varied career as a military officer throughout the American West. The grandfather of the present Cornelius — Gilbert Cole Smith — served as quartermaster for Fort Lowell in the 1860's.

I recall the warm summer afternoon in Riverside, California, in 1962 when I first had the pleasure of meeting Cornelius at his spacious home where his father had lived in retirement for many years. The living room of the old California mansion had resounded to the voices and stories of those men of action who subdued a wild and sparsely populated West. It was home first and secondly a treasure house of historical material and artifacts. As the author unfolded his concepts of the book it took little imagination to realize that here was one of the truly fascinating unwritten stories of the American West. The personalities to be revealed in the book were not padded with the materials of fiction; rather they were flesh and blood men imbued with a desire for personal freedom and a place somewhere in the West to call home where they might use their talents to create a stable and recognizable society in terms of Anglo-American ideals.

The story reads like all true pioneer adventures — involving action, a sense of desperation, a willingness to serve country, while adhering to a strict and unswerving code of frontier honor. This is not essentially a book that will delight the timid nor those who lament the violence of the nineteenth-century American West. Ruthless action, wars, and killings were involved in remolding a hostile terrain and an implacable, indigenous foe, the American Indian, into the West of today.

No apologies are extended for the actions of William S. Oury, the epitome of the man of action, or for his brother Granville M. Oury, who represented the learned man on the frontier as an attorney at law and the practical person who would defend his home, his country, and his honor. Imbued with the strain of fighting men and the clearness of vision that this was their land, William Sanders Oury and his brother moved westward. Born in Virginia, the mother of presidents, they sought their fortunes in the land of unlimited horizons and endless potential. It was also a land nearly devoid of organized civil government.

William S. Oury — already having been a courier from the Alamo and a Texas Ranger — left the hectic gold camps of California, and arrived by wagon with his wife and family in 1856 to become a leading citizen of the Arizona Territory. Here was a land marked by bold mountains, contrasting terrain — searing deserts, and refreshing alpine regions — bisected on the west by the mighty Colorado River, creating a natural boundary between California and the almost uninhabited area of a vast territory. Whatever law there was was ill-defined. Much of the territory was controlled by the ever-wary and unrelenting foe, the Apache.

William S. Oury played a bold and imaginative role as civil government took shape, and settlers, gold-seekers, speculators, farmers assembled in his adopted land. It was William S. Oury who in 1858 introduced into Arizona the first pedigreed, shorthorned cattle. He thus became a rancher and realized the potential of the grasslands then existing in southern Arizona.

In 1871, in the month of April, Oury was an instigator and participant in a singular campaign against the Apache Indians that resulted in a national scandal. The Camp Grant Affair, or, as some have termed it, massacre, shocked the east and caused a scandal throughout the nation. William Oury defended his participation in the affair in a straightforward manner, and a jury of his peers exonerated him from any wrongdoing. His conscience, never tarnished by his direct action in the Camp Grant Affair, remained singularly free of any guilt or remorse. His contemporaries on the scene may have been the best judges of this much-discussed and misunderstood sanguinary event.

From Indian fighter to sheriff of Pima County was a natural progression. As tax-collector, jurist, sheriff, Indian fighter, rancher, Oury cast his image and his resolute character on the face of southern Arizona. His brother Granville, cut from the same cloth, contributed to the refinement of civil government and a more stable social condition, which was the forerunner of the complex society now present in the modern state of Arizona.

The reader witnesses here the impact of the Anglo-Saxon on the West and the great Southwest. The Alamo, the independence of Texas, war with Mexico, the gold rush to California, campaigns against the Apaches, are coupled with the personal and amazing true adventures and escapades of William Sanders Oury. Truth, as usual greater than fiction, here reveals an exciting saga and the indomitable will of a western personality, adding new depth and understanding to the settlement of the nineteenth-century West.

JOHN D. GILCHRIESE
Field Historian
University of Arizona

*He brought me forth also into a place of
liberty; He brought me forth, even because
he had a favor unto me.* — Ps. 18:20.

Preface

ALL OF HIS LIFE WILLIAM SANDERS OURY searched for a place of liberty.
A free soul, a traveller, a looker upon far horizons, he sought new lands
for new freedom, and espoused the causes that spelled liberty for him.
He found freedom in Texas, and as one of the couriers of the Alamo he
helped to make that beleaguered fortress shine in the pages of history. He
marched with Houston from Gonzales to Buffalo Bayou, and sought
freedom in the swamps of San Jacinto. He rode with John Coffee Hays
as a Texas Ranger, and he marched through Mexico in chains with
William Fisher, Ewing Cameron, and "Bigfoot" Wallace. He drew a
white bean out of the jar at Hacienda Salado, and he rode with Zachary
Taylor at Palo Alto and Resaca de la Palma. He stormed the Bishop's
Palace in Monterrey with "Ad" Gillespie, and scouted Buena Vista with
Ben McCulloch.

When Texas began to fill up after the Mexican War he looked to the
goldfields of California, seeking his freedom and fortune in the icy
streams of the Sierra Nevada. When California got too tame he headed
for Arizona, to find freedom in the windswept vistas of that lonely land.
Here he fought Apaches, as he had fought Comanches in Texas. He

[xi]

raised stock in the sparse wastes out of Tucson, Sonoran longhorns at first, Illinois shorthorns later, ever harassed by marauding bands of Apaches eager to steal his beef.

Born in the green hills of Virginia, he could not remain in that pleasant and hospitable place. He had to follow the sun, move westward, seek liberty. "He had a favor unto me" — these words he could have said as he headed for Texas, a boy in his teens.

William Oury was my great-grandfather. I never knew him; he died twenty-six years before I was born. But I have heard about him all my life, listened to my father's tales of him, and browsed through the old papers and photographs since I was old enough to appreciate the life of that remarkable man.

In preparing this biography, I have augmented my private collection of papers with items obtained from the National Archives, The Texas State Archives, Arizona Pioneers Historical Society, and the State Historical Societies of Texas, Arizona, Pennsylvania, and Virginia. Copies of certain more important papers appear in the Appendices of this study.

Contemporary newspapers (1858–1887) have aided in shedding light on several of Oury's Arizona activities. A fair amount of material presented here has been taken from my father's reminiscences of William Oury, and from an unpublished manuscript prepared by my father on the Oury family. An early version of this work resides in the library of the Arizona Pioneers Historical Society in Tucson. My father had been revising this work for years, adding to it from the private papers mentioned, and was indeed working on it at the time of his death in 1936. This book, then, is a compilation of the spadework done by my father, and my own research, on a subject of great interest to both of us.

I have refrained, generally, from introducing conversation into this study. Oury's quoted remarks are listed as such, with the identifying source supplied. The few unverified remarks are secondhand, given to me by my father, who heard Oury make the statements. They may be considered as reasonably accurate, although many years have separated the hearing from the telling.

I had thought to write only of William Oury. In bringing pieces of his story into focus, I found it necessary to include much of the activity of his brother, Granville H. Oury. The lives of the two were inextricably woven; one man's story would be incomplete without a good portion of that of the other. Also, William Oury's son-in-law, Gilbert Cole Smith (my grandfather), has some recognition here, due chiefly to an interesting set of letters written by him while a member of Carleton's California Column in 1862–63. Still, William Oury is far and away the most important subject treated in these pages.

I have been as objective as possible in writing of William Oury, relating the shabbier aspects of his part in the Camp Grant Massacre, for instance, along with the heroic deeds accomplished as a soldier and Texas Ranger. These pages will please some and annoy others, but so will any definitive study of the life of a controversial figure. I can only hope that the work offered here may add something worthwhile to the literature of the Southwest, and bring to light an estimable life long neglected.

Acknowledgments

FIRST OF ALL, I must express thanks to my father, Colonel Cornelius C. Smith, U. S. Army. Prior to his death in 1936, he had done considerable research on the Oury family in general, and on William Sanders Oury in particular. It is largely from his unfinished manuscript, collected notes and papers and old photographs that I have based this biography of William S. Oury. The collection of papers while voluminous, was incomplete; I have filled the gaps with independent research in libraries and historical societies throughout the land.

I am especially indebted to the Daughters of the Republic of Texas and the Alamo Library, wherein I have gathered important information on the Alamo and its defenders, including some excellent photographs unavailable elsewhere. Mrs. Jacqueline R. Espy, curator of the Alamo, has been most helpful in assisting my research there, and Miss Catherine McDowell, assistant librarian and archivist of the Alamo Library has been of inestimable service to me in tracing down obscure dates, and aiding in the reproduction of exhibit material.

I am indebted to Pat Wagner, editor of *Frontier Times* magazine in Austin, Texas, for letting me use some of my grandfather's letters which had formed the basis of an article ("What a Life! U. S. Army, 1863") I did for *Frontier Times* in 1959.

Much of the basic research for this study was done in the Arizona Pioneers' Historical Society, Tucson, Arizona. A former director, Mrs. Yndia Smalley Moore, was of great service to me over a long period of time, making the society's facilities available to me whenever I have been in Tucson. Our correspondence over the past several years has been frequent. She has been of particular help in lining up old Arizona newspapers of the period 1858–1887.

Mrs. Virginia Taylor and Mrs. B. Brandt, archivist and assistant archivist respectively of the Texas State Library in Austin, have been most helpful in finding and reproducing William Oury's early military papers. Of aid to me in this matter also has been Mr. James M. Day, archivist for the state of Texas in Austin. Miss Winnie Allen, archivist at the Barker Texas History Center in Austin has been of service in this area as well. I must mention two more people in Texas who have helped in obtaining material; Mr. Richard C. Santos, Deputy Clerk of Bexar County who provided me with several records of William Oury's land transactions in San Antonio just after the Mexican War, and Mr. James C. Kenny, assistant City Clerk in San Antonio, who helped in tracing some of Oury's public service activities in the same period.

Mrs. Barbara Philpott, assistant archivist for the Division of Public Records, Pennsylvania Historical and Museum Commission, Harrisburg, has been very generous in obtaining obscure information on the doings of Wendel Oury in the Revolutionary War period. Mr. William H. Work, Chief, Division of Public Records, the Pennsylvania Historical and Museum Commission has reproduced early Oury commissions for me upon request.

Mr. James E. Crockett, Clerk of the Circuit Court in Wytheville, Virginia, has come upon early land transactions of the Oury clan in Virginia, reproduced them and sent them on to me. His assistant, Miss Carlotta A. Wilkerson has been helpful in this matter too.

I am very grateful for the help given me by Mrs. Fred Davis, secretary of the Washington County, Virginia, Historical Society in Abingdon. This generous lady not only opened up the archives of the Society for my research, but gave me a conducted tour throughout the entire Abingdon-Wytheville area, pointing out numerous places of interest pertinent to the Oury clan.

Mr. Dallas Irvine, chief archivist of the War Records Division, The National Archives, has found early records of Oury's military service, as has Colonel Richard Snyder, the deputy Adjutant General for the Commonwealth of Pennsylvania in Annville.

Mr. Jessie S. McCormick, Recorder of Deeds for Westmoreland County, Pennsylvania, has found evidence of land transactions by Wendel and George Oury in and around Greensburg. Mr. John Melville Jennings, Director of the Virginia Historical Society in Richmond has been helpful in genealogical matters concerning the Oury clan, as has Estelle Marks, State Registrar in the Department of Health in Richmond.

Reverend Stephen X. Winters, S. J., Administrative Assistant to the President, Georgetown University, Washington, D. C., has corresponded with me on the issue of William Oury's matriculation at that college in the early 1800s. Mr. E. E. Nichols, Managing Editor of the *Sacramento Union* has helped in providing background information on Sacramento in the gold rush period.

Miss Elizabeth F. Dunlap of St. Louis, dealer in rare books, and Mr. Marshall Jackson of Ovalo, Texas, have been especially helpful in tracing down existing copies of books long out of print. To Miss Dunlap especially do I owe a real debt of thanks.

Mr. Oury Jackson, a cousin now residing in Durango, Mexico, has helped in establishing dates and anecdotes of William Oury's stay in that city just after the Mexican War. His sister, Mina, has been especially helpful with personal anecdotes of her grandmother, Mina Sanders Oury, whose diary has been partially reproduced in these pages.

Father Juan Cisneros, curate of San Juan Bautista de Analco church in Durango permitted me to look at old mission records. Nothing definitive came of the search, but Father Cisneros did provide me with an excellent historical background of the city of Durango. Along the same lines, the author José Gallego (resident of Durango) was of service as well.

I must give thanks also to several libraries not already mentioned, and to the staff members of these institutions. Among these are: the National Archives and the Congressional Library in Washington; the California State Library, Sacramento; the Huntington Library, San Marino, California; the University of Southern California and UCLA Libraries in Los Angeles; the University of California at Riverside (UCR) Library; the Honnold Library, Pomona College, Pomona, California, and the Riverside, California, Public Library.

I am indebted to Harper and Row, publisher, for permission to use several brief quotes from Walter Lord's *A Time to Stand.* Also, I thank the McGraw-Hill Book Company for permission to quote from Lon Tinkle's *The Alamo: Thirteen Days to Glory;* and E. P. Dutton and Company for quotes from *Colonel Jack Hays, Texas Frontier Leader and California Builder,* by James Kimmins Greer. My thanks also go to the Bobbs-Merrill Company for permission to quote from *The Raven* by Marquis James; and to John Myers Myers for permission to quote from his book, *The Alamo.*

I owe much to my wife, Grace, for typing the first draft of this study, and to Mrs. E. M. Thrower for putting it in its final form. Thanks go to Staff Sergeant Rene Vega, U. S. Air Force, for making photocopies of the original documents forming the Appendix, and for making reduced (and enlarged) copies of original photographs. To everyone mentioned above, I owe a real debt of gratitude; without the help given to me by these people, I could not have written this book. My final appreciation then is voiced to the University of Arizona Press for its confidence, cooperation, and skill in projecting the written book into published form.

CORNELIUS COLE SMITH, JR.

Contents

Illustrations

Documents and Facsimiles

William Sanders Oury

CHAPTER 1

Legacy for a Patriot

IT WAS NIGHT ON THE WALLS OF THE OLD MISSION. From his place on the roof of the artillery barracks by the north wall, a lad of nineteen looked out across the clumps of sagebrush to the Mexican campfires half a mile away. His right hand grasped the stock of a Tennessee long rifle, and the slim barrel lay cradled in the other arm. Hatless, wearing a buckskin jacket and grease-spattered jeans, he stood motionless, looking out at the fires. The date was February 29, 1836, and the place was the Alamo. The boy had a date with history.

He had been in the grim bastion for a week, and although things looked hopeless he and his friends hung on. Behind him, at the far end of the enclosure, Jim Bowie lay sick and dying on a pallet. Hard by Jim's room and connecting it with the baptistry was the "weak spot," a palisade of logs defended by Davy Crockett and his sixteen boys from Tennessee. About midway down the west wall Colonel Travis sat in his little office wondering who to send out next for help. He had already sent eleven: Maverick, Sutherland, Smith, Dimmitt, Lewis, Johnson, Highsmith, Baylor, Bonham, Seguín and Cruz y Arocha, and no help had come. But "hope springs eternal. . . ." The last two to go had been Captain Juan

Seguín and his aide, Antonio Cruz y Arocha. The two had ridden hard for Gonzales, seventy miles away, and then on to the provisional government to ask for relief. Now the boy, William Sanders Oury, was about to ride for Gonzales to look for General Sam Houston.

He would be one of the few men to leave the place alive. Travis would send out another messenger (the last) three days later, and Bonham would return from Goliad with the bitter news than Fannin would not come with his garrison. But the others, save for a few women, two negro slaves, and several children would soon be dead. In another seventy-two hours the bodies of his companions would be tossed rudely onto a pile and burned. He would find General Houston, but it would be too late. The eagle and snake banner would already be flapping over the ruins. He would go with Houston to San Jacinto and watch the "Twin Sisters" cut down the Mexican skirmishers like wheatstalks. He would ride with Jack Coffee Hays at Plum Creek and Bandera Pass, and walk among the Comanche dead. He would draw a white bean out of the fateful jar at Hacienda Salado, and he would walk through northern Mexico in chains. He would ride with Zachary Taylor at Monterrey, and scout Buena Vista with Ben McCulloch and his fearsome band of irregulars. He would pan gold in the streams of California's Sierra Nevadas, and war with Apaches in the draws and canyons of southern Arizona. He would die on a ranch a few miles from Tucson over half a century later. But these things were in the future. Right now, a hard-looking Texan called up to him: "Hi, Bill, Colonel Travis wants to see you." Oury took a last look at the Mexican campfires winking in the distance, and climbed down the ladder.

He had just been chosen as a courier of the Alamo. Nothing he had done, or would do, would match this special moment in time, or be as filled with such portent of glory. With a light step he followed the messenger to Colonel Travis' quarters.

That was the way it was on that particular night in 1836, and we shall pick it up again a little later on. Let us go back in time now for a brief inspection of Bill Oury's people and his land.

Origins of the Clan

Williams's great-grandfather and the fountainhead of the Oury clan in America was Wendel Oury. There is some doubt as to his place of origin, some sources listing it simply as Germany, others as the Highlands of Scotland. A rather convincing case can be made for either claim. The Pennsylvania Archives would seem to indicate that Wendel Oury came from Germany. He is listed variously therein as Wendel, Windel, and

Vendel.[1] His great-granddaughter Senah Mathews (sister of William Oury) speaks of Wendel's "German descent" in a letter to a relative, going on to relate that he settled first in Pennsylvania, and some years later moved his family to Wythe County, Virginia.[2] Other members of the family trace Wendel's birthplace to Scotland. John M. Oury of the third generation (born in 1814) says: "My grandfather emigrated from Scotland, settled first in Pennsylvania, then in Abingdon, Virginia."[3] John speaks also of a noble Scottish family named Orry. This clan was prominent in the time of King James I (formerly James VI of Scotland). Dissatisfied with the change of titles and other aspects of James' reign, some of the Orry clan quit the country for France in 1604. In 1928, Colonel William O. Smith, grandson of William Sanders Oury, located seventeen separate families bearing the name Orry or Oury in Paris alone. Not as venturesome as their forebears, these people had settled for a variety of sedentary pursuits as furniture-makers, architects, green-grocers, and even a confectioner.[4]

The German claim may be partly substantiated by the fact that Wendel married Catherine Peterpenner in Pennsylvania, and by his close association with a community of friends and neighbors almost all bearing German names. Such "proof" must be inconclusive; it is mentioned solely as a factor lending some credence to the claim of German ancestry for the Oury family.[5] German or Scottish, the family took roots in the colony of Pennsylvania and made a home in the wilderness of the Western frontier. Wendel and Catherine had eight children: George, Thomas, John, Christopher, William, Elizabeth, Rebecca, and Margaret. The eldest, George, accompanied his father as a member of the Eighth Pennsylvania Militia to the battlefields of the Revolutionary War. A mere lad, he served as drummer boy for his father's company of volunteers.[6]

Life was perilous on the Oury farm. The Indians were a constant menace, and the young boys ploughing near the edge of the forest were ever mindful of ambush from the shadows. During the French and Indian War, Britain had formed alliances with members of the Six Nations Tribes, employing them as allies against the French or as paid neutrals to stay out of the fighting altogether. The establishment of peace in 1763 made occasion for the resumption of pillage by the tribes, and frontier settlers were constantly in danger of their lives. The Indian raids were terrifying affairs. Parties rarely exceeded forty men in number, and most of them were considerably smaller. Groups of six or seven were the rule, and were greatly feared because of their ability to strike quickly and retire. Clad in skins and hideously painted, the savages would descend upon a lone farmhouse, shrieking in such way as to make one's blood turn to ice. A whole family might be slain in a matter of moments, and the raiders gone to boast before the council fires of their brave deeds, wet scalps swinging from their belts. It was under such conditions that Wendel and his brood lived, in the years preceding the Revolution. Evidence of this is seen in the following petition, written by him and addressed to Governor John Penn in 1774.[7] The paper shows Wendel Oury to be a man of some education and feeling.

> *To the Honorable John Penn, Esquire, Governor and Commander-in-Chief in and over the Province of Pennsylvania and counties of New Castle, Kent, and Sussex upon Delaware. The petition of the inhabitants of West-moreland County humbly sheweth:*
>
> *That there is a great reason to fear that this part of the County will soon be involved in an Indian War; that the consequences will most probably be striking, as the country is in a defenseless state, without places of strength, stock of ammunition, or necessary stores.*
>
> *That the abandoning of the country must be attended with total ruin to great numbers who are now in an easy situation, but almost distracted with the apprehension of seeing their helpless infants fall sacrifice to savage cruelty. This will most certainly be the event unless they meet with some protection.*
>
> *In these circumstances, next to the Almighty, they look to you, your honor, and hope you will take their case into consideration, and afford them such relief as you shall seem meet. Your petitioners as in duty bound shall ever pray.*
>
> *Wendel Oury*

The paper must have had some effect, as the language of the next Oury petition shows that troops were sent to Westmoreland County. Unfortunately, the stint there was brief, and the troops were soon en route to the garrison at Kittanning.[8]

> *. . . your petitioners, in consequence of the first alarm did assemble at Hanna's Town, where at their own expense they erected a small fortification as shelter to their families . . . voluntarily taking up arms for the general defense of this part of the country until such time as your honor and the assembly were pleased to approve our proceedings. Your petitioners thought themselves happy and secure when the assembly so considerately ordered troops . . . for our general protection. We are now rendered uneasy by the removal of these troops upon which our dependence rests. . . . Left thus exposed . . . we conceive ourselves to be in great danger, and it is the general opinion that removing the troops to so distant and uninhabited a spot as Kittanning cannot answer the good purpose for which they were intended. . . . We must humbly request, therefore, that your Honor would be pleased to consider the alarming situation, and order such assistance as our situation requires.*
>
> *Wendel Oury*

This first petition was endorsed at Fort Allen, Hempfield Township, "between Wendel Oury's farm and Christopher Trubee's."[9] As shown above, the governor and his council sent troops, but the raids continued.

Fortunately, none of Oury's family were molested at that time, and possibly as a result of Wendel's petition, and others like it, the Continental Congress established three departments for Indian Affairs, each under the direction of an agent and three commissioners selected by the Congress.[10]

At first, Wendel's farm was in danger from marauding tribes wandering the forests and acting independently. When the British began to use the tribes as an extension of their own war arm, the American Congress, in retaliation, turned some of the Indians against the British. One way or another havoc and bloodshed were the order of the day.

In the Militia

Wendel Oury was commissioned a captain in the Eighth Pennsylvania Militia on 9 August, 1776,[11] and resigned October 16, 1777. His battalion commander was Col. Eneas Mackay; the regiment was commanded by Col. Daniel Brodhead.[12] The regiment was authorized by a resolution of Congress, 15 July, 1776, to defend the Western frontier, particularly the posts at Presque Isle, Le Boeuff, and Kittanning. By a ruling of Congress on July 20, county committees raising companies were to name the company officers. Thus Wendel was named by his county, Westmoreland, which contributed several companies to the regiment, as did neighboring Bedford.[13] David McClure was appointed chaplain, and Ephram Douglas quartermaster of the regiment.

On November 23, 1776, Congress directed the "Board of War" to move the regiment with all possible expedition to Brunswick, New Jersey, to join General Washington, "wherever he may be." [14]

The Pennsylvania Militia has frequently been confused with the Pennsylvania Military Association, which was recognized by the Provincial Assembly on June 30, 1775.[15] The Militia was not formed until almost two years yater, March 17, 1777.[16] Pennsylvania as a Quaker Colony at first had no miltary groupings of any sort. In 1775, as tension mounted with the British, there arose volunteer companies to form the Military Association, which was a civilian reserve subject to call in emergencies. Organization was by geographic district, so that men in a given company or battalion were likely to be acquainted with one another. Ages in the Association ranged from sixteen to sixty years. During the summer campaign of 1776, thousands of Pennsylvania Associators saw active service in New Jersey.[17]

As the months passed, men refusing to volunteer were dubbed "Non-Associators," and the stigma led many half-hearted patriots (both Whig and Tory) to enroll in the Association, thus watering down its elan and effectiveness, and bring about its collapse in the winter of 1776–77, and its subsequent replacement with a militia system.[18]

Wendel missed out on the New Jersey summer campaign, but his outfit was sent to Brunswick, New Jersey, November 23, to join Washington. It is apparent that he started out as an Associator although he probably transferred to the militia some time between March and October, 1777.

He would have been available to Washington for Trenton (December 26), Princeton (June 3, 1777), Oriskany (August 6), Bennington (August 16), Brandywine (September 11), Chad's Ford (September 11), Paoli (September 19–20), Germantown (October 4), and perhaps even Saratoga (October 7–17).[19]

At any rate, Wendel had been in active service for seven-and-a-half months before the militia was formed, and would be in the ranks for an almost equal period thereafter. Wherever he might have been in March of 1777, perhaps at Amboy (Punk Hill), or elsewhere in New Jersey, he was very likely transferred from the rolls of one outfit to another.

At the time of his separation from the Eighth Pennsylvania, Wendel Oury held a consignment of arms retained by his company, the lot to be delivered to the Council of Safety, and "the amount of their value rendered accountable." The arms were not listed by type or item, but those he kept for the company's further use were valued by him at £87, 15 shillings (those to be "delivered up" £43, 10 shillings).[20] Other companies surveying accountable property at the time list such fascinating items as: "blunderbushes," match rope, grape shot, flints ("very ordinary"), and "grannades."

Westward to Virginia

Some time later (about 1785), Wendel put his family and belongings in a couple of wagons and headed for southwestern Virginia. His route of travel may have been along the western slopes of the Appalachian chain, or perhaps along the Monongahela and Elk rivers to Charleston, and down to Kanawha, or he may have travelled down the Shenandoah Valley. Whatever the route, the trip must have been uncomfortable, even hazardous. The emigrant family seems to have arrived in the vicinity of Wytheville, Virginia, sometime in the summer of 1785.

Wendel Oury disappeared a year or so after establishing his family in Virginia. According to family legend, he had occasion to travel to Kentucky on business. He never returned or was heard from again, and was probably killed by Indians in the dark forests of the frontier. Whatever his fate, he left a heritage of vigor, determination, courage, and imagination, qualities which appear again and again in his sons and grandsons, and other members of a long line of bold men who fought their country's battles and pushed on to new and challenging places.

Of Wendel's life prior to 1774, the *Pennsylvania Archives* show that he served the British Crown during the French and Indian War. One entry lists him as "sick at Lancaster" on October 3, 1758.[21] Another shows him "present at Augusta" with Colonel Burd on December 24, 1760.[22] A latter-day relation (Eunice Oury of Kentucky) stated in 1907 that Wendel left a fortune to his family, and that the city of Greensburg, Pennsylvania, was built on his land. He did live there, or near there; the deed books of Hempfield Township, Westmoreland County, show that he owned numerous parcels of land in and around Greensburg,[23] but the fortune has not been substantiated.

George Oury was Wendel's oldest son and companion in arms. Some ten years after the Revolution he was apparently associated for a time with the Westmoreland County Rangers, as attested by the following:

We, the undersigned, do certify that we have received the several sums annexed to our names, under Captain Samuel Bell, Westmoreland County Rangers, for a party ordered on duty by Charles Campbell, Brigade Inspector of said company, in case of emergency, in the year 1793.[24]

Private George Oury is listed as having received a dollar. This incident took place eight years after Wendel moved his family to Virginia, so George may have stayed on in Pennsylvania in 1785, or gone to Virginia with his parents, and returned to Westmoreland County later. He was married twice: first to Elizabeth Adams, a lady of Scottish descent who claimed kinship to William Wallace,[25] and later to Nancy Sanders. Elizabeth bore him two sons: Augustus, father of Bill Oury, and Marius. Nancy bore eight children: Catherine, Elizabeth, Senah, Nancy, Malvina, Robert, Wendel, and John.

History gives passing glimpses of still other members of the Oury clan. Jacob Oury is listed as an ensign in the 133rd Pennsylvania Militia Company on July 22, 1813.[26] A relative, Francis Oury, was a private in the same company. Peter and Francis Oury are listed in the *Pennsylvania Archives* as owing taxes in Bedford County, Pennsylvania, in 1773, one Pound each.[27] Christopher Oury is shown as owning 150 acres, two horses, and two oxen.[28] Adam Oury has a similar entry,[29] and is listed as a pensioner of Crawford County in 1834. With these random bits of information the Pennsylvania phase of the Oury tale ends. The thread picks up again in the green and sunny hills of Virginia.

AUGUSTUS, father of William Sanders Oury, was an active member of his Virginia community. In 1820 he was postmaster at Abingdon, in 1830 on the Board of Trustees, and in 1834, "became a councilman along with nine other Abingdon men." He was born about 1786, the son of George and Elizabeth Oury.

CHAPTER 2

The Green Years

COLONIALS HAD BEEN DENIED ACCESS to western territories during the Revolutionary War. Now it was over, and Wendel Oury, who had helped to win it, in 1785 brought his family into a green valley about one hundred miles east of the Cumberland Gap. He could scarcely have made a happier choice than Abingdon, Virginia, then and now a fertile and lovely countryside located within walking distance of North Carolina and Tennessee. In pulling up stakes in Pennsylvania and heading west, Wendel had a head start on the great trek beyond the Appalachians which was not to begin for another twenty-six years. Between 1811 and 1817, from Pennsylvania alone, several thousand families headed for the Gap with all their earthly goods.

Still, Wendel was by no means among the first to move into the area. Colonel John Buchanan and Dr. Thomas Walker had pioneered the region as early as 1745. Walker's diaries are dramatic literary highlights on early American pioneering in wild country.

By 1760, Daniel Boone had come to Virginia enroute to Kentucky, and had given Abingdon its first name — "Wolf Hills" — after he and his companion had fought off a wolf pack that destroyed several of

Boone's dogs.[1] The name stuck until 1778 when the town built there was incorporated and named Abingdon, after the home parish of Martha Washington. It was the first incorporated town west of the Allegheny Mountains, and Wendel Oury built his first log cabin within one hundred yards of the wolf lair,[2] near the spring where Boone had camped.

This same spring was the location of the first settlement, in 1768. Eight years later, Captain Joseph Black built a stockade with palisades of sturdy oak, large enough to protect about 600 people from the Cherokees who were at least a match for the tribes the settlers had left behind.

A Town in the Woods

Abingdon was a primitive place when the Ourys arrived in 1785. All of the streets were in the woods, as there had been no general clearing of land for the erection of cabins.[3] There were no sidewalks, and the thoroughfares were simply deep ruts in the mud which was continually churned into a morass by the wheels of ox-drawn wagons. The first courthouse had been built in 1778, a twenty-foot square log cabin, followed the next year by a tavern across the way, from which more than a few late revelers were doubtless marched protesting back to the courthouse.[4] The latter structure was replaced in 1800, by a brick building at Main and Court streets, on the site that had earlier included the stocks, pillories, and whipping post of a justice that was primitive and immediate, but seldom kind.

The residents of Abingdon, although mostly church-going Presbyterians, could still raise a thirst, and the town had its share of such establishments. Besides the one across from the courthouse,[5] there was one near the stocks, and several in other sections of town, all typical taverns of early America. Picture the coach pulled up before the tavern door, the inn-sign slashed by rain and swinging in the wind. Inside, travelers and townfolk smoke long-stemmed clay pipes and hold great tankards of ale. In the fireplace the logs burn brightly, and the men talk of Kings' Mountain, just a few miles away, and of the good men who died there, or of the raid on Black's Fort.

In October, 1778, the trustees of Abingdon met at Christopher Acklin's tavern[6] and appointed Robert Preston to survey a township and lay out lots which Acklin was to sell to settlers. At the same time, Main and Water streets were laid off, with four cross-streets: Tanner, Court, Brewer, and Slaughter. It is not known just when Wendel purchased one of these lots, or precisely which one he bought from Acklin.[7] Although the fee, record, and chancery books of Washington County show many entries for George and Augustus Oury, they show none in the matter of property purchase for Wendel.[8]

In 1790, the population of Washington County was 5,625.[9] By 1810, the county had doubled its population to some 12,560.[10] The 1830 census shows a population of 15,614.[11] In 1785, the Oury family settled down, entered into community life, and began sending the children to school, except for George, now twenty-two. Within a year he was off for Pennsylvania to serve with Captain Bell and the Westmoreland County Rangers. Thomas, John, and Christopher attended a log cabin school taught by William Webb until he moved away in 1786.

There was a only a brief break in classes. Later in the same year an Irishman, Turner Lane, began to teach in Abingdon, and in 1788, the community built a school for him,[12] which was attended by both the younger and older children.

Years of Growth and Change

Augustus, father of William Sanders Oury, was born to George and his first wife, Elizabeth Adams Oury, about 1786. The latter years of that century and the first decades of the 1800's were times of growth, change, and turbulence for the Ourys, Abingdon, and the new Republic.

When Bill was just past twelve, he entered the Abingdon Male Academy and finished his studies there in 1832.[13] It has been reported over the years that he later attended Georgetown University,[14] but correspondence with that institution and with Georgetown College in Kentucky reveals no such records,[15] so his sole claim to an alma mater may have been the Abingdon Male Academy.

By 1806 the Ourys and their fellow townsmen were reading Abingdon's first newspaper, *The Holston Intelligencer and Abingdon Advertier*[16] which in the next two decades was the first newspaper to concern itself with such matters as the Tariff of Abominations and the brand-new Monroe Doctrine.

There were local problems as well. Between 1808 and 1812 the Abingdon Board of Trustees passed ordinances governing community life in such matters as the erection of outhouses (Sixth Act), the control of houses of "ill-fame" (Thirteenth Act), the "running around" of female dogs (Fourteenth Act), and the freedom of hogs on Abingdon's streets (a bylaw).

The War of 1812 seems to have had no profound effect upon the people of Abingdon. They were patriotic enough, many of the men proudly recalling service in state militias or the Continental Army against the British. It was simply that this war was primarily a naval affair, and the land battles were far away, in places like Canada and New Orleans. Still, some of the young men must have marched off, incensed at the burning of

Washington and tired of listening to the vets boast about Saratoga, and Yorktown, and King's Mountain. For the most part, though, there was plenty of work in the pioneer community to keep hands busy; men of Abingdon had no need to take up arms against a distant foe.

There are no records to indicate what part, if any, the Virginia Ourys played in this war. Kinsmen in Pennsylvania, Jacob and Francis Oury, served with the 133rd Pennsylvania Militia Company. Bill's grandfather George Oury is referred to as "Major" Oury in old family letters. As he was a drummer-boy in the 8th Pennsylvania Militia in 1776, he scarcely would have attained the rank of Major in that war. If the title is valid, he must have gained his majority in the War of 1812, and as a soldier from Abingdon.

By 1820, thirty-four year old Augustus was busy in civic affairs. On August 28, 1820, he was appointed postmaster in Abingdon.[17] By 1830 he was a member of the Board of Trustees,[18] and in 1834, Augustus Oury was elected a councilman along with nine other Abingdon men.[19] Names of Oury family members are mentioned numerous other times in the Washington County records.[20]

A Pleasing Community

By 1833, Abingdon had more than 250 dwellings and nine whole-sale houses.[21] Many of the homes were colonial brick structures with the large white Grecian columns peculiar to Southern architecture. The mansion of General Preston was then as now the showplace of the region, a genuine ante-bellum house with great ballrooms, sparkling crystal chandeliers, and French antique furniture.[22] Many of the homes of other leading Abingdon citizens are still standing: the William King house, the James White house, the Andrew Russell house, "Montcalm" (Governor David Campbell), "Panicello" (Judge Peter Johnson), and others.

These people — all known to the parents of William Sanders Oury — have gone to rest in Sinking Spring Cemetery at the west edge of town. There has been no attempt to beautify or manicure this place, but it has a desolate, wild beauty all its own, with the long grasses waving, and the huge gnarled oaks standing guard over the tilting headstones.

Bill, the oldest of the children of Augustus and Catherine Oury, was born on August 13, 1817. His early years epitomized the pleasant childhood days of countless pre-industrial Americans. Summer would find him fishing on the banks of Wolf Creek or Eighteen-Mile Creek, tributaries of the South Fork of the Holston River. Winter would see him sliding down the steep, snow-packed hill north of Court street, and in the fall he would hunt with his father for deer, possum, and wild turkey.

In Bill's early years, Abingdon was no longer a pioneer area, but it was a place of simple tastes peopled by good hardy stock. The few wealthy families rode in carriages and dressed in "store bought" clothes, entertained lavishly, and sent their children off to school. Most people had few conveniences, whether living in town or on a farm, made their own furniture and utensils, and wore clothes woven on homemade looms. Material for the clothing of Bill and his brothers and sisters was fashioned from wool carded by hand in the Oury home, and Elizabeth made her bedlinens from flax purchased from nearby farmers. Augustus bought shoes for the family from an Abingdon cobbler, and purchased his beaver hats from itinerant peddlers. Fare in the Oury household ran from the domestic ham and mutton available in local markets to the wild game in the surrounding forests.

The Oury family, like its neighbors, was self-sufficient, independent, and capable of meeting emergencies, but it was a friendly clan, and would give assistance to friends in need. It was an honest and law-abiding clan also; there is no record of malfeasance; rather a record of loyal service to the community in small civil posts without fanfare.

These were the green years, in a quiet countryside carpeted with sweet grasses and brilliant blossoms. Bill was to walk soon in a harsh country where grass was scarce, and there were thorns instead of flowers. Doubtless he would think often of the cool shade of Abingdon's old trees, and the clear sparkling waters of the Holston River, and would recall the refrain, "Virginia, Virginia, what a lovely land to grow up in!"

CHAPTER 3

I'm Going to Texas

"A LOVELY LAND TO GROW UP IN," but the West beckoned, even to settlers in the green valleys of Virginia. Bill Oury, like his forebears, wanted
to go West. And he was not alone in his desire. Countless young men,
some with families, were poling down the Ohio in flatboats or pushing
through the dark forests of the Cumberland to start life anew in vast
uncharted lands.

Moses Austin (1767-1821), father of Stephen Fuller Austin, was
one Virginian who was not only restless but quick to sense an opportunity.
Why not work up a scheme to colonize a portion of the vast wilderness
beyond the Sabine? He would have to go out there and see the Spanish
governor in San Antonio; after all, the Spanish government wasn't going
to give him the territory for his own. Roads leading to San Antonio were
all but nonexistent, hardly more than trails, really, and impassable in any
sort of poor weather. He would have to stay clear of Galveston Island;
there Jean La Fitte ruled like an emperor, bringing to the desolate spot
loot taken from New Orleans and the hapless ships plundered in the
Mexican Gulf.

In his fifty-third year, Austin set out for San Antonio to ask for a grant of land from the king of Spain. After weeks of travel, he arrived in the forlorn little village dishevelled, tired, and dirty. Martínez, the Spanish governor, gave Austin an audience, but seemed to be contemptuous of him, and before long asked him to leave.[1] With great good fortune, Austin was befriended by one Baron de Bastrop, a Prussian refugee and friend of Martínez. Far from having to go home empty-handed, Austin was soon able to obtain from the touchy official his promise of help in obtaining a land grant from the Spanish Crown. In time the grant was realized, a huge tract large enough to settle several hundred families on. Fate had provided him with the land he sought, but fate decreed that he should not see his dream materialize. He died in Natchez, Mississippi, on June 10, 1821, but not before passing on to his son Stephen his own burning enthusiasm for the Texas colonization scheme.[2]

It was in Wytheville, Virginia, that Augustus Oury knew Stephen Austin, who was born about twelve miles from there in 1793. Augustus and Stephen were childhood friends, and it was because of this lifelong association that Augustus moved his family to Missouri in 1833, and eventually on to Texas after the Mexican War.

In 1834, however, the Oury family was still settled in Pike County, Missouri, but Bill, drawn by tales of adventure and future wealth, was heading for San Antonio.[3] He had announced his plan simply by saying: "I'm going to Texas." No effort was made to stop him. Augustus gave him his blessing and a few dollars, and the whole clan saw him off.

Soon he would see "Uncle Stephen," whom he scarcely remembered, although of late the name had become a household word. Eventually of course Stephen's name would be synonymous with "the Father of Texas."

In the Streets of San Antonio

When Bill pulled into San Antonio's dusty streets and asked for Stephen, he was shocked to hear that Austin was languishing in jail in Mexico City. Well, it was sad, and he would write his father in a day or two; right now he had to settle himself. He looked around the sunbaked street, and he liked what he saw.

Texas was different. It was new, beckoning, inspiring. Here a man might make a fortune if he tried hard enough, or he might see the beginning of a new empire. And so Bill elected to stay, not knowing that a little over a year later he would be trapped in history — in an old San Antonio church surrounded by several thousand of Mexico's finest soldiers, that he would be one of a handful of couriers to ride for help, or that 183 of his comrades would die within the thick adobe walls.[4]

The year after Bill Oury arrived in San Antonio, Stephen F. Austin

STEPHEN F. AUSTIN. When Bill Oury arrived in Texas in 1834, he was shocked to hear that his father's old friend was "languishing in jail in Mexico City." A year later he was freed to return to the action and pursue the course of events that made later chroniclers of American history call him "the Father of Texas."

was winding up his second year in a Mexico City jail as a result of a stormy fourteen-year period of struggle, setback, and indebtedness incurred in his efforts to build colonies in Texas. When General Santa Anna was swept into the Mexican presidency in 1835 on the winds of revolution, Austin was freed for the second time, and returned to Texas.

He found the colonists in open revolt against Mexican rule. Continued martial law and the callous treatment of Austin had turned virtually all Americans against Mexico. And now new names were to be reckoned with: William Barret Travis, the fiery young lawyer from Alabama; James Bowie, the Louisiana knife-fighter; Jim Bonham, the chivalrous South Carolina lawyer; Col. James Fannin, the West Pointer; Sam Houston, one-time governor of Tennessee and later emissary to Washington for the Cherokee Nation, men such as Sam Walker, "Big Foot" Wallace, Ben Milam, and others.

And Bill Oury was in Texas also, ready to take up arms in its defense. He was nineteen years old, a sturdy, stocky youngster, tough as a hickory stick, and as full of fight as a rooster. Soon he would have the chance to show his mettle.

CHAPTER 4

We Would Fight

ON GAINING THE MEXICAN PRESIDENCY, General Santa Anna became a virtual dictator. He dissolved the state union of Coahuila, making Texas simply a province of the state, and soon thereafter dissolved the Coahuila legislature by force. He sent General Ugartechea to San Antonio to put down further colonial resistance, and re-imposed the ban on immigration of American colonists into the territory. Prohibitions were placed upon commerce so that colonists could conduct business in the area only with great difficulty. Then Santa Anna put out a fateful order. He decreed that all cannon in the possession of colonists would be seized by Mexican troops, and that small arms (for use in hunting game) would be held in the ratio of one rifle to each five inhabitants of the territory. An immediate showdown over the decree took place in the dusty little village of Gonzales, which later became known as "The Lexington of Texas."

Under Santa Anna's new edict, the one cannon in the Gonzales town square was to be seized. After a series of small episodes, a group of 168 colonists banded together to re-enforce the town. Stephen F. Austin arrived at Gonzales, October 19, 1835, to command the little army and to lead it off to San Antonio. Simultaneously a provisional government of

Texas was formed at San Felipe de Austin, to proclaim that the Texas colonies were in open revolt against Mexico.

There followed a number of small and sharp encounters leading to the first battle of the Alamo, outside of San Antonio in December, 1835. The Texans had attacked the old church to draw the Mexicans away from the city, and after four days and nights of fierce battle, the Mexicans were defeated.

On the morning of December 9, remnants of the Mexican army streamed into the Alamo and ran up a white flag. By the terms of surrender, General Cos and his officers were permitted to leave the area on the promise that they would go to Mexico and not return to Texas. It was a kind but foolish gesture; when the Mexicans came back, their numbers overwhelmed the defenders of the Alamo. Many of the officers now released would be returning soon.

Thus ended the first battle of the Alamo. A lull set in. Many settlers believed their troubles to be over and were willing to remain under Mexican rule if only the liberal policies of the 1824 Constitution might be re-established. And so the Texan Army began to disperse, some men returning to their homes, others gathering in small groups here and there to plan for an invasion of Mexico. But there was no lassitude in the Mexican capital. The self-styled "Napoleon of the West" was livid over the turn of events in the north; the ignominious defeat of Cos by a ragged handful of Texans was more than he could stomach. He made plans for an immediate invasion of Texas.

Plans for Defense

As the enraged Santa Anna's plans crescendoed, William Travis and Jim Bowie, joint commanders of the San Antonio garrison, began to lay their own plans for the defense of the Alamo that was to prove the rallying point for Texas independence.

As the defense took shape, volunteers began to straggle in — thirty men with Travis, Davy Crockett with sixteen Tennessee mountain boys — and the garrison began to assume its final form around the middle of February, 1835.

William Sanders Oury went into the Alamo on February 23, to leave it as a courier one week later, just a few days before the tragic climax of events. Bill's entry into the Alamo coincided with the arrival in San Antonio of General Santa Anna and his troops. Abruptly at this point, the casual visits of the garrisoned Texans to the village ceased, and before another day passed, frightened refugees were streaming out of San Antonio on horseback, oxcart, and on foot.

DAVID CROCKETT AND WILLIAM BARRET TRAVIS. "As the defense took shape, volunteers began to straggle in, thirty men with Travis, Davy Crockett with sixteen Tennessee mountain boys . . . ," all future heroes of the Alamo.

The Alamo was now a forlorn little island of resistance surrounded by the infantry, artillery, and lancers of Mexico, some 4000 strong. Long afterward, Bill Oury would tell his grandson at Fort Lowell, Arizona: "There was no getting out now; we would fight until the last."

Memories of the Alamo

Bill Oury in later years remembered the long infantry columns of Santa Anna's army advancing upon San Antonio, the clattering artillery caissons jolting along, and the spear-tips of the lancers dancing in the sun. He remembered the cannon balls smacking into the walls, and the hard work he had done making parapets for the Alamo's own batteries. He remembered the sleepless nights, and the cold, and the ration of beef and corn. He remembered Davy Crockett and his mountain songs, and Colonel Bowie, sick in the little room by the main gate, and Colonel Travis in his dirty homespun clothing. Bill remembered the couriers leaving for Goliad, and Gonzales, and Washington, and he remembered the Mexican campfires winking brightly in the cold Texas nights. But most of all, he remembered the Alamo, the grimy, terrible, wonderful, Alamo where he lived for seven long days. He would remember it all the days of his life.

This former Franciscan mission, founded in 1718, had flourished for about a quarter of a century before its influence upon the Indians had dwindled. It had been abandoned in 1793. Named San Antonio de Valerio, it was called the Alamo because of the cottonwood trees (alamos) lining the irrigation ditches surrounding the mission. The chapel was in ruins from neglect. Long ago the roof had caved in but it was still a staunch fortress, strongest perhaps of any of the buildings in the compound. Directly in front of the chapel was a small courtyard, divided from the long rectangular court by a low wall. The southeast portion of the smaller yard, open when the Mexicans held the fort, was now closed by a log palisade and some earthworks stretching from the baptistry corner of the church to the south wall.

As the place had not been designed as a fort there was little of the prepared position about it — no enclosures, crenellations, loopholes, moats, or any of the other fortress-like qualities. Also, there were no outer works of any kind. Worse, there were in the near distance a number of jacales, small adobe and wooden shacks dotting the plain. These would offer excellent cover and concealment for Mexican patrols and snipers, and would have to be taken down.

Bill said he didn't "think much of the place," but that it "would have to do."[1]

And so the beleaguered men started "making it do." One of the first things to do was to erect parapets along the walls for the cannon, and for the riflemen. This was done primarily on the north wall, against the palisade on the southeast side of the fort, and at key places elsewhere for the placement of the cannon. Parapets were not needed on the west side; the men could take the prone position on the rooftops there although the small lip of protection afforded to a prone rifleman was very small indeed. In the chapel, a scaffold was erected to serve as a catwalk for riflemen. Here and there baffles of cowhide and earth blocked off key doors and passage ways.

It had been reported earlier that the Alamo had twenty or more cannon. There may have been that number, but recent sources inform that only fourteen were serviceable and were used during the siege.[2] There were four four-pounders at the palisade, and two guns of undisclosed size in the lunette just outside the main gate. All of these guns pointed south, or southeast. The eighteen-pounder, heavier than anything the Mexicans had, was placed upon an earthern ramp at the juncture of the south and west walls. In the chapel, a dirt ramp had been built to a height of some twelve feet. On its top, facing north, east, and south were three twelve-pounders.

Over on the west wall, somewhere near the center, was a single twelve-pounder. The north wall had three eight-pounders.

The Alamo had fourteen guns all told; not a very convincing battery when compared with the artillery Santa Anna would bring into play. Bill remembers "dragging these guns around," and probably sweating like a horse as he helped run them up the ramps to the firing platforms.

Asked about the rifles, Bill said he thought they were "mostly percussion caps," but that there may have been "a few flintlocks there too."

Queried about the number of defenders, Bill was understandably vague, putting his answer at "something over a hundred." Actually, there were "about 150" men there at the start, though even that figure is debatable.[3] When Albert Martin and George Kimball came in with the thirty men from Gonzales, the total increased by that number. The list of Texan casualties varies in different sources.

Some fifteen non-combatants got out of the place alive: Mrs. Dickenson and her daughter Angelina; "Ben," and "Joe" (negro slaves of Bowie and Travis) and ten or eleven Mexican women and children.

By mid-afternoon of February 23, Travis had almost his entire garrison within the Alamo's walls. The peril of his situation was obvious to him from the start. Santa Anna knew it too. It was not long before he ran up a red flag on the San Fernando tower to frighten the Texans into submission. Travis' answer was loud and clear: a single blast from the mouth of the eighteen-pounder. The ball went whistling over the heads of the surprised Mexicans, and the Texans cheered.

When sentry Daniel Cloud had set off his "false alarm" on the morning of the twenty-third, Travis thought he had better send out a pair of scouts to take a look anyway. Dr. John Sutherland and John W. Smith rode out of town. About two miles out, the two advanced cautiously over the crest of a hill. There, spread out in glorious array before them were some 1500 Mexican lancers drilling, their spear-tops gleaming in the morning sun.

The messengers wheeled about and raced for town. Sutherland's horse stumbled and fell, sending him sprawling on the rain-slick earth. Smith helped the doctor back on his horse, and although he was sorely hurt, Sutherland followed Smith on in to Bexar. The gallop was a signal. This time the bell was ringing wildly, and with reason. It was time for Travis to move the men into the Alamo.

The Siege Begins

The first day of the siege was a busy one. Jim Bowie seemed to be everywhere, directing things with a firm hand. Parapets were going up, cannon balls being stacked beside fieldpieces, stores being put away in safe places, and the livestock being led into the enclosures behind the hospital. With great good fortune, foraging parties had secured eighty bushels of corn and thirty beeves; these were now brought in and added to the stores. Out in the courtyard, some riflemen were molding bullets from whatever odd pieces of lead they could find about the place. Into the general work of preparing for siege, Bill Oury threw himself with a will. "I helped wherever I could, watering the horses, pulling the guns in place, and running little errands for Colonel Bowie."[4]

By dusk, the Mexicans had set up two batteries of guns on the far side of the San Antonio River. These guns rained shot and shell (both) on the fort for hours, but exacted no casualties. In all, it had been a hectic first day. But it was not quite over; there were more messengers to send out. Although stiff and sore from his nasty spill, Dr. Sutherland expressed his willingness to ride to Gonzales. John Smith would go with him. Soon the two were off with a note to Pontón, the Alcalde in Gonzales. As he had handed Sutherland the note, Travis said that he would fire three cannon shots each day, at dawn, noon, and sunset, to show that the Alamo still held out. The two riders had not gone far before running into Bonham, coming back to the fortress from Goliad. He brought stunning news; Fannin would not come. Upon hearing the report, Travis immediately sent out scout Johnson to ride to Fannin and urge upon him the gravity of the situation. Also, he sent Lancelot Smithers to Gonzales, and a little later on, Benjamin Highsmith to Goliad. The first day had been a busy one for couriers, five of them out in the space of several hours.

On the twenty-fourth the defenders suffered a real setback. In helping to pull one of the cannon into place, Jim Bowie was badly injured. The gun-carriage toppled over upon him, crushing him to the ground. He was placed tenderly upon a rude couch and given the best care possible in the circumstances. Thereafter, he was out of active engagement until the end, all command passing over to his co-equal James Barrett Travis. Bill Oury did not see Bowie under the cannon, but remembered the Colonel "sick in the little room by the main gate."[5]

On this day too, three more battalions of Mexican infantry and some cavalry reenforced Santa Anna's already overwhelming force. Things were beginning to look dark indeed.

It was on the twenty-fourth also that Travis sent out the most stirring of all his messages, and one which has lived through the years as the most glorious and ringing cry of the Texas struggle for liberty. This famous "Victory or Death" message was taken out by Captain Albert Martin who rode hard for Gonzales, reaching there on the evening of the following day. The message read:

Commandancy of the Alamo, Bexar, Feby 24th, 1836.

> *Fellow Citizens and Compatriots! I am besieged by a thousand or more of the Mexicans under Santa Anna. I have sustained a continual bombardment and cannonade for 24 hours and have not lost a man. The enemy has demanded a surrender at discretion, otherwise, the garrison are to be put to the sword, if the fort is taken. I have answered the demand with a cannon shot, and our flag still waves proudly from the walls. I shall never surrender or retreat. Then I call upon you in the name of liberty, of patriotism and everything dear to the American character, to come to our aid with all dispatch. The enemy is receiving reinforcements daily, and will no doubt increase to three or four thousand in four or five days. If this call is neglected, I am determined to sustain myself as long as possible and die like a soldier who never forgets what is due his own honor and that of his country.* VICTORY OR DEATH.

> *William Barrett Travis*
> *Lt. Col. Comd't.*

It is almost impossible to understand how such an impassioned plea might be turned down. But it was. Martin could raise no one at Gonzales, although he and thirty-one others would go back to the Alamo five days later. Martin gave the message to Lancelot Smithers to carry on to San Felipe de Austin, almost 100 miles away. Smithers arrived there on the twenty-seventh, but could raise no relief force. But the word did spread, to Washington-on-the-Brazos, to Columbia, Goliad, Brazoria, and on across the Gulf to New Orleans and eventually to the great cities on the

Atlantic seaboard. But by then it was too late. Travis needed help now —
and it did not come.

On the twenty-fifth Sana Anna moved his headquarters across the
San Antonio River and attempted to set up artillery batteries closer to the
Alamo walls. Protected by the *jacales* on the flat near the fortress, the
Mexicans moved the guns within 300 yards of their target. The Texans
opened fire at some time in the early evening, killing two Mexicans and
wounding six others.

It was time to raze the *jacales.* A party working under cover of darkness started out for the miserable little shacks. Suddenly a Texas "norther"
blew up, and it was instantly cold and windy. Fired from the inside with
torches, the shacks burned greedily in the high winds. The brave men
raced for the fort amidst a fusillade of Mexican bullets, but not a man
was hit.

It was on the twenty-fifth too that John Baylor rode out of the Alamo
to find General Houston.

On the fourth day, the Mexicans began to divert the acequia surrounding the Alamo, a serious threat to the garrison's water supply. The
old well dug by the padres years ago was of no use; it had been filled in
and was dry as a bone. A new well was dug in the courtyard, however, and
as the river was close at hand and the water table high from the winter
rains, the diggers did not have to go too deep.

But things were tightening up in other ways. The Mexicans numbered in regiments outside the walls, and could cannonade by day and
harass by night. The defenders, 150 strong, were forced to stay right at
their posts. There was no relief for anyone. Sleep was a luxury, and might
be had only in the shortest catnap on the walls. Bill spoke of this to his
grandson years later saying: "we were all tired; I didn't sleep much all the
time I was there."[6]

On the twenty-seventh, the Mexicans tried to put a bridge across the
river, but failed. More Mexican reenforcements arrived and additional
batteries were trained on the Alamo's walls. So far, no one from the outside world (except Jim Bonham) had come to help. Travis decided to
send Jim out again, and on the same errand — to Colonel Fannin at
Goliad. Good and close friends for years, the two men looked at each
other, thinking that this might well be the last time they would ever see
each other. There would be a signal in case Jim should make it back, a
white handkerchief tied to his hat to distinguish him from figures who
might be in chase. Jim would make it back on March 3, and he would be
chased in; the handkerchief was a good idea.

That Travis fully understood the gravity of his position is evidenced
by the number of couriers and scouts he dispatched — sixteen in all, and

all to no avail. While on the Colorado en route to San Antonio, he had sent two messengers for help. The first was sent to Governor Smith on January 28; the man's name is not known. The second message also to Smith, was sent on the 29th and carried by Captain Tom Jackson. After arriving at San Antonio, Travis sent several more men for reenforcements. One went out on February 12th, but history does not record his name. Erasmus ("Deaf") Smith took a message to the Governor on the 13th, and later in the day a second messenger, Williams, was sent upon an identical errand. Three days later, Sam Maverick carried a note on his way to serve at the Independence Convention at Washington-on-the-Brazos. "Not long after," Captain Phil Dimmitt and Nat Lewis were sent for whatever help they could find.[7] On the 18th, James Bonham rode to Goliad to get some help from Colonel Fannin. It was the last message sent before the siege.

By February 28, the garrison was almost completely boxed in; only the land to the north was free from Mexican troops. Two days later even that quarter was blocked.

By the seventh day, no courier had returned, nor had any reenforcements appeared. Travis decided to send out word of his plight again. A call for volunteers was made, but no one stepped forth.

Lots were drawn, therefore, and the task fell upon two Mexicans, Captain Juan Seguín, and one of his aides, Antonio Cruz y Arocha. Proficient in their own tongue, they might brazen their way through the Mexican picket lines if challenged. Seguín had no horse of his own. Would Colonel Bowie lend his horse? He did, but Seguín later said that Bowie was by then so delirious with fever that he was never certain that the gaunt man understood his request. The two Mexicans rode out late at night and soon came upon a roving patrol. They answered the challenge in Spanish, riding up to a few paces of the group before spurring their horses viciously. They escaped in a hail of bullets.

By now it was clear that Fannin was not coming. Had Bonham reached him not later than the night of the twenty-seventh, he should have reached the fort on the twenty-ninth, this day. Well, if Fannin was not coming, the next move was to try Houston.

It was that night, and just a little later on, as Bill remembered it, that someone called out his name in the dark. He was hunched over his place on top of the artillery barracks, and climbed down a ladder to follow the man to Travis' room on the west wall. He remembered that it was cold, and he shivered as he walked along. Ushered into the room, he stopped before Travis, seated at a table in the far end of the room. There were no formalities. He was asked if he could ride through the lines for help; he said he "thought he could. Yes sir, I'll try."[8] And that was it.

Travis told him to find General Houston, and tell him the whole story.

Bill was instructed to find General Houston "wherever he may be." Neither Travis, Oury, nor anyone else in the Alamo knew where Houston was. He had been seen last in Refugio; by now he might be anywhere in the sparsely settled countryside. Travis had a hunch that the general might be in Gonzales, and added: "You might try there first." There was some talk about sending Bill to Washington-on-the-Brazos, Goliad, or on to Refugio, some twenty miles south of Goliad. In the end, the Goliad-Refugio route was ruled out. Also, Washington was 150 miles away as the crow flies, and time was running out. Besides, Gonzales was on the way to Washington, about halfway; Bill could ride on to the Brazos if he had to.

Bill went to the animal pen to select his horse. It was black-dark, and the feeble light from his lantern cast its rays but a few feet. There were only a few beasts milling around as he approached, and one looked about the same as another. Throwing a saddle on his horse and adjusting the saddle bags, he led the mount to the gate on the south wall. No one said anything to him as he left, and he eased out into the night. He decided to sneak his way slowly and quietly at first, lest he rouse some Mexican sentry or patrol. The hard riding could come later. Clearing the lunette, he wheeled his horse sharp left and walked it past Davy Crockett's palisade, the baptistry, and then headed due east for Gonzales, seventy miles away.

Young, imaginative, riding through the enemy lines at night, Bill remembered that he thought every sound in the velvety darkness announced the presence of a Mexican. His heartbeats grew louder in his ears, and even the soft clop of the horse's hooves on the ground sounded like cannon shots. Yet he saw no one and was never challenged. With the first rays of dawn he gave his horse the spurs, keeping up a gruelling pace until he dashed into the main street of Gonzales on the afternoon of March first. Bill had no way of knowing that on the same day he left the Alamo, Houston was riding out of the wilderness and into the muddy little main street of Washington,[9] where two days later he signed the Declaration of Independence and on March 4 was appointed Commander-in-Chief of the Armies of the Republic.[10] Bill may or may not have gone on to Washington but he was in Gonzales when Houston arrived there on March 11.[11] He made the long retreat with Houston's column to Buffalo Bayou, and there fought in the Battle of San Jacinto on April 21, 1836.

The final days of the Alamo form a tale as stirring as any episode in American history — Jim Bowie firing from his hospital cot with both hands, Davy Crockett felled by a sabre-blow, Travis shot, and finally, all of the garrison's defenders lying dead upon the ground. By nine o'clock in the morning, it was all over; thirteen long days of agony had come to an inevitable end. In the old state house at Austin there would stand a monument. On each of its four sides would be a name: Bowie, Bonham, Crockett, Travis, beneath the last name this brief inscription:

"Thermopylae had her messenger of defeat — the Alamo had none."

Visitors to the Alamo will see a series of bronze tablets running around the inner walls of the reconstructed chapel. Look at the first one to the right of the main entrance to that building. There you will see the name, William Sanders Oury, as one of the courier heroes of the Alamo.

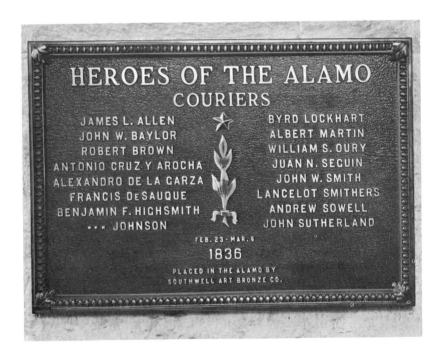

HEROES OF THE ALAMO
COURIERS

JAMES L. ALLEN   BYRD LOCKHART
JOHN W. BAYLOR   ALBERT MARTIN
ROBERT BROWN   WILLIAM S. OURY
ANTONIO CRUZ Y AROCHA   JUAN N. SEGUIN
ALEXANDRO DE LA GARZA   JOHN W. SMITH
FRANCIS DeSAUQUE   LANCELOT SMITHERS
BENJAMIN F. HIGHSMITH   ANDREW SOWELL
... JOHNSON   JOHN SUTHERLAND

FEB. 23 - MAR. 6
1836

PLACED IN THE ALAMO BY
SOUTHWELL ART BRONZE CO.

CHAPTER 5

The Twin Sisters

ON MARCH 13, HOUSTON SENT OUT A SCOUTING PARTY under "Deaf" Smith and Henry W. Karnes to verify the news about the Alamo. Some twenty miles out of town, the scouts came upon Mrs. Almarón Dickenson, Angelina, and the two Negro slaves; Mrs. Dickenson tearfully confirmed the tragic news. Bill had seen Houston upon the latter's arrival in Gonzales on the 11th, telling him that the place was intact when he left it on the twenty-ninth, but that "things looked pretty bad."[1]

Houston then sent orders to Fannin to blow up Presidio La Bahía and retreat to Victoria. Again Fannin hesitated, and this time it was fatal. He received Houston's message on the 13th, but did not move until six days later, going instead to rescue beleagured settlers in Refugio. En route, General Urrea intercepted him at Coleto Creek on the morning of the twentieth. Surrendering to Urrea, Fannin and his force of 390 men were marched back to Mission La Bahía and imprisoned. One week later, on Palm Sunday, the entire garrison was taken out of the mission and slaughtered.[2] The Texans were shot from behind as they walked along the road under guard. Surviving the first treacherous fusillade, Fannin requested that he be spared disfigurement and that he receive a Christian burial.[3]

GENERAL SAM HOUSTON AND COLONEL JAMES FANNIN symbolized respectively the ultimate success of U.S. troops in Texas and their earlier tragic defeat at the Alamo. Andrew Jackson called Houston's victory at San Jacinto "greater than New Orleans." As for Fannin, ". . . as the couriers from the Alamo had come . . . Bonham, Johnson, Highsmith and Bonham again . . . he had turned them all away." Shortly after, the enemy had Col. Fannin executed.

Both requests were denied, although he was taken a few paces aside and shot alone.

It seems likely that Fannin and his troops could have made the Mexican victory at the Alamo more costly than it was, or even turned the tide completely! But as the couriers had come to Fannin; Bonham, Johnson, Highsmith, and Bonham again — he had turned them away. In the end, all of the gallant men fell, some swinging rifle butts in the Alamo, some into the executioner's ditch at Goliad.

Houston organized his army immediately. He had 374 untrained and ill-equipped men to start with, most of whom had no rifles or even sidearms. Stores, clothing and ammunition were all but non-existent. Still, the men were willing, and imbued with the idea of a free and independent Texas. So Houston formed them into the First Regiment of the Volunteer Army of Texas.[4] Edward Burleson was appointed as the regiment's colonel, Sidney Sherman a lieutenant colonel, and Alexander Somervell a major. Bill Oury was sworn in as a private in the ranks.

Houston's strategy would be to retreat to the north, keeping out of Santa Anna's reach, making him extend his supply lines, and at the right time and place turning upon him for a showdown. The delaying tactic would baffle and frustrate Houston's officers and men, but it would pay off handsomely in the end. He lost no time in putting it into effect.

At midnight, March 13, Houston began his famous retreat. Burning what supplies he could not carry, and sinking two twenty-four-pounders in the cold waters of the Guadalupe, he headed north. The townspeople, swept up in the enormity of the situation, loaded everything movable into wagons and carts and joined the fleeing column. Someone fired the forlorn clapboard houses, and soon the whole village was ablaze.[5] It was sad, Bill said, "sad but pretty, bright in the night — like the beginning of a new day."[6]

Column Travels North

This exodus of the people would gather momentum as the column travelled north. Called the "Runaway Scrape," it would slow the column and impede its progress all along the way, and act as a demoralizing factor for an army already on the run yet eager for battle. Later, the fleeing civilians would take the left fork in a road several miles beyond McCurley's ranch on Spring Creek, and continue on to the Sabine and safety. The army, to the loud cheers of the battle-hungry men, would take the right fork for Harrisburg, San Jacinto, and the glory of April 21, still more than a month away.

By sunset of March 14, the column reached the LaVaca River, and about noon on the following day came to the banks of the Navidad. Here

Houston let the van rest a bit while he went in to Brazoria to get some artillery pieces — if there were any around. He ordered the troops to join him on the Colorado.[7]

Until now, the column had followed the main road between San Antonio and San Felipe. On the banks of the Navidad, Houston swung his army due north for Burnham's Ferry on the Colorado. Several of the officers grumbled audibly over this, but Houston swung nimbly out of the way of General Sesma's pursuing force, and luckily so.

The army and its band of civilian stragglers reached Burnham's Ferry on the seventeenth.[8] By now, volunteers picked up along the way had swelled the ranks to almost six hundred. On the twentieth Houston crossed the Colorado, but not before burning the buildings at the landing and the ferryboat itself. Bill remembered the burning of this place — "solitary little buildings going up in smoke."[9]

The army marched down the east bank of the Colorado to Beason's Ferry, where some seventy-five men from the towns of Beaumont and Liberty joined the ranks.

On the twentieth, scouts brought in a Mexican prisoner who divulged valuable information on the movements of Sesma's force. Three days later, this force appeared on the river's west bank with some 750 men. The next day, almost an equal number (Tolsa's Column) joined him, bringing the total to about 1400 men. Figuring to route the ragtag mob across the river, Sesma looked for a crossing. There were three in the area: Beason's Crossing; Deweese, about three miles to the north; and Atascosita Crossing, some five miles to the south. But Houston had anticipated him and put up stiff resistance forces at the crossings.[10]

The two armies faced each other thus for three days, trading only desultory rifle shots across the swollen Colorado. Then, on the night of March twenty-sixth, the Texas army broke camp and marched off under cover of darkness, leaving camp fires burning cheerily on the banks. On the morning of the twenty-seventh the Texans were reenforced; now their total strength was almost equal to that of Sesma.[11]

The retreat continued on the twenty-seventh and twenty-eighth. The subordinates were furious, some threatening to depose Houston should he take another step to the north.[12] Turning an ugly situation to his advantage, Houston gave assignments of merit and significance to his two loudest dissidents. He sent Moseley Baker to defend the San Felipe Crossing, and Wylie Martin to the crossing at Fort Richmond. Still sullen and rebellious, both men marched off to their assignments.

Bill remembered that all along the way the column had been plagued by cold, driving rains. Rain literally drenched the countryside. The men slogged along in mud that clung to their boots like glue. Near Mill Creek another cloudburst opened up and all but inundated the weary marchers. Horses and oxen mired in the gumbo, and through the dark hours of the night men placed themselves in harness beside the straining beasts to free the imprisoned loads. Once, Houston spent the whole wet night sitting in the saddle under a sodden blanket.[13]

On the twenty-ninth, the column hacked away at the bracken all day long to clear a path for the wagons, but made less than three miles. One month ago this day Bill had left the Alamo, and here he was — cold, wet, and on the run.

On the thirty-first, Houston reached Groce's Landing on the Brazos River with a dwindled force. Illness, privation, and hardships of the march had caused some 500 desertions along the way. From an original 1400 men, he would take only about 900 into battle three weeks later.[14]

On the first of April, Houston made a permanent campsite near Groce's Landing to rest and train his army. Also, he commandeered the steamboat *Yellowstone* to ferry the troops over the Brazos later on. At Groce's Point the ragtag band was reorganized and drilled, and it was here that Lieutenant Colonel Sherman was put in command of the Second Regiment of Volunteers. Conditions could scarcely have been worse. The rains continued, drenching the earth, spirits flagged, and there were desertions.

Houston sent scouts to see what the Mexicans were up to. "Deaf" Smith rode out from the camp, and Juan Seguín, and so did Bill Oury.[15] These men, and others like them, were literally the commander's eyes and ears.

Houston was not to fight Sesma alone. Santa Anna had decided against returning to Mexico and Houston learned on April 11 that the general was at Thompson's Ferry; it was the first knowledge he had of the fact. Also on the eleventh, Santa Anna ordered Filisola and Sesma to join him forthwith. On the fourteenth, with his subordinates, he decided to march on the seat of Texas government at Harrisburg, with about 750 men. Better hit it hard and have this Texas foolishness over with, once and for all!

Houston quit his camp at Groce's on the twelfth, and moved the troops across the Brazos on the *Yellowstone,* a steamboat which Bill recalled puffing majestically down river after it had ferried all the men across. Bill was glad Houston didn't burn it — as he had the smaller one at Burnham's Landing.

The next day, Bill actually watched a working party uncrate the "Twin Sisters."[16] Later, on Buffalo Bayou, he was near the guns as they raked the Mexican line, and he never forgot them.

Two days later, the Texas column came to the famous "fork in the road." Would ol' Sam keep on high-tailing it, or would he fight at last? As the head of the column veered east for Harrisburg the men cheered. The time had come.

On the morning of the eighteenth "Deaf" Smith caught a Mexican courier and brought him in. He carried dispatches indicating that Santa Anna had already been in Harrisburg, had burned it to the ground, and had thrown the press of the *Telegraph and Texas Register* into the bayou.[17] From Harrisburg the Mexican general had gone on to Washington and just missed capturing President Davis G. Burnet. The captured messages disclosed also that Santa Anna was in the vicinity of Lynchburg on the San Jacinto River.

At Lynch's Ferry

The two armies arrived in the area of Lynch's Ferry at about the same time, on April 20. Houston chose his position in a wood of oaks draped with long streamers of Spanish moss. He put his infantry and cavalry out of sight in the woods, and the two field pieces, the "Twin Sisters," on the edge of the clearing. Another wooded patch lay on Houston's left, hiding a treacherous swamp running into the San Jacinto River. The river and the swamp then curved around and enveloped the entire Mexican force. Santa Anna was in an impossible tactical situation. If he was to reach Lynch's Ferry, he would have to pass through Houston to do it.

The Mexicans discovered Houston at about 2:00 p.m. on April 20. And the Texans saw the Mexicans, bobbing lances of the cavalrymen, the sun glinting on the slender blades held aloft. Loaded with broken horseshoes, the "Twin Sisters" waited.[18] Joe Neill opened fire with one of the ladies and the skirmish was on. The first shot splintered a Mexican gun carriage and killed a horse. The Mexican gun crew fired the shattered piece anyway, but ineffectually. Colonel Sherman dashed across the open space to silence the Mexican gun, but got two men wounded and two horses killed. A private, one Mirabeau Buonaparte Lamar, did so well in this skirmish, however, that Houston put him in command of the cavalry for his coolness and tactical sense.[19]

At about 8 o'clock on the morning of April 21, General Cos joined the Mexican van with an additional 500 men. This was the man who had lost the "First Battle of the Alamo" and been paroled to his own country on promise not to return to Texas. His reenforcement brought Santa Anna's army to almost 1500 men.

As dawn broke the Texans were eager. If anything, the brief encounter of the day before had served only to whet their appetites for revenge.

Oddly, no one gave the signal to attack! The great leader lay sleeping, and no one would wake him! It was full day when Houston opened his eyes. Then came the words: "The sun of Austerlitz has risen again."[20]

At about noon, Houston called a council of war. Burleson was there, Sherman, Millard, Barnett, Somervell, Wells, and Lamar. The decision was made to take the fight to the Mexicans, and the Texan army formed up. Lamar's cavalry was on the right flank, and next to it the Regular Infantry Battalion commanded by Lt. Col. Henry Millard. The "Twin Sisters" sat proudly in the middle of the line. The First Regiment of Texas Volunteers came next, commanded by Burleson. And in that eager line Bill Oury held his rifle, ready to advance. The Second Volunteer Regiment formed the left flank; it was commanded by Sherman.

Just before the battle, Houston ordered "Deaf" Smith to destroy Vince's Bridge; if Santa Anna was to have reenforcements — at least they would have to flounder in swamp water!

It has been commonly accepted that the long line advanced into battle to the tune of "Will You Come To The Bower I Have Shaded For You," played by several fifes and a drum.[21] Reminiscing on this point years later, Oury was not sure: "All I know is that we just started forward on order." Bill recalled the air itself, well enough, saying that he had whistled it "many a time."[22]

The "Twin Sisters" were brought up on the line at about 3:30 p.m. Sam Houston rode up and down the line on a large white stallion shouting: "Hold your fire, men! hold your fire!"[23] Then down came Houston's arm and the Texas rifles cracked. The two cannon opened up and the enemy fell like wheat under a sickle.

The whole Texan line surged forward. Bill was near the cannon and recalled that the boom "was as loud as thunder." He remembered also charging into the Mexican camp wildly, and shouting with his fellows. Once his rifle was emptied, he used it as a club, swinging it savagely at the terror-stricken Mexicans around him.

Incredibly, Santa Anna and his staff were taking a siesta to the rear! Perhaps he had such supreme faith in his own powers as a tactician that he disdained the Texan force as wholly unworthy. Whatever the reason, as Houston's howling mob bore down upon him, Santa Anna lay sleeping! Surely, "the most costly nap in history."

In the sudden din of battle, Santa Anna and his men now rushed wildly about trying to make some sense out of chaos. Col. Juan Almonte, after the first hectic moments, did gather together some 500 cavalrymen in a grove of trees. When he gave the order to charge, no one did. The Texans, foot and horse alike, were upon them with piercing shrieks, and the force surrendered in a body.

GENERAL D. ANTONIO LOPEZ DE SANTA ANNA was "swept into the Mexican presidency in 1835 on the winds of revolution." But in 1836, at the Battle of San Jacinto, "as Houston's howling mob bore down upon him, Santa Anna lay sleeping." For a leader, it was "surely the most costly nap in history."

Gaining the Mexican breastworks, Houston's men fell to with Bowie knives and rifle butts. Sadly for the Mexicans, their field pieces had been put out of commission before they could get a shot off. General Castrillón who had led the final attack on the Alamo tried valiantly to protect a Mexican gun. He was killed on the spot. As they jumped over the clubbed bodies of the enemy and swarmed past the breastworks, the Texans yelled fiercely: "Remember the Alamo!," "Remember Goliad!" Santa Anna rushed from his tent, vaulted upon a horse and galloped away to the rear.

Houston, now on his third horse, rode about the wreckage of the Mexican bivouac. The mopping up was vicious. "Me no Alamo!" "Me no Alamo!" cried the fleeing Mexicans. They dived into the black swamp waters. They hid under branches and rotting logs, or in thick patches of grass. But they were found and killed on the spot. One mounted group made for Vince's Bayou. They were herded over a precipice; almost one hundred men and horses plunged over the cliff into the swamp water and were drowned or shot to death as they floundered. A few managed to crawl away from the vile-smelling morass, and surrendered meekly.

Santa Anna could not be found. As prisoners were brought into camp, each one was closely regarded, lest he be Santa Anna disguised. It was of the greatest importance to catch him. Escaped, he might reach Filisola and fight again. His capture, on the other hand, would signal the war's end.

Alone, he spent the terrible night of his Waterloo crouched in the branches of a tree. Wolves had come to feed upon the corpses of the slain, and he had climbed the tree for fear of them. About sundown on the twenty-second, he was apprehended by a small Texan patrol and taken into camp.[24] Disguised in rough clothing, he was not identified immediately. His own men, at once innocent and pathetic, betrayed him as they murmured in low voices; "El Presidente, El General!"[25]

Brought before Houston, the general bowed and identified himself. As neither man spoke the other's language, they communicated through an interpreter. Santa Anna made an oblique plea for mercy; Houston reminded him of the Alamo, and of Goliad, but could bring forth only nervous and evasive replies. Santa Anna then agreed to the evacuation of all Mexican troops still in Texas, and penned a note to Filisola to that effect. Houston gave the note to "Deaf" Smith and sent him off to find Filisola.

By now, Houston was almost done in. He had been hit in the ankle by a rifle ball, and the bone was shattered. Even as he questioned Santa Anna, his boot filled with blood.

But the battle was over, and Texas had won. If Houston was in pain, it was a happy sort of hurt. The long retreat was over, and Texas was free.

The Mexicans had lost 630 men killed, 208 wounded, and 730 captured.[26] The Texans had eight killed and 25 wounded!

End of the Battle

So ended the Battle of San Jacinto. Houston, like all great men, had his detractors. Even in the hour of victory, President Burnet, consumed with jealousy, discredited Houston by making a secret agreement with the vanquished Santa Anna. Burnet claimed to be offended by Houston's coarse language. Still, he was among those who later swarmed over the battlefield picking up souvenirs. Burnet even forbade Houston passage on a Texas naval vessel; the aching hero made the trip to New Orleans in a small, dingy gulf trading schooner. When Houston arrived in New Orleans on May 22, a month after the battle, surgeons removed two dozen pieces of shattered bone from his supperating wound. Andrew Jackson, on the other hand, was delighted with Houston, magnanimously stating that San Jacinto was a greater victory than New Orleans.

On October 22, 1836, General Sam Houston was sworn in as President of the Republic of Texas. The astute young cavalryman, Mirabeau Buonaparte Lamar, became his vice-president.

Many of the veterans of San Jacinto drifted with the four winds after the battle, going back to their homes or to beckoning horizons. Bill was among these, although he rejoined the army some seven months later. After San Jacinto he headed south for Bexar to visit the ruins of the Alamo; it was something he had to do.

CHAPTER 6

A Serape and a Sombrero

BILL'S DATE OF REJOINING THE ARMY was November 5, 1836. He became a private in "D" Company (Captain Irvine) of the First Regiment of Regular Infantry. The first official record of that service shows Bill's entitlement to pay between that date and May 31, 1837, and "$24.00 bounty," the latter not explained.

The next record indicates that Bill had been promoted to corporal, and received a furlough on 28 May, 1837.[1] Captain James Moncur signed this voucher in Houston on January 1st, 1838. The voucher also shows that Oury was discharged on December 30, 1837. On draft number 7373, Bill was paid off on January 4, 1838, in the amount of $135.31.[2]

Bill's service with the Regular Texas Infantry, therefore, lasted for a little over one year. Some of the time the company was quartered with the regiment in San Antonio; at other times it served actively in the field presumably in hit and run skirmishes with the Comanches.

The following year, Bill occupied himself with a variety of pursuits. He engaged in surveying for awhile, a job he liked because it kept him out of doors. He worked in several stores, but the life of the petty merchant palled. He tried ranching for a spell, but quit that as he wasn't keen on working for someone else. In the summer of 1838, the Republic of Texas gave him a grant of land in gratitude for his services at the Alamo and at San Jacinto. The certificate awarding the land was made in Polk County, on Aug. 15, 1838 (Certificate #111); it was issued by the Board of Land Commissioners of Harrisburg County.[3] Bill was then only twenty-one and full of vinegar and he never worked the land nor did he register the certificate.[4] As a consequence, he forfeited the title.

Bill need not have worried about leading a sedentary life. In the early months of 1839, settlers on the frontier were having a rough time. Comanche raids were frequent and bold; clearly something had to be done, and something was.

John Coffee Hays was born in Tennessee, January 28, 1817, six months before Bill Oury. He had missed the fight at San Jacinto, but hurried on to join the Texas army less than a month later.[5] Assigned to a spy company, his first assignment had been the sad duty of burying the remains of Fannin and his 390 men at Goliad.[6] Later, he served as a member of "Deaf" Smith's Rangers, and showed a remarkable aptitude for the mobile guerilla tactics used by that body.

With General Houston's furlough order of May, 1837, the army ceased to be a real protective force. It was up to the militia and a few companies of Rangers to provide protection for settlers and veterans opening up new lands. It was time for Jack Hays to think about forming his own ranger company. He was a natural for it. Bold, fearless, yet prudent, he was as skilled in the tactics of warfare as the enemy he stalked. When he fought Comanches, he fought their way; open, in the free prairies, but drawing the enemy in with a sagging center, only to envelope him with the wings. When he fought Apaches he used cover and concealment, and played the waiting game. Here was a man who could beat the Indian at his own game and did it often. And here was a man Bill Oury could cotton to.

A Friendship Begins

It was in the summer of 1839 that Bill began his long association with Jack Hays. The friendship was a strong one from the beginning, established by trial under fire in a series of military engagements and kindred episodes to include Plum Creek, Bandera Pass, the fight against Matthew Woll, and the storming of the Bishop's Palace in Monterrey in the war with Mexico. Later, Oury and Hays would go to California to seek fortunes in the gold fields, and their descendents would be friends in San Francisco over the years.[7]

By the summer of 1839, many of the old hands of the Texas frontier were in San Antonio itching for action: Ben McCulloch, "Big Foot" Wal-

— *Daughters of the Republic of Texas Library, The Alamo*

JOHN COFFEE HAYS. "With General Houston's furlough order . . . the army ceased to be a real protective force. . . . It was time for Jack Hays to think about forming his own Ranger company. He was a natural for it. Bold, fearless, yet prudent, he was as skilled in the tactics of warfare as the enemy he stalked."

lace, C. W. Weber, Bill Oury, Walker, McMullin, and others. Most of the men were mere youngsters in their early twenties, yet a tougher bunch would be hard to come by, then, or in any age. As the government provided no money for arms, mounts, or equipment, the men supplied their own. A more motley crew could scarcely be imagined. Most wore buckskin suits with the Mexican serape thrown carelessly over the shoulder. Some wore the black slouch hat, others the great-brimmed Mexican sombrero. All wore a brace of pistols and a knife of terrifying proportions. Even on a tough frontier where every man was rugged, the Rangers were a breed apart.

It was in 1839 that Mexico began actively to incite the Comanches to wage all-out war against the Texans.[8] The memories of First Alamo, La Bahía, Goliad and the other defeats stung; San Jacinto hurt the most of all, and Mexico was determined to win back Texas one way or another. And so the Comanches took to the warpath, not so much for Mexico as for themselves.

There were a number of minor run-ins between the Rangers and the Comanches during this period, and Bill was in most of them. The one he remembered best of all was the fight at Plum Creek, on August 11, 1840.

A band of wild Comanches had swept down the Guadalupe Valley killing settlers and plundering their holdings. Coming to the little community of Linnville, they burned it to the ground.[9] The town was left a shambles, many of its inhabitants dead upon its streets. Several of the more fortunate were spared and led away into captivity. Felix Huston, Mathew Caldwell, Edward Burleson, Jack Hays and some others, assembled a force of volunteers to punish the raiders.[10] In all, there were about seventy men from Austin, Victoria, Seguín, and Goliad. Bill Oury rode out with Jack Hays, his rifle slung over his shoulder and his Bowie knife tucked away in his belt.

The Indians were not hard to find. In the excitement of victory at Linnville, they had stolen all manner of goods and were loaded down with the plunder. Some of the warriors had been attracted by gaily colored ribbons found in a house or store, and distributed them to the jubilant fighters who draped them over the ponies' rumps and manes. Some, snagging in the bushes, fell off. As the Texans closed in, they could follow the trail by the gay streamers laced through chapparal and greasewood. The Texans caught up with the war party at Plum Creek (near the present town of Lockhart) on August 11, 1840. The ensuing contest was sharp and brief. Weighed down with plunder, the Comanches were no match for the angry Texans. A number of the Comanches were killed, and the rest captured.[11]

CAPTAIN CREED TAYLOR shot Comanche Indians side by side with Bill Oury in the Indian skirmish with Jack Hays' Texas Rangers at Bandera Pass in 1842.

During the fight, the Texans were treated to an extraordinary show by one of the Indians. The man had tied a long ribbon to his horse's tail. He wore a high-topped hat, stolen in Linnville, a swallow-tailed coat which he had put on backwards, a breech clout, and carried an open umbrella.[12] More, he rode about the field singing at the top of his voice. The Texans were convulsed with laughter.

In a macabre sidelight, several of the friendly Indians of the Texas party dined on the roast hands of the dead Comanches. Judge Waller was offered one of the delicacies, "browned and done to a crackling."[13] Undismayed by Waller's refusal to join in the feast, the friendly Indians went about eating the grisley morsels "with gusto."

Until Plum Creek, Jack Hays' Rangers had no official status. Reports of his extraordinary soldierly qualities in the fight so impressed President Lamar that Hays was given a captain's commission and directed to enlist a company of Rangers. He had turned twenty-three in January.

Hays lost no time in recruiting. Because of the high standards he established, he was soon able to put together "the best set of Indian fighters, taken as a whole, that Texas ever produced."[14] Rangers had to furnish their own equipment, as before, including a good mount, serviceable saddle, rifle, two pistols, knife, *reata,* and hair rope for staking a horse to the prairie. The dress was about the same as before also; buckskin jackets, cowskin (or buckskin) leggings, sombrero, serape, and roweled spurs.

Bill was by now a valued member of Jack Hays' band, and went along on its forays against "all enemies of Texas," participating in scrapes on the Guadalupe River, the Nueces, Sabinal, Uvalde Canyon, and others in and around central and southeast Texas.

In 1842, Hays led his Rangers against the Comanches at Bandera Pass. The pass, near the border line of Bandera and Kerr counties, is a gorge 100 yards wide, and some 500 yards long. It cuts the range of mountains separating the Medina and Guadalupe Valleys. The hills on either side of the gorge rise precipitously to a height of 250 feet.

Bandera Pass had been the scene of an earlier battle between Indians (Apaches) and Spaniards in 1720. In that encounter, General Bandera had marched out of San Antonio with a fair-sized complement of cavalry and infantry, catching up with his quarry at the pass. The battle lasted for three days, ending in defeat for the Apaches who left the area for the safer lands to the west. The pass was named after the victorious general.[15]

Hays had started for the pass from a camp on Leon Creek, a few miles outside of San Antonio. His intention was to go through the pass, and scout along the Guadalupe River. Taking his band of forty men, he traveled up the Medina, making camp about where the present town of

WILLIAM ALEXANDER ANDERSON WALLACE, better known as "Big Foot," was with the Rangers at Bandera Pass; later, like Bill Oury, he "lucked out" in the dreadful drawing of lots that meant life or death at Hacienda Salado.

Bandera stands. He arrived at the head of the gorge at about ten o'clock on the following morning. As usual Hays had an advance guard out, but somehow these men had allowed the Indians to escape their notice. The Comanches, about 100 strong, had seen the Texans first, entered the pass by its north end and set up an ambush.[16]

When the Rangers had gone about halfway into the defile, the Comanches fell upon them with wild and savage shrieks. Cool under fire as always, Hays restored order at once and a sharp fight ensued. When rifles and revolvers could not be loaded in the close-in fight, hand-to-hand struggles followed. Sam Luckey went down with a ball in his body. Kit Acklin was wounded at about the same time, but managed to kill the Comanche chief in a fearsome and bloody knife fight before toppling over.[17] Creed Taylor saved Andrew Erskine's life; a Comanche was about to stab Erskine with an arrow when Taylor's bullet laid the Indian low. Bill Oury got one Comanche with a rifle shot, and saw a Ranger go down "with an arrow sticking clear through him."[18]

After a while the Comanches withdrew to the north end of the pass, and the Texans to the south end, both taking their dead and wounded with them. Five Rangers had been killed and six wounded; the dead were buried in a common grave. The Indians kept up a great commotion throughout the night, but left the scene in the early hours before the dawn. No pursuit was made.

Also present at Bandera Pass were Ben McCullough and "Big Foot" Wallace. Bill Oury and "Big Foot" were to draw white beans out of the olla at Hacienda Salado a little later on, and Bill would serve briefly in Ben McCulloch's spy company before the great battle at Buena Vista four years later.

Many years later (1895) Bill Oury's daughter, Lola Oury Smith, was with her husband at Fort Sam Houston where Smith was the post quartermaster. Sitting on the front porch of her home in a rocker, she saw an old man approach. It was "Big Foot" come to say hello to the girl of his old comrade-in-arms. As the afternoon's shadows grew long on the parade ground, she listened in emotional silence as the old man told her about Bandera Pass and Miér, Hacienda Salado and Monterrey.

The Indian menace had been put down, but now there was something more serious to think about. Mexican troops would re-cross the border and bring the fight to the Texans once more. There was no rest for the weary.

CHAPTER 7

Lord, Make It a White One!

BY LATE SUMMER OF 1842, Santa Anna had launched three of the four invasions he would make on Texas soil: the one led by his brother-in-law, Martín Perfecto de Cós in 1835; the one which ended in disaster for him four month later at San Jacinto; and the one led by Rafael Vasquez which had captured San Antonio in March, 1842. It was time for him to try again. This time he would send General Adrian Woll to retake San Antonio and annihilate the Texans — or so he thought.

For their part, the Texans would try to turn the tables on Santa Anna and invade Mexico. A force would assemble at Laredo, and lose a battle at Miér, some eighty miles away. Those who lived would march cross-country to Matamoros and be driven through the streets like dogs. Before all this should come about, one more battle in Texas would whip the Texans into a frenzy.

It was not long before the news of Woll's capture of San Antonio reached Gonzales. Matthew Caldwell in charge of the garrison there, was soon joined by about one hundred Texas patriots; the small force hastened to the relief of San Antonio. En route, Caldwell was joined by Jack Hays, Ben McCulloch, and some 125 additional men.[1] Bill Oury was one of these. On September 14, Hays made a scouting foray on the outskirts of San Antonio and was discovered by Woll's Mexicans. Woll announced: "The second campaign against Texas has been opened."[2]

By now, Caldwell's entire force numbered 225; Woll's force at 1800 had a decided advantage. A council of war was held in the Texan Camp to map strategy, and the flat land by Salado Creek was selected for the battleground. On the following morning, Hays led about forty of his men to the outskirts of town to draw the Mexicans out. Bill made this patrol, and recalled shouting, yelling, and "cutting the fool" to gain attention from the city's guards. In a matter of minutes, some 600 furious soldiers were in the saddle and rushing toward the noisy Texans.

The big chase was on. Most of it was made at a gallop. When the decoy party careened through Caldwell's camp, the men were cooking at small fires, and were taken completely by surprise. Seeing more formidable opposition, the Mexicans pulled up short, and the sniping began.

Early in the afternoon, Woll arrived on the scene and set up his cannon. Soon grapeshot was whistling through the trees, the broken branches clattering down among the Texas riflemen. But as the afternoon wore on, the fight turned against Woll, and by dusk, many Mexicans lay dead. W. W. Lastinger has put the number at 400, probably a high figure.[3] In any case, it was time for Woll to retreat.

On the way back into the city, fate offered him sweet revenge. Captain Dawson and fifty-two men from La Grange, hurrying to help Caldwell and Hays, were jumped by the leading elements of Woll's retreating column. Dead tired, the intrepid men of La Grange had ridden for more than thirty hours without rest and were in no shape to fight.[4] But they were Texans; if they had to die, the enemy would pay for it.

White Flag Ignored

Surrounded on all sides by Colonel Carrasco's lancers (about 150 of them), and facing an artillery piece, the small band fired until its ammunition was almost gone. In the end, Dawson himself raised the white flag. About thirty-five of his men lay dead about him; it seemed pointless to sacrifice the remaining handful. But his men kept firing. Either they did not see his signal or felt the Mexicans would not honor it.[5]

Dawson died with the flag in his hand. Of the fifty-three men in the party, only fifteen survived the final assault. Except for these and three men who escaped,[6] all the others lay dead among the greasewood trees. The Dawson affair was not known to Caldwell until the following morning. Several of his men informed him that they had heard artillery fire in the distance. As the night was wet and stormy, inspection of the noise

had to be put off until daybreak. Then Caldwell sent out William Burnham, Caleb Brown, John H. Brown, and Griffith Jones to investigate.
Riderless horses grazing in the mesquite groves led the men to the awful
scene.

Dawson's men lay all about, hacked and mutilated, wet in icy pools
of water turned red. Having to pursue Woll, and not having digging tools
of any kind, Caldwell had to let the bodies lay where they had fallen, food
for the coyote and the buzzard. Later the remains were recovered and
buried at La Grange with full military honors.

Woll did not stop in San Antonio, but headed for Mexico. The
Texans overtook him at Hondo, once again inflicting casualties. Carrasco,
the man who had surprised poor Dawson, later said that if the Texans
had supported Hays' at the Hondo, Woll's army would have been routed.[7]
Because of differences between James Mayfield and Hays over pursuit
tactics, and because Caldwell bogged down, the gallant charge of the
handful of Rangers went for naught, and Woll got away to Mexico. Bill
Oury was one of a small patrol that tagged Woll's men some thirty miles
south and west of the Nueces. As the fleeing army continued on for Mexico, the patrol turned around and rode back to San Antonio. These men
and other small detachments of Hays' Rangers were the last ones to
re-enter the city.

Volunteers for Mexico

Late in September, Edward Burleson issued a call for volunteers for
an expedition into Mexico. Some 1200 Texans were assembled in San
Antonio ready to go. Houston could scarcely give open approval of the
scheme, as he had recently expressed a desire for peaceful relations with
Mexico. He had said as much in a letter to Jack Hays written on Sep-
tember 14. Still, when he heard about the clamor for invasion in San
Antonio, he gave tacit approval of the idea by naming General Alexander
Somervell to assume command of forces there. In his letter to Somervell,
Houston had paid homage to "the gallant Hays and his companions."[8]

Somervell was not much of an organizer, and the 1200 ardent inter-
ventionists soon began to drift away. So dilatory were Somervell's moves
that indeed he received a sharp censure from the War Department. Hays,
on the other hand — now a major at twenty-five — was eulogized by
Houston before members of the Congress. He was placed in command of
a battalion of scouts numbering about 120. Once again, Bill Oury cast
his lot with the man from Tennessee.

On November 22, the column started for Mexico, some 750 strong.
Hays' battalion led the way with several Indian scouts. Hays himself rode

frequently as the point of his own outfit, to insure it against surprise. When the column reached the Nueces, the river was swollen with winter rains. Bill remembered swimming his horse across the cold, swirling waters, thinking at any moment to go under and snag on some submerged tree trunk.[9]

With a scouting party, Hays reached the outskirts of Laredo on December 3. From two captured Mexicans, they learned that no Mexican force was in the vicinity. The main body of troops was still some thirty miles north of the river. One of the Mexican prisoners escaped and got back to Laredo with the news that Somervell and his army were not far away. When the column reached the river the town was virtually abandoned, and Hays had one of his men run up the Texas flag on a church steeple.

It became apparent, after a few days of rest, that Somervell had no plan for going deeper into Mexico. On December 11, he addressed his troops, announcing that any who wished to return to San Antonio might do so without prejudice. Some 200 men and a few officers took the offer. The remainder of the force, some 500, camped near Carrizo, a few miles from the dirty little village of Guerrero.[10] Within a week, a second crisis arose concerning the expedition, and Somervell issued a general order directing that the force return to Texas. Some 300 men refused the order; they had not come all this way just to turn around and go home. Many of them had stood on the rain-soaked ground and seen the mutilated corpses of Dawson's men lying in the icy pools. Others, like Bill, had been at San Jacinto, or in the scrapes preceding the Alamo. Some, present at none of these places, wanted to go just for the hell of it. No, they would not turn back now. Later, "Big Foot" Wallace would say: "I had a good reason afterward to regret that I had not continued my retreat . . . for verily, discretion is the better part of valor."[11]

These men were the hard core of the expedition — tough, resilient, and bold. And they were cocky individualists.[12] Authority had no meaning for them unless it was earned. They would despise a weakling, but follow a good leader. These men, Bill Oury among them, held a council and elected William S. Fisher to lead them to Miér.

It was at this point that Hays' outfit began to break up. Hays himself would not go, and spoke to his men against the move. It was not that he was afraid; he simply saw the effort as a colossal strategic and tactical blunder, and said so. But many of his men had made up their minds, and nothing he could say would deter them. And so Walker, "Big Foot," Oury, and a few others elected to put in with Fisher. Soon they would wish they had listened more carefully to Hays.

On to Miér

On December 20, Fisher formed his men up and started to move downriver in some boats he had confiscated near Guerrero. Only a few men could use the boats at a time; the trip downriver seemed to take forever. Three days later the little army came to Miér and pulled up on the Texas side of the Rio Grande. Hays, who had covered the flotilla on the Mexican side, rode on into Miér and found it deserted. He apprised Fisher of the news and left for San Antonio soon after, early on the morning of December 24. Bill would march with Jack Hays again, but it would be many months from now, and after some hair-raising experiences.

Fisher was a good choice for leader of the expedition. He had served in the Mexican Liberal Army throughout this very region, and knew it well. His second in command was Captain Ewing Cameron, also a veteran of the Mexican Liberal Army.

Fisher's band did not have long to wait for action. On Christmas Day, a scout reported to Fisher that General Ampudia was approaching Miér with a very large body of troops. The colonel took up a position on the outskirts of the city and saw the difficulty of his situation at once. Most of the town's buildings were of stone, with only tiny, aperture-like windows facing the street. In these little fortresses Ampudia soon placed his men, and then put several artillery pieces in the main plaza. The guns could be wheeled about by serving crews to fire down any of the narrow streets coming into the square. These guns were the key to the Mexican defense.

By nightfall of the twenty-fifth a small detachment of Texans had worked its way to the plaza, going from house to house, through rooms, over courtyard walls, and had even battered down a few crumbling adobe walls to gain a good position. ". . . Some of us were busily engaged, with crowbars and picks in breaking through the stone walls of the buildings, and in this way rapidly advanced toward the square in the center of town."[13] From this vantage point, snipers were then able to pick off almost the entire battery serving the guns in the plaza. Bill was in this party and remembered killing a Mexican "by mistake." The ball from his rifle had hit the barrel of one of the guns and ricocheted into the gunner.[14]

With the guns silenced, it would seem that victory was at hand, but it was not. The expedition's surgeon, Dr. Sennickson, had been captured in a house where he was attending a wounded man. He was taken to General Ampudia's headquarters where he was told that the Mexican forces had just been reenforced, and that more were coming in from Monterrey. In reality, Ampudia and his staff were poised for flight. So

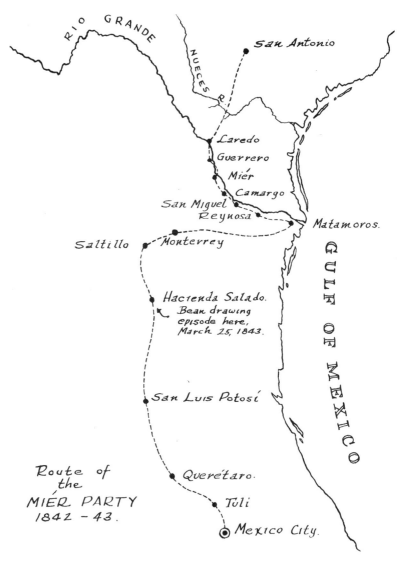

RIO GRANDE

NUECES R.

San Antonio

Laredo
Guerrero
Miér
Camargo
San Miguel
Reynosa
Matamoros.

Saltillo • •Monterrey

GULF OF MEXICO

Hacienda Salado.
Bean drawing
episode here,
March 25, 1843.

San Luis Potosí

Route of
the
MIÉR PARTY
1842 - 43.

Querétaro.
Tuli
Mexico City.

GENERAL SOMERVILLE'S Volunteers for Mexico started as 750 men on the rugged route to Miér; dwindled to fewer than 300 willing to continue the expedition without a commander. Bill Oury voted to push on with the "diehards."

successful was the lie, however, that Sennickson was taken in completely, and passed the story on to Fisher. The latter, sick and wounded, and not wishing to pit his hundreds against thousands, surrendered.

Some of the Texans wanted to fight on. After all, they had had the best of it so far, and suspected a trick. A man named Green "stepped out of the ranks and called for a hundred volunteers to go with him and cut their way through the Mexicans."[15] No one responded to his call, and the men were soon taken under guard and imprisoned in the very storehouses they had fought through just hours before. Wallace was outraged.

We were led off ignominiously by a guard of swarthy, bandy-legged contemptible greasers ... bound hand and foot and delivered over to the tender mercies of these pumpkin-colored Philistines — and all through the workings of the miserable little white flag.[16]

Thus the two missions, Woll's and Fisher's, ended in failure. The difference was that Woll got away. Under the terms of surrender, the Texans were to be treated with clemency, and were not to be sent to Mexico City for incarceration. Once the Texan arms had been put down, however, the agreement was ignored. For the next few days the men were kept huddled together in the stone houses, living "like pigs."

On the twenty-eighth, the hungry Texans were assembled outside, tied in pairs, and marched off under guard for Camargo. There they were given quarters in a cattle pen. From this dismal and wretched little place the prisoners were marched around the public square. According to Oury, the people behaved in various ways, some showing embarrassment or compassion, others hooting and howling, and some throwing stones at the filthy marchers. His remark years later was: "I guess people are about the same, anywhere."[17]

The next town to greet the van was Reinosa, where people acted much as those of Camargo, but added the gayety of musket-firing and bell-ringing. After a day's rest in Reinosa, the column resumed its march for Matamoros. Herded like cattle all day, crowded together in huddled bands at night to lie unblanketed on the prairie, the men vowed revenge should the chance for it ever come.[18]

The band entered Matamoros much as it had Reinosa, to the wild demonstration of the townspeople. Bill, paraded with his comrades through Matamoros streets like a chained animal, remembered the "welcoming committee" coming out to meet the column in carriages, on horseback, and on foot.[19] Chained to a ragged companion, Bill shuffled along in disgrace, thinking of his long personal war with the Mexicans (seven years now), and ruing his decision to go with Fisher instead of

Hays. But he would return to this town four years later to see the remnants of Ampudia's army hightailing it before Taylor for Monterrey. Now he was gathering what little strength he had for his own march to Monterrey, footsore, hungry, and dispirited. At the moment, there was very little to give heart to him or his fellow-Texans.

After six miserable days in Matamoros, the weary van started for Monterrey. A few miles outside the town, the column stopped to eat. While the Mexican guards had roast kid bought (or commandeered) from a rancher, Bill and his friends shared some impalatable roast dog, one of the poor, sore-eyed little creatures which had run up to the train to see what was going on.[20] The column kept on for Monterrey. At each little collection of mud huts along the way the usual gang would gather to shout imprecations and pelt the marchers with dirty missiles. Bill was interested to see the grip of the church on the people. The strongest and most often repeated epithet was: "Herético!"

En route to Monterrey a plan had been made to make a break at Sacata, but Cameron (the leader in the escape plan) decided against it and failed to give the signal.

At Monterrey the men were greeted with the usual noise-making, but were given cleaner quarters and better food than in any Mexican community along the way. Bill and "Big Foot" admired the beautiful Bishop's Palace on the hill, little dreaming that a few years later they would be storming the place in one of the bloody battles of the Mexican War. In Monterrey a few of the townspeople brought food to the prisoners, but it was noticed that Catholics in the group fared better than Protestants or "heathen." Wallace spoke of "sudden conversions" in Monterrey, but added: "I remained constant to my heretical opinions . . ."[21]

At Monterrey, Colonel Baragán had been put in charge of the Texans, and a few days later marched them off for Rinconada. It was on this march that the question of escape was again brought up. It was resolved that a try should be made at the earliest opportunity.

The column reached Saltillo within a few days, and here the guard was reinforced, undoubtedly aware that an escape would be attempted somewhere along the way. Remaining in Saltillo for a couple of days, Baragán then resumed the march for San Luis Potosí, but stopped to rest at a little place some 125 miles south of Saltillo. It was here, at Hacienda Salado, that the escape would be attempted, ending in one of the most gripping episodes in the annals of Texas history.

The break was made on February 11, the day following the arrival of the column at Hacienda Salado. Prime movers in the affair were Captain Ewing Cameron, Sam Walker, and "Big Foot" Wallace. A little after sunrise while the guards were cooking breakfasts over open fires outside,

Cameron let out a mighty shout and the Texans poured out of the adobe huts. Falling upon the surprised Mexicans, the Texans soon overpowered them and took possession of the rifles stacked nearby.

Sadly, in this melee, five of the Texans were killed: Fitzgerald, Lyons, Haggerty, Rice, and Brennan.[22] Also, five were wounded.

Colonel Baragán soon rallied his men and came back to Cameron, offering clemency if the Texans would surrender. The offer was rejected, but Baragán's horse and sword were returned to him in recognition of his humane treatment since taking over the column at Monterrey.

A Miserable March

Before taking the road for Agua Nueva, Bill and his comrades broke up all the Mexican guns and equipment they could not carry. On the first day the escapees covered about fifty miles back toward Saltillo, and after grazing their horses set out again at dusk, leaving the Saltillo-Monclova road and heading for the mountains to the west. From the thirteenth to the eighteenth of February, the men made their way up and down draws of the mountains desperately searching for food and water. Time and again the weary stragglers would come to sheer walls of rock, only to retreat or flop down upon the road exhausted. Bill recalled this miserable march vividly, telling his grandson of the cold, hunger, and despair of himself and his fellows.

Some of the horses were killed, and the sweet, stringy meat roasted on sticks over small fires. On the fourth day out Bill Oury killed a huge rattlesnake, skinned and roasted it, sharing the white slabs of meat with his famished companions. Actually there were several snakes found in the same den, hibernating in the cold Mexican winter; all were killed and eaten.[23]

The men climbed all day, up the face of a steep mountain. Gazing upon the scene below they could see the carcasses of the dead horses in a little flat, the buzzards at work on the offal.

The terrible problem for the next several days was water. There was none to be found; no streams, springs, not even a stagnant or gummy pool. The men grew crazed with thirst. Some gave out, done in by thirst and fatigue and simply laid down to die. The more hardy struggled on. The place was as barren as the craters of the moon. "Not a living animal was to be seen, nor was the song of a bird, or even the chirping of a cricket heard during our wandering in this wilderness . . . night at length overtook us again, and worn out, despairing, we threw ourselves upon the ground to pass away, as best we might, the wretched hours till morning."[24]

By the seventh day, the party had pretty well broken up. Many had fallen dead on the rocky slopes, and the survivors had wandered off singly or in small groups in the desperate search for water. By now many were seized by delirium, and began to shout, pray, and sing in cracked voices. Bill did not, but remembered "the eerie sound" of the men piping off in shrill screeches.

That night the survivors were captured by a Mexican searching party, trussed up, and thrown upon the ground. They drank their first water in six days, from small gourds dipped into an olla.

The survivors of this ghastly march offered so piteous a countenance that even the Mexican guards were touched at the sight of them. Many were without shoes, and the remnants of their clothing hung in shreds. All were gaunt, bearded, and wild-eyed, like men without reason. The men were kept in camp for three days before being marched off for Saltillo. During this time, Mexican searching parties rounded up a dozen or more stragglers in the hills. Once on the road for Saltillo, the men had their hands tied behind the back to prevent escape; the entire distance to Saltillo was covered in this cramped position.

Bill and his companions remained in Saltillo for several weeks, recuperating and awaiting their fate. The worst thing about the detention place was that it abounded in vermin and lice. Bill's hair and beard became literally infested with the elusive bugs.[25]

Finally, President Santa Anna issued orders that all the survivors of the escape were to be shot at once. Fortunately, the commander at Saltillo, General Mexia, refused to carry out the barbarous order. As a result, he soon resigned his commission in the Mexican army. The foreign ministers in Mexico City protested the harsh decision; to appease them, Santa Anna countermanded the order and changed it to one of decimation. The men were soon marched back to Hacienda Salado, where every tenth man would be shot.

The ragged Texans were brought into the large courtyard of the Hacienda and formed into ranks. An officer read the decimation order. John Brennan, W. Moore, and A. S. Thurman were used as interpreters.[26] In a loud clear voice, Thurman read the final paragraph carrying the death order. The men were shocked even though they knew that some dread punishment awaited them.

Of the 304 men who had started to invade Mexico with Fisher, and the 204 who had made the break here at Hacienda Salado, only 174 men were now alive.[27] An earthenware olla was placed upon a table and 174 beans were dropped into it; 157 white, 17 black. Each man would approach the table and withdraw a single bean. Those drawing black beans were to be shot when the grisly lottery was over.

The Fateful Drawing

The drawing began with commissioned officers. Captain Cameron pulled out a white bean. Captain Eastland drew next, extracting one of the fateful black beans of death. He would write in a letter: "Let no Texan lay down his arms until peace has been permanently established. It has been said that I am a timid man, but as God is my witness, I am not afraid to die for Texas."[28]

The enlisted men of the party were called by muster. By the time it came Oury's turn to draw, several men had already drawn out black beans. Bill approached the jar. He dipped his hand into it and stirred his fingers through the hateful pile for a moment. Years later, he told his grandson that he had shut his eyes and offered a silent prayer: "Lord, let it be a white one!" When he withdrew his hand, a small white bean lay cradled in the palm.

The doomed men were taken aside from the others and given a few minutes to write final messages to loved ones. One of these, written by Robert Dunham, hangs framed upon a wall of the Alamo chapel now. It is one of the most poignant letters of all time. It reads as follows:

Dear Mother:

I write you under the most awful feelings that a son ever addressed a mother, for in half an hour my doom will be finished on earth, for I am doomed to die by the hands of the Mexicans for our late attempt to escape the [blur] Gen'l. Santa Ana that every tenth man should be shot; we drew lots. I was one of the unfortunates. I cannot say anything more. I die, I hope, with firmness. Farewell, may God bless you, and may He in this my last hour, forgive and pardon all my sins. D. Headenburg will get this to you — Farewell,

Your affectionate son,
R. H. Dunham.

James N. Torrey drew a black bean, his brother a white one. James had a wife and children waiting for him; the brother had no one, and insisted upon taking James' place. But James went to his death like a soldier.[29]

The seventeen were marched from the courtyard to the eastern wall of the Hacienda. A priest who had accompanied the march from Saltillo was present to hear confessions. Of the seventeen, two men made confessions. The rest, Protestant or nothing, made peace with God, each in his own way. Robert Dunham was asked by one of the group to offer a final prayer. As he began, he was rudely stopped by the officiating officer.

Two files of Mexican infantry and an escort of cavalry led the men

EWING CAMERON AND ROBERT H. DUNHAM were among the Texans taking part in the grisly lottery for life ordained by General Santa Anna. Dunham was one of seventeen to draw a black bean from the earthenware pot and face the firing squad. Cameron, like Bill Oury, drew a white bean but quarreled with a Mexican officer and was shot on the grounds that the number executed thus far had not constituted the prescribed numerical one-tenth of the group.

to the wall. Those who had been left in the courtyard were ordered to keep absolute silence on pain of being shot for any demonstration. In this circumstances, they could hear the proceedings plainly — the death march of the tinny little Mexican bugles, the roll of drums, and finally the sharp rattle of the muskets. And then silence.

Not quite. Henry Whaling was wounded in fifteen different places by the erratic marksmen just a few yards away. At each volley he would curse them roundly for their clumsiness. Finally, one of the riflemen walked forward and placed the muzzle of his piece against Whaling's head. He could scarcely miss.[30]

The Mexican burial squad was astounded on the following morning to find only sixteen bodies by the wall. James L. Shepperd had disappeared. A bullet had ripped away a portion of his cheek, but he had not been hit in a vital spot. In the night he arose, cold and stiff and almost dead from loss of blood. Somehow he managed to crawl away in the darkness. He was able to keep going for several weeks, suffering unspeakable torture as he clawed his way through the wilderness. At last he was captured and taken to Saltillo, where he was executed before a cheering crowd. His body was left unburied at the edge of town.

On the morning following the execution the survivors were marched off for San Luis Potosí, but not before being made to view the corpses of their late comrades. Bill later spoke of the despair he felt at seeing the men lying on the ground before him, grotesque in the attitudes of death.

Within several days the marchers came to San Luis Potosí, where they rested for a day or two. The march continued then, first for Querétaro, then for Tuli. At Tacubaya Captain Ewing Cameron was taken from the ranks and shot. It seemed that sometime before, Cameron had quarreled with a Mexican officer named Canales over ownership of a horse. Cameron took the animal, and Canales swore revenge. Later, at Hacienda Salado, Canales had been present when Cameron drew the first bean out of a jar (a white one). The craven official then petitioned Santa Anna for Cameron to be shot, on the ground that the seventeen men executed did not constitute a numerical figure of one-tenth of the 174 present, that in effect four men were "unaccounted for." The embittered Santa Anna complied with Canales' petition, and Cameron was shot.

From Tacubaya, the men were herded into the city of Mexico, residing first at Santiago prison, then at San Ángel prison, and finally within the dank, ancient fortress of Perote. There they joined prisoners taken by Woll in San Antonio. Bill Oury said that as they languished and rotted in the fetid place, never knowing whether each day might be the last, some died and a few escaped. The remainder were finally released on September 16, 1844. When at last they walked out of the gloomy dungeon,

Bill remembers scarcely being able to stand the fierce glare of the sun. Months later he crossed the Rio Grande into Texas, trying his best to forget the past two gruelling years. But he could not forget them; too much water had gone under the bridge. He would go back, but he would bide his time. Right now, he needed to rest, and think, and plan for a future.

An interesting fact about the seventeen men slaughtered by the Mexicans at Hacienda Salado was that their bones were collected by American army personnel during the Mexican War and returned to Texas.[31] Major Walter P. Lane is credited with exhuming the bones, at the suggestion of Captain John E. Dusenberry of his command. Dusenberry had been a member of the Miér expedition, and had himself drawn a white bean; he still felt keenly the death of his comrades.

The exhuming took place on May 3, 1847, and the bones placed in several boxes which were lashed to the backs of mules, the animals carried the sad packages to Buena Vista, where they were turned over to General John E. Woll. Oddly, these boxes were transported all over Mexico with the army, and were not taken to Texas until the war was over. At the war's end, Captain Dusenberry escorted the bones to La Grange, Texas, home of William Mosby Eastland, one of the officers shot by the Mexicans. On September 18, 1848, the bones, along with the bones of the men killed in the Dawson Massacre, were buried at La Grange with full military honors. Sam Houston was there that day, thinking, as Captain Dusenberry spoke, of the long, long, struggle with Mexico and of all the men who had crossed over the river.

CHAPTER 8

With Us at Monterrey

SOON AFTER ARRIVING BACK IN SAN ANTONIO, Bill acquired some land near Misión San José de Aguayo. This was one of the loveliest of all the Texas missions, and stood on the banks of the San Antonio River some four miles from the city. Oddly, it was named after a patron saint (Joseph) and a Spanish governor of the Province of Texas (Aguayo), but it was generally called Mission San José. Bill's place was but a short distance away and he could see the mission's unique Gothic tower as he ploughed his fields. Once again the sedentary life of the farmer proved burdensome to him, and his thoughts turned to the Texas Rangers. It was a harum-scarum life to be sure, and dangerous, but it "beat farming any day." Bill quit his place on the river and went to look up his friend, Jack Hays.

Anson Jones had been inaugurated as President of the Republic of Texas in December, 1844, and had from the first spoken out in favor of Texan Independence over annexation to the United States. Hays, on the other hand, favored annexation and lost no opportunity to further its cause. In the summer of 1845 the Texas Congress approved annexation, and President Polk ordered General Zachary Taylor to take his troops to Corpus Christi. On the assumption that the United States Army then would take on the responsibility of defending Texas, the Texas Congress directed Hays to disband his Rangers. It was seen almost immediately that the action was premature; it would take weeks, perhaps even months, before a sizeable army force could arrive in Texas. The Congress then reversed itself and asked Hays to raise a new battalion of Rangers at once. Hays complied, naming several of his comrades as company commanders, and directing them to fill out their companies at once. The subordinates set about their tasks, and President Jones confirmed Hays' commission as leader of the new battalion in December, 1845.

Records in the War Department Adjutant General's office show that William S. Oury enrolled in the First Regiment of Texas Mounted Rifles (subsequently the First Regiment of Texas Mounted Volunteers) on 28 September, 1845.[1] He was assigned to Capt. R. A. ("Ad") Gillespie's company for a six-month enlistment. While the official records of enlistment (and discharge) show a three-month break in his service (March 28 — June 29, 1846), the fact is that he was an active member of Captain Gillespie's company during the entire period. He was a participant in the engagements at Palo Alto and Resaca de la Palma, and in the events leading to both.

In late March, 1846, General Taylor was ordered to take possession of the disputed territory lying between the Nueces and Rio Grande Rivers. A Mexican army of some 6000 had assembled on the Rio Grande near Matamoros under General Ampudia. On April 12 Ampudia issued an ultimatum informing Taylor that unless he would break camp within twenty-four hours he must be prepared to suffer the consequences. Taylor ignored the warning. Ampudia was soon replaced by General Arista, but the ultimatum was not withdrawn.

On the twenty-fourth, Arista ordered General Torrejón to cross the river near La Palanga and to shoot any Americans who would resist him. Not far from the crossing place, Torrejón jumped a scouting party of the Second U. S. Dragoons under Captain S. D. Thornton. One American officer and sixteen American soldiers were killed by Torrejón's men, and the remainder of the patrol taken prisoners. This was the spark igniting the flame of war between the United States and Mexico. General Taylor immediately called upon the Governors of Texas and Louisiana for four regiments (each) of volunteers. Troops began to pour into Corpus Christi and within fifteen days two of the bloodiest battles of the war had already been fought. Bill Oury tells about these terrible days in his own words.

I was mustered into the U.S. Service at San Antonio, Texas, shortly after the annexation of Texas to the Union. I was placed under the command of Captain R. A. Gillespie. General Taylor, who was at Corpus Christi with his command, had said that our company should take the field at the first appearance of war. Sam Walker, who was also with our company, had gone down with our Captain from San Antonio to Corpus Christi, and remained there to obtain permission to raise a small company of scouts. This body was to accompany the army on its march from Corpus Christi to the Rio Grande. Learning from Taylor that Captain Gillespie's company would not be called to the front, but instead would remain in Texas to protect settlers from Indian forays, Walker wrote to Gillespie, and requested that the latter send Sy Taylor, Jim Taylor, "Shap" Woolfolk and myself down to Corpus to help him. This was readily agreed to, and we set out the same evening for the army, which by then had gone on to Fort Brown. We were welcomed by our old companions, arriving just before the Mexicans commenced bombardment of the fort. General Taylor, with the greater part of the army, had gone down the coast to Point Isabel to see to the landing of supplies and troops. General Arista took advantage of our divided condition to cross the Rio Grande and throw his whole force between Fort Brown and Point Isabel, thus cutting our small army in two.

Several attempts were made by Major Brown to communicate with General Taylor, but the Mexican lancers were scouring the whole plains, and every party making the attempt was driven back to the fort. In this emergency, Walker went to Brown and told him that if he would allow him to mount his men upon the pick of his artillery horses, he would engage to deliver any despatches he might desire to send to Taylor. The Major agreed at once, and at dusk Walker with 14 men started upon a most perilous journey. I was one of the 14 men. Every pathway was watched by Mexican cavalry. They saw us leave the fort at dark, and their vigilance redoubled. Finding it impossible to go by any of the regular paths, Walker resolved to cut a new one. With hatchet and Bowie knife, through the thorniest thicket it has ever been my bad luck to encounter, we cut our way for six hours. The night was so dark, too, that one could not see the hand before the face, and we had not even a star to guide us. There you have one of the gloomiest pictures that might be painted.

Fortunately, we had a man equal to the task. Sy Taylor, born on the Texas frontier, and possessed of an instinct equal to that of the most acute animal, led us through. Under his guidance, a path was hewn through the jungle, and at dawn we emerged upon the prairie to the astonishment of the Mexicans; they had cavalry pickets stretched along almost the whole front of the thicket. Luckily for us, there was no picket in our immediate front, and we had just time to mount and fly over the prairie with about 500 lancers in full chase. We were pursued all the way to Point Isabel, where our guns gave us protection. We were received with the wildest demonstrations of joy by General Taylor and his whole command. The distance from the fort was about 23 miles, and every report of cannon during the bombardment there had been heard at Point Isabel. The General and his command were kept in continual uneasiness for the fate of the garrison until our arrival. The general, when told that the stars and stripes were still saucily flying over Fort Brown could scarcely contain himself, and at once resolved to take up the line of march for the fort on the next morning.

No one can describe the joy with which this news was hailed by the whole *command, notwithstanding that all knew that General Arista with an army of over 8000 regular Mexican troops stood ready to dispute their march. On May 8, the forces met on the plain at Palo Alto, where an artillery duel was kept up all day with no result. We lost Major Ringgold, one of the most gallant artillery officers the army ever had. That night General Arista withdrew to Resaca de la Palma, and the next day occurred the action named for that place. The meeting resulted in a complete triumph of American arms. The next day, General Taylor marched to Fort Brown, where the whole garrison was mourning the death of their gallant commander, Major Brown.*

Two days after that, Captain Gillespie arrived at the fort from San Antonio, and at once taxed General Taylor for not keeping his promise made at Corpus Christi. He further stated that if he and his men were not ordered into actual service immediately, he would take his company back to San Antonio and disband it. To his credit, Taylor acknowledged the justice of the demand, and at once gave the order for the company to be brought to Mexico. Those of us who had been with Walker were permitted to remain at Fort Brown until our company could be brought down from San Antonio. This permitted us to participate in the several skirmishes incident to the occupation of Matamoros by the U.S. Army.

Our Captain lost no time in taking the company down to Camargo, and we very soon had the pleasure of receiving an order from him to join the company at that place. In the meantime, General Taylor had sent a requisition to Texas for mounted troops, and two regiments had been raised and brought into the field in the shortest time imaginable. The first regiment was commanded by Col. Jack C. Hays, and the second by Col. Woods. Our company (Capt. Gillespie's) became "A" Company in Col. Hays' regiment, and with that famous command I served through the siege and fall of Monterrey. Col. Hays regiment was in turn attached to the Second Division (General Worth's) during the siege and battle at Monterrey. This division consisted of the fifth, seventh, and eighth regular infantry regiments, an artillery regiment, Col. Hays Regiment of Texas Volunteers, and the Phoenix Company of Louisiana Volunteers. There our gallant Captain [R. A. Gillespie] lost his life at the head of the storming column on the heights above the Bishop's Palace. Our company was thus left without a commander until the battle ended.

In late September (1846) our company was honorably discharged, with the most flattering compliments of our grand old Division Commander, General William Worth. The company marched back to San Antonio, leaving me and two others of the command as a guard of honor over the grave of our revered captain. Shortly afterwards, and as soon as the proper arrangements could be made, my two companions left Monterrey with the disinterred body of our beloved Commander, and carried it to San Antonio, where it now rests beside that of the gallant Walker, killed at Huamautla. In life they were fast friends, and they sleep sweetly together in death; a grateful people have erected a monument over their graves to perpetuate their memories.

Here ended my service as an enlisted solidier, and I remained in business first in Monterrey, and after, when we advanced into Saltillo, in the latter place. At the time of the Battle of Buena Vista, I joined Ben McCulloch's spy company, making reconnaissances with him to Encarnación, mentioned by General Taylor in his report of that great battle. I remained with Ben until after the Battle at Buena Vista, 23 February, 1847.[2]

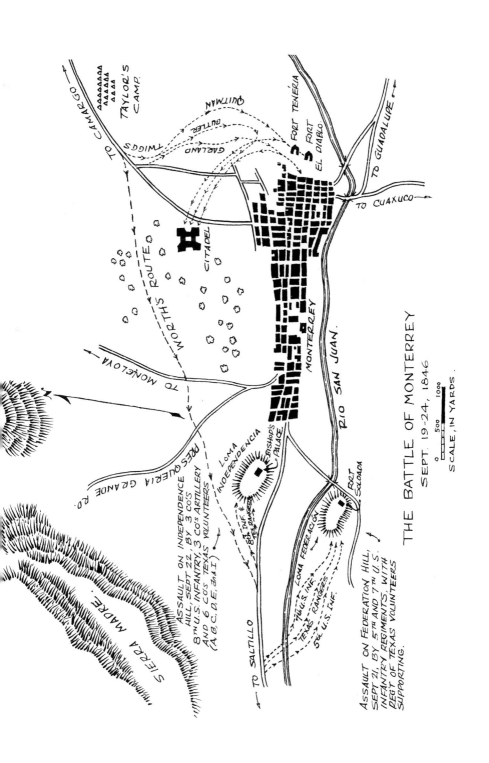

THE BATTLE OF MONTERREY
SEPT. 19-24, 1846

SCALE, IN YARDS.

0   500   1000

TAYLOR'S CAMP.

TO CAMARGO

TO TWIGGS

QUITMAN

BUTLER

GARLAND

TO GUADALUPE

FORT TENERIA

FORT EL DIABLO

TO CUAXUCO

CITADEL

WORTH'S ROUTE

MONTERREY

TO MONCLOVA

RIO SAN JUAN

PRESQUERIA GRANDE R.D.

LOMA INDEPENDENCIA

BISHOP'S PALACE

8TH U.S. INF.

TEXAS RANGERS

ASSAULT ON INDEPENDENCE HILL, SEPT. 22, BY 3 CO'S 8TH U.S. INFANTRY, 3 CO'S ARTILLERY AND 6 CO'S TEXAS VOLUNTEERS (A,B,C,D,E, 2nd I.)

LOMA FEDERACION

FORT SOLDADA

7&6 U.S. INF.

TEXAS RANGERS

5&U.S. INF.

ASSAULT ON FEDERATION HILL, SEPT. 21, BY 5TH AND 7TH U.S. INFANTRY REGIMENTS, WITH REGT. OF TEXAS VOLUNTEERS SUPPORTING.

TO SALTILLO

SIERRA MADRE

The Fray Reviewed

It is well known that Arista's delay in crossing the Rio Grande at Longoreño was the cause of his inability to reach Point Isabel before Taylor. Had he crossed sooner, Taylor would have been in a bad way, cut off from his supply depot on the coast. The Mexicans did cross the river, but not until after Taylor had reached the coast as he had planned. A week later the two forces met at Palo Alto, a small village about half-way between Point Isabel and Fort Brown (Brownsville).

Taylor's force, Oury with it, started for the relief of Fort Brown on May 7. By then, Ampudia had ceased his bombarding of the fort and was hurrying toward Palo Alto to lend Arista a hand. When the opposing forces met there, an artillery duel ensued, "being kept up most of the day without result."³ General Cadmus M. Wilcox makes a similar assessment, saying: "The action of May 8 . . . was, on the part of the United States Forces, defensive and mainly of artillery against Mexican artillery and cavalry supported by infantry."⁴

At dawn on the ninth, the two armies had moved closer together. Soon after, Arista began to pull his troops back toward Matamoros, looking for an advantageous place to make a stand. A few miles to the southwest of his dawn position he found the place, a narrow defile running at right angles to the road, either extremity ending in a shallow pool. The battle fought there took the name of the place: Resaca de la Palma.

The dense chaparral precluded maneuvering about, but one bold assault on the Mexican positions was led by Captain Charles A. May in the face of head-on fire. Leading his charge in a column of fours, and shouting: "Remember your Regiment!" May stormed the astonished Mexicans who broke at the unexpected charge. May captured a battery of enemy guns on this foray and took as his prisoner a Mexican general.⁵ Bill was not in position to see May on this occasion, but he remembered seeing the captain on several occasions, noting that "he had long hair falling down past his shoulders."⁶

The fighting was alternately slack and sharp. In the end, Arista's forces quit the field and streamed back towards the river in confusion. Had Taylor possessed the means of crossing the river in pursuit it is likely that he would have taken Matamoros then and there. At that, Arista did not get off scot-free. The guns of Fort Brown were trained upon the Mexicans as they crossed over the Rio Grande in small boats; many were hit, the screaming passengers dumped brutally into the swirling waters. The American losses for both engagements were less than two hundred. Arista lost about 1000 men.⁷

At the close of day on May 9, 1847, Bill surveyed the field; it was littered with the Mexican dead. "Dead men, dead horses, and broken guns carriages lay strewn all about — it was a terrible and sickening sight. I had seen it before, and I would see it again, but it was always the same, fearful and shattering to the soul."[8]

Another veteran (Samuel C. Reid, Jr.) makes much the same observation, although he arrived upon the scene two weeks after the battle had taken place.

At about 12 o'clock we arrived at Resaca de la Palma which still bore the fresh signs of recent and terrible conflict. Strewn about on every side were the hats, cartridge boxes, belts, broken bayonets, and torn and bloody garments of the Mexican soldiery. The free fresh air of heaven was tainted by the horrible effluvia arising from the dead bodies of horses, mules, and oxen which lay on every side. To avoid inhaling the horrid incense, we rode on, leaving the wolves and carrion birds to gorge upon the dainty feast prepared for their revolting appetites by man . . . civilized warfare . . . has no more disgusting sounds than the snarl of the wolf as he tears his prey, or the flapping wings . . . of the carrion bird as he stoops to his hateful feast.[9]

For about a week before the taking of Matamoros, Taylor harassed the Mexicans with scouting and raiding parties while consolidating his supply lines with the aid of Commodore David Connor.[10] Barita, a dusty little village some fifty miles up river from Matamoros, was receiving Mexican reinforcements. Bill Oury was one of a detachment of volunteers sent to Brazos to intercept the buildup. Brazos, on the Texas side of the river, was about twelve miles downriver from Barita. There was not much for the advance party to do. The march from Brazos to Barita was not heavily contested, and the sad little place capitulated on the seventeenth day of May. On the following day, Taylor crossed the river and took possession of Matamoros uncontested.

Victorious At Last

Bill Oury, entering the city as a soldier of a conquering army, could scarcely help thinking about his last visit to town. Four years ago he had walked these streets in rags, chained to a fellow Texan, shuffling along barefooted and dispirited, a prisoner tormented by the slurring insults and well-aimed missiles of the crowd. And he thought of his luck at Hacienda Salado, and of his comrades who ran out of luck there, and the shooting of Ewing Cameron at Tacubaya, and the rotting months of prison in Mexico. But it was different now, and it would not have been surprising if a bit of swagger had replaced the usual steady gait.

Although the victories at Palo Alto and Resaca de la Palma gave Taylor control of the Rio Grande, he was unable to pursue the Mexican army. Before he could do so he had to wait for several months in Mata-moros, building up supplies, recruiting, and training. When finally he did move, he selected Monterrey as his objective and Camargo as his base of operations.

Camargo was a natural choice. It lay directly on the road to Mon-terrey, and it provided access to water, forage, and wood. By mid-August, Taylor had his force concentrated there, and divided into two divisions of regulars, under Generals Worth and Twiggs, and one of volunteers, under General Butler. The regular divisions pulled out of Camargo on August 19, and within three weeks had reached Cerralvo (along with Butler's Volunteers who had left Camargo a few days later). On September 19, Taylor encamped his force about four miles out of Monterrey. General Ampudia (who had replaced Arista after the disastrous routs of May 8 and 9) had moved into the city and established its defenses. The stage was set for the first large-scale engagement on Mexican soil.

The city was enclosed in a elbow of the San Juan River which came in from the northeast, looped around the main part of town and ambled lazily on westward. The main citadel was a masonry fort located about three quarters of a mile due north of town. There were several smaller forts scattered around the perimeter of Monterrey, and the Bishop's Palace stood in solitary grandeur (as it still does) on the crest of a hill nearby. Ampudia's main line of communication ran along the Saltillo road leading westward. Taylor planned to gain control of this road and cut off Ampu-dia's supplies. Worth's division was assigned the task of taking the road. He began his turning movement on the afternoon of September 20. One of the first tasks would be the reduction of Federation Hill, a steep, thicket-covered out-cropping just across the river from Independence Hill and the Bishop's Palace. Mexicans swarmed all over both hills, and had cannon trained on the flats below.

Worth sent his troops up the Saltillo road. When they arrived at a good jumping-off place, the men left the road and started through the cane fields for the base of the fortress. Soon discovered by the Mexicans, Tay-lor's men were engulfed in a deadly plunging fire. Bill recalled crossing over a small stream as he broke out of a cane field, and hearing the grape-shot whistle over his head. Although grape and ball crashed into the trees and water around him, he was not hit. Neither, remarkably were any of his comrades.

As the Americans moved closer to the base of the hill, the Mexicans came pouring down from the crest to take up better positions about half-way down the slope. Perceiving this, Worth ordered the Seventh U. S. Infantry to support the attacking column.

Once the column reached the base of the hill, the Mexican guns could not depress so as to bear upon it. Still, the volley of musket fire was extraordinarily heavy. Up and up went the Americans, slamming rifle fire into the Mexican emplacements, and frequently over-running positions to engage in hand-to-hand encounter with the desperate defenders.

At last the crest was taken and the U. S. flag planted upon it. A nine-pounder was captured near the top and turned upon the erstwhile defenders, now fleeing in confusion down the backside of the hill.

Bill had not made this first assault up the slopes, but sat waiting at the bottom with the men of his company. As part of a general support force to aid in mopping up the hill, Col. Jack Hays' Rangers joined with the Fifth and Seventh Infantry Regiments at this time. The next objective was Fort Soldada, a fortress standing on the crest of Federation Hill at its far end.[11] Men of the Regular Army vied with the Texas Rangers in getting to Fort Soldada first. Again, the way was impeded by heavy musket and artillery fire, and a number of men fell in the assault.

It was Bill Oury's own Captain, "Ad" Gillespie, who first reached the enemy's works, and a shout went up from the proud Texans.[12] Within minutes, the flags of both the Fifth and Seventh Infantry Regiments arrived upon the scene.[13]

The combined forces had captured the hill and with it some 1500 Mexican soldiers and a large quantity of ammunition. But the job was only begun; some 600 yards away, Independence Hill poked its nose into the sky. It too was crawling with enemy soldiers and would have to be taken. At the moment, Bill and his Ranger companions were exhausted. Victorious but tired, they flopped down upon the ground seeking rest.

Early in the morning of the twenty-second, Bill and his messmates were roused from their slumbers to begin the assault on Independence Hill. It was a dark and misty morning, overcast, and gloomy. The assault force numbered some 465 men and their officers.[14] It was comprised of three artillery companies, three companies of the Eighth U. S. Infantry, and six companies of Col. John Coffee Hays' Regiment of Texas Rangers. The latter companies were: "A" Co., Capt. Ben McCulloch; "B" Co., Capt. C. B. Acklen; "C" Co., Capt. Thomas Green; "D" Co., Capt. Ballowe; "E" Co., Capt. C. C. Herbert, and "I" Co., Capt. R. A. Gillespie.[15] It is possible that one more Ranger Company was included in this assault force — either "F," "H," or "K."

Independence Hill is some 700 to 800 feet high, and rises almost perpendicularly from the floor of the valley. It is covered with rock ledges, and thick, almost impenetrable bramble bushes. On its crest stood the Bishop's Palace, turned into a grim fortress by the Mexicans within its walls. Left intact, it could menace Monterrey with its guns; it was obvious to Taylor that its defenses must be reduced. So impossible did the task seem that officers and men alike paled at the thought of negotiating the steep slopes under concentrated fire.

At the base of the hill, the command was divided. Capt. J. R. Vinton with a company of the Third Artillery was detached to move off to the left and proceed up the northwest slope of the hill. With him were one company of the Eighth Infantry and three companies of Texas Rangers, all under the command of Lieutenant Colonel Walker. The rest of the command, under Colonel Childs, veered right to make an ascent on the southwest slopes.

The ascent was even more difficult than had been imagined. The great rocks were hard to negotiate, and underbrush clawed at the clothing like fishhooks. Miraculously, the climbers were able to advance within about 100 yards of the hill's crest before they were discovered. It was still dark, but noise and falling rocks gave them away. Now a steady stream of fire poured down upon the advancing columns, but few men were hit in the dark.

A Captain Lost

With a final surge, the exhausted climbers gained the hilltop and fell upon the Mexicans with wild and jubilant shouts. The Mexicans broke and ran in their confusion, some towards the Bishop's Palace, some plunging headlong down the hill. It was in this part of the battle that Captain "Ad" Gillespie fell, mortally wounded. His men, Bill Oury among them, tried to assist him, but they could only offer comfort.[16] Gillespie was not the only one hit; Herman S. Thomas, Lt. We. E. Reese, and Daniel McCarty were badly wounded here, McCarty dying shortly thereafter.

There followed a general regrouping of forces in preparation for the assault on the Bishop's Palace. Elements of the Seventh Infantry joined the victorious Texans on Independence Hill, along with several companies of the Eighth Infantry, and Capt. J. B. Scott's Company of the Artillery battalion. Soon thereafter, the Fifth Infantry and Blanchard's Louisiana Volunteers crossed over from Federation Hill to join the growing assault force.

The Mexicans were not idle. General Berra began to reenforce also, and would make a concerted effort to drive the hated gringos from the hill. Several battalions of Mexican infantry then formed in line across the front of the Palace. On their flanks were squadrons of light and heavy cavalry, with speartips gleaming in the morning sun, and pennants fluttering. A Mexican bugle sounded the advance and the whole line moved forward. On the line came, the riflemen with arms carried at high port, bayonets glinting in the sun's rays, the lancers at a trot.

But fate conspired against these brave men. Captain Blanchard's

Company of Volunteers had been ordered to fall back in the middle of the line, with the Texas Rangers holding their positions on the flanks. As the Mexican line sucked into the funnel, the Rangers hit from both sides with deadly effect. Then the whole American force was up, yelling and lunging at the astounded Mexicans. As at Fort Soldada, the surprised Mexicans bolted, and the battle was over.

A short struggle occurred with the few troops left inside the Palace, but all therein were captured and led away. The total American force (with reenforcements) was numbered at about 800 men; the Mexicans defended the Palace with some 2000 troops.[17]

The entire command of General Worth then moved bag and baggage to the Bishop's Palace for the night. The men had not had a warm meal in three days and were soon cooking some captured stores of rice and flour into cakes over open fires. The resulting biscuits, heavy pieces of dough, were consumed eagerly by the ravenous men, soon joking among themselves and calling each other "doughboys."[18] This name stuck. It has since been used as a synonym for the infantry soldier, and had special currency for the American troops of World War I. Another "first" accredited to the storming of the Bishop's Palace was the use of the "rebel yell." Although often associated with the Confederate Army during the War between the States, it was first sounded by the Texans of Hays' Rangers as they swarmed over the defenders on Independence Hill on September 22, 1846.[19]

The only troops not encamping in (or upon the grounds of) the Bishop's Palace were the Texas Rangers and the Fifth Infantry. The Fifth recrossed the San Juan and took up positions again on Federation Hill. The Rangers took up places in the small buildings and ranchos at the bases of both hills. In one of these rude huts the body of Captain Gillespie was brought, and Bill Oury sat up with him all night, attending to his wounds, and offering prayers for his life. In vain. Gillespie and Thomas (of "A" Co.) died the next day and were buried on Independence Hill.[20]

On September 24, General Ampudia surrendered his force in the main plaza of Monterrey. Once again the victorious Americans permitted the defeated force to withdraw (as after San Jacinto). It was felt that with the crushing victory at Monterrey, a general peace would follow. Ampudia assured Taylor that his government was already treating for peace, and Taylor believed him. It was known that Santa Anna had returned to assume control of the government in the capital, and it was rumored that he wanted peace. Consequently an armistice of eight weeks was arranged at Monterrey, so that both factions might gain definitive word from their governments.

On several occasions during the surrender ceremony, Bill Oury acted as General Taylor's interpreter.[21] Years later he told his grandson that he had had doubts about the terms even as he was engaged in translating them for the General's Commission. The Mexican cavalry and infantry were permitted to retain their arms, and the artillery units were allowed to keep half a dozen field pieces. Moreover, the force was allowed to withdraw to Linares and San Fernando, along the road to Saltillo. Bill was only a private, but the proceedings made no sense to him.[22] What he could not know was that Taylor's lack of wagons and mules made immediate chase of other elements of Santa Anna's army impractical. In any case, if Bill had to translate, he did not have to agree with Taylor's decisions, and it did not much matter in the outcome whether he did or not.

The Mexican Army, or what remained of it, marched off to San Luis Potosí, where Santa Anna hurried to assume command. Thereafter, he was in full control of the army until its final defeat at Chapúltepec. With victory in its grasp, the American Army let its quarry go, to fight again at Buena Vista, Contreras, Churubusco, and all of the other delaying actions down to the capital itself.

Bill had seen Santa Anna riding on his white charger outside the Alamo's walls ten years earlier. He had seen him again after San Jacinto, a comic-pathetic figure in ill-fitting clothes. At the Alamo he was out of range; at San Jacinto he was a captive. Bill wished he might get Santa Anna in his gun-sight just once. He never saw the Mexican President again.

End of the Rangers

On September 30, the Rangers were mustered out of service. Bill stayed in Monterrey long enough to guard the grave of his fallen commander before disinterment and removal of the remains to Texas. He related that he "engaged in business" in Monterrey for about six weeks, until the army took Saltillo in mid-November.

Not long before Buena Vista, Bill joined Ben McCulloch's Spy Company, and with it made forays into such places as Encarnación, Jesús María, Hedionda, Agua Nueva, and other Mexican way-stations in the Monterrey-Saltillo-Linares triangle. It was a typical decision for the bold and youthful adventurer at that time and place in history. In McCulloch's Spy Company, Bill saw both danger and the threat of death but joined it anyway. Then, as now, proper military planning called for knowledge of enemy capabilities — knowledge only to be obtained directly by spying.

McCulloch had been mustered out of the service after Monterrey on September 30, 1846. Now he was back in Monterrey again, having arrived there on January 31, 1847.[23] He went on to Saltillo, reporting to General Taylor on February 4th, with twenty-seven men. Bill joined him there

SAM WALKER AND BEN McCULLOCH were both companions of Bill Oury in the war with Mexico. Sam headed a company of fourteen scouts, including Bill, who volunteered to carry hazardous messages for the Company under Captain R. A. Gillespie at San Antonio. Ben was later to become a Confederate general, but when Bill knew him he was in charge of a spy company.

for a six-months tour of duty. A few days later McCulloch met with Taylor again at Agua Nueva, and was ordered out on a reconnaissance mission to Encarnación.

The several spy companies were all very colorful.[24] Many of the spies were Mexicans, enlisted by the company commanders because they could infiltrate more readily than Anglo-Americans. Sometimes the companies were composed entirely of Mexicans — as the one commanded by Manuel Domínguez at Vera Cruz. Some companies included soldiers-of-fortune, ex-U. S. Army soldiers, and the frontiersmen of Texas, Louisiana, Kentucky, and Tennessee.

When bivouacked with U. S. troops, they had a uniform of sorts. The jacket was green, piped in red, the trousers dark blue reenforced with leather on the inside of the pants leg — for better wear in the saddle. The hats were wide-brimmed straws, banded on the crown with a wide red cloth that fell away behind like a sailor's ribbon, or a veil. The spies were armed with lance, carbine, sabre, and pistol.

On missions behind the lines all of the gaudy apparel was ditched for Mexican peon clothing. Spies let their beards and hair grow long, unkempt

MISSION OF SAN JOSE DE AGUAYO. As Bill was plowing near San Antonio he could see the beautiful church tower by the river. But the tranquil life of the farmer soon proved burdensome, and Bill returned to the Rangers.

and matted. Shoes were cast aside for sandals, and serapes replaced shirts and jackets. Major General John Herr in *The Story of the U. S. Cavalry* describes the spies in these words: "These men in outlandish dress and with huge beards looked almost like savages and kept the Mexicans in mortal terror."[25]

Without doubt, Bill Oury was as dirty and ornery-looking as the rest. Bill scouted with McCulloch right up to the Battle of Buena Vista, gaining valuable information for Taylor on the whereabouts and strength of Santa Anna's troops. The great battle commenced on February 22, 1847. Bill was not a participant; his service in the Mexican War ended with his participation as a spy leading up to Buena Vista.

In recounting the days and deeds of those years to his grandson, Bill remembered something of all his adventures, but he remembered Monterrey the best of all. In different words, but with the same thought, he made the story sound like Charles Fenno Hoffman's famous words:

> *We were not many, we who stood*
> *Before the iron sleet that day,*
> *Yet many a gallant spirit would*
> *Give half his years if but he could*
> *Have been with us at Monterrey.*

Bill drifted back to Texas, and to have something to do, he got another piece of land close by Mission San José.[26] It was here that his father, mother, and several of his brothers and sisters joined him. He could scarcely recognize Sally Woods and Susan; they were babies of five and two respectively when he had left for Texas. As for Senah, Catherine, and Elizabeth — well, they hadn't even been born! Now here they all were, young ladies and teen-age girls, and each one pretty as a picture.

But the reunion was short-lived. In Senah's words: "After being in Texas some eight months we decided we did not like the Mexicans and father took us back to Pike, where we have been ever since. I was married in San Antonio on February 8, 1849. Brother William would not go with us to Missouri, and his spirit of adventure carried him off to California in 1849 . . . in the new El Dorado, he amassed a goodly sum of money."[27]

If indeed Bill did "amass a goodly sum of money," no one else has mentioned it over the years, including Bill himself. In any case, he did not share his family's antipathy towards Mexicans, even though he had been busy fighting them for a dozen years, and had languished in their jails. As if to balance the scales, then, he went back across the Río Bravo to Durango and there met and married Inez García, a lovely Mexican girl.

CHAPTER 9

The Golden Fleece

BILL OURY HAD AN AFFINITY FOR THINGS LATIN — the language, the customs, the people; it is not surprising then that he should have fallen in love with and married a Mexican girl. Her ancestry was Spanish — in fact, both parents had been born in Barcelona, and had come to Mexico in 1827. After living a short time in Mexico City, Señor García established a ranch in Poanas, a few miles north of Zacatecas. His place was bordered on the north by the *municipios* of Peñon Blanco and Cuencamé, and at some distance on the south by Nombre de Dios, and Suchil. Inez García was born on the ranch in 1828. The family made only occasional visits to Durango in her girlhood years; the visits became more frequent when she reached convent age.

Bill had left Texas late in 1848 and had gone first to Saltillo, back to another of the very places he had shuffled through in chains five years before. He stayed on in Saltillo for a couple of months "in business," and then pushed on for Durango.[1]

In the heart of the city is a large plaza, El Zócalo. On its north side is the huge cathedral begun in 1695 and finished over 100 years later. It was and is the tradition for townspeople to promenade about the square on warm evenings, to see and to be seen. It was on one of these *vueltas* (walks) that Bill Oury first saw Inez García. Just how a bold "gringo"[2] may have bypassed the reserve and formality so dear to the Latin heart remains a poser. In any case, the two met and were married, after a respectable waiting period and the posting of the banns. Bill and Inez were married in one of Durango's churches — there is no record of which one.

Durango has modernized and spread out considerably in the last 117 years. Still, much of the colonial architecture remains, and is in use and in a sense, one walks the same streets in Durango today as Bill and his bride might have walked in 1849.

Just off the plaza, south of the Cathedral is Universidad Juárez. In Bill's day, the place was known as Seminario Conciliar (1767-1856). It was founded as Colegio de Los Jesuitas in 1594,[3] going by that name until 1767. From 1856 until 1872 it was known as Colegio Del Estado, and from 1872 until 1964 as Instituto Juárez. In 1965 the college received its fifth name: Universidad Juárez de Durango.[4] It is a large colonial building with a patio full of brilliant flowers. Bill and Inez must have strolled past it many times, pausing perhaps to study the intricate and lovely stone carvings on its columns and facade.

A few miles out of town looms the famous Cerro de Mercado,[5] an iron mountain whose rich ore has yielded 60 per cent pure iron ore for many years. A going concern in 1848, it was a comfortable carriage-ride away from town. At its base, picnickers might gather baskets of great mushrooms after a rain.[6]

Bill liked Durango and was fascinated by its history. Founded in April, 1563, by Don Francisco de Ibarra, the place was first called Guadiana. The name Durango came later, in honor of the city of that name in the province of Vizcaya, Spain.[7] The Valley of Durango had probably first been seen by Oñate and Angulo of Nuño de Guzmán's command, although Ibarra gets credit for actually founding the city.[8] Some fifty-seven years later, in 1620, the place became a bishopric when Fray Gonzalo de Hermosillo arrived to assume his Episcopal duties. It was in 1621 that the place was given the status of a "city," when it received its coat of arms from King Philip IV of Spain.

A Romantic Town

Romanticists, Bill and Inez liked the old legends of Durango, and there were many.[9] A favorite was the one about the White Nun. A young Mexican girl, Beatrice, loved a captain of the Royal Spanish Army. It was in 1810 during the period of Mexican revolt, and in a reverse of fortune, that the soldier had to flee Durango for Mazatlán. Beatrice entered a convent in Durango. Each evening she would accompany the sisters to the Cathedral to pray, and would slip away to the bell tower to scan the horizon for signs of the Loyalist column bringing back her lover. One night she fell from the high place and was killed — an accident? a suicide? No one knows. But each night she returns to the east bell tower in the white robes of a novice, searching the plain for her gallant captain who never comes. When the shadows are just so, her form is visible in the tower far above the city street, so thousands say.

As much as Bill liked Durango, there was no real place for him there. Word had come of a fabulous gold strike in a place named Sutter's Mill in far off California. Gold! With some luck he might strike it rich in no time at all, and perhaps come back to establish the finest hacienda in all the land. Well, why not?

And so Bill and Inez left Durango and headed for Mazatlán. There he could catch one of the side-wheel packets or the stern-wheelers running between San Juan Del Sur, Nicaragua, and San Francisco. Inez left home with some misgivings. California was far away and she might not see her people again for a long time. She was never to see them again.

The first leg of the journey was rugged. Durango is high, something between 5000 and 6000 feet, and sits in a valley on the plateau of Central Mexico. Going east to Vera Cruz or Tampico, or west to Mazatlán or Culiacán, one must cross the great barrancas separating the plateaus from the coastal areas. These are huge canyons, dropping away from the escarpment in dizzying plunges, the bottoms seemingly lost in the cavernous depths below. On the top there are pine trees, and the weather is cool. On the bottom there are luxuriant growths of jungle, and snakes, and "tigrillos" and parrots. If a mule makes a false step, he hurtles through space, to be dashed on the rocks below. At any rate Bill and Inez did make it to Mazatlán.

The sea voyage to San Francisco was vexing in the extreme. Instead of salt-spray stinging the cheek, gulls wheeling overhead, blue waters sparkling, and a romantic landfall in the distance, for Bill and Inez it was mostly a case of sea-sickness, dirtiness, and poor food. A "poor sailor," Inez stayed in her cabin most of the time, a wretched little space shared with several other women, and wholly unconducive to physical comfort. Bill was impressed with the plight of fellow passengers who had boarded the ship in Nicaragua. Already out of the Atlantic coast ports for months, and likely with harrowing overland journeys through the jungles behind them, they were still faced with weeks at sea in a rolling little tub.[10] Like most of the ships in this trade, this one was old, small, and terribly overcrowded. It had not been fitted to carry large numbers of passengers for long periods of time, but it was doing both. Fresh provisions were scarce, and the drinking water was stale and brackish. The decks were so small that proper exercise was made difficult; most of the passengers listed about aimlessly, deriving what pleasures they might from visions of wealth waiting in the goldfields of California. By any standard, Bill and Inez were on no excursion. Seasickness was common, and there were two burials at sea — two poor souls sliding down into the cold waters of the Pacific, their dreams of glory vanished forever. There were no tears of farewell for the sad little packet as her weary pasengers stumbled ashore in San Francisco.

A Man's Town

And what awaited them at rainbow's end — gold? wealth? glory? Not exactly. A veteran of frontier and soldier life, Bill could hold his own in any society, but he was astonished at the wild depravity into which he had brought his bride. In 1849, San Francisco was a man's town. Men swarmed over the hills of the city, living in mean tents and lean-to shacks of the flimsiest design. In these rude places, a dozen or more men might bunch together, sleeping on boxes, crates, or even on the floor. Men who owned stores generally slept on the premises, perhaps on the counter or under it. The streets were thick with an oozing black mud after a rainfall, and were the dumping places for all manner of trash. Rats fed from the piles of offal like guests at a banquet, and were so numerous as to ravage whole sacks of grain or flour in a single night. Men walking the streets at night frequently stepped upon the horrid, bloated creatures. Drainage was poor, and pestilential pools collected in low places giving off offensive and sickening odors.

There is no record of where Bill and Inez stayed on arriving in San Francisco, but they had a limited choice as all living space was at a premium. Still, there were hotels, and Bill might have chosen the City Hotel (corner of Clay and Kearny), the Union (Kearny, between Clay and Washington), Tehama House (Sansome and California), the Oriental (Bush and Battery), the International (Jackson, between Montgomery and Kearny), or the Rossette House (Bush and Sansome). Single rates at these places ran from two to ten dollars per day.

Meals were taken at eating houses, and of these there were a great number, catering to almost every taste. A few were elegant; most were atrocious with poor food and outlandish prices. Bill and Inez did their stint in these places, but later enjoyed such places as Delmonico's, Franklin House, the Lafayette, and others of equal stamp. If he wanted a drink with friends, Bill could go to Winn's "Fountainhead," the Barry and Patten place on Montgomery street, Allen and Parker's, Fish and Patten's, the El Dorado, Arcade, or the Polka.

The San Francisco of 1849 was afflicted with the presence of such rogues and villains as the western world has rarely seen.[11] The lure of gold had attracted the bold and lawless of every land, who were turned loose in an astonishingly free environment. Attacks upon individuals upon the city streets were common; one went out into the open at his peril. Long before any great numbers of people had arrived from the Atlantic states, San Francisco was overrun by the roughest elements from Australia and the hard-bitten water-fronts of the Pacific. The English penal colonies in Van Dieman's Land and New South Wales had spewed forth an assortment of rogues, freed from the misery of penal servitude and capable of terrorizing San Francisco.

Bill Oury was not personally bothered by these brigands. Wherever he went, he carried a pistol and the same Bowie knife he had used as a Texas Ranger. He looked like, and was, a fighter. As a rule, depredations of the lawless were directed against the helpless, and these were mostly foreigners: Chileans, Mexicans, Chinese, and others. Understandably clannish, these ethnic groups gathered in small knots about the city. The roving gangs of cutthroats would fall upon these people, almost always at night, steal everything in sight and club their victims into insensibility.

The most notorious of the gangs was known as "The Hounds" (an apt description); it was the excesses of this brutal lot which gave rise ultimately to the vigilante movement. After a particularly fiendish attack by these desperadoes upon one of the foreign settlements, the weary citizens of San Francisco decided to act. The mayor, T. M. Leavenworth, called a protest meeting to plan reprisal action against the Hounds.[12] At the gathering, Samuel Brannan denounced the group in forcible terms, and called for immediate action.[13] Some 230 people were deputized and armed as a vigilante group.

By 1851, conditions in the city had again become so riotous that a Vigilance Committee was formed to cope with the situation. It became a major factor in this period of San Francisco's long and colorful history.

Bill apparently had no part in the committee. His old friend, John Coffee Hays, at that time sheriff of San Francisco, was sent by the governor to remove two confessed criminals from the hands of the vigilantes. Fearless as ever, Hays entered the premises and marched the prisoners away. Three days later the scene was reversed; an armed party of some thirty-six vigilantes broke into the jail, took the hapless two, and hanged them at the vigilante meeting house. This was the last violent act of the Committee.[14] It had done its work. From there on, law enforcement on the San Francisco streets, such as it was, became the province of the city officials.

Apparently Bill's only participation in the vigilante period was as a viewer at one of the hangings performed by the Committee in July of 1851.

Among the most vivid of Oury's memories of San Francisco were the great fires. Of the first six, he saw them all, and was indeed "burnt out" by the sixth on June 22, 1851.[15] Early San Francisco was a "natural" for fires. Fashioned largely of clapboard shacks and canvas tents, any portion of the city might be swept by fire at any time. A single blaze started anywhere along the line could be whipped by winds into a raging inferno in a matter of minutes.

The Sixth Great Fire

On Sunday, June 22, 1851, Bill and Inez were on the way to mass at the Catholic church on Vallejo street, between Dupont and Stockton. Church bells were calling the faithful to worship. Soon, the bells changed tone, and in the language of Poe became: "loud alarum bells, brazen bells . . ." The sixth great fire of San Francisco had started,[16] at a store on the corner of Pacific and Powell streets. Before it was put out, twenty blocks of the city would be reduced to rubble and ashes.

Fire companies arrived on the scene. With primitive equipment and no water pressure they could do virtually nothing. The intense heat drove the crowd back. The more audacious ran into buildings to retrieve goods, but soon these too were burning in piles up and down the line. Like the others, Bill could only stand and watch as his place went up in smoke. Inez wept.

As it turned out, several arsonists were caught applying the torch. It was commonly held that gangs of men started the blaze in reprisal for the hanging of John Jenkins twelve days earlier. It was a terrible vengeance. A complete area of the city was burned out, from Sansome street on the east to Powell on the west, and from Clay street on the south to Broadway on the north. The burden fell upon merchants and shopkeepers, and a great number of families who lost their worldly goods on that fateful Sunday morning. Many moved away then — to other cities, to the mines, and some, weary of it all, just headed for home.

When he lost his place in the fire, Bill decided to move on. He had heard great tales of sudden wealth acquired in the Mother Lode country and decided to try his hand. He had planned to go to the goldfields upon his arrival in San Francisco, but circumstances forbade it. The gold camps were no place for a woman, and he would not leave Inez behind in San Francisco. Now he heard that Sacramento and Marysville and Placerville were not such bad places — why not give them a try?

From the outset, Sacramento held little promise for Bill. Although the local war over squatter's rights on Sutter's lands was over by the time

Oury arrived, the town was hectic and uncomfortable. The streets were as dirty, the lodging as poor, and the jobs as scarce as ever they had been in San Francisco. Several months after Bill and Inez were settled, a fire swept the city destroying almost two-thirds of it. This time they were not in the fire's path.

The one big event on record for Bill and Inez in Sacramento was the birth of their first child, Lola, in 1852. Bill did take a turn at panning gold, but had none of the luck romantically associated with the occupation. He tried the various streams feeding into the American River, camping on their banks for days at a time. Up early in the morning, he would pan all day, occasionally sifting out a small nugget of gold, or leaving a residue of dust in the bottom of the pan. But now the streams were pretty well panned out; the real finds were taking place where hydraulic equipment was knocking down whole mountainsides, leaving great ugly slashes upon the land. The open air and towering pines were therapeutic, but the gold-panning was a frost. Like Jason, Bill followed the golden fleece, which turned out to be a fleece of another kind. He couldn't make it in the goldfields. His only diversions were to be found in Grass Valley and Nevada City, or in the rough little places like Red Dog, You Bet, and Rough-and-Ready. This was all very exciting, but he had a wife and baby girl in Sacramento. It was time to go home.

For the next several years Bill remained in Sacramento. His activities in this period are not known. He had worked in a saloon in San Francisco.[17] Sacramento was full of them. Perhaps he resumed his place not "before," but behind the bar.

CHAPTER 10

The Most God-forsaken Spot on Earth

IN 1856, BILL AND HIS WIFE AND DAUGHTER in a covered wagon left Sacramento for Texas. He had not found his fortune in the cold streams of the Sierra Nevadas, nor had he been able to make his mark in Sacramento or San Francisco. Besides, these places were becoming cities at a rapid pace, and Bill was not a city man. If the towns were raw frontier by Eastern standards they were too settled for Bill, and so he headed back for Texas. He never got there, but he found his home along the way.

The trip was leisurely, down the San Joaquín Valley where the going was easy and the scenery pleasing. As Inez was expecting a child, Bill covered but a few miles each day, making camp in the waning hours of the afternoon, and providing what comfort he could for his wife and four-year old girl. When he could, he would stop at one of the California missions. Coming out of Sacramento towards the coast the little party came first to San José de Guadalupe, a lovely shaded mission founded by Father Lasuén in 1797. Bill stopped there for a day. The priest heard Inez' confession, and she enjoyed conversing with him in Spanish.

Continuing down the eastern slope of the coastal range of mountains, Bill stopped at most of the missions: San Juan Bautista, San Antonio de

Padua, San Miguel Archangel, and others. Indeed, the missions had been so placed by the founding fathers as to require a day's travel from one to the next. Bill missed a few because of his inclination to travel fast or slow as the occasion required, or because as in the case of Misíon La Soledad, the place lay in ruins. Wherever he stopped, the treatment was always the same — hospitable, warm, gracious. Coming from the rude and bustling air of the mining camps and San Francisco into the old-world atmosphere of the missions, Inez felt at home; it was like riding a stagecoach between Durango and Zacatecas, in the land of her youth.

The three weary travelers rested for awhile in Los Angeles, then a dirty sprawling village still sleeping and totally unconscious of the cataclysmic growth that was to make it one of the largest cities on earth. The party continued on along the coast, making stops at San Juan Capistrano, San Luis Rey, and finally, at the end of the Alta California Chain, at San Diego de Alcala. From San Diego, Bill headed his wagon due east, climbing over the Laguna Mountains (in the present-day area of Alpine and Descanso), and then slugging it out across the blistering sands of the California desert. A few miles west of the Colorado River they passed through the sand hills, great sweeping dunes of fine-grained sand, ever-shifting and blowing with the hot desert winds. The wagon would sink to the hubs in the mushy sands and the mules would strain at their halters until it seemed that the harnesses would snap. Bill was forced, time and again, to push away the sand around all four wheels, place coats and blankets under each, and put his shoulder to the task of aiding his weary beasts. Finally, the tired little crew reached the Colorado, and were ferried across the river to Yuma City.

There Inez was delivered of her second child, a daughter who was named Louise. The other little girl, Lola, had just passed her fourth birthday. Bill stayed in Yuma for several weeks while Inez rested, then the party of four began the trek across the Arizona desert. The route lay eastward along the south bank of the Gila River to where it bends away to the north towards Phoenix. At that junction Bill headed southeast for Tucson, right through the heart of the Papago country. In later years he mentioned passing through several of the villages, where he was courteously treated by the inhabitants. With the passing of time he had forgotten the names of these little communities, but thought he might have stopped at Wohok Hotonok, Sil Nakya, Ali Ak Chin.

Arrival at Tucson

The Ourys found Tucson a small adobe town surrounded by a wall for protection against the Indians. It was a dirty, wild, undisciplined place, filled with roistering trail drovers, ranchers, and its share of brigands, and cutthroats. There was little or no law, and virtually no one present to enforce whatever laws abided. Water was scarce, and the climate hot and arid. In fact, Tucson in 1856 was not a very pleasant place. Indeed, even nine years later, Bill's sister-in-law, Mina Sanders Oury, made an even less enthusiastic appraisal of the old Pueblo. Coming into the town from El Paso in 1865, she wrote:

. . . For nearly five months we have been wanderers, have endured hardships, privations, dangers and trials of every description. At last we have drifted into port, but alas! I look around me with sinking heart and wonder if this can be the goal we have been striving so hard to reach. Excepting the wretched, squalid town of Janos, in Mexico. . . .I do not remember ever having seen a less inviting, less promising prospect for a home. Tucson is certainly the most forlorn, dreary, desolate, God-forsaken spot on earth . . . there are but one or two glass windows in town, and not a single board floor. . . . Mr Oury [Bill Oury] lives more comfortably than any other person here. He keeps a splendid Durham cow that gives an abundance of the richest milk and from his ranch they get delicious butter, an unknown luxury (here) outside their establishment.[1]

In the beginning Mina Oury found not a soul, other than her in-laws, with whom to form a friendship, and rarely left her quarters for any reason. Five years later, in 1870, John G. Bourke saw very little improvement in Tucson. ". . . streets and pavements there are none; lamps are unheard of . . . drainage is not deemed necessary."[2] J. Ross Browne voiced a similar opinion: "Tucson is . . . a place . . . for traders, speculators, gamblers, horse thieves, murderers, and vagrant politicians. If the world were searched over, there could not be found so degraded a set of villains as from the principal society of Tucson."[3] John C. Cremony, an interpreter for the Bartlett Boundary Commission of 1850 gave poor Tucson an equally caustic appraisal:

Tucson is cursed by the presence of two or three hundred of the most infamous scoundrels it is possible to conceive. Innocent and unoffending men were shot down or Bowie-knifed merely for the pleasure of witnessing their death agonies. Men walked the streets with double-barreled shot-guns, hunting each other as sportsmen hunt for game. In the graveyard . . . there were 47 graves of white men in 1860, and of that number only two had died natural deaths.[4]

There can be no doubt that when Bill and his family arrived in Tucson in 1856 they entered a real frontier town. Tourists cruising through its streets today can have no idea of the raw aspect of those early years. But Bill liked Tucson. If Mina hated the place, that was her affair, and Bourke, Browne, and Cremony were entitled to their opinions. Bill saw something there he had missed in the gentler communities — a free place where a man could stretch out and make his own way without the hand of authority to molest him. He could grow up with this land, and become a part of it, and so he decided to stay.

Texas held a spot in his heart like a man's first love, that no other place would ever take away. He would never forget Travis, and Bowie, and Crockett. He would never forget Houston, and Jack Hays, "Ad" Gillespie, or General Taylor. In his half-dreams he would close his eyes and think of a soft summer's night in San Antonio, remembering the sybilant voices of Mexicans, and the sweet notes of a guitar strumming in the distance. But these were things of a time past. He had lived these days; it was time to turn the page and begin another chapter. And Bill had made up his mind about Tucson almost as soon as he had driven his wagon down the dusty main street. With the exception of a few trips he never left it thereafter, living wholeheartedly in the community and helping it to grow and prosper for the next thirty-one years.

In Cattle and Politics

Within a few days of his arrival, Bill acquired a small cattle ranch on the Santa Cruz, about half-a-mile south of a small lake (in later years called Silver Lake). This was to be his livelihood, but it was not long before he also became engaged in politics. For the remainder of his life, Bill was in and out of Tucson politics, and although he held several offices of importance, he was never as agile or successful a politician in the Territory as his brother Granville.

Granville, Bill's junior by eight years, had been practising law in Los Angeles since the early part of 1855. Seeing the possibilities inherent in the new Territory of Arizona he followed his brother there in 1856, arriving in Tucson only a short time after Bill. Soon after "Grant's" arrival, a convention was held (August 29, 1856), wherein it was resolved to send a delegate to Washington urging the organization of Arizona as a Territory. The petition was signed by some 260 persons, and Nathan P. Cook was selected as the delegate. The Committee membership was made up of Grant Oury, N. P. Cook, H. Ehrenburg, Ignacio Ortez, I. D. C. Pack, and Mark Aldrich serving as president. Grant was selected then as a member of the New Mexico Legislature (at Mesilla) while the group awaited word on its petition for territorial status.

It was in this year of 1856 that Bill and Grant met the men who would be their friends for the next several decades No oldtime record of Tucson would be complete without a mention of a few of their names: Solomon Warner, Charles D. Poston, Sylvester Mowry, Charley Brown, Leopoldo Carrillo, Mark Aldrich, and Charley Myers.

Of these, Solomon Warner was perhaps the most engaging personality. A former storekeeper in Yuma, he had moved to Tucson when the Gadsden Purchase opened the area to Americans. He arrived in Tucson a little before Bill Oury, on February 28, 1856, and for the next few years hauled freight between Tucson and Fort Yuma, guiding his mules over the treacherous rocks and sands of the long desert. Bill and Grant spent many a silver dollar across the rude counter of his store which was located near the present corner of Main and Alameda streets.

When the Civil War came to Tucson, these old friends aligned themselves on different sides. Bill and Grant were fiery Southern sympathizers, hating Yankees almost as much as they did Apaches. Warner, on the other hand, was a loyal Union man. When Captain Sherod Hunter of the Confederacy entered Tucson on February 28, 1862, Warner left town, the Rebel troops confiscating all of his goods and property. Still, this deep ideological difference between the Ourys and Warners did not mar their friendship. Bill Oury always liked Sol Warner. In a community where there were relatively few white residents, it was natural that close friendships should develop. When Bill died in 1887, Sol Warner was one of the sad pallbearers.

Sol himself prospered over the years. At the close of the Civil War he came back into Tucson from Sonora and started in business again. Sugar was selling for 75 cents a pound, soap for 50 cents a bar, and flour at the rate of eighteen dollars for 100 pounds. There was plenty of money around and people were willing to spend it. Warner was fortunate too in that Tucson had become the supply depot for the entire Territory. Camp Crittenden inaugurated and continued a policy of placing large orders for Warner's supplies. Sol built a flour mill near Sentinel Peak ("A" Mountain) in 1874. Bishop Salpointe gave him a right of way through the grounds of Misíon San José del Tucson for this purpose. The right of way permitted him to build a canal to carry water to his mill wheel. But Sol Warner died almost penniless. He had claims against the government for some $20,000 for losses incurred by Apache attacks on his wagon trains, and it is said that the government never paid the claims. He died on November 14, 1899, forty-three years after coming to the old Pueblo with his first muletrain of goods.

CHAPTER 11

Jacks and Jerklines

In August, 1856, the federal Congress passed a postal bill making possible the establishment of an overland stage passenger and mail service across the wastelands of the American Southwest. James E. Birch, a California stage operator, obtained a contract for a line to operate between San Antonio, Texas, and San Diego. He organized his company early in 1857, and began to advertise in the leading papers of the country. Operating on a shoestring, Birch was barely able to fulfill his contract with the government. His early stages would leave Fort Yuma and probe but a few miles into the desert, there to relinquish the mailbags to a relay of horsemen who carried the mail on to Tucson.

Just as he was beginning to operate efficiently, a rival operator pulled the rug from under him. John Butterfield, of Utica, New York, obtained a government contract for a stage to run between St. Louis and San Francisco, the contract to run for six years for $600,000.00 per year. As Butterfield's enterprise was bigger than Birch's the government selected it for backing, Birch as a consequence was out of business. Butterfield met the government's franchise terms in the first year of operation, although he was pushed to make it. His stages were required to cover almost 2800 miles in twenty-five days (or less), operating on a semi-weekly basis. Even with the setbacks occasioned by Apache attacks upon his stages, Butterfield was soon able to inaugurate daily trips; this gained him an increase in government subsidy to $1,300,000 per year.

Agent for Butterfield

Bill was one of Butterfield's first employees, named as Tucson agent early in 1857.[1] Later, when the line was well established and running on a daily schedule, there would be some 750 employees, twice that number of horses, and over 100 large Concord coaches and spring wagons.[2] The selection of stations required the eye of a tactician. Each station must be near water, be defensible against Indians, have good grazing land nearby, and be within reasonable proximity to its adjacent station in the chain. This meant that the stations were generally about twenty miles apart. Most of them had small blacksmith shops for maintenance and repair of the coaches. Today of course, all of the Arizona stations, except for a few stone or adobe ruins are gone.

Regular ads for the line appearing in Eastern papers by 1859 carried the following interesting information.

Coaches of our line leave semi-monthly from each end, and on the 9th and 24th of each month at 6: A.M. An armed escort travels through the Indian Country with each mail train for the protection of mail and passengers. Passengers are provided with provisions during the trip, except where the coach stops at public houses. . . . Each passenger is allowed 30 pounds of personal luggage, exclusive of blankets and arms.

Passengers coming to San Antonio can take the line of mail steamers from New Orleans, and travel a week to Indianola. From the latter place there is a daily line of 4-horse mail coaches direct to San Antonio. On the Pacific side, the California Steam-Navigation Company runs a first-class steamer semi-monthly between San Francisco and San Diego. Fares on this line are as follows, including rations:

San Antonio	San Diego	$200
San Antonio	Tucson	150
San Antonio	El Paso	100
Intermediate Stations		15c per mile.[3]

At the Tucson agency, Bill put out similar ads, but tailored them to local needs. Many of these appeared in the Tubac *Arizonian* during 1859.[4] One of these simply lists "running time" between Tubac and San Francisco (eleven days), and between Tubac and St. Louis (sixteen days). Another of Bill's ads reads:

Notice is hereby given that packages, boxes, or parcels brought by the Overland Mail, if kept in the office over one day will be at the risk of the owner as the company makes no charge for storage. It will not be responsible for any loss that may occur.[5]

William S. Oury,
Agent, O.M. Co.

Another of Bill's ads read:

The line, which has been in successful operation since July, 1857, is ticketing passengers through to San Diego and intermediate stations. Passengers and express matter forwarded in new coaches drawn by six mules over the entire length of our line, excepting the Colorado Desert of 100 miles, which we cross on mule-back. Passengers [are] guaranteed on their tickets to ride in coaches, excepting the 100 miles as stated above. Passengers ticketed to and from Fort Lancaster, Fort Davis, El Paso, Fort Fillmore, La Mesilla, Tucson, Fort Yuma, and San Diego.[6]

On April 28, 1859, this news item appeared in the Tubac *Arizonian.*

O.M. train attacked by Indians. The conductor of the O.M. coach which arrived at Tucson on the 25th reports that a Mr. Buck, in the employ of the O.M. Co. as a teamster, was attacked by a party of Tonto Apaches a short distance below "Murderer's Grave" station, and so severely wounded that it is thought he will not recover. He received three arrows in his back. . . . The wagon he was driving and the mules were captured. . . .[7]

These ads today evoke a primitive and colorful institution — the Overland-Mail! Picture the poor wounded man toppling from his seat, three arrows stuck securely in his back — or the passengers loading at Tucson for the long, hot, jolting trip to Yuma, Bill giving last minute instructions to the driver and the man "riding shotgun." See the drummer nervously scanning the horizon for Indians, the bored cardsharp en route to San Francisco, and the pretty young girl wondering how 100 miles on mule-back will be!

The line had several names. Generally, it was referred to as the "Butterfield Line," or the "Overland Mail." In Missouri people called it the great "Southern Overland," while those in the far west gave it the name "California Overland Express." The coaches were of two types; the heavy "Concord" wagon and the lighter and faster "Celerity Wagon." The latter was one of Butterfield's own innovations and was used in the western end of the run, being better adapted to negotiate mountain roads, desert sands, and to giving its occupants a speedier getaway when Indians attacked. Both coaches were ordinarily painted a russet-red, or a deep green color. Many had hand-painted scenes on the doors.

The coaches were drawn by four, five, or six horse or mule teams. In the west, mules were preferred, not only because they were stronger, but because Indians would not steal them or run them off as readily as they would horses. The coaches averaged about 120 miles per day, the passengers breakfasting early in the morning at the starting station and taking supper at the sixth station down the line. Occasionally, the driver would try another twenty, perhaps even another forty miles. Like as not, however, it would be the other way around, particularly in rugged terrain or in Indian country. Passengers (women and children excepted) frequently had to get out and walk alongside the coach; the poor horses or mules could not pull dead weight up some of the mountain passes or through the deep sands. At times, when the weather was good, the run was delightful. Mostly it was an endurance contest, punctuated with blazing sun, high winds, mud, sleet, snow, sleeplessness, poorly prepared food, and coach sickness. There are cases on record where passengers because of fear, overactive imagination, and constant motion lost all contact with reality, and were temporarily reduced to howling maniacs. One thing, the run was seldom boring.

Perils En Route

The theme for the ever-present danger of Indian attacks was set in a colorful report made by W. L. Ormsby, a reporter of the New York *Herald.* He was a passenger on the first through East-West Butterfield Coach, leaving St. Louis September 15, 1858, and arriving in San Francisco "23 days, 23 hours later." He wrote:

I am safe and sound from all the threatened dangers of Indians, tropic suns, rattlesnakes, grizzly bears, stubborn mules, mustang horses, jerked beef, mountain passes, fording rivers, and all the concomitants which envy, pedantry, and ignorance had predicted for all passengers of the Overland Mail route. . . ."[8]

Although he warned of the dangers of coach travel, Ormsby was not molested in his hectic run. But the dangers were not imaginary, and both travelers and residents were well aware of them.

Mina Oury, Granville's wife, wrote of the danger along the Overland Mail route. By the time she made the following entry in her diary (November 3, 1865) the line was no longer in operation. The perils along its old route, however, were as fearsome as ever.

Every foot of ground for hundreds of yards around our camp has been the scene of the most heart-rending murders and butcheries. The stage has been attacked twice very recently at this very spot (Apache Pass), the passengers

and driver killed, the horses either killed or carried off, and the stage burned.
A train of four wagons and nine men were attacked, five of the men shot,
and the other four tied to a wagon-wheel and left to burn to death. Their
charred remains were seen long after. Within 30 steps of us, the mutilated
bodies of five Mexicans were found burned, and nearby is a tree where the
skeletons of six Indians swung for two years. . . .[9]

Still, all was not grim with the Butterfield Line. When the coaches came into town they did so with a flourish and a bang, after careening down the main street of the old Pueblo to pull up in a shuddering stop at the office on the corner of Pearl and Pennington streets. A man seated beside the driver would blow loudly upon a long horn to warn teamsters, pedestrians, urchins, burros, and ox-drawn wagons to make way for the Tucson stage.[10] Just about everything and everybody would pull aside at the sound of the trumpet to let the big stage come shooting through. Now and then an oxcart would hold its place, and soon the street would be a welter of kicking legs and tumbling wagons.

Bill Oury watched the stages come and go hundreds of times in his four years with the line. The old rounded adobe tower, with the words, "Stage Depot, Tucson," became a familiar and beloved sight. It was his bailiwick, his province, from the business office inside to the corral in back where he kept spare parts for the stages and great mounds of hay and grain for the horses.

Bill kept his job as Overland Mail Company agent until the beginning of the Civil War. Service was then disrupted until the war's end, when it was resumed until the coming of the Southern Pacific Railroad in 1880.

As Tucson grew and the needs of its citizens multiplied, a rival line appeared. The Texas-California Stage Line moved in from Yuma about 1879. The Overland Mail established an office on South Convent Street for its Tombstone run, and another nearby for its run to Guaymas. Bill had nothing to do with the new line or the branch offices. His heyday was the line's early period, 1857–1861, the most colorful years of all, when the town was at its rowdiest, the trips the most hazardous, and the mules probably the meanest. The old Butterfield Line was a tough, rugged outfit; Bill loved it, and talked about it to his dying day.

CHAPTER 12

Brother Granville

LIKE BILL, GRANVILLE WAS BORN IN ABINGDON, VIRGINIA, but a few years later, in 1825. He was eight when Augustus moved the family to Pike County, Missouri, and according to Bill was "in and out of the wagon like a jack-in-the-box" as the family moved west. He spent his boyhood on the banks of the Mississippi, like Huck Finn, poling homemade rafts in the shallows, and angling for catfish.

On reaching young manhood he began to study law with Judge Ayler Buckner, a local jurist who had served in the Congress as a Representative from northern Missouri for a dozen or more years.[1] Judge Buckner's offices were in Bowling Green, a town some twelve miles from Grant's home in Louisiana, Missouri. Grant studied with Buckner for two years, and was admitted to the bar in the fall of 1848.[2] He hung out his shingle in Louisiana at once.

He did not practice long in Missouri, for he succumbed to "gold fever" and headed for California. By now, Bill had arrived there from Mexico with his bride. He had written to Grant, painting an exciting picture of life in the gold camps, and urged him to come west. Grant did come, on horseback with several friends. Considering the dangers of such a journey and the times in which it was made, it was a singularly uneventful trip. The little party saw not one Indian along the entire route. Grant scratched about the streams of the Mother Lode country for a spell, even finding a few bright nuggets. But he was unable to find the wealth he sought. Bidding Bill and Inez farewell (in Sacramento) he drifted south, and soon took up the practice of law in Los Angeles.[3]

Another Oury in Town

Granville arrived in Tucson just a few weeks after Bill in 1856, following a different route from Bill's between Los Angeles and Yuma. At Warner's Ranch, he found Judge Peter Rainesford Brady ill and feverish to the point of death. Grant remained there with Brady for six weeks, nursing him slowly back to health.[4] When Brady was well enough to travel, Oury arranged for his passage to Los Angeles. It was a kindness Brady never forgot.

Grant was very active in the fight to establish Arizona as a federal territory, and more of this will appear later on. In 1862 he raised a battalion of troops sympathetic to the Southern cause and took them to Mesilla. His entire service in the Civil War seems to have been with Colonel P. T. Herbert's battalion of Arizona Mounted Volunteers. The War Department records of the Confederate States of America show that Grant was enrolled in Colonel Herbert's outfit on May 21, 1862, at Mesilla, New Mexico Territory.[5] The company muster roll shows that he was "elected" captain on the same day.[6]

Grant served with General W. H. Sibley in the latter's Louisiana campaign. Although a brave and fearless man, Grant seemed not to have the same feeling as Bill for the military. He became engaged in some sort of quarrel with his superior officer, and as a result offered his resignation just nine months after the promising start at Mesilla.

The documentation of the incident is very scarce. The note carried a Pattersonville [Louisiana] dateline of 22 February, 1863, and was addressed to Brigadier General Sibley.[7] Two days later, at New Iberia, Sibley "respectfully recommended" that Oury's resignation be accepted.[8] The Division Commander [Taylor] returned Sibley's recommendation for clarification, stating (that) "simple tenders of resignation without sufficient cause [given] . . . will not be accepted."[9] Sibley then came back with these unflattering words:

Captain Oury's war savvy is so small that his services can readily be dispensed with. He desires, moreover, to go to Arizona where he can be of great use.[10]

W. H. Sibley,
Brig. General
Army

This time the recommendation was approved. Things moved swiftly, and Grant was paid off on 8 March, 1863, with severance pay of $1141.33.[11] With the major battles of the war yet to come (Gettysburg and Vicksburg less than four months away), it seems strange that release from the service could be effected simply by requesting it. Rather frequently employed, however, this practice, coupled with short enlistments, made for a sort of huge floating population — in both armies.

Grant moved on to San Antonio, and there in the latter part of 1863, married his cousin Mina Sanders, of Seguin, Texas. She was a remarkable and strong-willed woman, as may be seen from portions of her diary interspersed in this narrative.

His quarrel with Sibley notwithstanding, Grant was a loyal and outspoken sympathizer for the Southern cause. In fact, so keen was his enthusiasm for the South that at the war's end, he fled the country into Mexico rather than give allegiance to the victorious Yankees. If his zeal was genuine, so were his discomforts in the wilderness south of the border. After several remarkable months, the expatriot was willing enough to come back home. On October 8, 1865, at Fort Mason, Arizona, Grant did what he had sworn never to do — offered his oath of allegiance to the government of the United States of America. The oath was written in Grant's own hand, and receipted by Lt. W. H. H. Fellows, 7th U. S. Infantry, California Volunteers.[12] Fellows, in making an entry in his "description list" speaks disparagingly of Oury as having served with the "so-called Confederate Army" although to Grant, his keenest aspirations and fondest dreams had coincided with the Southern cause.[13]

Grant in Politics

In 1866, Grant was elected to the Arizona Legislature and made Speaker of the Assembly, a position he held also in 1873 and 1875.[14] In 1869, he served as District Attorney for Pima County. In 1871 he moved to Phoenix where he served as District Attorney, and was elected as Speaker of the Arizona Legislature for the second time. His service in that capacity seemed to impress his colleagues; he was the recipient of a warm testimonial from the collective assembly attesting to his "great fairness and impartiality."[15]

Grant ran for Congress on the Democratic ticket in 1879, but was defeated. He returned to Florence (where he had taken up residence) and served as District Attorney for two years. Then he ran for Congress again, opposing one H. W. Stewart, and this time he was successful.[16] He ran again in 1883, defeating Judge DeForest Porter.[17] He came home to Florence in 1885, again to be D.A. for the township.[18]

Despite his meagre war record, there is no doubt that Granville Oury was a brave and resourceful man. His accomplishments show that he was suited more to statesmanship than to fighting, and in this he was the antithesis of Bill who was a fighter, not a diplomat. Still, when physical danger threatened, Grant was right there.

The Crabb Filibuster

This is demonstrated by the following bizarre incident in which Granville played a part. The famous Crabb Filibuster which ended in disaster, costing the lives of sixty-eight men, took place in 1857. Henry A. Crabb was a Stockton, California, lawyer who envisioned a new frontier in northern Mexico with himself as leader. The wide-open land there seemed an inviting target for conquest, and he set out to push the natives aside and move in. In the end, Crabb was caught by a detachment of Mexican soldiers. His head was severed, and placed in a container of mescal for preservation. Later, the grisly object was mounted on a spike and paraded about the town. Granville ("Grant" to many or "Gran" to his brother Bill) didn't even know Crabb, but on hearing of the expedition's predicament in Mexico, gathered up Crabb's rearguard of twenty men in Sonoyta and set out to rescue the ill-fated buccaneers. Grant's motive for making the trip has never been ascertained. No one has been able to say whether he went to join the expedition or advise against it. On arriving in Sonoyta, he learned that Crabb had not been reenforced as expected, and that he was holed up in a convent, surrounded by Mexican troops. Grant assumed command of the rear-guard of twenty men and hastened off to rescue Crabb and the others.

The brave little band had seventy-five miles to go over rough country. By the time it arrived at Caborca, its position was perilous. Grant and his men concealed themselves in some chapparal just outside of town, and pondered what to do next.[19] But they had been seen. Soon a Mexican army officer appeared before them, relating that Crabb and his men had surrendered, and that if the relief party would quit the fight, their lives would be spared. One hour was allowed for an answer.

Oury called back that "not one moment" was needed, whereupon he and his men fired a volley at some soldiers waiting in the distance.[20] The fighting then started and Grant began his rear-guard action which lasted in varying degrees of intensity all the way back to the Arizona border.

Bancroft states that the Oury party lost four men on its retreat. An old time Tucson resident, Ed McGowen, said: "Captain Oury and his band of twenty heroes cut their way out, although surrounded by the enemy, and every man but one got safely back to Arizona." Grant never had very much to say about the affair, one way or another.

MR. AND MRS. GRANVILLE H. OURY. Bill's sister-in-law, Mina, like her husband, was an articulate Confederate sympathizer. In her diary of Arizona frontier life, she was forthright in describing Tucson as "the most Godforsaken spot on earth." More politician than soldier, Grant Oury led his wife and an embittered group of Arizona Confederates to Mexico to avoid swearing allegiance to the United States, returning three months later, "weary, sore, and chastened." Grant later became a respected figure in Arizona politics.

Running for Office

Grant's political efforts were far more successful. Morris Goldwater, great uncle of the defeated candidate for the U. S. presidency in 1964, ran for the Territorial Assembly in Maricopa County in 1874 (on the Democratic ticket), with a running mate, Winchester Miller of Tempe. They were opposed by William Long and John T. Alsap, probate judge and trustee of the Phoenix Townsite. When the votes were counted, Alsap came out ahead with 324; Long and Goldwater had tied at 204 votes apiece, while Miller trailed with 120. A special runoff election was ordered for December between Long and Goldwater.[21]

The Republicans had done better than their rivals, receiving 528 votes against Goldwater's and Long's combined total of 324. Rather than see his party go down to defeat, Goldwater withdrew, yielding his runoff post to Grant Oury, by then well known in Arizona political circles. Oury won the runoff post with ease, and gained a strong friend in young Morris Goldwater who supported the older man in his successful bids for a seat in the U.S. Congress in 1880 and 1882.[22]

In his try for the U.S. Congress, Grant had the solid support of his old friend Solomon Warner. In a statement entitled: "To the People of Arizona," Warner made these remarks:

Since this political campaign opened, attacks have been made upon the Honorable G. H. Oury, which for injustice and recklessness have few equals in the political history of any country. . . . I have known Mr. Oury since February, 1856, as an official and as a private citizen, have watched his course closely, and am intimate with the part he has taken in many trying events, and know, in a general way, his entire course in Arizona. Speaking from what I know, I feel that I am entitled to a hearing from the people, who always desire fair play and truth. Knowing then the injustice done him, I cannot remain silent.

Most of them who slander him now came here long after the trying times of our early history were over, times in which Oury demonstrated his manhood, and left an impression of respect and kindness in the memory of all who knew him then. I propose to tell you a few of the early incidents of which I have knowledge, in support of what I say, to prove that Grant Oury has always reached out his arm in defense of the weak.

In 1857, when we had little or no law . . . a band of desperadoes headed by J. G. (Billiard) Ward, and one Redding, followed a pack train from Sonora with flour for Fort Buchanan. Near Nogales, the gang attacked it, killed several of the party, and drove the animals away into this Territory. Grant Oury came to me for animals to go in pursuit of them. He followed the band, captured the animals and returned them to their rightful owners. He was assisted by a few of our people, but he was the one who got up the party.

About 1859 a man named Miles lay sick and wounded in Tucson. He was set upon by one Byrd, and some others, who claimed Miles owed them

*$1,600. . . . Byrd and his gang were about to take all his property when . . .
Grant Oury demanded proof of Byrd. Under the pressure made by Oury and
others, the plunderers desisted. . . .*

*These are not the only instances; many others can be told and the proofs
furnished. . . . I am now in my old age, unable to get out and see the people
and tell them what I know, hence this message. I cannot feel that it is right to
forget the services of a man now that the trying events are past. A grateful
and kind remembrance should always be accorded to those who have been
true in the dark days. . . . I cannot refrain from saying to the people that Grant
Oury has been the friend and supporter of the right from our early days to
the present hour . . . there is no more fitting person for these considerations
than Granville H. Oury.*

Solo (Solomon) Warner.[23]

Grant had his enemies and he had his friends. What a good friend
was old Solomon Warner. Bill always spoke affectionately of his brother
"Gran" — until the latter years of his life. Then in-law trouble arose and
the two became estranged. In the main, however, and over the years, close
association and sharing of mutual hardships made for a strong bond
between the brothers.

CHAPTER 13

You Shoot First

LIKE A GREAT MANY MEN OF HIS DAY, Bill Oury believed implicitly in the Code Duello, and indeed risked his life twice on the "Field of Honor" to prove it. In the far west of the frontier period, duelling was an established and acceptable way of settling even the most trifling differences. Bill's quarrels were of no great moment, to him or either of his adversaries, yet "honor" was gained only at the expense of human life in both contests.

In the first of these two affairs, Bill engaged in a dispute with one Benjamin H. Miles, an ex-politician in the California State Legislature. Miles had a brother, Edward, who had come to Tucson in the mid-1850's and established a trading post. Benjamin had come to Tucson to see his brother, and got into the altercation with Bill on April 27, 1858.[1] There is no known record on the subject of the quarrel, but as Miles was as ardent a Republican as Oury was a Democrat it is possible that politics was the issue.[2] Actually, it was Edward, the storekeeper, who first had words with Bill. In the course of the wrangle, Benjamin interceded and challenged Oury to the duel. As the challenged party, Oury was permitted to choose the weapons. He chose rifles, the distance between duelists to be thirty paces.

A news item in the July 5, 1858 issue of the Santa Cruz (California) *Sentinel* provides a cryptic footnote to this tragic episode in Tucson's history. In an almost casual manner it dismisses the event with these words: "Miles was shot through the neck and fell dead upon the field. He was unaccustomed to the use of firearms."[3]

Bill's second duel was fought in Tucson in 1860, with one Benito Flournoy. According to Lázaro Borquez, an eyewitness, the duel was performed under unique circumstances. Instead of following the custom of stepping off so many paces, whirling and firing, the antagonists faced each other squarely to begin with, fifty paces apart. The arms used were muzzle-loading muskets, each loaded with a lead slug.[4] Borquez recalled that the entire male population of the Pueblo turned out to see the duel. The principals, their seconds, and the gallery gathered at Elysian Grove. Oury and Flournoy were dressed in black, and two coffins draped in black were placed a few yards to one side of the field.[5]

Oddly enough, Benito Flournoy was a stand-in, and had no business in Elysian Grove on that cheerless morning. The quarrel was actually between Oury and Benito's brother Eduardo Flournoy, and had occurred over something no less trivial than the ownership of some adobe bricks. Charley Meyers and Juan Elias had tried to stop it since Oury was a married man with children and Eduardo was single. Rather than compromise family honor, Benito, also married, stood in his brother's place.[6]

Borquez related that Flournoy called out: "You shoot first, I am a better man than you are!" Oury replied: "No sir, you shall shoot first."[7] As neither man would take the first shot, the seconds tossed a coin; Flournoy lost and had to shoot first. His musket roared and the slug grazed Bill's cheek and neck. The blood splashed upon his collar and the shoulder of his dreary dark suit.

Ordinarily, Bill might have fired in the air, and both men could have walked from the field satisfied. In this peculiar affair, the condition had been set that alternate shots would be fired until one of the men was dead. Bill took aim and dropped Benito in his tracks. His seconds believed him to be wounded only, and rushed up to get him ready for the next round. He fell limp in the arms of the man who reached him first. He was placed in a coffin and carried away to the cemetery.

Bill never had much to say about either of these affairs. When his grandson asked him (in 1885) if he "had really killed two men with rifles," his only reply was: "Yes, I did."

CHAPTER 14

Oury and the Pioneer Press

ODDLY, IT WAS ANOTHER DUEL that occasioned the purchase by Bill Oury of Arizona's first newspaper and press, the *Tubac Arizonian*. Its owner, a Mexican War veteran, Colonel Edward Cross, was an enthusiastic supporter of the newly formed Republican Party. His editorials were offensive to Oury and his good friend Sylvester Mowry, both ardent Democrats.[1] Mowry engaged Cross in a duel over one of the latter's editorials, but the affair ended harmlessly; Mowry fired in the air after Cross missed his first shot.

It was Oury who suggested purchase of the paper. He and Mowry bought it from Cross for $2500 on the same day that the duel was fought. The best account of the duel and subsequent acquisition of the paper was written by Oury himself for the Arizona *Daily Star* some twenty years after.[2] It was titled: "A Brief History of Early Journalism in Pima County." Salient portions read as follows:

In the year 1858 the Santa Rita Mining Company, under the direction of Messrs. Wrightson, Thomas, and William of Cincinnati, arrived in the old village of Tubac making it the headquarters of its operations temporarily. The Wrightsons were both practical printers and brought out from Cincinnati . . .

one of the best printing establishments . . . ever brought into the territory. . . .³
Before the end of the year, the Weekly Arizonian, *edited by Colonel Cross was ushered into existence in the ancient burg of Tubac.⁴ The editor and all the proprietors of the paper belonged to the party then newly born, y-clept "Black Republican," and hoped through the influence of their paper . . . to mould the political complexion of the territory in that direction.*

In this however, they reckoned without their host, as at that time nearly the entire American population of the country was decidedly Democratic, and through the untiring activity of Sylvester Mowry had already undertaken the task of obtaining from Congress a territorial organization.⁵

The undertaking proved fruitless, not for lack of ability or perseverance on the part of our champion, Mowry . . . but [because] although the administration was Democratic, the Republicans had a majority in the Lower House of Congress. To the charge that their opposition was factious (made by Democratic friends of the measure in the House), the Republicans replied by producing editorials from the only newspaper printed in the territory, opposing organization. In one of these editorials, Colonel Cross criticized very severely the part taken by Mowry in the matter. . . . Upon his return, Mowry . . . demanded a retraction of the offensive language, and was peremptorily refused. This led to a duel, in which an amusing interpretation of the Code of Honor was rendered.⁶

The weapons chosen were Burnside rifles; distance, twenty paces. The day was exceedingly windy and the guns light in weight. Consequently, the first fire resulted in a clear miss by both. The guns were promptly reloaded and the word given for the second fire. Mowry's gun failed to go off; Cross fired and missed. . . . Mowry's second, Mr. Mercer, now argued that in order to "make things even," Colonel Cross must stand up and allow Mowry to take a shot at him without returning fire. After considerable argument on both sides, this was agreed to. . . . As a result, Cross stood with his arms folded . . . as calmly and coolly as a knight of the Middle Ages. At this stage, your correspondent . . . stepped up to Mowry and asked him what he proposed, and if he intended to fire at Cross with intent to do him bodily harm — to which he indignantly replied, "Do you think I would kill a defenseless man?" To this I simply remarked that I was glad. . . . However, as the thing had been agreed upon, and no harm was to be done, it would give Mowry the appearance of magnanimity to waste his shot. Time was called, and Mowry fired in the air. Here the duel ended, both parties retiring from the field.

Upon the return of all hands to Tubac, I suggested to both belligerents that in order to avoid future unpleasantness, Mowry and I would purchase the press . . . at a fair price, and remove the paper to Tucson. The price was arranged at $2500, the press taken down the same day and a wagon to transport it engaged. The next morning, the whole thing was loaded and taken to Tucson. From its first issue there it nailed the Democrats flag to its masthead and I can proudly say that from that day down to the present . . . it has never displayed the Republican colors. ⁷

From the spring of 1859 to the fall of 1860, under the able editorship of J. Howard Wells, it battled sturdily for the Democratic cause and earned the confidence and patronage of the federal administration. . . . After he retired, a young man from San Francisco named Gelwick took charge, and Frank Higgins did the type-setting. About this time clouds began to gather over the political horizon and government patronage was withdrawn. Although the paper struggled on for some time, sustained almost entirely from my own private purse, in May, 1861, the editor Thomas J. Turner, announced the last issue of the Weekly Arizonian *on account of the approach of Civil War.*

The material of the printing office was now carefully packed away and the press taken down and stored by its owner, who expected it to rest peacefully until the civil strife was over. Alas! how vain are all human calculations. In the summer of 1862, when the California Column arrived in Tucson, commanded by the superzealous General Carleton, everything in the land was considered disloyal, even down to the press and type out of which the old Weekly Arizonian *had been produced. It was ruthlessly torn from its secluded resting place and paraded as a great trophy of war, and finally put up as the organ of the "great I am," James H. Carleton. In spite of all the efforts of all the soldier printers of the Command, the old press, true to its Democratic instincts, refused to perform service for the Republican cause.*[8] *After considerable pounding and destruction of a great part of its material and furniture, the press was given over to continancy.*

*After the departure of the "great I am" for New Mexico, I gathered together the scattered fragments of furniture, and sadly stored them away to rest, from which they were not dragged forth until 1866 when Sidney DeLong . . . again brought the old press into requisition, I agreeing to give him its use free of charge. . . . First edited and printed by a crazy-brained fellow named Pierce, afterwards by Shearer, the paper under its old name (*Weekly Arizonian*) struggled along for a year or so and again went to sleep, from which it did not wake until the summer of 1870, when it was revived under the management of P. W. Dooner.*[9] *This was to advocate the cause of P. R. Brady, Democratic Candidate for Congress against R. C. McCormick, candidate of the federal ring — which at the time ruled the territory with an iron rod. . . . Needless to say, the ring triumphed and . . . Dooner was driven out of Arizona and his paper sent to grass when the campaign was over. . . .*

In the course of years, the remaining material was sold to the Citizen. . . . *the press lay exposed to the action of all weather, in my yard, until the latter part of 1876, when it was sold to D. Velasco for $100. After cleaning and putting it up . . . he sold it to C. H. Tully who in connection with Mr. L. C. Hughes (in 1877) started the Arizona* Star, *which was printed in the same faithful old press until recently. After separation from Tully, Hughes brought out a power press and left the old one to print "Dos Republicas." Tully purchased a new press for his paper and sold the grand old relic to* The Nugget, *which sprightly sheet it still sends forth with unremitting faithfulness every week.*

W. S. Oury.

So much for bygone days, when the way to silence the opposition was to shoot it or buy it out. It may be of some interest to list here a few of the items which appeared in the *Arizonian* during its short life in Tubac. These are taken at random, and provide nothing more than a look at the character of the historic paper.

A March 3, 1859, item expresses awe over the fact that a Navajo Indian was killed by a Minie ball "at 400 yards" (on "one of Lindsay's recent scouts").[10] Had the writer guessed what damage the Minie ball would do in the next five years, he would have real cause for wonder.

Mincing no words, one Palatine Robinson asked on March 17, 1859 that: "All persons indebted to the firm of Hayden and Robinson are requested to come forward and settle without delay."[11]

A chilling little story appeared in the paper on June 16, 1859.

Ran away from the employ of Hoppin and Appel at Tubac on the night of June 12, a peon named Juan José Arenas. He stole a Mississippi rifle and other articles belonging to his employers, and was in their debt $82.68¾. He has probably gone to Sonora. The subscribers will feel obliged for any information as to his whereabouts and will pay a suitable reward for his arrest and delivery at Tubac.[12]

A search through later issues of the *Arizonian* failed to shed any light on the fate of Arenas.[13] One wonders how he got himself indebted to the tune of $82.68¾, and while sympathizing for the losses of the merchants rather hopes that Juan José made it to Sonora and safety.

The October 6, 1859, issue carried this piece on its co-owner:[14]

On the 4th inst., W. S. Oury, Esq., left for the East by the Overland Mail Route, on a visit for a few months. He took with him his oldest daughter, Lola, a very interesting child. It is his intention to place her at school in Missouri, in which state he has many relations. Mr. Oury, since the formation of the Overland Mail Co. has held the position of general agent of this place, where he has been of great service to the company. In the impartial discharge of his duty he has endeared himself to our citizens. As one of the earliest settlers of the Territory, and possessing a high tone of character, and unyielding will with conservative principles, he has been able to exert an unusual influence for the good and welfare of this community. He carries with him the warm wishes of hosts of friends.

Songs of Early Days

Students of the military will be interested in the "Song of the Dragoons" published in the *Tubac Arizonian* on April 14, 1859. The dragoons had not much time left to use that romantic name. On August 3, 1861, Congress passed a bill organizing all mounted troops, dragoons and mounted riflemen into one branch, thereafter called Cavalry. The name dragoon disappeared from the U.S. Army rolls, and as Major General Herr has said: ". . . caused confusion then, and has ever since."[15]

The following song was written by a Lieutenant Anderson of the First Dragoons, and was a parody on the popular tune "Some Love to Roam." It was sung to the same air, and (according to the press item) was "highly popular in the 1840s and '50s." One might think about the hardbitten horse soldiers sitting around their camp fires before Buena Vista, or with Kearny on his march to California singing this song. If its literary style leaves something to be desired, it does offer an authentic bit of nostalgia for a most colorful type.

THE DRAGOON'S SONG

O sabre bright is my delight
    And a steed that loves the lea,
A hardy hand at a word's command,
    The life of a dragoon free.

Now stirrups all, at the bugles' call
    We're over the prairie wide
While every bound o'er Indian ground
    Is pulse to our roving pride.

The bending sky is our canopy
    And the turf shall our pillow be,
No city clown, in his bed of down
    Sleeps half so sweet as we.

No care have we for a ship at sea
    Nor the miser's hoarded store
A steed, a sword — is the dragoon's word,
    He cares not a jot for more.

With these my boys, and the maid that joys
    In the love of our heart so true.
We'll live and roam o'er our prairie home
    'Til death's bugle sounds tattoo.

A set of sun when our march is done,
    Bright burns the bivouac,
A song we troll, and pledge the bowl —
    Here's health to our friends a-back.

In his days with the Texas Rangers (at Corpus Christi and Brownsville in 1836) Bill had listened to the song of the famed Second Dragoons,

Oh! the dragoon bold — he scorns all care,
    As he goes around with uncropped hair,
He spends no thought on the evil star
    That sent him away to the border war!

Bill recalled that many of the dragoons of the Mexican War period had long, flowing hair. Captain Charles A. May, the hero of Palo Alto and Resaca de la Palma charged into battle, "his dark brown locks falling well over his shoulders."[16]

As described above, the *Arizonian* had a short but eventful life. Its copies are now collector's items; even those in the vaults of the Arizona Pioneers' Historical Society are so brittle with age that they are not available for public inspection. Fortunately, most of the old issues have been put on microfilm and thus are not lost to researchers interested in early Arizona history. What a story their pages tell, and what things the rusting old hulk of a press might recall if it could speak.

CHAPTER 15

Since My Return From Richmond

GRANVILLE WAS THE POLITICIAN of the Oury family, very much in the thick of things when the residents of Tucson sought to name a delegate to the Confederate Congress in Richmond in 1861. This, therefore, is Grant's story rather than Bill's, and a glimpse of Arizona's brief history as a Confederate territory.

As a provision of the Treaty of Guadalupe Hidalgo, all of that portion of Arizona lying north of the Gila River became American territory. Six years later, in 1854, the Gadsden Purchase added almost 30,000 square miles of territory in southern Arizona to the United States. On September 9, 1850, the Organic Act of Congress had established the Territory of New Mexico, with its capital in Santa Fe. The same act gave territorial status to Utah and permitted the entry of California into the Union as a Free State. There were no restrictions on slave-holding either in New Mexico or Utah.

This was supposed to be a "compromise," but it satisfied no one. Agitation over the slavery issue continued, and in 1854, the Kansas-Nebraska Act brought an end to whatever conciliatory provisions the Organic Act of Congress had offered. Over the next few years, smouldering feelings kindled; northerners became even more adamant on the isue of abolition. Southerners became increasingly more vocal and truculent in defense of their peculiar institution.

Arizona wanted territorial status for several reasons. More and more people were settling there, and most of them found the Indians to be enough of a menace to require the presence of federal troops. Also, a transcontinental railroad running through this harsh but beautiful land would open up the entire area for development.

Still, the Congress was not in any hurry to give territorial status to Arizona. The reasons for Congressional delay were plain enough. There were those in Congress who thought the idea premature on the grounds of insufficient population, but mainly opposition was occasioned by the fact that the more prominent citizens of Tucson and Mesilla were rabid and outspoken Southern sympathizers. What good would it do the North to give Arizona territorial status, argued the northern senators and representatives, only to see the territory espouse the Southern cause in case of conflict? And so the petitioners suffered rebuff and delay.

With the Gadsden Purchase, residents of southern Arizona (Doña Ana County) began to think seriously about gaining territorial status for that area. Part of the unrest was caused by reports that rival factions were competing for land to use for a railroad which would link California with the East. One group favored northern Arizona, the other southern Arizona. It was soon determined that the northern route presented too many terrain problems for any such venture; the people of Tucson were elated.[1]

A Plea for Status

A convention was held in Tucson on August 29, 1856.[2] Nathan B. Cook was elected to serve Arizona in the U.S. Congress, and the Arizona petition was presented to the Congress at one of its early sessions in 1857. The effort came to naught. If Arizona was ready for the U.S., the feeling was not reciprocal.

The August 29 petition listed the several grievances of Tucson's residents, enumerating among other things that the Pueblo's citizens were "isolated and cut off among savage tribes," had no law courts, and were "without any of the privileges of citizenship."[3]

This petition bore some 260 signatures, Granville Oury's name being the top one in the lefthand column — immediately opposite the signature of Mark Aldrich, the convention's presiding officer. Nathan Cook carried the petition to Washington, where it was introduced before the House on December 11, 1856 (by delegate Miguel A. Otero of New Mexico Territory).

In his message to Congress in 1857, President Buchanan recommended that Arizona be given territorial status. At about this time another convention was held in Tucson, in which Sylvester Mowry was selected as Arizona's delegate to Congress. Mowry, a close friend of both Bill and Grant Oury, fared no better than his predecessor. With admirable consistency, Buchanan reaffirmed his stand on Arizona territoryhood in his messages to Congress in 1858 and 1859, pointing out in one speech that some 10,000 residents of the area were virtually without law.

Arizona did achieve territorial status finally, but was to experience interesting and tortuous politics before gaining that end. In March, 1862, a bill was introduced before the Congress, passing the house in May. The Senate then debated the bill, postponing action until February 1863, when it was passed by that body and became law with President Lincoln's signature on February 24, 1863. But the Civil War was on in full swing now, and implementing the order presented difficulties. It was not until December, 1863, that Governor John Goodwin (first governor of Arizona Territory) established the Territory and announced an election of representatives for July, 1864.[4] From that time on, Arizona had a recognized government in national affairs.

Activity of Mowry

Mowry's disappointment before the Congress did nothing to dampen his ardor for the cause. He stayed on in the national capital to lobby for Arizona, moving in Washington society with ease and aplomb. His letters to Grant during this period are worthy of note. Writing from the New York Hotel on March 11, 1859, he addressed Oury as follows:

Dear Grant:

Congress adjourned leaving the country in a beautiful condition. The House not only defeated every territorial bill, but adjourned without giving a single day to territorial business. . . . There is not a dollar to carry a single letter to any part of the country, and the postal department owes several millions. Telegraph from Washington says an extra session will be called in June or July.

I shall be out in May and arrange with you the plans of next session's work. I have no idea of giving it up. We must succeed sometime, and I will have a few thousands left to spend on it. A regiment is ordered to Arizona to make war on the Apaches. I shall, I think, be able to get you something in connection with the Army that will pay, if you desire it.

General [name illegible] goes out with several hundred men to locate on the San Pedro or thereabout, making a depot for future operations against Sonora of course. You will like him very much; he is every inch a soldier and a gentleman. The country just now is being much excited about Cuba, and

there is a meeting Monday night at Tammany Hall in which Benjamin,
Mallory, Pugh, and your humble servant are invited to speak. I shall probably
decline, as I do not desire to excite any more opposition than I have now. I
sent by last mail a host of garden seeds to yourself, brother, and others. I hope
to find you well, and strong for Arizona.[5]

> *Ever yours,*
> *Sylvester Mowry*

This letter hints at two possibilities. Both men had a keen appreciation of the times, Mowry especially from his vantage point in the East.
Even at this early date, he had a premonition about Civil War, and was
worked up about the Kansas-Nebraska Act, Abolitionism, the Dred Scott
Decision, and similar matters. His offer of a position for Grant with federal
troops in Arizona might well be interpreted as a means of keeping tabs on
Union troop movements in the event of Southern secession. The reference
to the establishment of a depot for future operations against Sonora is
interesting too. Did he mean that federal troops would employ depot
resources against Confederate forces when war came, or was he thinking
about filibuster? The Crabb expedition had met with disaster in Sonora
just two years earlier. Still, might the game be worth another try?

Another Convention Held

Still trying for recognition, interested parties held another convention in Tucson on April 2–5, 1860. This one aimed at setting up a provisional government "to ordain and establish a provisional constitution
to remain in force until Congress shall organize a territorial government,
and no longer."[6] The meeting brought together thirty-one delegates from
the surounding settlements, including Tucson, Mesilla, Las Cruces, Tubac,
and Santa Rita del Cobre.[7] James A. Lucas presided over the meeting and
Dr. L. S. Owings made several appointments after being elected governor.
One of these was Grant Oury, named by Owings as chief justice of the
Second Judicial District. Interestingly, Oury's certificate of appointment
carried the same date as the convention's adjournment, April 5, 1860.

Sylvester Mowry was in the East, still trying to serve Arizona as its
delegate to Congress, but having no official status. Forlornly, the convention hoped that its eloquent spokesman, accredited or not, might make
Congress aware of Arizona's problems. In any case, the Tucson group had
no intention of letting the grass grow beneath its feet and began again to
agitate for territorial status. Many of them wrote letters to men of influence
in the East, and the men answered. Seventeen days after the convention's
close, Mowry wrote to Grant again, this time from the national headquarters of the Democratic convention in Charleston, South Carolina.[8] This

letter is of interest not only because of its reference to Arizona politics, but for its coments on national politics as well.

Dear Oury:

I am in receipt of yours of March 28 and am here at the convention. The Arizona bill is reported in both the Senate and the House, thereby giving the lie to all cross statements. I hope and think it will pass. If you have not received the appointment of Marshal please write me at once. I have neither seen nor heard anything of the paper you speak of Walker and Company getting up. He does it at his peril. He professes great friendship in his letter to me, and I have plenty of influence to get him removed if he plays me false. Mr. Thompson thinks him worthless anyhow.

I hope you have put the Provisional government through in good shape. It is going to help our cause very much.

There is hell to pay here in the national convention. The South will bolt if Douglas is nominated. If he is not, it looks as if the Douglas men were anxious to break up the convention in a row, in order that Douglas may run outside as a stump candidate. Breckinridge is the favorite now, although Guthrie of Kentucky and General Lane have strong friends. Senator Slidell, Knight Bayard, Mr. Barlow and Butterworth of the New York delegation, Brown, the editor of the Constitution, and myself have a private house, the finest quarters in town. You would be delighted to see how wonderfully Slidell manages everybody; he is positively great in that character. It was a sore day for Douglas when he quarreled with Slidell.[9] I don't think Douglas has any chance, although he will poll over 100 votes at first. It requires two-thirds to nominate out of 303.

Fort Buchanan is to be moved to the Aryvypa, [sic] and increased to six companies. A large post, six companies, to go to the Mimbres, and a camp of six companies to go to the Santa Cruz, somewhere in the heart of the silver district, near Patagonia or thereabouts. I am afraid they will carry their settlers with them. I will find out if anything can be done, and will do it for you.

There are to be no more Indian agencies created, the superintendent having decided against it. I will write to you as soon as the nomination is made.

Ever yours,
Sylvester Mowry

This letter underlines the strong feeling of the opposing factions of the Democratic party in its stormy convention at Charleston. The northern wing, declaring that each territory ought to control slavery as it saw fit (the doctrine of squatter sovereignty) championed Douglas. The southern wing felt it the duty of Congress to protect slavery in the territories. Breckinridge was the darling of this faction. The remnants of the old Whig and Know-Nothing groups formed the Constitutional party, declaring for "the Constitution, the Union, and enforcement of the laws." John Bell was the candidate of this party. It is easy to see from Mowry's letter that he held Douglas in no great esteem. Again, Mowry hints at secession in mentioning "our cause," and he is not so certain at this point that he will be able to put Oury in touch with movements of federal troops. Whether he had tried to get Oury an appointment as Indian agent is not known. It is assumed, from the letter's closing remark, that he may have tried to do so. More than likely Oury was out of a job, and his friend Mowry was doing everything he could to get him one. Here was Grant, first named as secretary of the 1860 Tucson convention, then appointed chief justice by Owings, but neither of these activities carried a salary. Then comes Mowry, speaking to Grant about something in connection with the Army, an "appointment as marshal," and, finally, hinting at a position as Indian agent. As it turned out, Grant got none of these jobs.

Mowry's sentiments about secession were no secret. Two years later (in June, 1862) they were to get him in trouble. He was arrested on the charge of treason, tried by a military court, found guilty, and sent off to prison at Fort Yuma.[10] Grant escaped a similar fate by joining the Confederate Army and going off to war with General Sibley.

The 1860 convention put Arizona no nearer territorial status than the previous meetings. Petitions had been made and fiery orations delivered, but to no avail. The country drew nearer to war with each pasing day. On January 9, 1861, the Union steamship, *Star of the West,* en route to provision federal troops at Fort Sumter, was fired upon. A few months later (April 12) Fort Sumter itself was fired upon by Confederate shore batteries and the garrison forced to surrender. But the agile Arizonans had beaten the rebel gunners to the punch. A secession meeting was held in Mesilla on March 16, promoted by Lucas, Grant Oury, Dr. Owings, Robert Kelley, and other staunch Southern sympathizers. Two days later, the preamble and resolutions of this meeting were sent to the provisional Congress of Confederate States then meeting in Montgomery, Alabama. The Mesilla convention named no delegate to Richmond, but a subsequent convention did.

Grant as a Delegate

Encouraged by Lt. Col. John R. Baylor's proclamation of August 2, 1861 (creating the Territory of Arizona), the citizens of Tucson held a meeting three days later and elected Grant Oury to serve as the new territory's delegate to the Confederate Congress. Oury went to Richmond soon thereafter, and even addressed the Congress on December 18. But he had no official status. It was not until late in November of 1861 that the subject of Arizona territorial status came up for discussion before the Congress. By then, Grant had been in Richmond for three months, a duly elected delegate — with no seat in the legislature. The Arizona bill was not passed in its final form until January 13, 1862.[11] President Jefferson

Davis signed it five days later, proclaiming the bill to be in force as of February 14th.

Oury then had a brief seating in the Congress, lasting less than two months, from January 24 to March 11, 1862. It ended because Baylor, not knowing Oury and not concerned with the Tucson convention at which Grant had been elected, put forward M. H. MacWillie as Arizona's delegate to the Confederate Congress, and proselyted for his election.

Soon after MacWillie replaced Oury in Richmond, Baylor got into trouble with President Davis. No "Indian-lover," Baylor had issued a rash order the intent of which was to exterminate all hostiles in the territory. As a result he lost his position as governor of the territory. Actually, it mattered little who was in the position at this stage. Federal troops were coming into Fort Union under General Canby, and with the help of Major John H. Chivington's forces would soon send Sibley's Confederates reeling down the Rio Grande Valley. And Carleton's "California Column" was closing in from the West. Oury had mixed emotions. Although he and Baylor were at odds, their sympathies were on the same side, and Grant despaired at the news of Sibley's retreat before the Yankees.

Before his ouster took effect, Grant had written two letters to President Davis — one on November 7, 1861, the other on January 27, 1862. The first letter, a brief one, simply requested Davis' consideration of territorial status for Arizona, and read as follows: [12]

His Excellency
Jefferson Davis, President, C.S.A.

Dear Sir:

   As a delegate elect from the Territory of Arizona to the Confederate Congress, I would earnestly invite your attention to the subject of her wants and necessities, her present isolation and unprotected condition, and the position she has assumed towards the Confederacy . . . with a request that if consistent with your excellency's views, you will in your message to the next Congress recommend her organization as a Territory at the earliest possible moment, with such facilities, civil and military, as the urgency of her case demands. I am, sir, your excellency's most obt. humble servant.

Granville H. Oury

The second letter, somewhat lengthy, did nothing more than carry Oury's recommendations for appointment to key positions in the new territory when it should become established. It is ironic that in this letter he recommends M. H. MacWillie for the office of attorney general.[13] Just forty-three days later MacWillie would take Grant's place in the Confederate Congress!

The Mesilla *Times* of July 29, 1861, carried an interesting account of the occupation of Mesilla by Confederate forces under the command of Colonel John R. Baylor of the Texas Mounted Rifles. In a ringing statement beginning with the words "Arizona is free at last!" the account goes on to describe Baylor's advance from El Paso to the outskirts of Fort Fillmore, and his subsequent occupation of Santo Tomás, Mesilla, and Fort Fillmore itself. These events, and the abject flight of the Union forces under Major Isaac Lynde on the twenty-seventh, set the stage for the proclamation of Arizona as a Confederate Territory by Colonel Baylor, and the subsequent relationship between Baylor and Granville Oury.

A Confederate Territory

On August 2, 1861, several days after entering Mesilla, Baylor issued a proclamation in the name of the Confederate States of America establishing the Territory of Arizona.[14] He organized a military government, and named himself as governor, soon thereafter turning command of his troops over to Brigadier General Albert Sidney Johnston. In his proclamation, Baylor cited the anarchic social and political conditions of Arizona, and the obvious need for the introduction of proper law and order. He abolished all offices, both civil and military, established by the United States or the Territory of New Mexico, and organized the territory under a military government of two departments; one executive, the other judicial. The executive power he vested in the commander of the Confederate Army in Arizona (himself); the judicial power was vested in a Supreme Court, two district courts, two probate courts, and a justice of the peace for each township. The district and probate courts were to be "holden" at Tucson. He designated Mesilla as the seat of territorial government. Apparently the Colonel was not only a man of military skill and daring, but a first-class organizer as well.

It was at about this time (three days later, August 5) that Grant was elected at the Tucson convention to serve as territorial delegate in Richmond. It was not until some six months later (February 14, 1862) that President Davis proclaimed that the territory belonged to the Confederacy. In a real sense, this hiatus proved Grant's political undoing, at least as far as his position as territorial delegate in Richmond was concerned. True, he had been duly elected in Tucson, but Baylor did not know him, and had his own candidate for the office of delegate to the Southern Congress.

Grant, going to Richmond in September, 1861, was "recognized as a delegate" from Arizona Territory, but was not admitted to a seat. Marcus MacWillie was admitted on March 11, 1862, and held his position until the close of the war. Working in the twilight zone of official sanction and legitimacy, Grant was in reality only a quasi-delegate; elected, yes; "official," no. He blamed Baylor for his troubles, and in a somewhat florid burst of righteous indignation, he stated his case to the public in an open letter on his return from Richmond in May. The handbill, bearing the date May 21, 1862, is a lengthy statement now residing in the files of the Arizona Pioneers' Historical Society. It begins: "Since my return from Richmond, I have been delayed by unavoidable circumstances from giving to the people of Arizona an account of my stewardship while engaged in the provisional Congress of the Confederate States of America as their representative." It goes on, then, to lambaste those who had in his opinion played him false.

From that unpublished statement it appears that Oury had reason for pique, if not for bitterness. He had been duly elected to the Confederate Congress by an authorized and representative body of Arizona citizens who had sent him to Richmond. He had served his constituents as best he could, although denied official status by the dalliance of President Davis in officially proclaiming Arizona as a territory of the Confederacy (and subsequently appointing its officers). His nomination for appointment went unheeded, and upon arrival back in Mesilla, he found that far from having his efforts appreciated, another was being groomed to take his place. It was more than his sense of fair play could endure.

A forerunner to Grant's handbill was a letter he wrote to the members of the Provisional Congress from the State of Texas (February 1862). In it, one senses Oury's kinship with the Texans, as though they are willing to see Arizona seated, even though others were not. He says:

Gentlemen:

I have now been here nearly three months awaiting the action of Congress upon the question of the recognition and organization of the Territory of Arizona by the government of the Confederate States of America, without as yet effecting anything decisive. As the peculiar circumstances of my situation forbid longer delay on my part, I am constrained to ask you the withdrawal of the papers deposited in your hands; to wit, my credentials, and the bill for the organization of the Territory, which I consider my own private property, being the work of my own hands.

I had thought and hoped, when despatched upon my present mission that the Confederate Government was one conducted upon the great principles of justice and right, and that the people of Arizona, loyal and devoted to the South, would receive that attention which common justice and precedent on the part of this government would naturally accord them. I find that I have been incorrect in my conclusions.

While yet the Southern Confederacy was composed of the seven first seceding states, Arizona, fearless of consequences and acting upon principle, made her stand in favor of the South, absolving herself from all allegiance to the Federal Government, and assisted with her arms in driving the minions of abolitionism from her soil. She expected, as she had a right to do, that the government to which she was bound by all ties of birth and education and sympathy would extend to her the help necessary to save her from her enemies, and secure to her the prerogatives of freedom. The same time that we have been knocking at her door for admission, the states of Missouri and Kentucky, where treason to your cause and to your institutions are the strongest elements on their borders, have been received with open arms, while we are neglected and refused.

You will bear in mind that you gentlemen represent a sovereign state of the Confederacy, that through convention of her people inviting, or rather exhorting the people of Arizona to connect their destiny to the South — how well the State of Texas has been sustained in her action towards Arizona is plainly indicated by the refusal of Congress to take notice of her.

In conclusion, I have only to say that I have no complaints against the Texas delegation; on the other hand, I have to thank them for the interest they have taken in Arizona and the politeness extended to myself.[15]

Oury's attempts at recognition before the Confederate Congress passed with this final venting of feelings. Coincidentally, Grant was mustered into the Confederate Army on the same day that his handbill hit the streets of Mesilla, May 21, 1862. His record as a soldier is related elsewhere in this study. Surely his experience as a politician, at least in this instance, must have seemed to him cruel and disheartening. That he yearned to serve the Confederacy in the role of delegate from Arizona Territory is beyond question. The exigencies of war, the more pressing problems of the national scene, and the means of his political antagonists conspired to thwart him for a time. He turned to other activites but perhaps it was in his star to become a delegate to Congress regardless of obstacles. Years later, he took his seat as the Democratic representative from Arizona Territory to the Forty-Eighth U.S. Congress in Washington.

CHAPTER 16

All Honor to Arizona's Seven Heroes

BUT FOR BILL OURY'S CHANCE KNOWLEDGE of one of the great tales of the early West, it might have been forgotten with the passing years. Just where Bill picked up the details of the Cooke's Canyon Affair is not certain. He had no part in the episode and was far from the scene of battle when it occurred. Still, circumstances made Bill perhaps the chief chronicler of the event. He closes his printed story with the statement that Cochise himself told the tale at Corralitos in Chihuahua, "just as it is given here," further reporting that Cochise paid rare tribute to the gallant men,[1] saying that with such men he [Cochise] could undertake to whip the whole United States, confessing that of the combined Apache forces, 185 men were killed, and 125 "came out alive." Bill's own assessment of the battle is summed up in these words:

Of the many deeds of desperate bravery performed all over the frontier of America by her hardy pioneers, probably none can compare in dogged determination and persistent fighting with those displayed in the affair at Cooke's Canyon in July, 1861.[2]

High praise indeed from a man who had fought at the Alamo, Miér, and Monterrey!

On July 21, 1861, Mimbreño and Chiricahua Apaches jumped seven Americans in one of the passes of the Peloncillos, some 100 miles east of Tucson. Although the ensuing struggle ended in the killing of 175 men and the wounding of an undisclosed number, it was not until some twelve years later that news of the affair began to trickle out.[3] Bill, in talks with some of the Indian participants, had learned the facts, or some of them, and told the story to friends in Tucson. Even then he put down nothing of the tale on paper. He did so on July 27, 1879, in a story published in the Arizona *Daily Star,* eighteen years after the tragic and heroic episode.

Member of the Party

Bill starts his story by listing the white participants as members of a mail party setting out from Mesilla for Tucson on June 20, 1861. They were Fred Thomas, "conductor and manager," Joe Roacher, Mat Champion, John Portell, Robert Aveline, E. Mills, and John Wilson. One month later, after having crossed New Mexico, the party entered Arizona in the vicinity of Cooke's canyon, a cleft in the rugged Peloncillo chain. They were attacked by some 300 warriors of Mangas Coloradas and Cochise, ambushing from points of vantage in rocky defiles of the canyon. "Conductor," Thomas, realizing the terrible disadvantage of the party's exposed position, ordered an immediate run to the crest of a nearby hill. Here the tables would be turned, and the attackers would be forced to show themselves in order to come within effective firing range. Reaching the hill was no picnic; the besieged men ran a fearful gauntlet of rifle fire and arrows, one of which caught Johnny Portell, wounding him slightly. When they had reached the crest they stopped the coach, and under what Oury calls "a galling fire," unloaded all arms, ammunition, and water, and set up a perimeter defense. In an effort to appease the attackers, Thomas then whipped the mules off the hill. The ruse failed. After a short run, the frenzied beasts capsized the coach. Now the beleagured men had no transportation, and nothing to bargain with.

The men raised up a rude sort of breastworks with the slabs of slate covering the hill. So protected, they were able to resist an almost continuous fusillade until nightfall. Under cover of darkness they raised the parapets to a height of about three feet. Thomas ordered a reconnaissance, finding to his chagrin that the group was surrounded on all sides.

The next day was sheer torture. The fight lasted from daybreak until dark. As the morning sun cast its rays down the slopes of the canyon, the Apaches began firing. Some of them attempted to use the slabs of slate as shields, crawling behind the upraised sheets on their bellies. The slightest exposure of the body brought a crashing rifle ball into the crawler, and before long many who advanced in this way lay dead or dying on the slopes. The sun was fierce, a brassy ring in the sky grinding down on white man and Apache alike. As night fell, the water supply was almost gone. Clearly it must be replenished, or the sun would accomplish what the attackers could not.

At this point, the field was littered with Apaches, but the mail party (except for Johnny Portell) was unscathed. Thomas tried to get water but could not; all approaches to the water hole were zeroed in. "Nothing remained but to lay down and seek that rest which their exhausted condition demanded."[4]

The third day was even more gruelling than the other two. Wave after wave of braves rushed the revetments, only to fall kicking, or be driven back by murderous fire, and the sun pressed down upon the seven men — lips cracked, throats parched and bone-dry. With the next day, they could make one more stand. As Oury puts it: "the heroic little band solemnly collected . . . for a last supreme effort to obtain that which was life itself — water."[5]

The Dash for Water

Thomas volunteered to make a dash for water, and asked for two men to join him. Bob Aveline and John Wilson stood up. The three collected every canteen on the premises and began a stealthy trip down the hill. The Indians, spotting them even in the dark, closed in. Soon Thomas was dropped, shot through both legs above the knee. Almost immediately, Aveline and Wilson both pitched forward, shot dead in their tracks.

Thomas was down, but he was not out. With both legs shattered, he began advancing on the stumps, firing at each searing step. His life's blood, according to Oury, "smeared every stone for more than forty feet."[6] Firing until his last cartridge was gone, he brought up his six-shooter and emptied its chamber at the merciless foes. At the last, he picked up rocks and threw them, until riddled with bullets he pitched over dead. The Indians, sensing the end was near, rushed the four survivors, and soon the grisly affair was brought to a close.

While the casualty figures given by Oury and the contemporary chronicler, Douglas D. Martin, are far apart, acceptance of even the conservative number does nothing to downgrade the heroism of the participants. One wonders at the dogged persistence of the Apaches in pressing the fight against the mounting losses. One applauds the gallant and hopeless resistance of seven men against 300. And no matter where Bill Oury picked up his information — whether in Corralitos, Sabinal, Carrizal, Tombstone, or Tucson, in a stage station or a saloon — it is history's gain that he picked it up at all. As Bill said in finishing the epic tale: "All honor to Arizona's Seven Heroes!"[7]

CHAPTER 17

Oury and Cochise

ON FEBRUARY 4, 1861, Lt. George N. Bascom, Seventh Infantry, U.S. Army, tried to arrest the Chiricahua Apache Chief Cochise at Apache Pass. Cochise was nimble enough to get away. One of the men in his party (Cochise's nephew) was clubbed by one soldier and bayoneted by another; neither wound proved fatal. Ensuing events growing out of this unfortunate affair ended in the grisly torture and killing of sixteen Americans and Mexicans by Cochise's band, and the hanging of six Apaches by the Army. War broke out then, a long drawn-out bloody struggle between Indians and whites lasting for a dozen years. There was an intermittent peace of sorts for about four years, but after the death of Cochise in 1876 the wars were resumed, lasting until 1886 with the capture of the renegade Geronimo.

The Bascom affair has probably generated as much intellectual and historical heat as any of the important episodes of the Far West. No two chroniclers of the event seem to be in complete agreement on it, and there has grown up a sort of feud; one side supporting the action taken by Bascom, the other sympathizing with Cochise and his people.[1] Like all arguments of this sort there are elements of truth on either side. In any case, it is likely that students of the affair will go on thinking just about as they have, even in the light of new evidence.[2]

Until the recent publishing of Lieutenant Bascom's report to Colonel Morrison on February 25, 1861 (from Fort Buchanan),[3] information on the affair came chiefly from the reports or statements of five white participants. One of these participants was Bill Oury, involved in his capacity as the Butterfield Stage Agent at Tucson. The others were Assistant Surgeon B. S. D. Irwin, U.S. Army; William Buckley, Superintendent of the Butterfield Division including the Apache Pass station; A. B. Culver, the conductor of the west-bound stage stopped at the Pass when the first incident occurred; and a man named Oberley, a former color sergeant of the Seventh U.S. Infantry.

Bill Oury played a very minor role in this drama, but his contribution is a report, written from memory several years later.[4] Errors of a failing memory and personal bias notwithstanding, it nonetheless serves as one of the chief written records of the Bascom affair.

In characteristically florid and indignant style, Oury begins his statement with a slap at A.P.K. Safford for the latter's remarks in an article printed in the Tucson *Citizen*. The story begins with these words:

Prompted by a desire to vindicate the memory of the dead, and to acquit of blame any who may still be alive of those who were actors in the drama so graphically painted by his excellency, I have determined to give to the world a true history of every incident connected with what was called the outbreak of Cochise's Chiricahua Indians in the month of February, 1861.... I will here state that I was an eyewitness of, and participator to some extent, in the drama.[5]

Oury went on then with his story. In the autumn of 1860, some Apaches made a raid on the Sonoita Valley near Fort Buchanan. Some twelve miles away from the post lived Johnny Ward, a rancher, with an Indian woman and a son she had borne him.[6] The boy, Mickey Free, was about six years old at the time of the raid. Ward was away when the raiders arrived, so there was no resistance of any kind. The Indians ran off Ward's stock and picked up the boy.[7] Upon his return and the discovery of his loss, Ward trailed the raiders to the banks of the San Pedro River, and there decided to enlist the aid of the Army. He proceeded to Fort Buchanan where he implored the commander, Lt. Col. Pitcairn Morrison, to send a detachment out after the marauders. For reasons of his own, Morrison failed to act until three months later, when he sent Lt. George N. Bascom with about sixty men to retrieve the stolen child if they could find him. John Ward accompanied the group taking with him one Antonio, an interpreter fluent in the Apache tongue. It is important to note that Bascom's instruc-

MICKEY FREE, a half-breed youngster, unwittingly brought down the wrath of Cochise upon the whites for more than a dozen years. At six years of age, Mickey was the central figure in the Bascom Affair. He later became an Indian Scout.

tions included the employment of force, if necessary, to retrieve the boy and the stolen property.[8]

Bascom arrived at Apache Pass on February 3.[9] He made a brief marching halt, and got a drink of water from one of the attendants at the stage station there (A. B. Culver). Besides Culver, there were two other men present at the station; Walsh, his assistant, and James F. Wallace, a stage driver. All were destined to die. After taking his drink, Bascom marched his column about three-quarters of a mile from the station, to a place called Siphon Canyon. There he made camp.

On the fourth, Cochise came down from the hills with five companions: his brother, two nephews, a woman, and a small child. He asked Culver where the soldiers were headed. Culver repeated what Bascom had said — that the column was headed for the Rio Grande. Supposing that the soldiers were indeed headed there, Cochise entered Bascom's camp voluntarily. By Oury's account this was the case, and there was no "beguilement by a White Flag," as charged in Governor Safford's letter.[10] Cochise asked for Bascom's tent, was shown which it was, and headed for it. In the tent were Bascom, Ward, and the interpreter, Antonio. Ward saw the Indian approaching and said: "Here comes Cochise."[11]

As Cochise entered the tent Ward slipped out to alert the soldiers outside and the tent was soon surrounded. It was at this critical moment that the whole tragic episode really began. It has never been established what band of Apaches really ran off with Ward's boy. Some make the claim that it was indeed Cochise and his Chiricahuas; others feel that it was a roving band of Coyoteros. In any case, the fat was in the fire when Bascom bluntly charged Cochise with the theft and informed him that he and his companions would be held as hostages until the boy and the stock should be returned. Antonio made the translation. Oury says:

The words were scarcely out of Antonio's mouth when Cochise sprang like a tiger, at the same time drawing his sheath knife with which he made a rent in the tent, and his head following the stroke of the knife, he landed outside amongst the astonished soldiers, who being recruits with no Indian experience let him escape in a flurry . . . although they fired perhaps fifty or more shots after him, he escaped unhurt. Another of the bucks leaped through the hole in the tent, but a different fate befell him, he being knocked by a soldier with the barrel of his musket, and another pinned him through the body to the ground with a bayonet. The rest seeing the situation remained quietly in the tent, and were held as prisoners.[12]

Events then moved swiftly. Cochise disappeared into the hills but soon came back to the stage station on the following day with a band of warriors. The three men there, Culver, Walsh, and Wallace, knew nothing of the episode in Bascom's Camp, and so had no reason to suspect Cochise of treachery. Cochise beckoned them out of the station. Suspecting nothing they came out, and "after a few words spoken and some maneuvering," the Indians rushed the three.[13] Walsh and Culver broke away and made a dash for cover. Wallace, a small man, was held securely by his captors.

Culver ran for the station, Walsh for the stone corral behind the building. As Culver reached the front door, he was felled by a bullet, badly wounded. At this dramatic moment Bascom and his men appeared on the scene and joined the fray. A trooper spotted Walsh dodging into the corral, and thinking him to be an Apache, shot him. The luckless Walsh died instantly.

The drama continued and more innocent people were drawn into it as actors in a vicious and deadly play. On the evening of the same day a train of wagons headed for the East arrived at the Pass and camped in a spot about two miles west of the station. Never was the selection of a campsite more costly. Two miles down the trail were soldiers and safety, but the leader of the unfortunate train had no way of knowing it. In a few hours nothing remained of him and seven Mexican companions except charred skeletons.

Two Americans traveling with the party (Jordan and Lyons) were taken captive, and spared for no apparent reason, while the eight other men of the party were lashed to the wagon wheels and set on fire. It is interesting that in his report to San Francisco on September 20, 1862 (twenty months later), Brigadier General James H. Carleton of the California Volunteers mentions coming upon the remains of these unfortunate men. He said: "Two miles beyond Apache Pass I found the remains of nine white men . . . one of them had been burned at the stake. We saw the charred bones and burnt ends of the rope by which he had been tied. . . ."[14]

With the capture of Jordan and Lyons, Cochise had three hostages to bargain with. On the following day (Tuesday), he appeared near the station with a large band of warriors and the driver Wallace, trussed up and held securely with a length of rope. Bascom and two of his men went out for a parley and Cochise put forth his terms for Wallace's release. If Bascom would free all of the Indians in his custody, Wallace would be freed. Bascom asked about Jordan and Lyons and was told they were still in custody. Bascom then offered to release all of the Indians for the three whites; Cochise refused. Bascom remained adamant. Poor Wallace — trussed, frightened half out of his wits — begged Bascom to accept Cochise's offer, but he would not. Sergeant Reuben F. Bernard, a dragoon from Fort Breckenridge and one of Bascom's party, protested Bascom's decision so violently that he was later charged with insubordination.[15] And so poor innocent Wallace was once more led away at the end of his rope, this time forever.

The bloody affair dragged inexorably on. The westbound stage was due at Apache station on Wednesday night. Cochise had his warriors pile stacks of dry grass on the mail road in Syphon Canyon, scheming to divert the stage and shoot down the fleeing occupants by the light of the flames. Luckily, the coach was ahead of schedule and reached the canyon in broad daylight. It passed on unmolested, reaching the Apache Pass stage station at about 4 P.M. The driver, A. B. Culver, brother of Charles Culver, decided to lay over until the following morning.

The eastbound stage was also due at Apache Pass on Wednesday evening. Aboard were eight persons: six passengers including William Buckley, superintendent of the Tucson-El Paso division of the Butterfield Company, and two employees: King Lyon (the driver), and the conductor. Bill Oury gives this account of the dash made by this stage:

Let us ascend by the road, in the mind's eye, to where looking out of the pass upon the broad plain extending as far west as the eye can reach, a speck, barely seen, under the gleaming rays of the setting sun, is gliding rapidly towards that fatal pass. Hark! the savage yells of Cochise, and his fellow demons . . . who have discovered that this is the stage from Tucson, freighted with precious Christian life, whirling rapidly and all so unconsciously into the jaws of death. Now all is hurry and preparation amongst that band of savage devils as they come sweeping down from Chiricahua's lofties to place themselves in ambush and coolly await the approach of their unsuspecting victims. . . . Will it not occur to the officer at the mail station that a strong escort should be sent out to warn them? . . . Alas, he is young and inexperienced, his men are raw recruits, and none of them think of anything but the horrors which have surrounded them during the evening. Meanwhile the sun has disappeared in the west; twilight has faded into night, and now the coach is slowly moving up the hill into the Pass, every rock of which conceals the carcass of a barbarous foe.

Now the stage has entered the Pass, and the passengers [are] cheered with the prospect of speedy arrival at the station, and the enjoyment of a good supper. All is mirth and contentment amongst them. The next moment all is changed to horror and dismay. Every rock sends a blaze of fire almost into their very faces, and now the driver, King Lyons is shot, his leg broken, and he can no longer guide the team. Almost at the same instant one of the lead mules falls dead, and out into the deadly fire springs every brave man, some to cut out the dead mule, others to attend the wounded driver. Quick as thought, William Buckley ascends the box . . . and away they go at lightning speed through a perfect storm of bullets which riddle the coach, but providentially, no one else is hurt. Just ahead of them is a very steep pitch down into a rocky ravine, across which a stone bridge has been built. Cochise, with his usual sagacity has torn away part of the bridge, calculating that . . . the coach will be precipitated into the ravine, and all that survive the smash will fall in easy prey. . . . He has made a bad calculation. Instead of tearing the lower side of the bridge away only, he has torn both sides, and left the middle solid. Down the steep pitch speed the flying mules. They huddle together and leap

across the broken bridge — the wheels fall down on both sides [of it] and the
velocity slides the iron axles across the solid center, and strange to relate, the
stage flees on. . . . Cochise, believing that there is some witchery, abandons
the chase and soon the coach arrives at the station, and as soon as it stops one
of the wheel mules falls dead. Had this occurred before they reached and
crossed the bridge, not one of those . . . brave men would have been left to
tell the tale.[16]

At this point, Oury sums up the casualty rate to date: ten white men killed, two badly wounded, and three taken prisoners "by the noble Cochise." Only one red man has received any injury at the hands of the whites, and that very slight.

Bill then reports that on the same night a courier was dispatched to Tucson to obtain troops from Fort Breckenridge to escort the west-bound stage through the Chiricahua country. Also, Lieutenant Bascom sent off to Fort Buchanan for supplies and medical assistance. A. B. Culver made the ride to Tucson, and a soldier rode off for Fort Buchanan. They rode together as far as Dragoon Springs and there parted company. Both arrived at their destinations on Friday night, February 8.

With Culver's departure for Tucson, Buckley decided to go on east to Mesilla as planned. In preparation for the trip he had to water his stock, and so drove the beasts (in the company of some twenty soldiers and a handful of Butterfield men) to a spring about 700 yards east of the station. Cochise had hidden some warriors near the spring. When the animals had watered and were being returned to the station the Indians opened fire, killing one Butterfield employee, wounding a soldier, and making off with all of the mules. Without mules, Buckley had no choice but to delay his trip.

It was with Culver's arrival in Tucson on the eighth that Oury became engaged in the famous Bascom affair. Prior to this time he had no real knowledge of the events described above except as related to him by Bascom, Buckley, Culver, and others who had experienced them at first hand. Happily, his chronicle agrees with their reports in all major aspects of the events recorded. On Culver's arrival Oury requested that the latter send a messenger to Fort Breckenridge to enlist aid from the military garrison there. Oury sent off such a request also, asking that the troops meet him at Ewell's Station, some fifteen miles west of Apache Pass.[17] Oury started out for Ewell's Station on Saturday morning (February 9) in the company of four men. On the following day "G" Company of the First Dragoons left Fort Breckenridge under the command of First Lieutenant Isaiah N. Moore. Also present was "D" Company with Second Lieutenant Richard S. C. Lord.

The military column reached Ewell's Station ahead of Oury, leaving a message that it would wait for him just west of the Pass. It did so, "at the rock tank six miles west of the Pass,"[18] and all continued on to the station arriving a little after sundown and imediately after Irwin's arrival from Fort Buchanan.

Irwin, enroute to Apache Pass at the urgent request of Bascom, jumped some Coyotero Apaches in Sulphur Spring Valley. Here he recaptured some stolen stock, and took three Apaches prisoner, running the total of Apache bucks held by Bascom and Irwin to six. This figure is significant in the light of ensuing events.

Oury Learns the Facts

On his arrival at Apache Pass, Oury learned of the pitiful tale of Wallace, led to the hilltop parley at the end of a rope. At Cochise's bidding, Wallace had written a cryptic message on a sheet of paper with charcoal, and the note had been stuck in the ground. It read: "treat my people well, and I will do the same by yours, of whom I have three."[19] This was the first time Bascom had any knowledge of captives other than Wallace, knowing nothing of Jordan and Lyons.

On the morning following his arrival at Apache Pass, Oury set out with the troops for Cochise's village. Near the western edge of the Pass, the column saw buzzards wheeling about slowly in the sky. Soon the men came upon the bodies of three men, gaping with hundreds of lance holes, and mutilated beyond recognition. Oury, as Butterfield agent in Tucson, knew most of the men employed by the company in the Arizona area quite well; he was able to identify one of the bodies as Wallace. It was assumed that the other two bodies were those of Jordan and Lyons. A party of dragoons buried the three men there on the spot.[20]

Next there occurred the final incident in this tragic affair. Bascom is generally blamed for the event, but the truth of the matter is that he wanted no part of it. Let Oury speak:

As we wended our way slowly back to the station, a discussion commenced among the men . . . whether it would not be best to take all the Indians held by Lt. Bascom and hang them to the trees that shaded our new made graves. Before we reached the station it was so decided. Soon after we unsaddled our horses, Lt. Moore went to Bascom in whose charge the Indian prisoners were and told him what it had been determined to do. He [Bascom] objected to the proposition, *saying that he was in charge of the Indians and would be censured for allowing such disposition to be made of his prisoners. Moore then said that he was the ranking officer and would assume full responsibility. This settling the dispute . . . arrangements were made by the dragoons and early next morning the Indians were marched out to the mound of the grave and six were hanged upon the oak trees. The boy and squaw, after witnessing the hanging were set free.[21]*

The so-called "Bascom affair" so angered Cochise that he launched a long and terrible war against all whites until Maj. Gen. O. O. Howard was able to make peace with him in 1872.[2] Bascom fell at the Battle of Valverde, New Mexico, while fighting against troops of the Confederacy in February of 1862, just one year after the episode for which he has been made infamous. It is of interest to note that he was commended in official orders and promoted to First Lieutenant, and to the grade of Captain prior to his death at Valverde.

But it must be concluded that Bascom was really the only person in the party who opposed the hanging of the six captives. At least there are no records to indicate that any of the others protested Moore's decision. Irwin favored hanging the men on a "one for one" basis.[22] Six Americans had been killed: Wallace, Whitfield, Sanders, Jordan, Lyons, and Brunner.[23] Therefore, he ruled that six Apaches ought to be hung.

There can be no doubt that Bascom's intemperate detention of Cochise in his (Bascom's) tent triggered the action. But it should be remembered that Bascom was under orders from Lieutenant Colonel Morrison to use force if necessary in recovering Ward's stolen boy and cattle. It is demonstrable that the subsequent torturings and killings were wholly on the Apache side until the hanging of the six captives on the nineteenth.

CHAPTER 18

My Dear Uncle

As THE CIVIL WAR began, leaders of the Confederacy seemed to be more aware of Arizona's importance than were their counterparts in Washington. President Davis had been interested in the area as early as the 1850's when as Franklin Pierce's Secretary of War he had experimented with camels for use by the military in the dry desert regions. With the abandonment of forts Buchanan and Breckenridge and the withdrawal of the federal garrison from Tucson, the entire area between Fort Yuma and Fort Fillmore at Mesilla was without protection.

It seemed that whichever side should put up a show of force might keep the Territory. Public sentiment in Tucson was predominantly Southern, although there were a few prominent names in the other camp. Also, the selection of Grant Oury as the Territory's delegate to Richmond on August 5, 1860, had literally pushed the political border of the area west to the Colorado River. To add to the confusion, the Overland Mail stopped its Arizona run and was not reopened until the fall of 1862. One of the minor sidelights of this development was that Bill Oury lost his job; he had been the agent for the line since 1858.

Alert to the vacuum created by the withdrawal of Union troops, the

Confederacy decided to move in. First to move was Lieutenant Colonel John R. Baylor marching north from El Paso to Mesilla with four companies of the Second Regiment, Texas Mounted Volunteers. The battle of Mesilla and the evacuation of Fort Fillmore were quick Southern victories, accomplished by Baylor almost without the firing of a shot. The retreating Union officer, Major Isaac Lynde, surrendered his force of some 400 U.S. regulars to Baylor's smaller command, against the angry petitions of his pluckier Yankee subordinates. Baylor then proclaimed himself military governor of the Arizona Territory and established Mesilla as the capital.

Thus the stage was set for the coming struggles in New Mexico and Arizona between Union and Confederate troops. Colonel Edward R. S. Canby chose Fort Craig on the Rio Grande and Fort Union east of Santa Fe as the two best points from which to check raiding Confederate columns coming in across the Texas Panhandle via the Pecos and Canadian rivers.

The "Johnny Rebs" had no idea of permitting Canby to establish himself in New Mexico, however, and so they moved north. In January, 1862, Brigadier General Henry H. Sibley joined forces with Baylor at Mesilla and marched off for Fort Craig to take on Canby. The two columns met on February 21 at Valverde, some six miles north of Fort Craig.[1] Both sides had losses and the outcome was indecisive. It was here that Captain George Bascom fell, just a year after the running battle with Cochise at Apache Pass. After Valverde, Sibley and Baylor continued on toward Fort Union; Canby remained in place at Fort Craig.

Sibley fared no better at Fort Union. Colonel John Slough of the First Colorado Volunteers got there ahead of him, and on March 11 sent out a column to meet Sibley coming in from the west. The advance columns of both forces met near the mouth of Apache Canyon two weeks later (March 26), and exchanged shots. The ensuing battle at Glorieta proved to be Sibley's undoing in the Far West. The engagement might have gone in Sibley's favor had not Major John Chivington[2] slipped in behind the Confederate train and made off with most of its supplies. Sibley's disastrous retreat down the Rio Grande Valley was the result of Chivington's bold stroke. Also, the victory put a sudden and conclusive halt to further Confederate invasion of Arizona and New Mexico territory by way of Texas. But the rebs had one more card to play.

Just before Valverde, Sibley had ordered Captain Sherod Hunter and "A" Company of the Second Texas Mounted Rifles to proceed to Tucson and occupy it. The object of the move was to secure a good position for the establishment of a chain of posts which was to stretch from Texas to California.[3]

Hunter reached the Old Pueblo on February 28, 1862, and was met with wild acclaim by the rebels of the town, Bill Oury as elated and noisy as any of them. Bill did in fact "dance a jig" when Hunter and his Texans came marching in. He did not have long to dance. Just sixty-five days later, on May 4, Hunter evacuated Tucson. In another sixteen days Captain William P. Calloway entered the town with "B" Company of the First California Cavalry, and raised the Stars and Stripes.[4] There were a few who danced in the streets on this day too — Bill was not among them.

The Column in Arizona

The presence of the California Column in Arizona turned out to be decisive. Like Caesar, it came, saw, and conquered. Also, it stayed. And with "B" Company, Fifth California Volunteers, came Second Lieutenant Gilbert Cole Smith of Sacramento. He stayed on to garrison the town, and he later married Bill Oury's oldest daughter, Lola, just past seventeen on her wedding day. That gay affair came later, in 1868. When Gilbert Smith came to town with the Union Army, Lola was a twelve-year-old girl, still in pigtails.

A graphic picture of the troubled times is given in the personal letters of Lieutenant Smith to his uncle, Cornelius Cole, soon to be a U.S. senator from California. Excerpts from several of these letters will be given in the following pages — but first a sketch of the origin of the famous California Column.

When the war began, California had been a state for more than a decade. Due to the tremendous influx of people seeking fortunes in the goldfields, the political complexion of the state was mixed. Abolitionists took the stump on the streets of Sacramento and San Francisco (Cornelius Cole among them) and delivered tirades against the slaveholders and secessionists of the South. Then a rebel would shout his opinions to the crowd, and like as not fisticuffs would follow.[5] In this climate, the federal government moved fast to keep California for the Union.

After the first battle of Bull Run, Governor John G. Downey of California received a communication from the Secretary of War suggesting the establishment of a volunteer group, to consist of one infantry regiment, and five companies of cavalry. The men would serve a three-year enlistment and be employed mainly in protecting the Overland Mail route from the west coast to Fort Laramie. The volunteer force began to gather, and on September 7, 1861, Gilbert Cole Smith received his commission as a Second Lieutenant in "D" Company, Fifth California Volunteer Infantry.[6]

Soon after Smith joined the regiment, word spread that his battalion was going to Texas to take on Twigg's Confederates, and regain the loot

GILBERT COLE SMITH, a Union Army officer, came to Tucson with the California Column in 1863. He stayed on to garrison the town and finally, in 1868, to marry into a former Confederate family. His bride was Oury's daughter, Lola.

taken by them from U.S. government posts. The unit was slated for a sea voyage as far as Mazatlán, and then an overland march across northern Mexico to west Texas. There it would engage Twigg and draw off the rebels from Arkansas and Missouri.

The idea died a-borning. Secessionist demonstrations in southern California caused the diversion, and Smith's outfit moved south at once. Colonel Carleton's First California Infantry, and the First California Cavalry under Lt. Benjamin F. Davis, arrived in San Pedro within a matter of days of each other, and established themselves at Camp Latham, near present-day Santa Monica.

From this position, Carleton sent garrisons to Los Angeles, San Bernardino, San Diego, and Yuma. Lieutenant Smith's outfit drew San Diego, and within a week or two he was off for his new post. The garrison life there proved indolent and pleasurable, with fandangos and the courting of dark-eyed señoritas occupying as much or more time than soldierly duties. The idyllic life came to an end with General Sibley's invasion of New Mexico Territory, and Carleton's Column began its historic trek eastward. It fought only one battle, at Picacho Pass, on April 15, 1862, where one officer and two enlisted men of the First California Cavalry Volunteers were killed.[7] At this time, Smith was still in San Diego with the rear echelon.

Smith's letters were written to his aunt and uncle in Santa Cruz, California, and follow his company's moves from San Diego to Fort Yuma, Gila Bend, and Tucson. The first one, written to his aunt, Olive Cole, bears the date May 7, 1862.[8]

> *New San Diego Barracks, Cal.*
> *May 7th, 1862.*

Dear Aunt:

Your very kind and welcome letter of April 20th reached me a week ago today, and on account of my being engaged in making out the monthly report of the post for the last month, I did not have time to write you by return mail.

The steamer Narragansett *of the U.S.N. made us a visit about ten days ago. She is a steam gun-boat or Man-of-War, manned by about 110 officers and men, and carrying four thirty pound guns and one larger shell gun or Columbiad, which, to give you an idea of its size, weighed eight tons. It was thirteen feet in length, and took a shell eleven inches in diameter and of 120 pounds weight, which it could throw about three miles with great precision. It beats all the guns I ever saw.*

The Officers of the ship were mostly from the N. E. States, and were as intelligent, free-hearted and liberal a set of men as we commonly meet. We were invited on board and spent nearly a whole day there, and I was very much interested with the strange things I saw there.

I am studying the "Lingua Española." We do not have much use for the language in our business, but in getting acquainted with some of these Spanish people, I find the need of it. I attended a party the other night and had quite a pleasant time, danced all night and we did not get home till after sunrise the next morning. I find these Spanish people differ from ours in their manners and customs, but they are polite, and sociable, and quite accomplished for the ostensibly limited advantages they have.

Well, I have written enough, and hope that I may hear from you again soon.

Your aff. nephew,
Gilbert

There is not much information available now on the *Narragansett,* but according to the above letter it was very likely a forerunner of the low free-board, single-thrust monitors especially designed for service in 1862. These ships, the *Lehigh, Mahopac, Nahant, Nantucket, Ajax, Jason,* and others all carried two fifteen-inch smooth bore rifles as main batteries, and a couple of twelve-inch howitzers as secondaries.[9] They averaged about 225 feet in length, forty-four feet in breadth, and had an average displacement of 2,000 tons. They could make about six knots.

The gay life in San Diego continued. In a short note to his aunt of July 2, 1862, Smith said:

I went to old San Diego to attend a wedding. Saw the marriage ceremony and kissed the bride. . . . We danced all night again, and an hour after broad daylight this morning. Came home this morning at about six or seven and slept until Guard Mount at nine, and then I arose and took the duties of Officer of the Day.

Preparations are being made to celebrate the fourth in San Diego. Our company is to be marched into Old San Diego, and arrangements are made by the citizens to give us a reception. We are to have a ball at night, and I expect that I shall have to be up again all of tomorrow night, but we shall have a very pleasant time . . ."

The next letter was written almost a year later. The main events within the time lapse seem to have been a move to Fort Yuma on the Colorado River, and understandable complaints at not being paid. This letter reflects the low morale of the command as a result of that condition.[10]

Fort Yuma, Cal.
March 27, 1863.

Dear Aunt:

I am very well and enjoy myself as well as could be expected in a God-forsaken country like this. There are but few people living here who have an approximation to civilization, and among that few, virtue, honesty, candor or any other moral principle is at a great discount. licentiousness, dishonesty, intemperance, avarice, duplicity and every other evil that you can think of are above par.

As far as my own experience goes however, I like Fort Yuma. The weather has been very pleasant since we have been here. I regard it about the same as I once heard a drunken man assess the world. Said he; "The world is good enough, damn it. It is the people that make it bad!"

We expect soon to be enroute to Tucson, and so on to Texas, though we have not received orders to go yet. I shall be glad when we get on the way, as I always prefer the field to garrison. We understand from the Vedette this morning that the paymaster is pretty near this place, and will probably be here tomorrow. We all think it time he should come. Our company has not been paid in thirteen months. We shall probably be paid in paper too, which the people here are trying to depreciate fifty per cent. The merchants who have got rich here by government contracts ask double prices for goods paid for in paper. Thus a poor soldier, who must needs have some little necessaries, is swindled out of his money and realizes only half his pay.

We have been denied the long standing custom and privilege of officers to have credit in the commissary department, and this too when we have not seen any paymaster for over a year. That is, the government refused, even with our pay in its hands as security to do for us what the meanest person would not have denied us. It almost seems that the goverment does not consider us honest men.

Some officers have been obliged to draw their rations in kind, and even that is forbidden. If we could sell our pay accounts as of old, then we could get along without trouble. That too has been forbidden. So you see, everything seems to work disgust in the minds of our officers. Many have resigned, but now if one offers resignation, it will not be accepted on his assigning as his reason that he will starve to death.

I have between four and five hundred dollars due me now, but cannot tell when we will be paid again. I have one satisfaction however, I owe no one.

I have no objection to your having parts of my letters published, but your judgment will dictate what is better to suppress. Kiss the children on my account, and write soon.

> *Your affectionate nephew,*
> *Gilbert*

A couple more months saw the unit on the move again, still unpaid, still hoping to encounter the Rebel army in battle, and winding slowly across the scorching sands of southern Arizona in early summer.

> *Gila Bend (Camp)*
> *Arizona Territory*
> *June 1, 1863.*

My dear Aunt:

It is now about noon and we have have been in camp an hour or more. I am reclining on the ground beneath the shade of a mesquite tree which serves as a partial shelter from the burning rays of the desert sun.[11] We are now about 150 miles from Fort Yuma on the Gila River, and enroute to Tucson, A.T. We have been out on the road for about ten days, and have encamped on the Gila every night, so that I have had the pleasure of taking a bath every evening. There is not a trace of civilization along the route, except that the wagon road looks about the same as in a civilized community.

The day before yesterday I saw a carcass of an Apache Indian hanging on a tree by the roadside. I was informed by the man who hung him there, (Mr. Woolsey), that a party of about a dozen Apaches attacked him about a year ago on the spot. He turned on them with a gun and pistol and succeeded in driving them off by shooting at them. . . .

It is a rule among the Apaches never to touch one of their warriors when killed or wounded after he has been touched by a white man. The circumstances of this one being left there so long, and not taken down by his friends gives this rule a shade of truth.

The night before last we encamped at Oatman Flat, near the place where the Oatman family was killed by Indians in 1851. You have probably heard the narrative of this family. I visited the graves, or rather grave, as they seem all to have buried in one grave. There is a pine board which marks where they lie, on which is rudely carved: "The Oatman Family, 1851." The grave is surrounded by a little fence made of poles.

We have seen signs of Indian tracks along for the last day or two, and have to keep a good lookout as we are now in Apache country. Colonel Bowie is along with us. [Not the Col. James Bowie of Alamo fame.] I do not think much of him as a military man. This march rather gets him. Everything he does is with an eye for politics, and you know those are not the men for the army. A good officer should be honest instead of a selfish, political trickster.

Lieutenants Glasby and Zabriskie are lying here sleeping under the trees. Zabriskie is a fine, clever, and witty fellow, much like Uncle Wash.

When I get to Tucson, I can send a letter home in 14 or 15 days, and with three cents postage. That will seem like getting near home. Remember me to all, and please write soon.[12]

> *Your affectionate nephew,*
> *Gilbert*

The dead Apache seen by Lieutenant Smith was very likely the same one seen by J. Ross Browne several years later. In his famous book *Adventures in the Apache Country,* published by Harper and Brothers in 1869, Browne dwells upon the incident at length: [13]

The chief lay just where he had fallen, stiff and stark. It is a curious fact that the Apaches never move their dead. A superstition seems to prevail upon them on this point, and I have been told that they will not approach a spot on which one of their comrades has been slain. Woolsey and his party determined to make a conspicuous mark of the dead Indian Chief from which marauding Indians might take warning. They dragged him to the nearest mesquite tree and hanged him up by the neck, leaving the feet to dangle about a yard above the ground.

Browne, having listened to Woolsey's tale asked to be shown the spot where it had happened. Woolsey took him there and the Indian was still hanging on the tree. Brown wrote:

"I stood by the tree and gazed with strange feelings upon the dead Apache. The body was dried and shrunken, and of a parchment color.

CORNELIUS AND OLIVE COLE of Santa Cruz, California, were the "Dear Aunt and Uncle" of Gilbert Smith's letters, written from the bleak desert encampments on the trek across Arizona to Tucson in 1863, with the California Column. "Uncle Cornelius" represented California in the United States Senate.

One of the feet and both hands had been cut off or torn away by coyotes."[14]

If Browne saw this grisly sight in the same year his book was published, then the body had been hanging there for six or seven years. This is not too surprising, however, in view of the loneliness of the spot, and of the dry desert air which tends to preserve rather than destroy human tissue.

The "Uncle Wash" referred to in the above letter was Cornelius Cole's brother, then a colonel in the Third New York Volunteer Cavalry in the Army of the Potomac. He later attained the rank of major general and remained in the regular army for a number of years.

The main body of the California Column had been in Tucson for almost a year by the time Smith's battalion arrived there. Captain Calloway had entered the place on May 20, 1862, followed soon after by Lt. Colonel Joseph West who took possession. Captain Sherod Hunter had left well ahead of the California troops, having a field day in appropriating or destroying the property of the few Union sympathizers in town. Carleton would turn the tables on the rebel sympathizers, however, and Bill Oury would feel the full weight of Carleton's power. By June, 1862, there were eleven companies of Union infantry, two of cavalry, and two artillery batteries stationed in and around a military plaza established to accommodate the force.

Tucson was a wild, rough place in 1863. J. Ross Browne had said of it: ". . . Volunteer soldiers are stationed all over the town at mescal shops, the monte tables, and houses of ill-fame for the preservation of public order."[15]

It was into such a place that the young officer Smith came, yet it seemed to dampen his spirits not at all. In a letter written on June 24, 1863, just a few days after his arrival he tells of a Mexican fiesta.[16]

> *This is the day of San Juan and is being duly celebrated by the Mexican population here. The day was ushered in with the firing of rockets and a sort of spasmodic performance of four or five Mexicans on some antiquated fiddles and drums, which they think makes very fine music, but I differ with them considerably.*

The back pay issue was still a problem at this writing.

> *We have been in the service nearly two years and have been paid only twice, the last time in a currency depreciated almost one-half. We, of course, have had to get credit or we could not have lived.*

His next letter was written about a month later from the Pima villages near Phoenix. He had been sent there with a small detachment to see what had been holding up mail shipments. Whatever it was is not mentioned in the letter, but his observations of Pima life are the chief topic.[17]

Pima Villages, Arizona
July 20th, 1863

My Dear Aunt:

. . . I was much pleased to hear from you again, and especially to hear of Uncle Cornelius's nomination for Congress which took me by surprise. I had not anticipated, not even dreamed of such a thing, but it is an agreeable surprise to me and I must congratulate him on his success.

I hope that he may use some of his influence to get me transferred to the Eastern Army, or to the Regular Army which I should like better. If I can get into the Regular Army with a second lieutenancy I should remain there and make the military my study for life. I like the service as well as ever, but this particular service, I am sick and tired of. Perhaps you have heard and know enough of the general management of the California Column to give you some ideas of matters here. If the most forbearing man would not get tired of this humbugging it would be because he had not a proper manly spirit.

The news which we have had lately has been rather discouraging, but our hopes are as high as ever. The news has just come that Vicksburg is taken. This is encouraging and if true will be apt to wipe out the war from Mississippi and the Southwest, and if matters could only be fixed that Lee's Army could be captured in its raid on Pennsylvania, then I think the rebellion would be crushed and we should have peace again in a short time.

I am looking and hoping for these things to come to pass before President Lincoln's term of office expires. I do not want to see a dough-faced copper-head for our next President, but I feel afraid of it if some decisive turn does not take place before the next presidential election.

I have been here nearly two weeks. I came down here accompanied by an escort of men to see what was the reason the mail did not come when it was due at Tucson. I am expecting to receive orders from Tucson to return in a day or two.

The Pimas are a very industrious, peaceful, good-hearted and virtuous tribe of Indians. . . . They cultivate some fifteen or twenty thousand acres of the rich bottom lands of the Gila River, and raise large quantities of the finest wheat I ever saw, and corn, peas, squashes, melons, etc. They irrigate their lands by large ditches called Asecas [acequias] and some of them are miles in length. They have many very good ideas about farming, and are far above any other Indians I have seen before in every respect.

The men are generally good sized healthy looking fellows, but like other Indians they do not work much themselves, the women doing most of the hard work. The women are generally short and strong, own the lands, and do the hard work. They bring wheat here to sell every day, and I am sometimes provoked to see a great big lazy Indian on horseback, and his wife trotting along after him on foot, with from two to three bushels of wheat in a sort of basket on her head and shoulders.

They seem to have a horror for blood, and you never hear of them maliciously killing anyone. They seem to have an idea of capital punishment, as one of them heard that the Indian agent had killed a man in Tucson. [He] asked me in Spanish why the people did not kill the agent for it. They never *have been known to kill a white man, but they are enemies of the Apaches and have no scruples about killing them in battle. When they come back from their war path those who have killed any of the enemy have to stay outside their houses and fast for several days in order to get the enemy's blood off them, after which they have a fine reception by the young ladies and a feast. The men generally dress in an old shirt or soldier's coat of which they have a great many. Some have a great roll of beads around their neck, or hanging from their ears, and occasionally one has some funny trinket hanging from his nose which looks most disgusting.*

They tattoo themselves just under the eyelashes with a streak of black which extends back from the outer corner of the eye to the hair on the side of the head. They paint their faces with red and black paint which gives them a hideous appearance.

Their hair is very coarse and thick, [and] they cut it off in front so that it extends just down to the eyes, but let it grow to a great length on the back of the head and twist it up in ropes, which on some hang nearly to the knees. Every little while they do it up in mud for a day or two at a time. I think they do it to prevent it from fading.

The women wear no other clothing than a sort of skirt . . . which they wrap around the waist, and it extends down about to the knees, the upper part of the body being naked. They wear their hair about a foot long hanging naturally about the shoulders. They are tattooed about the eyes the same as the men, and after they are married they have two black streaks from each corner of the mouth, and perpendicular to it, extending down to the bottom of the face. Some of their women are very pretty, and they are generally modest and virtuous.

Their language is a sort of harsh gutteral like other Indian languages, but much different from the Yuma, or their nearest neighbors, the Maricopas. Though the language is very harsh to the ear, there is a great deal of poetry in their expressions. . . . A man asking another to make a light at night would say, "make a moon." . . .

I have learned to count. They count by tens. Their word for ten is "westa-mah," and for two, "kok" — thus, twenty becomes "Kok-Westa-mah", thirty, "Vik-Westa-mah," etc. I think from this they must have considerable of a system to their language.

The population of the Pimas is now from 6,000 to 7,000 persons, a very large tribe. But I am writing a lot of stuff which may not interest you, so I will stop here and not commence another page.

Please remember me to all the family and write soon,

Your affectionate nephew,
Gilbert.

Communications were not very good between Tucson and the outside world in 1863. Vicksburg fell to Grant on the fourth of July, yet Smith informs his aunt on the twentieth, that news of the victory has just come. Also, at this writing, the Union forces had prevailed at Gettysburg, and Smith's beliefs that such a victory would crush the rebellion were beginning to come true, although he had no way of knowing it. Indeed, by the time the news of Gettysburg reached him, the whole eastern seaboard knew the smallest details of the fierce struggles at Cemetery Ridge, and Culp's Hill, and Round Top and the Devil's Den. Will Thompson's "High Tide at Gettysburg" would later bring tears to the eyes of many Americans — Yankee and Rebel alike:

> *Fold up the banners! Smelt the guns!*
> *   Love rules. Her gentler purpose runs.*
> *A mighty mother turns in tears*
> *   The pages of her battle years,*
> *Lamenting all her fallen sons!*

But on the twentieth of July, 1863, Gilbert Smith had never even heard of Round Top, or Little Round Top, or the Devil's Den. Six days later, however, he knew of the momentous battle, and mentioned it in the last of these letters:[18]

> *Tucson, Arizona*
> *July 26, 1863.*

Dear Uncle:

We are much elated with the good news from the East. Some of our men have not yet got sober on account of it.

I am appointed A.A.Q.M. and A.C.S. at this post by orders from District Headquarters and am to commence receiving the government stores and property here tomorrow. . . . It will be a good business schooling for me. I will write and tell you how I like it when I have had some experience.

I hope that your election may come to pass.

Lieutenant Dutton of Captain Tidball's Company has just arrived here from Apache Pass. He reports that a party of Apaches have driven off the stock at that post, or a part of it.

I received a letter from home by last mail. All are well except grandma who is failing very fast. I have several other letters to write and will not weary your patience longer.

> *Your affectionate nephew,*
> *Gilbert*

Here the letters end, and with them a nostalgic link with the hectic days of yesteryear. Gilbert Smith stayed on in the army, attaining the rank of colonel before his death in St. Louis, Missouri, on July 14, 1899.

When Carleton arrived in Tucson he found things in bad shape. The townspeople were hostile, but to hear Carleton tell it, one might think the entry of Union troops into town was the occasion for the greatest joy by Tucson residents. Carleton's remark was: "Our arrival is hailed with great joy by all the people who remain."[19] A few there may have been who were glad to see the blue coats; most of the people were of an opposite persuasion, however. Off in the hills the Apaches were on the rampage, taking full advantage of the struggle of white man against white man. Pillage, looting, and murder were common. The stage line had ceased operations, and traffic in and out of town had come virtually to a standstill. In all, the situation was desolate and forlorn.

Under Two Governors

Accordingly, Carleton placed the Territory under martial law and proclaimed himself governor. Thus, the unhappy land had two governors at once; one in Tucson, another in Mesilla. The latter was a governorship in name only, however, as by this time Baylor was out of Mesilla and in retreat before elements of Carleton's force.

As Carleton himself would press on to the Rio Grande and eventually to Santa Fe, he created a special district in the Tucson area and placed it under the authority of Major David Ferguson of the First California Volunteer Cavalry.[20] The district took in all of Arizona Territory west of a meridian line running through "what is known as Apache Pass, on the Butterfield route, hence to Mesilla."[21] The area was named the District of Western Arizona. Major Ferguson selected Tucson as his headquarters.

Carleton wasted no time in putting Tucson's house in order. First of all, he placed all capital offense trials under the jurisdiction of a military commission,[22] and arrested a number of desperadoes right away. The fact that he promised that the rules of evidence would be "those customary in practise under common law" did little to reassure the roughnecks caught in his net. The added warning that no execution would follow conviction until the determination of the President should be known, "unless the public safety absolutely requires it," did little to cheer the hard characters sitting in Carleton's military stockade.

Carleton decreed that no man might reside within the Territory who would not swear an oath of allegiance to the United States.[23] He also forbade words or acts which might "impair that veneration which all good patriots should feel for their country," and threatened punishment for any who spoke ill of, or acted against the Union. He dealt loafers a mortal blow when he wrote: "No man who does not pursue some lawful calling or have some legitimate means of support shall be permitted to remain in the Territory."[24]

In rounding up undesirables of the town, Carleton promised to arrange it "so that when a man does have his throat cut, his house robbed, or his fields ravaged," he might have comfort in knowing that the guilty would be punished.[25]

Apparently not satisfied with arresting only the hardened criminal types of Tucson, Carleton went after the rebel sympathizers too. Tucson at the time consisted of some 450 to 500 people, mostly Mexicans, with only a handful of Americans in permanent residence. Among these were:

Bill Oury, Sam Hughes, Mark Aldrich, Solomon Warner, Peter Rainsford Brady, John Sweeney, Hiram Stevens, Charley Brown, Hill de Armitt and Philip Contzen. A few, like Sol Warner, were loyal to the Union; others (most) were almost hysterically pro-Southern — Sylvester Mowry, for example. On June 13, 1862, he was brought before a military tribunal, tried, convicted, and relieved of his property, including his silver mines in Patagonia. There was some talk that this was done out of spite as the result of an old quarrel between Mowry and Carleton.

Bill Oury's brush with the conquerors involved not Carleton, but his second in command, Joseph R. West. After Carleton's promotion to brigadier general in 1862, West succeeded to colonelcy, and later, on October 25, 1862, was himself appointed a brigadier general of volunteers. He had been appointed as the military commander in Mesilla on August 13 of that year, but was in residence in Tucson when he and Oury had their run-in.

Bill's account of his experience with West is a reminiscence, written some seventeen years after the incident, and published in an 1879 issue of the Arizona *Daily Star*.[26]

I had with scrupulous care preserved every number of that first newspaper ever published within the limits of Arizona Territory from the time it was founded in Tubac in 1858 to the last issue of the same in Tucson in 1861 — in which the editor announced the closing of his office and advertised the sale of his pair of pocket derringers as useless furniture on account of the prospect of civil war — which so soon thereafter became a verity.

In June, 1861, I was called by business to San Francisco, and carried with me on horseback, at great inconvenience, the valuable little journal containing a complete epitome of the early history of Arizona. At considerable expense, I had it bound in book form in the bay city, bringing it back to Arizona in November of the same year. As a bona fide Arizonan, I looked upon the trouble of transporting it as trifling compared with the value of the work [I believed] I had secured for the future historian of my beloved land.

The year 1862 brought into Arizona the ever-to-be-remembered California Column, the first regiment of which was commanded by a colonel ever-to-be-execrated by every lover of the territory, who immediately upon his arrival in Tucson commenced sticking his nose into everything (the filthier the better, for him). In an evil hour, some unsuspecting resident gave him the information that the only history of the early settlement of the country was in the possession and property of your correspondent.

Soon after, I was waited upon by an orderly with the Colonel's compliments, and ordered to appear before him, bringing the history with me. Under the peculiar circumstances then existing, I could not afford to disobey. Consequently, with my darling child under my arm, and sad forebodings, I was ushered into the august presence.

After the customary salutation, I was relieved of my highly prized burden, and after a few common-place remarks, permitted to retire. Time passed, but not a word was ever uttered about the return of my book. On learning casually

*that the redoubtable Colonel was about to take up the march for the Rio
Grande, I called upon him for the return of my book. I was coolly informed
by this valiant warrior (in books) that the work was packed up in his luggage
and that he could not take the trouble to look for it — that "if an opportunity
offered" he would send it back from the Rio Grande.*

*I mustered the courage to protest the carrying of the book out of the
country, and pronounced it an act of vandalism. No prayer or argument I had
wit enough to make availed ought with this son of Mars. My book was
ruthlessly torn from me, and the following year Charles O. Brown finding it
kicking around Mesilla, kindly returned it to me, but so mutilated by the
gallant Colonel's keen scissors as to be absolutely worthless. The name of this
plumed knight is Joseph R. West, whilom carpetbag senator of the proud state
of Louisiana. Pass him around, hold him up to scorn and contempt of every
true Arizonan and oblige,*

W. S. Oury

Obviously Bill had no love for the Union Army, and particularly none
for the censor of his papers. Regardless of Bill's assessment of West,
Carleton could not agree. In his report to San Francisco, dated September
20, 1862, he said: "Much of our success was dependent on his [West's]
energy, perseverance, cheerfulness, and high soldierly qualities. I cannot
too strongly recommend that this officer be promoted to the grade of
Brigadier General of Volunteers as a reward for these services."[27]

·Although Carleton had forbidden remarks in derogation of the Union,
the real rebels of the town grumbled amongst themselves anyway. At the
war's end, their chagrin heightened by defeat, such individuals loosed
their pent-up emotions and spoke out at will. Granville Oury was one of
these. An article appearing in a San Francisco paper in December, 1866,
took Grant to task on this score.[28]

*We consider it very unfortunate that the speaker (Granville Oury in the
Territorial legislature) thought it necessary in support of Andrew Johnson to
eulogize Jefferson Davis, or any other engaged in the late attempt to overthrow
the government.*

Carleton and West might forbid public talk against the Union and
make the ban stick during hostilities, but with the armistice all bets were
off. Enforced silence could never change the spots on the brothers Oury,
nor keep them long tractable.

CHAPTER 19

The Occupation Blues

AND SO THE CALIFORNIA COLUMN had come to town, and was there to stay. Any hope that Confederate forces would take Tucson back went winging with Sibley's defeat at Glorieta. The Southern sympathizers grumbled at the restrictive measures levied upon them but they had to go on living, and there were many things to do. To begin with, the town was badly in need of law and order. It was as unruly now as it had ever been, as undisciplined perhaps as even in its Anglo and Mexican periods.

In the early American or "Anglo" period, Tucson was a wild, rough place, full of gunmen and swaggering desperadoes. Shootings on the street were not uncommon, and disorder was the rule rather than the exception. In Spanish and Mexican times, the whipping post was used, and many a luckless peon had his back torn to ribbons by the cat o'nine tails. Tucson's first American Judge was Marcus A. Aldrich who arrived in the old pueblo in 1855, a few months ahead of his good friend, Bill Oury. Aldrich, like Oury, had come to Tucson from the California gold fields. He had left a promising law career in Illinois, having been a member of the Illinois legislature in the 1830's. His wife, Margaret Aldrich, never came to Tucson, choosing to remain in the East, probably waiting for her husband to come to his senses and quit the awful, western country. He never did. Reluctant to break the marriage bonds, even with what most contemporaries would have considered just cause, Aldrich solved his problem of loneliness by taking up with a Mexican woman, Teófila León. A daughter, Faustina, was born of the union. She was seven years older than Bill's daughter, Lola, and the two were good and close friends for many years.

Aldrich and a few of his contemporaries did what they could to maintain order, but it was not enough to make Tucson a safe and orderly place. Aldrich appreciated the deterrent qualities of the whipping post and continued to sentence men to public flogging. But even the revolting spectacle of a man whipped to shreds was not sufficient to deter boisterous bullies and drunks from creating all sorts of mischief. On August 26, 1860, a meeting of the citizens of Tucson had been held and a code of laws was adopted for the suppression and punishment of crime. Two months later, on November 1, Aldrich was so disgusted with the cowardice of the townspeople in failing to press charges against felons that he resigned his post as judge. This also had no visible effect on the people of the town. Desperadoes of all sorts made the streets a sort of no man's land and the gentle people stayed at home, or ventured upon the streets at their peril.

A strong municipal government was needed to cope with the lawless character of the town, and a handful of persons moved to bring the idea into reality. Governor John Goodwin had initiated civil government in the Territory of Arizona by a proclamation made at Navajo Springs on December 29, 1863. The Tucson group thought it time to ask the chief executive for some sort of city government, and so held a meeting on May 8, 1864, to discuss the issue. It is doubtful whether Bill as a participant of the convention thought about it, but it was eighteen years to the day since he had ridden with General Zachary Taylor at the battle of Palo Alto.

Bill Oury rose to nominate General W. Claude Jones as president of the convention, and Gregory P. Harte as secretary; both men were installed on a voice vote.[1] The object of the meeting was then discussed, and the secretary was called upon to read several resolutions which had been prepared by Oury, Aldrich, Sol Warner, and a few others in advance. It was resolved that in the absence of any law preventing the establishment of self-government, the citizens would act on their own until the governor might provide the legal machinery for government. A mayor and five councilmen would serve the government. The resolution then went on at some length outlining the duties of these officers, and a move was adopted to have the mayor and the councilmen make a report on their doings to the next legislature, the object in view being a city charter from the governor's office.

The last resolution was one petitioning the governor to appoint a mayor and five councilmen, "to hold office until a government is established by legislative enactment." All resolutions were then placed before the meeting for discussion, and were adopted on the spot. Sixteen men signed the petition; Bill Oury's name was first on the list. The petition was sent on then to Governor Goodwin and the council sat back to await his pleasure. They did not wait long. Goodwin was on an inspection tour of the Territory and passed through Tucson just three days later (May 11th). He took the occasion to issue a proclamation "in accordance with the request made to me by the citizens of Tucson."[2]

The Town is Established

Thus the municipality of Tucson was established. Bill Oury was appointed the town's first mayor on that same day, with a council consisting of Mark Aldrich, Juan Elías (Sr.), Hiram S. Stevens, Francisco S. León, and Jeremiah Riordan.[3] With reference to Bill's appointment, an Arizona paper said: "Mr. Oury is an old and well-known resident of the Territory, a gentleman of culture and character. His appointment and that of his associates . . . will ensure a strong municipal government."[4]

Thus Tucson became a legally established municipality with at least the rudimentary means of establishing law and order. It was some time, however, before a move was made to incorporate the town. Yuma was the first of the larger Arizona towns to incorporate, and Tucson followed its lead. On 22 April, 1871, almost seven years after the governor's municipality proclamation, a petition was submitted to the Board of Supervisors of Pima County by the townspeople requesting incorporation. It read, in part:

Sirs; we the undersigned, have the honor . . . to show . . . that whereas the Congress of the United States has passed certain acts by which they propose to donate to towns or villages, situated upon the public lands, a certain amount of land, the amount graduated to the population, either to the municipal authorities or county judge in trust for said town or village, and where this town has no corporate existence, and the county no Judge, your petitioners respectfully request your honorable body that you would order an election . . . for the purpose of electing municipal officers according to law.[5]

The petition goes on to list the population of Tucson at 3,200 people (based on the 1870 census) and to request 1920 acres of land as prescribed by Congress for municipalities of between 3,000 and 4,000 population. Bill Oury signed this petition, along with the usual group interested in city affairs at that time: P. R. Tully, Estevan Ochoa, S. R. DeLong, Sam Hughes, Sol Warner, the Zeckendorfs, S. H. Drachman, and a few others.

Two days later, the Board of Supervisors acted favorably on the petition, and appointed Sidney R. DeLong, John Anderson and Sam Hughes as inspectors for the election which was to follow. On the following day, April 25, the inspectors issued the call for a town election. The election was scheduled for Wednesday, May 17, and called for naming a mayor, four councilmen, a marshal, treasurer, recorder, and, of all things, a pound-master. The election was held as scheduled, but no new office-holder could claim to have been catapulted into office by surging popular acclaim. Sixty-six votes were cast, and the election was termed "a quiet affair." Sidney DeLong became the new mayor, and Charley Brown, Sam Hughes, W. W. Williams, and Bill Oury became aldermen. William Morgan was voted in as marshal; W. J. Osborn became the new assessor; Hiram Stevens took office as the city treasurer, and Juan Elías "went to the dogs."

A little over a year later, on July 9, 1872, Mayor DeLong petitioned the U. S. Land Office for 1,280 acres of land for the official townsite of the city of Tucson.

And so the town became incorporated. The officials were at least successful in bringing law and order to Tucson, although it was not easy, what with the frontier element. Mark Aldrich died two years later, on September 21, 1873, not missed by the tough characters he had punished, but bereaved by his many friends. His place was taken by "Judge" Charley Meyer, a homespun jurist of the Roy Bean type ("Law West of the Pecos"). Meyer had no legal training at all, and was in fact a druggist. He kept up the tradition of the whipping post, and invented a new system for keeping the peace. Men convicted of crime or felony were gathered into chain gangs to work the streets of Tucson publicly.[6] This had little effect upon hardened criminals but it devastated the Tucson residents caught in Charley Meyer's net. Harsh in concept, the measure had a most sobering effect. Although the unfortunate "one-timers" had to suffer humiliation on Tucson's streets, the town was becoming a safer place to live.

Bill Acquires Property

In addition to taking an interest in public affairs, Bill began to look around for city property in the early 1860's. He was never able to acquire parcels of great value, but he did gain possession of numerous small pieces of land about town. In one of his first orders as commander of the Western District of Arizona, Major Ferguson took up the subject of real estate. He directed that all Tucson property holders (to include those living within three miles of town) must register their property with a suitable description, and present an abstract of title for each piece owned.[7] He named Bill

Oury as registrar and recorder,[8] with power of attorney to name his own deputy. Oury was directed to open his office on 10 August, 1862, and to proclaim that all property-holders were expected to register their holdings before September 10th. Oury was to receive a fee of one dollar for each parcel he recorded. The order was printed in English and Spanish and circulated about the town.

The *Index of Deeds of Real Property* (kept in the Pima County Courthouse) shows that the listing of parcels began on September 4, 1862, just six days before Ferguson's deadline. On this day, Bill listed his own land, seven small lots; 73 through 77, 79, and 101. These were lots he had acquired at different times, from different people, and for varying amounts of money.

Lot number 73, for example, had been purchased from Miguel Pacheco and Guadalupe Sáens on Nov. 26, 1856, for the princely sum of thirty dollars.[9] It was located on Calle de La Misión, just south of what later became Levin's Park. Lot 74 was just north of the old Military Plaza, at about where the corner of Court and Telles streets would later join. Bill had acquired this parcel from Nelson Van Alstine in September, 1857, for sixty dollars.[10] Lots 75, 76, and 77 were in what later became the Chinatown District at the confluence of Calle del Correo (Pearl Street now) and Calle de las Milpas. Bill had obtained lot 75 from Steven Ramírez in May, 1861;[11] lot 76 from Francisco G. Torano on November 28, 1857,[12] and lot 77 from Guadalupe Santa Cruz at an undisclosed date.[13] Description of these adjoining lots places them almost exactly across the street from land later occupied by the business establishment of Tully and Ochoa.

Lot 79 was purchased from Richard M. Doss for $800, and was situated just south of Calle de la Guardia (Alameda Street now).[14] Lot 101, acquired by Bill from Hiram Stevens for $125, appears to have been on Calle del Arroyo (Pennington) between Calle Real (Main) and Calle del Correo (Pearl), in the exact spot where Tully and Ochoa put up their corral in the late 1870's.[15] Later, Fish and Silverberg built a drygoods store across the street. The dry goods store location was later taken over by William Zeckendorf.

In these six lots, Bill had the nucleus of what would later become very valuable land. From 1857 through 1861 he had paid out a little over $1600 for these parcels. Like all other outspoken Southern sympathizers, Bill suffered confiscation of these properties during the Civil War. In a sort of tragi-comic affair, he saw himself recording his own land, only to have it taken away from him. The Río Abajo Press of Albuquerque for June 28, 1864, carried an item concerning the sale of confiscated property by the U. S. marshal. The sale was made under the direction of the U. S. District Court of the Second Judicial District of the Territory of New Mexico. In this sale, Bill lost lots 75, 76, 77 and 79 in Tucson, and his cultivated field out near Warner's Mill.

These suits were begun in May, 1864 (in the Pima County District Court), on the charge that speaking out against the federal government was tantamount to waging war against it. Hence the litigants were in rebellion and vulnerable to the confiscation order. Granville Oury had served in the Confederate army; there was little doubt that his land would be taken from him. Bill, on the other hand, had not borne arms, but his remarks were as caustic and vexatious as ever. As a result, the property listed above was taken away from him on July 28, 1864. Happily, all of his confiscated lands were returned to him under the provisions of a general amnesty order signed by President Andrew Johnson on July 4, 1868.

In 1959, while in Tucson researching for this biography, I called upon Mr. Arthur Jacobs, a grandson of Leopoldo Carrillo. He said that he had heard that Bill Oury had once owned all of Chinatown, the "Wishing Shrine," and Elysian Grove. He added that there was a small zoo in the latter place in the 1880's, and that a bear owned by Oury got out of its cage and killed a Mexican. Property records as described above would indicate that Mr. Jacobs was essentially right about the Chinatown holdings. I have been unable to verify his interest in the other places, or to learn any more about the rapacious bear.

Bill had several other holdings in town, listed in later records. In the field notes of W. W. Foreman, made for entry into the map of surveys for Tucson in 1872 (Book of Deeds nr. 2), Bill is listed as owning lot #3 of Block 183. This was a small 60 x 60 lot on Main Street just west of the Military Plaza, and south of Washington. He sold it to Hiram Stevens on Nov. 12, 1880 for $350.[16] Bill later acquired lot 4 of Block 221,[17] and lot 2 of Block 186.[18] Also, he owned all of Block 123,[19] an area consisting of twelve small lots, bounded by 4th and 5th Avenues, and 17th and 18th Streets. This land is still enclosed by the same streets and lies three blocks east of the present Drachman School. It was deeded by Bill to his wife Inez on January 4, 1884. In the same year, Oury paid one Chan Tin Wo $2700 for lot 1 of Block 188.[20]

On November 10, 1877, Bill acquired 160 acres in Florence under the provisions of the Congressional Land Act of 1820.[21] There is no record of his use of the land. He also had a sizeable piece of cultivated land out near Warner's Mill at the foot of Cerro del Tucson ("A" Mountain). It was an irregularly shaped piece about 1500 feet long, lying adjacent to fields owned by his friends Manuel Romero, Pedro Burruel, Jesús and Juan Elías, and Mark Aldrich.[22]

The only other property interest worthy of mention was that connected with a joint venture undertaken by Bill and Charley Brown,

Abraham Lyon, George Bryant, and Michael Leydon. It involved a mining claim in the Cokespa Mining District, and bore the pleasant sounding title Keo-chin-i-cum. Whatever became of the venture is not known. Although Bill recorded the claim on February 4, 1864, nothing was heard of the property thereafter. Very likely it was simply another of the hundreds of mine sites ringing Tucson on all sides.

Although his lands were confiscated during the war period, Bill got them back eventually, and was able to keep most of the lots while he lived. After his death in 1887, his widow was hard-pressed for cash. She was forced to sell what she could, and even lost several of the lots for taxes. She tried valiantly to hold on to these, but lost all but one or two, which she left to her heirs.

Bill's first property in town was on South Main Street, about where Jackson Street came in from the east to join it. It was only a block away from Barrio Libre, and hence right on the edge of the civilized portion of town. It was from this house that he walked to work when he was agent for the Overland Mail Company. His early neighbors there are not known. By the 1870's, Pancho Gómez had moved in on one side of him and William Zeckendorf on the other. Leopoldo Carrillo, Theodore Welisch, and Charley Meyers were living across the street. To the south, within the next couple of blocks lived Judge Scott, Sabino Otero, Pete Kitchen, Juan Elías, Governor Safford, Joe Phy, and Bill's relative by marriage, Adam Sanders. Oddly, Bill's property on Main Street is not recorded in the Index of Deeds made by him on Major Ferguson's order, although all of his other properties were duly registered.

The "Map of Tucson," 1862, surveyed by Major Ferguson (and drawn by J. B. Mills, surveyor) shows no lot number where Bill Oury's house stood, but the house itself is indicated on the map, number 30. A map prepared by A. W. Patticini, draughtsman for the U.S. Surveyor General in 1880, shows the dwelling located on "plot #5." The George Roskruge map of 1893 gives the same information.

Bill had lived first on a cattle ranch on the Santa Cruz River. Not long after (in 1856), he moved into the house on South Main, where he lived until his move to the ranch he called Tanque Verde.

On moving into town from the place on the Santa Cruz he could not be close enough to his stock to keep the animals safe from predators. In addition to normal losses from mountain lions, he soon began to suffer regular losses at the hands of "moonlight requisition" squads. Suspecting Apaches, Bill decided to spend a few nights near the herd, sleeping on the ground with a rifle at his side. He hired four Mexicans and posted them at strategic places among the rocks.[23]

On the third night, he heard an owl hoot. Soon three Apache bucks moved silently into the ocotillo corral. Bill had told his gunmen to let the Apaches kill a steer, figuring that the men would present a bunched target while skinning the animal. He was right. One volley brought down all three men. Bill was censured for this in town, but cattle theft along the Santa Cruz came to an abrupt halt. In fact, Mexican ranchers living inside Tucson's walled village began to move out to their ranches in permanent residence after this episode.

It was in February, 1864, that Grant Oury and several of his friends wrote a remarkable letter to Lt. General Edmund Kirby Smith of the Confederate army.[24] Things were not going well for the South. Since July, its position had become precarious. Lee had lost some 28,000 men at Gettysburg, 10,000 at Vicksburg (with twice that number taken prisoner), 18,000 at Chickamauga, and almost 7,000 at Missionary Ridge. Worse, his armies were in retreat almost everywhere along the line.

Still to come were the grinding clashes at The Wilderness, Spotsylvania, and Cold Harbor, where Lee's army would inflict aggregate casualties of 39,000 men on Grant's juggernaut, as against less than 19,000 losses of its own. Even so, Northern superiority in numbers and Grant's tenacity would enable the Union commander to push on to the inevitable victory, past Atlanta, Franklin, Nashville, and Five Forks.

In this gloomy climate of retreat, Grant Oury and his friends were undismayed. And so they decided to strike "one more blow" for the Confederacy. Fourteen of them got together in San Antonio and drafted the letter to Kirby Smith. Actually, not all of the signers were in San Antonio at the time. Dan Showalter sent the letter on to Tucson where several men signed it and returned it to him. In its entirety, it read:[24]

To Lieut. Genl. Kirby Smith, C.S.A.
D. Sir.

The few Arizonans and New Mexicans that have survived the exigencies of the service, seeing but little hope of a restoration of their country under existing circumstances, and desirous of making one more effort, striking one more blow for their homes and property, earnestly appeal to you for the relief and assurance that the necessity of their case demands.

We are assured not alone by the signs of the times, but by the arrived sentiments of members of the Confederate Congress, that should offer of a peace treaty be made, conditions for the surrender of all Territories by the South, the same would be accepted by our government, and we believe that however repugnant the measures might be to the existing powers, the pressure of the people in their great desire for a speedy conclusion of the present war would be such as to override all argument and powers of the administration. We have no country, no home, but Arizona and New Mexico, and if these are given up we will have fought and many have lost their lives to no purpose. Almost the entire American population of these Territories are now in the ranks of the Confederate Army and join us in making this last appeal for help.

We propose to take one hundred chosen men under the command of Lieut. Col. Dan Showalter, traveling in detachments of twenty-five through Mexico, for the ostensible purpose of visiting the late rich gold discovery made in the Territory of Arizona, concentrate our force at Tucson (at which point a large supply depot has been established, guarded by about one hundred men from the best information gotten yet), take that place, and move directly forward to the gold mines between the headwaters of the Salinas and Gila Rivers, where we are assured that our numbers will be augmented to at least five hundred men, and perhaps many more. Thence we march directly on Fort Yuma, destroy that point and open up communication with Southern California from which a sufficient number of men can be drawn to sweep the entire Territories east, and establish beyond cavil the claim of the Southern Confederacy to the country. We ask that the numbers of men under the command above-mentioned, together with seventy thousand dollars in specie or its equivalent be granted us, and we solemnly pledge our lives for the success of the undertaking.

> *Very Respectfully.*
> *Yours, etc.*

San Antonio, Texas
Febry 14th 1864

> *Lt. Col. Dan Showalter*
> *F. E. Kavanaugh*
> *G. H. Oury*
> *C. C. Dodson*
> *Fred A. Neville*
> *M. Oury*
> *Henry McNamee*
> *Joseph Franck*
> *H. H. Holmes*
> *Joseph (Rins?)*
> *William Willon*
> *David Young*
> ————— *. . . Mas*
> —————*Brevoort*

There is no record of any answer by Smith to this wild suggestion. A mere glance at its parts shows that failure anywhere along the line would prove disastrous. First, there was the business of trespass in Mexico, then the necessity for reducing the garrison at Tucson. Fort Yuma would then be taken (after 500 men should rally to the Stars and Bars), the victory to be followed by a general uprising in California, whose jubilant and enthusiastic participants would "sweep the entire territories east." Still, if the scheme was brash, its authors were in earnest.

In any case, there was not much General Kirby Smith could do about it. He was then in command of Confederate forces west of the Mississippi, but as the Federals controlled the river he was virtually cut off from the seat of war. By now, the South would live or die depending on what Lee and Johnston might do, a fact appreciated by Grant whose entire plan for 1864 centered upon destroying the armies led by these two men. In the far west, Carleton had secured the forts from Yuma to New Mexico. It is unlikely that any one in the Southern military establishment gave much thought to Oury's letter. Besides, at this late date, where would Kirby Smith get seventy thousand dollars?

In any case, nothing came of the offer. By the following spring, Lee had surrendered to Grant at Appomattox courthouse (April 9, 1865), and some thirteen weeks after that, Grant Oury, Dan Showalter, and several other irreconcilables were off for Mexico.

The year 1864 was saddened for the Oury family by the death of an infant son of Bill and Inez· The child's name appears nowhere in the family records, indicating that it may have died soon after birth. But Bill's sister, Senah, writing from Louisiana, Missouri, mourned with the bereaved parents, and in the same letter took her brother gently to task for remaining in the wilds of Arizona.[25]

Most deeply do I feel for you in the loss of your boy, but if it is one of God's providences, I thank him with a heart overflowing with gratitude.... The little one was taken from the evils to come, and can you, my brother, lay your treasure in the cold grave, around which the sweetest, tenderest affections of your heart had gathered, and feel he has gone to dust forever? ... Will he, the bright blossom of an hour, and you, the worn out veteran of the world's service, have no meeting point in the future? ... Oh, my brother, if your reason is to tear from you the sweet hope of immortality, it is a curse.... I do not believe that God will pass unheeded the tears I have shed, and the agonizing prayers I have sent up to his throne.... I was not at all surprised to hear of your visit from the Apaches. I had been looking for that very news for some time, believing that they would take advantage of the distractions of the times to make such a raid. You will never be rid of them until you come out of Arizona. Why can't you do it? Are there not other places you can make a living easier, be more secure in your property, and have better educational and social advantages? It will hardly be right, I think, to take Lola from civilization with her knowledge and taste for the same, and bury her among the rocks of Arizona. And you who have been hiding your light — come out and let others see it.

CHAPTER 20

Rebels to Mexico

BY SPRING 1865, THE CONFEDERACY — worn out, tired, and defeated — collapsed. Lee had surendered the remnants of the Army of Northern Virginia at the McLean House, Appomattox, on April 9. Under the terms of surrender, officers of the Confederate army were to give individual paroles promising not to take up arms again against the United States.

Grant Oury had been out of the army since his run-in with Sibley, but he remained a staunch supporter of the Confederacy, and was heartsick at the news of Lee's surrender. He was, like many of his companions, bitter, disillusioned, and angry. The prospect of life under the Yankees seemed appalling. There was only one thing to do — head for Mexico and a new life.

After his release from the army, Grant had gone to San Antonio, and married his cousin, Mina Sanders, of Seguin, Texas. She was as bitter as her husband over the South's defeat and agreed in an instant to take up the trail for Mexico. A few weeks after Lee's surrender, Grant and Mina climbed into a wagon and headed south. The date was June 20, 1865. Within three months, they (and others of their party) were back in the United States, weary, sore, and chastened from the gruelling trip that took them all over northern Chihuahua and Sonora. No matter how miserable the journey, Mina kept a diary in which she put daily entries. This remarkable paper presents firsthand a number of unique and truly hair-raising adventures. It has been printed in its entirety in the *Arizona Historical Review,* running serially from April 1931 to June 1935, with comments by my father. Excerpts from the original diary are interspersed throughout this chapter.

Grant and Mina left San Antonio at about four o'clock on the afternoon of June 20, and made camp about nine miles southwest of town. Great was Mina's joy when out of the evening shadows rode a lone horseman. It was her brother, Adam Sanders, whom the family had thought dead on the field of battle at Franklin. Adam had ridden some fifty miles that day already, and learned of Mina's departure upon arriving home. An irreconcilable himself, he decided to join the party. She records that she was overcome with tears at the reunion, and "at twelve o'clock we retired, a heavy dew falling upon us, and the mosquitoes were troublesome."[1]

On the twenty-first, the party made about thirty miles, passing through Castroville and crossing over the Hondo River. As she places quotation marks about the word "Hondo" (deep), it is likely that the river bed was dry and the wagonwheels simply churned through loose sand.

It is at this point in her story that Mina first mentions the others in the exodus into Mexico. "Our mess consists of Capt. Dodson, Mr. Neville, Mr. Billy Wilson, Mr. Oury, Addy, myself, and the teamsters — Mr. Collier who drives an ambulance, and Silvario, a Mexican."[2]

The June 21 entry also mentions Colonel Dan Showalter, one of the co-signers of the letter to General Kirby Smith mentioned earlier. Showalter, a flashy individual, was quitting the country too, probably more in the spirit of adventure than for sentimental reasons. Noted as something of a trouble-maker, he had been run out of California by General Carleton several years earlier. Showalter had killed a man in a duel in California, and was himself killed in a riotous brawl in Guaymas some months after Mina's entry of June 21. On that day, Showalter was ill, as Mina writes:

Mr. Oury had been disposed to ridicule my culinary knowledge, but was so pleased with the result that he took some to Col. Showalter who is crippled by a fall from his horse, and is suffering greatly.[3]

Mina's entry for June 22 mentions two more persons fleeing southward; one Oldham and David S. Terry. Oldham had been a political opponent of General Sam Houston in the 1850's. Terry, a violent man, had killed Senator Broderick in a duel in California in 1858.[4] Like Showalter, he was to die as he lived, violently. Apparently the two parties travelled a parallel course, but made separate camps. On June 24 Mina writes: "We camped on Turkey Creek . . . Colonel Terry's party camped near us, but each kept his distance."

The first stages of the trek seem to have been made in comparative comfort; Mina writes:

Mr. Oury has a wagon drawn by four mules, loaded with provisions and baggage, and he allows two soldiers (picked up in San Antonio) to ride in the wagon. I am very comfortable — have a bed in the ambulance and sleep half the day. It is a small room, and I keep things hanging all around for convenience. The gentlemen are all very kind and attentive to me, especially Mr. Oury and Addy, who anticipate every wish, and so far, I have enjoyed the trip exceedingly.[5]

On the twenty-sixth, the parties made preparation to cross into Mexico. Grant arose at daylight and rode over to Terry's camp, and the two then crossed the Rio Grande to speak to a Mexican general, described by Grant as "an intelligent and polished gentleman." Mina and the others brought the wagons into Eagle Pass, just opposite Piedras Negras, the point of entry.

General Joe Shelby

It is at this point that Mina mentions General Joe Shelby of the Confederacy. On this day (June 26), he was apparently held up on the American side while trying to dispose of a rather sizeable stock of firearms and ammunition to the Mexican government. Mina reports that Shelby wanted to serve Benito Juárez in the latter's fight with the Emperor Maximilian. This does not jibe with sources pointing to Shelby's efforts to join the other side.

Like Grant and Mina Oury, Joe Shelby could not accept the South's defeat. With the awful news of Lee's surrender, he addressed his men on the subject of flight into Mexico. Many of them had been with him at Prairie Grove, Wilson's Creek, Westport, and Pea Ridge; they trusted him implicitly. Now, on the muddy banks of the Rio Grande, a final vote was held. Some of the men had soured on the scheme and wanted to go home; others chose to follow Shelby into Mexico. Some favored Juárez, some Maximilian. Once the decision to quit the homeland was made, Shelby ceremoniously sank his Confederate battle flags in the Rio Grande and walked ashore on the Mexican side. Shelby was the only Southern commander who refused to surrender at the end of the Civil War. Now he was an expatriate roaming the hills of a hostile land.

Shelby and his men had been in Mexico only a few hours when they fell to fighting some guerrilla bands of Juárez. Shelby made immediate contact with the French Army commander in Monterrey advising him that he would like to join forces with the French at once, adding that although he "preferred peace to war," he would attack forthwith unless his offer was accepted. The Frenchman was glad enough to accept the offer, but Maximilian was not. Nothing came of Shelby's military efforts in Mexico. Eventually his men scattered and drifted back across the border. Shelby spent a couple of years in Mexico, trying his hand at coffee-raising and freight-line operation. He failed at both. Upon his return home he became a U.S. marshal in Missouri.

The Oury party crossed the Rio Grande on the late afternoon of Wednesday, June 28th. Of this episode, Mina relates:

We did not commence crossing 'til late, and it required some time, as the boats are miserably constructed affairs. I remained on the bank 'til the last, and had ample opportunity for observing. On the Texas side, a great many of Shelby's men were selling flour, etc., to the Mexicans. The bank is lined with the lowest class ... half-clad women and men, peddling bread and water melons. That which most excited my disgust was a number of Mexican men in a perfect state of nudity, running up and down the river and parading the banks. I learned that these creatures are employed to assist cattle in swimming across. ... At last our turn came, and the boat had to be dragged up the river some distance by those thinly clad bipeds, and there attached to the cable. The river is muddy and swift. Piedras Negras is an abominable place, with narrow, crowded streets, where we were compelled to remain while the gentlemen rushed around buying onions, frijoles, pickles, bread, etc. ... We left town late, drove fast, passed through a little settlement, and camped a short distance beyond.[6]

Here Mina had the first inkling of what the Mexican venture might be like. But "hope springs eternal" — and the party pressed on. On this day too, "several negroes took leave of absence." Captain Strobe, a member of Terry's party had lost forty slaves between San Antonio and Piedras Negras. If the white Southerners had their way of expressing a yearning for freedom, so did their silent charges.

To wind up this hectic day, a furious storm broke over the little caravan.

The boys hopped around briskly in search of shelter. Mr. Oury crept into my apartment, which was dry but crowded. Addy found a snug place underneath the wagon. The lightning was vivid, accompanied with continual roars of deafening thunder.[7]

On the twenty-ninth the several parties consolidated and "forced Mr. Oury, greatly against his will," to take charge of the train. That night one of the Mexican drivers stole a horse and vanished in the darkness. A negro slave belonging to Judge Terry was less fortunate. Caught in the act of escaping, he was stripped of his provisions (by Terry) and sent on his way. Of this mean episode, Mina wrote: "The negro was very penitent

GENERAL JOE SHELBY could not accept the South's defeat. When news came of Lee's surrender, Shelby took a vote among his men on the banks of the Rio Grande. "Once the decision to quit the homeland was made, Shelby ceremoniously sank his Confederate battle flags in the Rio Grande and walked ashore on the Mexican side." The Southern leader never returned to his native land.

and begged hard to remain, but Dave was immovable and left the poor fellow alone, miles from anywhere. I hope he found his way back to Piedras Negras."[8]

As the party was but a couple of days out of the border town, it is likely that the poor man found his way back. Still, the incident discloses the unsavory side of Judge David Terry.

On June 30, Mina expressed uneasiness at the reported presence in the vicinity of Comanches, Kickapoos, and Choctaws, although no Indians were seen that day. It was on the evening of the thirtieth that Mina first met Mrs. Terry, who for some reason had not stirred from her wagon. Mina speaks of her as "a fine-looking red-headed woman, whose complexion is preserved by the wearing of a brown linen mask."

On July 1st the Indians came.

. . . They are a degraded and uncivilized race of human beings. . . . As I had never seen an Indian, all my ideas of them were borrowed from Cooper's novels. I watched their movements with curious interest, which very soon resolved itself into extreme disgust and abhorrence. The filthy horrid creatures are the most persistent beggars I ever saw. Owing to their proximity, it became necessary to put out a double guard, which did not prevent the stealing of one of our horses. I spent a sleepless night haunted by the sight of those loathesome creatures.[9]

On the fifth, a band of Liberal soldiers (juaristas) came dashing into camp frightening Mina out of her wits. The sergeant in charge of the ragtag little army permitted his men to beg for bread, but slashed at the more impertinent with a quirt when they demanded tobacco. Mina observed that "the poor starved wretches are under perfect subjection, miserably treated and driven like dogs."[10] Mention is made here of the women in the Mexican band. Wives and camp-followers, the women were called "galletas" (cakes), after their manner of making and serving thin corn or flour cakes on the march.

Three days later (July 8) the Oury party arrived at Monclova, where it bought provisions and rested. Near the edge of town, Mina saw a group of some twenty-five to thirty Americans, enclosed in a corral and held under guard. These men had deserted from the Confederate army before the war's end, gone off to Mexico, and enlisted in the Liberal army. In Monclova they had been caught, stripped of arms and put under guard. Mina allowed that "they perhaps deserve such a fate, but my heart aches for the wretched creatures." Some inquired if the Confederacy wasn't "about played out."[11]

It was in Monclova too that Mina complained of thorns and mosquitoes.

. . . The terror of both man and beast in Mexico is the thorns. Everything is armed with them, the sharpest, longest, fiercest thorns in the world. You can't avoid them — they are everywhere, on everything. The very atmosphere bristles with them. . . . And the mosquitoes. . . . When the wind lulled, the calm brought myriads upon myriads of the most ravenous insects. . . . All our efforts to thwart them are ineffectual. The boys tied their heads up in towels and handkerchiefs, and each armed with a brush fought desperately with the malicious foe. I burned sugar in a frying pan, and while the smoke lasted, it kept them off. Afterwards they came in scores and devoured my face, neck, and hands.[12]

One wonders how keen now was the ardor for the good life in Mexico. There is no statement of remorse on this slapping, clawing night of the mosquitoes, but it is likely that the cooler greener hills of home loomed bright in the memory just the same.

On Monday, July 17, the party came into Parras, and saw the soldiers of Maximilian's army. Mina describes with enthusiasm this entry into the first Mexican settlement of consequence.

. . . Parras is a place of considerable importance. The warm plaza is very handsome, laid out in walks bordered with lovely roses, dahlias, and other flowers. The triangles and diamond plots are thickly carpeted with luxuriant grass, and dotted with shrubbery and flowers. . . . There is a fine brass band which discourses enlivening music during the evening. Altogether it appears to be an inviting resort. The streets are full of French soldiers. The officers wear elegant uniforms, scarlet pants trimmed with black, dark green and black jackets fitting closely, and the whole elaborately ornamented with silver braid and buttons. They are superbly mounted on beautiful Arabian horses, and it is a dazzling spectacle to see them fully equipped and mounted. The soldiers wear yellow linen blouses and pants with wide red belts, pants tight at the ankles, but very wide in the legs. Tiny red caps, tassel behind and no brim, adorn the backs of their heads. Several have loose slips of linen over the blouse and pants, extending to the knee.[13]

A few days later, after the animals had been given a chance to rest and recuperate, the party played host to a French officer and his staff. The officer, a colonel, brought not only his staff but an escort of twenty soldiers trotting and jingling into camp. The men were mounted "on their splendid Arabian horses, full armed with guns and sabres, and making a magnificent display in their flashing uniforms."

Mina inserts a wry little aside about the paucity of decent goods in the markets of Parras in her entry for July 23.

Capt. Dane and Mr. Wallace escorted Mrs. Terry and me to the stores for shopping, where we found poor assortments and high prices. Mrs. Terry needed shoes and couldn't find a number 5 in town. The Mexican women have very small feet, and the merchants told us that they rarely sold a shoe for ladies as large as number 3. I made no purchases.[14]

On this same day, after the abortive shopping tour, the foursome visited a local cotton goods factory, an establishment which seemed to interest Mina considerably.

I had become initiated into all the mysteries of cloth making by the primitive process resorted to by the poor blockaded southerners during the war, but had never seen it manufactured by machinery. What a contrast to the slow cards and wheels and clumsy looms of those trying times! Here, 250 looms, run by water power, turn out daily 45 yards of unbleached muslin cloth. . . . The factory is the property of a widow "over old to marry," and who has no daughters. Capt. Dane is inconsolable over this news.[15]

While marvelling at the efficiency of the cotton mill, Mina wonders in the following lines at the impoverished state of those living and working nearby.

In many respects these people have not advanced one step since the time of Moses. . . . We saw them threshing wheat in a most primitive manner. The wheat is piled on a hard spot of ground cleared for the purpose, having been thrown on raw hides, dragged by ropes attached to the pommels of saddles, and dumped in the pile. In the center of this pile is a post, and attached to it are two rows of horses, eight in each row, necked together. A man with a long whip drives the horses around, the outside ones in a gallop, the ones in the center having leisure to snatch sundry mouthfuls as they go — and thus the grain is tramped out. Afterwards, it is tossed up in the air by basketfuls, and winnowed, a slow and tedious process.[16]

Not satisfied with shopping and the inspection of the cotton mill, the party parked the ambulance and continued the tour of the winding, narrow streets of Parras on foot. Soon they arrived at the base of a steep hill and climbed until they had reached its summit, a vantage point reached by some stairs and a tunnel carved in the heart of a great boulder. There on top was a huge cross and an altar, reported by Mina as having been erected in a single night by a priest and two small boys. Of this scene, Mina says:

All the diseased and infirm of the countryside make pilgrimages to this shrine, and here find a miraculous cure for all the ills and ailments to which flesh is heir. A stream of women, many with children in their arms, and all bearing long tallow candles, were struggling up the hill, and we found several devotees on their knees, seeking absolution from sin and bodily pain. Poor ignorant wretches! Doubtless the exercise may benefit many, but I feel that no human afflicted with any serious ailment is equal to that climb.[17]

As the four Americans gazed upon the pilgrims, a light rain began to fall, and they started for their wagon in the streets below. Mina's eyes were the first to see the grim procession passing through the glistening streets at the bottom of the hill.

A brass band led, playing anything but a funeral dirge, then came men bearing on their shoulders an open coffin, exposing the corpse of a very dark, much wrinkled old man. The lid of the box was carried by a man in the rear, accompanied by mourners of each sex, bearing lighted candles. I had scarcely recovered from the effects of this repulsive sight, when an even more revolting one succeeded it. A gang of criminals, chained together in couples and wearing heavy chains 'round their ankles, were coming in from the fields, where they are taken daily and forced to labor.[18]

Mina's day was not quite over; after the funeral and chaingang processions, she was accosted by beggars before she and her friends could get on the buck-board and drive back to camp.

These are the most abject, degraded, wretched, decrepit, infirm, miserable specimens of humanity it has ever been my misfortune to look upon. I began by giving a silver dollar, but found that my means would be exhausted if I continued to give a cent, or even a quarter of a cent, as is the custom here.[19]

It was in Parras that the van began to break up. Colonel Showalter headed for Durango, stating that he would go on to Guaymas a little later on. Mina and Grant bade him an affectionate farewell. They never saw him again. On reaching Guaymas he quarreled with a man and was shot to death. A day or two later, the Terrys left the train.

On the day following the Terrys' departure, the party came upon a ranchhouse near the ruins of an old mission. In the courtyard were some huge old fig trees, whose gnarled trunks were carved with hundreds of names and initials. Imagine Mina's surprise, as she idly traced the deep cuts with her fingers to rest her eyes upon the name: W. Oury! Bill had passed this spot on his way to Durango seventeen years earlier (1848), and had added his name.

Mina Shows Doubts

On the next day, she made this little entry, a poignant one, but indicative of her growing awareness of the questionable wisdom in fleeing her native land.

Soon we had a visit by one of the most abject, wretched, hideous creatures I ever beheld — a superannuated old woman in tatters who trudged by mechanically mumbling a prayer — reiterating the sad fact that she had neither father, mother, sister, brother, nor rich relation. We all contributed to alleviate her wants, and I gave her a hearty breakfast. She then went to the road where Addy had dropped some corn in feeding his horse. She picked up each grain, going over her melancholy prayer. I never dreamed that in the whole world there existed so much destitution and want as I have already seen in Mexico.[20]

This entry was made on July 25. The party had been in Mexico 35 days and had come only about 200 miles south of the Rio Grande. The poverty and destitution of the peons dismayed the travelers, but they were almost as sorely tried by the arrogance of a wealthy young Hidalgo encountered a couple of days later.

On the twenty-seventh of July, they were in need of water and fodder for the mules, and stopped at the Hacienda Santa Rosa. It was one of the holdings of a wealthy Spanish absentee landlord, and was being run by his young brother-in-law. Mina tells of arriving at the place at two o'clock in the afternoon, and being made to wait in a cluster of flies in the broiling sun until the young administrator finished his siesta and would deign to listen to the party's wants. Even then, he would sell only the cut grass which lay about the place in dry heaps, even though there were acres of fresh green clover nearby swaying gently in the late afternoon breeze. Mina records that the poor old mules ate the brittle stalks "under protest." And who could blame them? The party was having great difficulty by now in obtaining stores or provisions of any kind. They were about two days behind a sizeable element of the French army which was literally sweeping the countryside clean as it advanced. In the matter of forage and subsistence, Mina made some observations pertaining to the Mexican peons seen each day.

They exist upon tortillas and atole (flour starch), and if required to furnish themselves, can live upon less than any human being I ever saw. But if fed by an American, they can consume more than wolves. We see this in our Mexican driver, who scrupulously cleans our board of everything left on it, often disposing of immense plates of fried bacon, while wearing the most forlorn aspect imaginable![21]

Perhaps the driver (Silvario) had made too much of scavenging or had given a surly answer to one of the party. In any case, it was just west of Mapimi, on July 30 that he wore out his welcome and was sacked. Mina's entry says that he "begun to assume too much authority and importance, and to issue peremptory orders to John Peterson (a Confederate soldier who had accompanied the van all the way from San Antonio). Mr. Neville scolded Silvario, who thereupon resigned, "to the gratification of all."

During the first week of August, the party was heading in a northwesterly direction, through Arroyo Salitre, La Parida, Refugio, and Santa Rosalia. Near Santa Rosalia, Mina reports considerable activity of the French again, writing that "every street, corner, and door was full of French troops." A few miles out of town two rivers came together (the Río Floridán and the Concho), and the waters were high, preventing a crossing by the French column. Mina reports five Frenchmen and seven mules drowned in the swollen waters, although a thousand infantrymen had made it across; the cavalry was "water bound," the troopers riding up and down the banks in vain efforts to find an easy crossing.

If the army couldn't cross, Grant could. He hired two Mexican dug-out canoes and lashed them together so that the inboard sides were about six feet apart. The wheels of his wagons thus fitted into the canoes, whose gunwhales were in constant danger of dipping below the water level. Each wagon had to be ferried separately in this way, pulled over by a gang of naked Mexican rivermen with much grunting, tugging, and shouting. All of the wagons were put safely across, and there was no loss of stores or provisions; the bill for the crossing was eleven dollars. A little further on, the party came to another river (the Santa Cruz), also swollen and turbu-lent. Grant and another man hurried the mules across a shallow but swift ford, "not daring to let the mules step slowly for fear of their being swept off their feet and carried along with the current." Henry Gillett did not fare as well. His wagon, "loaded with wife, three small children, a nurse, and plunder" sank into a hole and broke its single-tree. The mules reared and their harnesses broke, and in seconds mules and human beings were thrashing wildly about in the swift stream. No lives were lost, but it took two hours to pull the broken wagon to shore, and retrieve the wild-eyed animals who went flashing away down the river.

The harrowing day ended well however. On entering the town of Santa Cruz Rosales, the party was met by a detachment of French soldiers who ushered it into camp. There the colonel made hot toddies and fed them, and gave Grant some despatches to deliver to the general in Chihua-hua. As it happened, the party arrived in Chihuahua on the same day the troops did, August 15. As the weary travelers came into town, they watched the French troops celebrating the birthday of Napoleon Buona-parte (born in Ajaccio, Corsica, on August 15, 1769) by feasting, singing and dancing in the streets.

It was here in Chihuahua that thieves ransacked the Oury and Wil-son wagons, getting away with clothing and about one thousand dollars in gold. The discharged driver Silvario was suspected and arrested by the local *jefe de policia*. As no proof of his guilt could be established he was set free. The stolen goods were not recovered.

On Sunday, August 27, the party drew near Galeana, and Mina speaks of the numerous graves and crosses along the road attesting to the "atrocious work" of the Apaches. An American met in Galeana regaled the group with stories of the appalling outrages committed by the roving bands, the latest being the massacre of a Mexican family not far away. As the party came upon the scene of carnage, Mina saw pieces of crockery and fragments of bedding scattered forlornly about; the poor victims had been burned. On the following day, the party had to continue after dark, when the waterhole it had sought turned out to be dry. Mina creates a chilling atmosphere when she reports that in the dark the "huge rattlesnakes kept up a continual buzzing. The boys killed 15 or 20, and found it an unprofitable undertaking." [22] Late that night, the bone-weary travelers climbed a long sloping hill, and camped at its summit in the courtyard of a deserted mission.

On the following day, in Janos, the party learned that two large bands of Apaches were camped ahead on the road. A council was held, and it was decided that the best thing to do was to remain in Janos for awhile, "the most wretched, squalid, dilapidated spot on earth."

It was here that the whole Mexican venture was realized as a colossal failure. On September 10, after a week in Janos, Mina writes of Grant's frustration and anxiety, describing how both had begun to make inroads upon his "unusually sanguine temperament." The party, leaving Texas in anger, had expected to find all of the good things for a new life in Mexico — cheap land, freedom, business opportunities, a friendly people. Instead it had found a savage land — strewn with rocks, cactus, and rattlesnakes, and precious little water. The villages it had passed through appeared to the party as sad little gatherings of grass huts, peopled by disease-ridden and semi-naked savages. Prices for provisions were exorbitant, and the people surly and difficult to deal with. Altogether, the prospect of civilized life in this strange, raw land seemed remote as the dejected party huddled about its wagons in Janos. As Mina put it: "Oh God! how gloomy the prospect!" [23]

It was decided to sell all the wagons except one, which would take Mina and her brother Adam to El Paso. From there, having reentered the United States, Adam would head the wagon westward and go to Tucson by way of Mesilla and Apache Pass. Grant and the other irreconcilables of the party having fled the country without surrendering to the Federals could not risk the El Paso entry. They would have to go west from Janos over the roughest of mountain ranges, following no road or trail, but scrambling over the rocks as best they might. Grant gathered together all of the salable items owned by the various members of the party: ambulance, harnesses, clothes, casks, bottles, books, and a number of other things. One lame mule was sold for $30 to a Mexican, but then Mina laments that not another twenty dollars could be found in the entire town.

In speaking upon Grant's departure (with six of his companions), Mina wrote:

My heart stands still at the thought of danger besetting both our pathways, and nothing but desperation gives me courage. I had so earnestly hoped that the trying ordeal of being separated from my husband, which I had been called upon to bear through the long years of our struggle for liberty was over, but alas! I have conceived of nothing so terrible as this. He goes to the setting, I to the rising sun.[24]

Saturday, September 16, was the day of parting, a day of sheer misery for Mina who refers to it as

one of the darkest days of my short life. My husband is gone, God knows to what fate. This very night . . . or tomorrow, his precious life blood may flow to satiate the wicked thirst of the most fiendish savages the world has ever known. O, how can I endure the agony, the suspense, the terror of all this, where can I find the fortitude, the courage, the patience to sustain me through this trial?[25]

Mina and Addy teamed up with a Mexican wagon train heading north. It consisted of twenty-five wagons loaded with flour and other staples. Mina's wagon was placed in the middle of the van and the long, slow trek to El Paso began. Before joining the Mexican train, the Oury party had started and stopped as it saw fit. Now, route discipline called for halting early in the afternoon, and resuming march not long after midnight. Mina found it gruelling and monotonous. On the other hand, she said, "Our train presents a formidable appearance and is not likely to be attacked." She describes the morning harnessing up as a hectic welter of "yelling, screaming, lassoing, jumping, and prancing." Having slept but little through the night, both of the jaded travelers fell asleep on the seat not long after the train got under way again. The road was cut into deep ruts by the wheels of the dozen wagons ahead, and the Oury mules pulled their burden along in the deep tracks, unmindful of the exhausted drivers crumpled in the seat behind.

As the long, slow train moved north, Mina could appreciate the strain under which the men of the party had operated. Until now, her trip had been made in relative comfort; she could curl up in the back of the wagon and sleep, protected from the sun or rain, and free from the choking dust-clouds sent up by the mules and the lead wagons. Now, she was forced to take her turn driving, as Adam could not drive all of the time. She did well, but lamented aloud on the twentieth of September:

How dreary, how lonely in this Godforsaken part of the universe. . . . I have never in my life conceived of traveling under such adverse circumstances, and almost despair of getting through alive. Only those who have experienced this mode of traveling can realize the discomforts. . . . I am roused up night after night, after uneasy sleep, tired, in the dark, and have to fumble for my blankets, untangle the harness, and hitch up the mules . . . it is awful, but my greatest sympathy is for the poor, tired, hungry mules.[26]

Sometimes the going was easy, and the wagons rolled smoothly over solid ground. At other times, the train would hit sandy stretches and slow to a snail's pace. Mina tells of the continual stalling of the wagons, and the curses and screams of the drivers belaboring the straining mules, and the whips cracking. On one day, the whole train bogged down in what Mina described as the deepest sand she ever saw, and the teamsters went about their business "whooping, hollering, slashing, whipping, and yelling hideously in a monstrous effort to move their wagons." "At last," she says, "by hitching all the mules [300] to the wagons, they pulled them one mile."

Now the nights were bitter cold, and Mina and her brother shivered miserably in the back of their wagon. But the heat of the days was so intense that the pair were "literally roasted." "The sun blazes upon us without mercy, and the glare from the white sand is blinding me."

The going was so wretchedly slow that Mina and Adam decided to make the rest of the journey alone. On the evening of September 22, they talked over the idea with the wagon-master who advised against it, but "put up no strenuous argument in the matter." They started out at about eight o'clock on the following morning.

Actually, nothing exciting happened in the remainder of the trip to the border. A burro train passed by on the morning of the twenty-third, and that afternoon several horsemen waved to Mina from a distance. The pair reached El Paso on the evening of September 24, bone-weary but happy.

Three months and four days had passed since the party had left San Antonio. Mina, in exquisite relief from the trials of her arduous journey, stated that she didn't care if she never saw Mexico again. What had begun as a great adventure ended in failure, and she was the first to admit it. She was "home" again, but she still had a long way to go to join Grant in Tucson.

Mina had not been in El Paso a day before the bitter subject of the Civil War arose. Of this incident she writes:

In the afternoon Capt. Lent, an ex-federal officer called to see me, representing himself as an acquaintance and friend of William Oury and my husband. Very soon he broached the subject of our late Civil War, to which I protested, suggesting that all circumstances considered, I deemed it imprudent to discuss with me this very tender and sacred topic. I informed him that he was the first enemy of our cause I had yet had the misfortune to look upon, and that he must not stir up the bottled wrath I had not vented before. Withal, he submitted most amicably to "the benefit" I showered upon him from my long charged battery. . . . He insisted upon our going to hear the band play in the plaza, and the moment I made my appearance, the band struck up "Dixie." For a moment all the old joy and pride I used to feel upon hearing the loved air was revived, when, like a flash, the true state of things came to me, the dreadful calamity that had befallen our beloved South, that I was standing upon Federal

REBELS TO MEXICO.
Granville and Mina Oury headed south with a group of Confederate friends in June, 1865, to start a new life far from the bitter environment of defeat. The map shows their route south and the separate paths Grant and Mina had to follow for the difficult return journey to Tucson.

NUEVO LEON.

San Antonio
Castroville
Uvalde. Hondo
Eagle Pass
Piedras Negras.

COAHUILA.
Morelos
Sabinas
Monclova
Parras.
Santa Rosa

Carro Gordo
La Descubridora
Mapimí
Torreon.

RIO GRANDE

NEW MEXICO.

Mesilla.
El Paso.
Guzmán.
Corralitos.
Galeana
Carmen

Chihuahua.
Saucillo
Santa Cruz
Rosales.
La Florida
Santa Rosalia.
Valle de
San Bartolo.

Terrazas.

CHIHUAHUA

Juárez

Janos

SONORA

ARIZONA.
Fort
Fort
Bowie.
Tubac.
Tucson
Fort Cummings.
Santa Cruz
Fronteras.
Nogales
Bauispe.

SINALOA.

GULF OF CALIFORNIA.

soil listening to our glorious air being played by a Federal band — perhaps as an insult to my feelings. All the fire of my soul was aroused. I trembled with rage.[27]

Mina remained shaken and upset, even after the thoughtful Yankee captain had his men play "Maryland, my Maryland," and the "Secession Polka." He had meant the music as a gesture of kindness, and so it was, but the strains brought back the bitter memory of defeat and withdrawal, of a lost cause, dead kinsmen, and the sadness of a fruitless journey into an alien land. The tears rolled down Mina's cheeks as she listened to the music of her own beloved country.

From El Paso (or Franklin, as the American side was called at this time), Mina and Adam drove to Mesilla where they stayed with a Colonel and Mrs. Jones, friends of Grant from earlier times. Mina speaks of being within the "pales of civilization" again, exults over the coffee, rich cream and butter, and the splendid garden of their hosts. She mentions the house, commodious, handsomely carpeted, and with a genial atmosphere throughout — "such a contrast to the mud hovels and dirt floors of Janos."

On the Road Again

After a few days of luxuriating in the comfortable atmosphere of the Jones home, Mina and Adam headed west in the company of four men bound for Tucson. The little van was poorly equipped for Indian fighting, with only one rifle and three-six shooters. Providence was kind, however, and no Indians came. The wagons reached Fort Cummings on the twenty-first of October, and lingered for several days to pick up an escort of soldiers for the trip through Apache Pass. Captain Burket would have provided one but could not as most of his men were away on patrol. And so the party continued on its way, passing through Cook's Canyon on the twenty-fifth.

On the twenty-ninth, the little party came to Apache Pass. The place was rocky and precipitous, and the mules almost uncontrollable in the vicinity of clear mountain spring water; they had not had water for more than twenty-four hours. At Fort Bowie, Adam petitioned Major Gorman for an escort, but was refused. The major had troubles of his own. The road from Fort Bowie to Tucson was perhaps the most dangerous in the entire west, lying astride Chiricahua country, and zealously guarded by Apaches. It was here that Bascom had his brush with Cochise just four years before, and where single travelers and small parties of emigrants were ambushed with terrifying frequency. Mina's timing was unfortunate. As she arrived at Fort Bowie, Gorman was concerned over the possibility of an Indian attack to free Chief Francisco, an army prisoner at Fort

Goodman (about 120 miles away to the north). As Mina and Adam begged for an escort to Tucson, Gorman, with his field glasses was watching Indians making signal smokes in the hills nearby. It was soon reported to him that the Apache party was about 650 strong. With only four men and two guns, Mina saw the futility of trying to run against such odds.

It would be madness for us to venture out in this condition. They are watching our movements, know exactly our strength, and are anxiously anticipating our annihilation." [Even so, Mina's impatience and frustration at this point were well nigh unbearable.] *"My anxiety to see my husband is beyond expressing. . . . Today we could have been in Tucson had the heartless old major here furnished us with the necessary escort, and but for the delay at Cook's Canyon would have reached there five days since.*[28]

The Oury party did get off on November 2, and headed for Tucson via Apache Pass. It was at the pass that Mina saw the charred remains of the wagon ambushed by Apaches in 1861. On this last leg of the journey the going was slow, as the party had joined up with two mule-drawn freight trains carrying heavy supplies. One of the trains belonged to Señor Conrado Aguirre of Magdalena, Sonora, the other to the Tucson firm of Tully and Ochoa. "So much," says Mina, "for having to creep along with a Mexican train, sore trial to my already threadbare patience, but there is no remedy." Still, the train provided security, as had its predecessor between Corralitos and El Paso. The road, if such it might be called, now ran through the most dangerous kind of terrain. Frequently it snaked through narrow defiles where the rocks towered above on either side. As Mina put it, "whole bands of Apaches could secrete themselves, and by firing down from above . . . could annihilate at first fire an entire party."

A few miles out of Tucson, Mina saw a buggy approach, "containing two gentlemen." Instinctively, she jumped from the buckboard and ran to meet the oncoming vehicle. Her instinct was correct; in a few moments she was tight in the arms of her husband, tears of gratitude and emotion streaming from her eyes. The "other gentleman" was Señor Veramendi, an old friend of Grant's, and a relative of the man who had been Governor of Nuevo León at the time of the Alamo. Mina drove on in to Tucson behind a set of Bill Oury's grays, whose speed Grant "had to check continually." It was daybreak when the happy couple pulled up in front of Bill's house on Calle Real. A cheerful fire was burning, and the family arrayed to give the travelers a warm and hearty welcome.

Glad to be away from the wilds of Mexico, Mina nonetheless did not take to Tucson. As reported in another portion of this study, she assessed Tucson as "certainly the most forlorn, dreary, desolate, Godforsaken spot on earth." She further laments that "there is not an American woman in town, and but one or two American men whom I would be willing to know."[29]

Mina describes the effects of the Yankee occupation in Tucson, referring to the period as "the wreck." Bill Oury's household goods had in large measure been confiscated by the Federal troops on their entry into the town in May of 1862.

A few of Mr. Oury's books were saved from the wreck, and a few pictures and articles of furniture. The bulk of his possessions the Federals appropriated and ruthlessly destroyed. His horses were confiscated and are now serving at federal hospital and barracks. If we remain here, we must pay rent for a house, although he (Mr. Oury) rightfully owns several. Nothing offers in the way of a business, and the prices are absolutely appalling — lard, one dollar per pound, sugar, one dollar a pound, eggs, $1.25 per dozen. . . . I fear we have made a fatal mistake in settling in such a place. . . . Even Mr. Oury with his hopeful nature cannot disguise his disappointment. We are all blue.[30]

Here the diary ends, except for one brief entry made sixteen years later on October 9, 1881, at Florence, Arizona. In this entry, Mina simply relates what has happened in the ensuing years to the members of the party who made the long trip from San Antonio to Mexico; "Billy," Mr. Neville, Mr. Dodson, Captain Swope, Dan Showalter, and Judge David Terry. Most of them had died, several violently. The years had been good to Grant and Mina, however, and in this final entry she rejoices, as the couple are on the eve of making a visit to San Antonio, the first in sixteen years.

Although the terrain over which Grant travelled from Corralitas was considerably rougher than that passed by Mina and Adam, he arrived in Tucson almost a month ahead of his wife's wagon. As he and his companions were on horseback, they suffered no delays enroute. Almost immediately upon his arrival he was directed to go to Fort Mason and swear allegiance to the United States. A few months before, he and the other men of his party swore they would never do this, but "the best laid plans of mice and men 'gang aft agley. . . ." Judging from the papers in the case, the young lieutenant (W. W. Fellows, Seventh Infantry, Calif. Volunteers) was as staunch a Yankee as Grant was a rebel. Fellows, in administering the oath and describing Grant, refers to the "so called Confederate Army."[31] The oath was taken on October 8, 1865, just a few days after Grant's arrival in Arizona. It was a bitter pill to swallow, but all things considered, Grant was glad to be home.

CHAPTER 21

Camp Lowell and the Quartermaster

BY JUNE, 1862, a month or so after it had driven the small Confederate force out of Tucson, the California Column had placed eleven infantry companies in town, along with two cavalry companies and two artillery batteries. These troops were placed first in Military Plaza. Subsequently, a huge tent camp was set up a couple of miles away, in the place where the Carnegie Public Library and Armory Park now stand. The official title of the place was "Camp of U. S. Troops at Tucson, Arizona," and until the establishment was deactivated all official correspondence originating there was so headed.[1]

With the end of the Civil War, the camp was deactivated, but so loud were the cries of Tucson's citizens for protection against the Apaches that reactivation was effected some sixteen months later, on August 29, 1866.[2] The place was named Camp Lowell, and because of its temporary nature kept this title until a move to permanent quarters on the Rillito was made in March, 1873.[3] From that time on, the official title of the establishment became Fort Lowell, named for Colonel Charles R. Lowell, a captain of the Sixth U. S. Cavalry, who fell at Cedar Creek in the Civil War.

With the arrival of Carleton's California Column in 1862, a quartermaster supply depot was established in Tucson, and called the Tucson Depot. My grandfather, Gilbert Cole Smith, who had written the letters discussed earlier, was assigned as acting assistant quartermaster to this depot on May 18, 1864.[4] He was, at the time, a captain in the Fifth California Volunteer Infantry. Eventually, he was appointed Chief Quartermaster of the District of Arizona (June 11, 1866), and in January, 1868, as Chief of Commissary of Subsistence for the District.[5] He remained in this capacity until 1870, when he was sent to Corinne, Utah, for a short period of duty before settling down in the Presidio, San Francisco, for a tour of several years.

Soon after his initial quartermaster appointment (1864), Smith received orders to aid in the construction and provisioning of new posts built along the Arizona frontier. These posts were established by executive order for the protection of the Territory against the Apaches. His first assignment took him to Fort Bowie, a post established near Apache Pass two years earlier (July 28, 1862) by Brigadier General James H. Carleton after his arrival in Santa Fe. The fort was named for Col. George W. Bowie, Smith's regimental commander.[6] Smith remained at Fort Bowie until April, 1865, when he was ordered to San Francisco for consultation with the Chief Quartermaster of the Department of California concerning the work he was engaged in.[7] On the way back to Arizona, he was put in charge of a large wagon train of supplies at Fort Yuma. The train was part of a Cavalry Column under Col. Clarence E. Bennett, enroute to establish Fort McDowell on the Verde River.

Upon his arrival in Tucson, he was sent almost immediately to Fort Mason near Tubac to inspect the place for its building and provisioning needs.[8] Whatever plans he may have had for Mason died a-borning; the name of the fort was changed to Camp McKee on 6 September, 1866, and three weeks later the place was abandoned. On the same day of McKee's abandonment (1 Oct., 1866), Camp Cameron was established at Calabasas, a point about halfway between Tubac and Tucson. Named after Simon Cameron, Lincoln's Secretary of War, this place had a short life too, being deactivated on March 7, 1867, some five months after its inception. Smith went there however and made recommendations for the transport and storage of provisions for the new post.

Smith was sent next to Camp Wallen on Babocomari Creek, some 12 miles west of Tombstone.[9] He recommended that funds for building not be appropriated, as the camp was considered a temporary place. Although it lasted longer than either Mason or Cameron, it too had a short life span (May 9, 1866–Oct. 31, 1869).

In the summer of 1867, he was sent to reconnoiter the new Fort

Crittenden on Sonoita Creek. This place was commissioned on August 10, 1867, near the remains of old Fort Buchanan, abandoned in the summer of 1861. Crittenden served for almost six years to protect Arizona settlers against the Apaches; it was deactivated on June 1, 1873. It was Smith's job to requisition, obtain, and transport all of the goods necessary to build and provision these establishments.[10] His official log book is filled with entries showing the transfer of long wagon trains not only to the five places mentioned above, but to Camp Nogales, Camp Pinal, Camp Tonto, Camp Goodwin, and Fort Yuma as well.[11]

An Equitable Dealer

In his business dealings with the merchants of Tucson, Smith saw to it that the contracts were distributed as fairly as possible. By so doing, he became a well-known and popular figure with the Tucson citizenry, doing business with Tully and Ochoa, Hinds and Hooker, William B. Hooper, J. B. Cove, and many others.

Provisioning for the newly established posts was a task of considerable proportions. There were veritable mountains of supplies stacked about the depot, supplies obtained not only through local purchases from the merchants named above, but from California by way of Yuma, and from the East Coast via Guaymas, in Sonora, Mexico. So dangerous was the route of the wagon trains hauling supplies from Guaymas to Tucson, that special arrangements had to be made with the Mexican government for military escorts. One of the men doing business with Captain Smith was Sylvester Mowry, Bill Oury's old friend from Tubac days in the 1850's. In the late 1860's, Mowry was living in Guaymas in order to direct properly the loading and unloading of ships and freight wagons destined for the quartermaster depot in Tucson. A brief announcement in the weekly Arizonan told of the arrival in Tucson of Sylvester Mowry with 130 wagons loaded with 600 tons of government freight.[12]

One of Gilbert Smith's letters from Tucson on Sept. 5, 1868, suggests the transportation problems of the period. To W. B. Hughes, assistant QM at Fort Yuma, it reads:

Captain:

> *On the 29th inst, eight government teams left here enroute to Fort Yuma. . . . Two of the teams, with four mules each belong to Wilmington, Cal. The other six six-mule teams belong to me at this depot. We are very short of means of transportation here, and taking away these teams leaves us so that we hardly know how to get along. I hope that you will be able to furnish transportation (for some discharged troops) from Fort Yuma on, and let my six teams return to this place. They might be loaded with such stores as you may have for this place. . . .*[13]

Your obt. svt.,
Gilbert C. Smith

LOLA OURY SMITH was the daughter of William Sanders Oury. Her wedding to Gilbert Smith was "witnessed by perhaps the largest gathering of notables ever convened at a wedding in the Territory." As time passed, the Smith home at Fort Lowell became a mecca for Army officers.

While Camp Lowell was still a going concern, the officers of the regiment took quarters in town. Most of these were not very elegant, but in time they were made passably comfortable and attractive. These homes off-post enabled the young officers to meet and mingle socially with the townspeople. In this way a number of courtships flourished, ending in marriage between young officers of the military and the belles of Tucson. Some of these were the marriages of Miss Alice Goodrich with Lt. T. H. Slavens, 4th U. S. Cavalry; Miss Zettie Ezekiels with Major William A. Rafferty, 2d U. S. Cavalry; and Miss Lola Oury with Captain Gilbert Cole Smith, 9th U. S. Infantry.[14] Captain Smith had a house on the northwest corner of Stone and Ochoa streets,[15] the same house in which my father was born.

Why Bill Oury, the rebel and fiery Southern patriot permitted his daughter to be courted by a Yankee officer has never really been explained. Perhaps it was Lt. Smith's quiet good manners and respectful demeanor that won the old firebrand over; maybe it was all Lola's doing, regardless of parental objection. In any case, on July 1, 1868, the Reverend Salpointe joined the pair "in Catholic marriage."[16] Three days later, the Tucson *Weekly Arizonian* carried the following story on the wedding.[17]

"Although Cupid is not young," says a gifted writer, "he is not in the least the worse for wear. His locks are still golden, his cheeks glowing, and the bright kindling glance of his eye is as radiant as ever. So we must judge from his success in Tucson, for we today have to chronicle a wedding celebrated with much good cheer.

On Wednesday evening, Captain Gilbert C. Smith, U.S.A., long the popular Quartermaster of this place was joined in the holy bonds of matrimony to Lola, daughter of William S. Oury, Esq. The prominence of Captain Smith and the Oury family, one of the best known in Arizona, made the event the great one of the season. The din of generous preparation had been heard for many weeks, and the ceremony was witnessed by perhaps the largest gathering of notables ever convened at a wedding in the Territory.

The Governor and all the civil officers living below the Gila, General Crittenden, his staff and officers from nearly all the military posts, the leading American and Mexican citizens of Tucson and other towns, and the ladies (God bless them!) were all in attendance. The house had been tastefully decorated with evergreens and flowers, and was brilliantly lighted. The guests were dressed in a manner that would have been creditable in the large cities of the Atlantic, and the supper was a complete triumph. To say that all went "merry as a marriage bell" is to give but a poor idea of the hilarity of the occasion. Every one seemed in glowing spirits. The parents of the bride were wreathed in smiles, and had a hearty welcome for their guests. The bride herself was exquisitely dressed and looked better than ever before, which is saying much. The vicar and his assistant performed the wedding service according to the interesting form of the Roman Catholic Church, and the bride and bridegroom sustained themselves with admirable dignity, seeming fully to realize:

"That marriage rightly understood, gives to the tender
and the good, a Paradise below."

We can't pretend to say how many warm kisses the bride received, or
how many cordial, and we believe sincere, congratulations were showered
upon her and the gallant Captain. If good wishes avail anything, indeed must
then wedded life prove a Paradise below.

After the congratulations, the dancing began, the music being furnished
by the Camp Grant troupe, and it was kept up until broad daylight, with a
proper interval for the feast of edibles and drinkables which had been so
lavishly spread. Those who call Arizona a dry desert country should have
seen the groaning tables and tasted the various luxuries. The substantials were
washed down by some of the choicest wines ever brought to the Territory,
and the health, long life, and complete felicity of the newly married was the
ever-ringing toast.

As time passed, the post home of the Smith's at Fort Lowell became
a sort of mecca for Army notables of the era; Generals Adna Chaffee,
William R. Shafter, W. H. Carter, Nelson A. Miles, Arthur MacArthur,[18]
and many others.

Bill Oury was not a Catholic, but his wife was. No doubt she was
the prime mover in obtaining the services of the Vicar Salpointe. During
Holy Week, in 1864, she and Bill had put on a lavish entertainment for
Bishop Lamy, who had come to Tucson from Santa Fe for a visit. The
Bishop had been driven down Calle Real under a triumphal arch of cottonwood branches, and the streets were gaily decorated with flowers and
paper streamers.[19] Colorful blankets hung from the windows and door-
ways of the houses along his route, and there was much cheering as his
carriage rolled along the dusty street of the old pueblo. The procession
ended at Bill's house, and the party went in for a grand feast. As the years
passed, the Oury home became a frequent visiting place for the padres;
Lamy, Machebeuf, Reghieri, Bosco, Mesea, Boucard, Birmingham, and
others.

The days at Fort Lowell were happy ones for Gilbert and Lola Smith,
perhaps the best of their lives. Their first child (my father) was born not
at Fort Lowell, but in Tucson on April 7, 1869. His given name was
Cornelius Cole, after Gilbert's uncle, the United States Senator from
California. Within a few days after his birth, the baby was taken in an army
ambulance to San Xavier Mission, and there baptised, certainly one of the
first American children and perhaps the first, baptised in the "White Dove
of the Desert."[20]

As the lad grew older, he was sent away to school, but spent his
vacation periods at home with his family at Fort Lowell, and much of it
with his grandparents in Tucson. His grandfather's tales intrigued him,
and he plagued the old warrior with questions.

CHAPTER 22

Tales of a Grandfather

My father, Cornelius Cole Smith, was sixteen years old in 1887 when Bill Oury died. He remembered Bill well and with great affection. There follows my father's firsthand account, set forth in his diary, of the latter stages of his grandfather's life, and of the places where Bill Oury lived:

From 1876, the year we returned to Arizona from Fort Union, New Mexico, to 1884 (when we left for the East), I attended the Catholic Parochial school in Tucson (except for 1880 when I was enrolled at Brewer's Academy in San Mateo, California). During the school months of each year, I spent my vacations at Fort Grant, as my father was stationed there. Similarly, I spent my holidays at Fort Lowell when he changed station from the former to the latter place in 1882. The arrangement was convenient for all concerned, as my mother's parents lived in Tucson, and with them I had the advantage of school and a home . . . like the one under my father's roof. I remember having talks with my grandfather about "the old days." Oddly, though I was interested in the stories about the Alamo, General Houston and San Jacinto, General Taylor and Monterrey, and the drawing of the beans at Miér, I was fascinated by the picture he painted of old Tucson, I guess because I was born there; it was "my" country.

He had told me that with the coming of the Americans, the place passed from the sleepy, apathetic little pueblo to a rip-snorting, roaring town where it behooved the tenderfoot and the greenhorn to stay under cover. He told me that when he came there, in the late 50's, one might walk down the main street and see the lumbering Butterfield "jerkeys" coming into town, or see a small packtrain of Army camels coming in from Texas, or Fort Yuma over on the Colorado. He described for me the atajos of laden mules coming in from Hermosillo or Sonora, and how the dust-covered detachment of soldiers would straggle into town after a patrol on the desert. He painted vivid word pictures for me of the vaqueros riding down Calle Real on "grullos," and of the ox-drawn wagon trains coming into town from the mines, their thick wheels screeching under the enormous weight of rocks and ore. I knew he was right, because I remember some of these things myself. A few years later, in my time, I can see in my mind's eye one of Tully and Ochoa's fuel trains loaded with supplies for an army station. These wagons, frequently with one or more trailers attached, were drawn by many yokes of oxen. I can see a huge Negro driver, from Georgia or Texas, rawboned, in slouch hat, trousers tucked in boots, driving one of these trains. He would circle his great plaited rawhide lash, swinging it with both arms, and let it fly with a report like a gunshot on Goldie's or Blackie's rump. I remember the slow-moving burro trains coming in from Mexico, laden with sweet oranges, sugar cane, and panocha. I remember seeing a man lurch out of a saloon one day when I was about fourteen. He was trying to free his pistol from its holster. Seconds later a second man jumped out of the building and the two men began trading shots. One, the first one out, went down, and the victor went back into the saloon, probably to continue with his card game. I remember peeking over the shoulders of the crowd pressing in on the fallen man, and how odd it seemed to watch him breathing his last.

Although I was not allowed in them, I remember the saloons and gambling houses, like Charley Brown's "Congress Hall." I remember the cowboys and the miners going in and out of his place, and I suppose, horse-thieves, cattle rustlers, and bad men of all kinds. And there were soldiers there, and women, some quite pretty, whom the respectable people like my grandparents referred to as, "painted."

I remember the Clantons. As I recall it, they came to Tucson from the south, Georgia, I think, and settled on the San Pedro in about 1875. Old man Clanton feared nothing; his two boys, Ike and Bill, were of the same stamp. At the time I speak of, 1877-78, they were decent youngsters who came to Tucson from their father's ranch to attend school. I was younger than they were, but as they were my schoolmates, I remember them. This was the school conducted by the Catholic priests, one of whom, Father Antonio Juvançeau was a great favorite with all of us. He was a friendly man, of sunny disposition, and encouraged the boys in manly games and sports. We used to ride horses bareback at full tilt, and pick up a handkerchief on the ground. Sometimes we fell. We used to ride bucking calves with only a leather thong lashed about the animal's middle to hold to. I've never seen youngsters do these things anywhere else.

It was not until after the opening of the mines in Tombstone that the Clanton boys came into notoriety. Bill was killed there in Tombstone by Wyatt Earp, his brothers, and "Doc" Holliday. I never knew what became of Ike.

From the time the California Column came to Tucson in 1862, up to 1873, there was always a garrison of U. S. troops in the town. The approved

CORNELIUS COLE SMITH, grandson of William S. Oury and father of the author of this book, was born in Tucson on April 7, 1869. "Within a few days of his birth the baby was taken in an army ambulance to San Xavier Mission "... certainly one of the first American children" baptized at San Xavier.

military designation of the station to 1866 was, "Camp of United States Troops, Tucson, Arizona Territory." In 1873 the garrison was moved to Camp Lowell, and the name of the place was changed to Fort Lowell. I remember being told that the fort was named in honor of Col. C. P. Lowell, of the Sixth U. S. Volunteer Cavalry, whose troops relieved the California volunteers on their expiration of service in 1866. While I do not remember them, I do recall my father's telling me that the first regiment to garrison Lowell after the Civil War was the Third U. S. Cavalry, commanded by a Major William B. Royall.

I remember Fort Lowell pretty well, because my father was the post quartermaster there. I can recall talking, as a small boy, to his commanding officer, Colonel Eugene A. Carr, of the Sixth U. S. Cavalry. I recall that the post was in the form of a rectangle, and that there were seven sets of officers' quarters there, with the commanding officer's house in the center of the line (on the south side). The hospital and the band barracks were on the east side, and the troop and company barracks, the quartermaster and commissary storehouse were on the north end. On the west end were the quartermaster's office, the guardhouse, post bakery, and the adjutant's office. The post trader (or sutler) store was just outside the rectangle near my father's office. In rear of the hospital were some quarters for married soldiers. The stables were north of the barracks, and nearby was the post garden, cared for by some Chinamen.

On the Rillito, about a mile from the post was Dunn's Ranch where we kids used to go to pick gooseberries. Tanque Verde, nearby, was my grandfather's cattle ranch. I played there as a boy, and also on Fuller's ranch in the foothills of the Catalinas.

In front of the officer's quarters was a double row of cottonwood trees, each watered by an acequia. The parade ground was full of gopher holes, and it offered us amusement to flood the gophers out of their holes by pouring buckets of water in them carried from the acequias. I remember the excitement of the fort during the Feast of St. Augustine. There was baseball and horse racing for the troopers, dances, picnics, and gay good times all around. I remember riding Dougherty wagons into Tucson, and I can recall each Sunday morning the ambulance which took Mrs. Carr and my mother to attend Mass at St. Augustine church in Tucson. I remember Bishop Salpointe and Father Juvançeau, and the post surgeon, Dr. J. B. Girard (who married my mother's sister, Laura), because they were French and spoke in a tongue I could not understand.

I remember when the Southern Pacific Railroad came into town in 1880. There was a big celebration, and troops from Lowell marched into Tucson to parade for the ceremony. Also, my grandfather gave a very fine speech. I remember that there were always some cavalry and infantry at the post at the same time. As I recall it, they came in this order: the 3d Cavalry, the 6th, 4th, and 2d Cavalry; the 8th, 1st, and 12th Infantry. Growing up on Army posts, I liked them all, and I liked the different outfits that served on them. Somehow, I liked the cavalry the best, and used to hang around the stable to listen to the trooper's tales, and watch them curry their horses. The post was abandoned in 1890, but by then I was in the cavalry myself, running after the Sioux with "K" Troop of the 6th up in the Dakotas.

I remember the officers who visited in my parents' home, fine gentlemen all: Col. William R. Shafter, who commanded our Army in Cuba against

*Spain in 1898, Col. A. V. Kautz, Col. Orlando B. Willcox, Col. Carr, Lt. Wm.
H. Carter, Capt. J. B. Kerr, and Major Charles E. Compton. Captain Kerr, a
wealthy officer from Kentucky, brought his thoroughbreds from Kentucky
with him; "Butcher Boy," and "Childers." With them he beat the best horses
Arizona and California could bring against him, and he "cleaned up" regularly.
I remember General George Crook too, with his slouch hat and his side-
whiskers, a friendly, pleasant man, a great man.*

*. . . I did not fail to note the wild and woolly days of that epoch. Tucson
was a lively burg with many men dedicated to following the fickle Goddess of
Chance at Charley Brown's Congress Hall, on the corner of Myers and
Congress streets, and other places. . .* I

*The Fiesta de San Agustín (which lasted for ten days) was the occasion
for much out-of-door gambling, dancing, racing, and at times, bull fighting.
At the fiesta, I have seen around the "Chusas" and "Carcamen" tables officers
and ladies from Lowell "following a hunch," along with Mexicans, Indians,
and Chinamen.*

*. . . Perhaps some old timer will remember a famous race between a
horse called "Pumpkins," owned by a Tucson sport whose name I cannot now
recall, and Lieutenant Kerr's "Butcherboy." Butcherboy won the race, but
there was some dispute in which guns were drawn and trouble seemed
imminent. The judgment of cool heads prevailed, and the affair was satisfactorily settled. This race was run at the track near Jimmy Lee's Mill, afterward
known as Silver Lake.*

*Another famous horse of those days was Bullet Neck, and he too was
beaten by Butcherboy. The Mexicans also were much given to horse racing
with their smaller mustang breed. Their favorite distance was a four-mile race.
The most famous of these four-mile runners was a Sonora horse called
"Chanate" (Blackbird).*

*In the old days of Tucson things were wide open. For the Mexican popu-
lation the twenty-fourth of June (El día de San Juan) was a lively one, with
horse racing, and all sorts of mounted sports including the pulling of a live
chicken from the ground where it was loosely buried up to its neck. When the
rider came to the chicken, he made a low reach from the saddle, holding the
pommel with one hand, while endeavoring to grab the chicken with the other.
This was quite a trick, for enough of the chicken's neck was left free to give
him a chance to duck or dodge. Of course all of this was hard on the chicken.*

St. John's day was also a day for bailes *or dances. In fact, they were
ushered in with music, and the charging of horsemen up and down old Main
Street. The 16th of September and Cinco de Mayo were gala days for the
Mexicans too. On the night of the 16th of September, the front edges of the
roofs of houses were covered with hundreds of lanterns — made of tin cans
filled with earth, in which a candle was stuck. Pasted on the cans was red,
white, and green paper, the Mexican colors, so that the lanterns gave the
effect of red, white, and green light. In addition, there were many fireworks
and great bonfires in the streets lighted at dusk.*

*. . . One who thinks of Tucson in terms of today cannot appreciate the
hardships and discomforts of yesteryear . . . water was a very precious article
. . . it was sold by the bucketful, and this was done as late as 1882. Who of the
old timers will not remember Adam Sanders with his big Texas mule and water
cart, and his two buckets of water for five cents? Sanders obtained his water*

from the Ojito (Little Eye) spring under the cottonwood trees just to the south of the old Eagle Mill on Main Street. This spring was owned by Sanders and brought him quite an income.

In those days there was no ice, and the heat of the summer was intense. Butter, which always came by bull trains from the east in cans, was of the consistency of olive oil, and rancid, more like machinery oil than food. Ants were bothersome and into everything. . . . Is it any wonder that J. Ross Browne said that: "the best view one got of Tucson was leaving it?"

There was something else that Bill Oury had done and told his grandson about, although the event is not mentioned in the diary. He had introduced shorthorn cattle into Arizona Territory. In 1862, when his daughter Lola was ten, Bill took her to St. Louis and put her in the Convent of the Sacred Heart. Each year thereafter, she returned to this school until her graduation in 1868. When Bill went back to get her that year he met a drover in Illinois with a handsome herd of shorthorn cattle. Back in Arizona, the only cattle on the range were the tough, wiry, Sonoran longhorns; the Illinois herd looked fat and sleek by comparison. The idea of introducing this fine breed in Arizona appealed to Bill, so on the spot he bought four bulls and 102 heifers from the drover. He hired several drovers and started the long drive back to Tucson — across Missouri, northern Oklahoma Territory, the Texas Panhandle, New Mexico, and on into Arizona.

The drive, although made in Indian country much of the way, was without incident. Bill kept the herd in the Santa Cruz valley on the outskirts of Tucson until 1884, when he moved them to open range. Many factors combined to keep the herd small — drouth, natural predators, a limited market, and raiding Apaches. By 1880, the herd was not appreciably larger (at 400 head) than it was on the fall day in 1868 when Bill brought it though the dusty streets of Tucson.

CHAPTER 23

The Camp Grant Massacre

ON APRIL 30, 1871, a tragic event occurred in Arizona which rocked the entire territory. It has in fact come down through the years as a black mark on the pioneer shield, and in Arizona is still talked about with considerable heat and emotion. A party of 146 men, most of them Papago Indians, made a raid upon an Apache ranchería near Camp Grant, and killed a number of women and children. The provocation for the attack was presumably raiding parties of Apaches from the ranchería, which had been terrorizing the countryside. Also, the vigilante group had fully expected to find the Apache bucks in camp, and settle the issue with them then and there. As it happened, only a handful of Indian men were present when the raid began, and many innocent people were cruelly slaughtered.

Bill Oury was a prime mover of the punitive expedition, and was with it from start to finish. The story, with all of its ramifications, is one of the saddest yet most interesting in pioneer annals; it deserves re-telling here, and is related with the hope that the reader may view the affair with sympathy for both sides, and that he may view it against the needs and character of the times.

[*186*]

Bill told his grandson about the famous "Camp Grant Massacre" too, an incident which had taken place when the boy was only two years old. The story as it follows is compounded from my father's memories, interspersed with excerpts from Bill's account, written for the Arizona Pioneers' Historical Society.

Camp Grant was located some 60 miles northeast of Tucson. It had been founded as Fort Arivaypa late in 1859 or early in 1860 by a handful of men of the Eighth U.S. Infantry and the First U.S. Dragoons.[1] Shortly after its activation, its name was changed to Fort Breckinridge.[2] One year later, in July 1861, Capt. Isaiah N. Moore destroyed the post under federal orders so that it might not fall into Confederate hands. Stores of the post were placed in piles and burned along with the buildings of the camp. The place was reestablished on May 18, 1862, by elements of General Carleton's California Volunteers, and renamed Fort Stanford in honor of the California Governor Leland Stanford.[3] The following year, in October, the place was renamed Fort Breckinridge. Two years later, on November 1, 1865, the name was changed to Camp Grant in honor of the Civil War hero. There was one more name change, to Fort Grant on April 5, 1879, and the post was finally abandoned in 1895.[4] It was known as Camp Grant at the time of the bloody doings on the morning of April 30, 1871.

Prior to the Mexican War, the Mexican government had the responsibility of protecting its settlers from the Apaches. Apache bands roamed the countryside at will, from south-central Arizona down into Sonora, and from the Colorado river to the Rio Grande and beyond. While the raids were as vicious and depraved then as later, not much publicity attended them; there were too few white settlers around to make an issue of the situation. But white settlers began to trickle in after the ceding of the territory to the United States in 1848, and especially after the Gadsden Purchase arrangement six years later.

One of the provisions of the Treaty of Guadalupe Hidalgo forbade Apache raids back and forth across the new international border, and the Army (some time later) was sent in to enforce this decision. With the increasing influx of settlers into Arizona Territory, particularly after the Civil War, the Army had its hands full trying to protect, with a handful of men, literally thousands of square miles. The Apache was outraged at the invasion of his lands by the whites, and so continued his raids, if anything with increased savagery and malevolence. The settlers were vexed at the feeble protection given them by the far-flung outposts, and the Army was in the middle, despised by the Apache (as an adversary) and belittled by the settlers because it could or would not annihilate the red man.

A Hotbed of Discontent

So matters stood in the fall of 1870. The Apaches were making hit-and-run raids round about Tucson, and little or nothing was being done to punish them. Into this hotbed of discontent came one Lieutenant Royal E. Whitman, sent to join "H" Troop of the Third U.S. Cavalry at Camp Grant. As senior officer present at the post (although only a first lieutenant) he assumed command of the place. Because of his implacable nature and the stubborn quality of his policies, he was destined to become "the most hated man in Arizona." In a sense, the abuse heaped upon him was unfair; he was simply carrying out the policies of his superior, General George Stoneman, commander of the Department of Arizona. Stoneman, under orders from Washington had established gathering points for the surrender of Apaches, at which places the warriors, in exchange for their arms and a promise to stop raiding, might draw rations and clothing from the government. These "feeding stations" were highly unpopular with the citizens of Tucson and the farmers in the valleys beyond. Still, Whitman, because of his demeanor, was able to cause plenty of animosity all by himself, Stoneman's policies notwithstanding.

For a couple of months after Whitman's arrival things went on without incident at Camp Grant. One day in February, 1871, five Apache women came to the post looking for a lost boy. In the course of conversation with Whitman in this matter, one of the women let it be known that their chief, Es-kim-in-Zin would like to come in for a talk, and to this Whitman agreed.[5] Several days later, Eskiminzin came in with two dozen braves. The result of his parley with Whitman was the surrender of Eskiminzin and his people to the post commander. The group was placed in camp on Arivaipa Creek, almost half a mile from the post.

Upon establishing this camp, Whitman wrote to General Stoneman for instructions requesting authority to feed and provision the prisoners in the manner established by Stoneman at other places. His request drew no answer. In the meantime, the band on the Arivaipa had grown to several hundred. Whitman, on his own authority, began to count the prisoners and issue rations every third day.[6] Stoneman steered clear of the matter until April, when he sent a new commander to Camp Grant, one Captain Stanwood. By then, the ranchería had swelled in numbers to over 500, and Whitman had given Eskiminzin permission to move his camp some four miles upstream where the water supply was adequate. Stanwood brought oral orders from Stoneman to continue the policy already implemented by Whitman. Stanwood left the scene almost upon his arrival. After making a brief inspection of conditions at the post, he went to patrol the territory south of Tucson, and Whitman was again in charge of things.

Things had already begun to happen, presumably because of the presence of the concentrated force of Apaches on the Arivaipa, and the settlers grew restive. On March 10, Apaches killed a soldier and a Mexican passenger of a wagon train bound from Camp Grant to a station in the Pinal Mountains. Ten days later, a raiding part hit Tubac, killing L. B. Wooster, a rancher, and carrying off a Mexican woman, Trinidad Aguirre.[7] The Tucson *Citizen* cried: "Will the Department Commander longer permit the murderers to be fed by supplies purchased with the people's money?"[8]

Resolve for Action

As tempers flared in Tucson, Bill Oury resolved to do something about the deteriorating situation. His decision was based not only upon the two incidents listed above, but upon a string of outrages authored by Eskiminzin and his band of Pinal (or Arivaipa) Apaches dating as far back as March, 1866. In that month, they killed Captain J. E. Millar of the Fourteenth U.S. Infantry and Dr. (1st Lt.) Benjamin Tappan, enroute from Fort Yuma to Camp Grant.[9]

A year later, April 1867, they killed a man named Valentine at the nine-mile crossing of the Santa Cruz, and several months later shot and wounded one Adam Linn.[10] In September, 1867, Irwin, a post sutler at Grant, left the post to inspect crops along the Santa Cruz nearby. Eskiminzin's braves murdered him not far from the protection he had just left.[11] His partner, Israel, started out to avenge him, but could not pick up the trail of the Apaches. Later, enroute from Tucson to Camp Grant, he with a man named Kennedy, and Sam Hughes, Jr. were ambushed at Cañada del Oro by Eskiminzin. Israel was shot from his horse, tied to a wagon wheel and burned alive by the Indian bushwhackers.[12] Kennedy was wounded, but crawled away into the bush. Found by a party of soldiers a day later, he was rushed to Tucson, but died there on the following day. Hughes escaped.[13]

A few days later, Eskiminzin's braves jumped Harry Long and Sam Brown near Tres Alamos, and a day or so later killed all the members of a small haying party near Camp Grant.[14]

Bill Oury remembered these things as he was appointed head of the Committee of Public Safety by the aroused townspeople of Tucson. In writing of his participation in the appeal to General Stoneman and the subsequent raid upon the Apache ranchería, Oury said:

During the winter of 1870–71 Apache murders and depredations were so numerous as to threaten the abandonment of nearly all the settlements outside of Tucson, especially on the San Pedro . . . presentations were made to the right-Royal Whitman that his Indians were plundering and murdering our

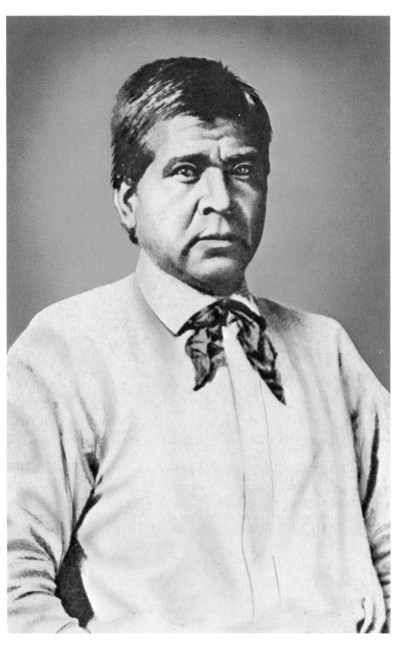

ESKIMINZIN was chief of the Camp Grant Apaches who became a national *cause célèbre* when Bill Oury and Jesús María Elías led five other Americans, 47 Mexicans, and 92 Papagos in the so-called "Camp Grant Massacre."

people, which he denied, and stood ready to prove by every striker on the reservation that his Indians never left the place."[15]

With the continuing pattern of Apache hit-and-run raids, Oury continues in his paper:

It was determined to raise a military company at once, for which a paper was drawn up, and signers called for, to which 82 Americans signed their names. The writer was elected captain, and all hands pledged to eat up, blood raw, every Apache in the land, immediately upon the occurrence of a new outrage.[16]

General Stoneman at this point was not in Tucson, but on the Gila River, near Florence. Undismayed, Bill in the company of Sidney R. de Long, and J. W. Hopkins called upon him at his place in the field. The date was March 25, 1871. The reception was not a warm one. Bill's exact words on that meeting are:

The result of the conference with that august personage General Stoneman was that he had but few troops, and could give us no aid, that Tucson had the largest population in the territory, and he gave us to understand that we must protect ourselves. With this cold comfort, after a trip of 150 miles and the loss of a valuable mule, we returned to our constituents, and although no public demonstration was made, at a quiet assemblage of some of our oldest and most influential citizens, it was resolved that the recommendation of Gen. Stoneman should be adopted, and that to the best of our ability we would endeavor to protect ourselves.[17]

It is clear that Bill left the meeting with the same impression of Stoneman that had found currency with the public; namely, that in matters where the Apache was concerned, the general was an appeaser. Oury considered the pow-wow a flat failure, saying: "We can expect nothing more from him than has been done, and if anything further is expected, we must depend upon our own efforts for its consummation."[18]

Two weeks after the parley on the Gila (on April 10), an Apache raiding party hit the little Papago settlement at San Xavier, and ran off nineteen head of horses and cattle. A posse was formed in Tucson and chased the thieves some fifty miles, killing one, and returning the cattle to the village. Three days later, Eskiminzin killed Alex McKenzie at his farm on the San Pedro. The two men had become friends, and McKenzie suspected nothing when the Apache rode up to his ranch with several companions. McKenzie killed a beef· for the visit, and the party feasted. Later, pretending to leave, Eskiminzin hid in the bushes near the farm, and as his host passed by, ran a lance through his heart.[19] Asked later why he had turned on McKenzie, the Indian said: "I am a great chief . . . it takes a great and brave man to kill his best friend."[20] A group formed to hunt down the killers, but after chasing them for several miles ran headlong into a party of some 100 Apache braves. In the ensuing fight, three whites were killed.

By now, the *Citizen* was labelling the Camp Grant truce "a cruel farce."[21] It was obvious to Bill that the town could expect no help from the Army or from the community. If anything was to be done at all, he, Elías his friend, and a few others would have to do it themselves. On Friday morning, April 28, 1871, Bill met with Jesús Maria Elías on the banks of Pantano Wash outside the town. With them were five other Americans, forty-seven Mexicans, and ninety-two Papagos, a force of 146 all told.[22] Sam Hughes, the Adjutant General of the territory, was there to deliver a wagonload of guns and ammunition. He did not go on the raid, although he was "heart and soul in it" according to William Bailey, a participant.[23] Mrs. Hughes had helped mold the bullets and load the cartridge belts for the expedition. Bailey states that the rifles were government issue, Springfields, each numbered, and each coming from a government crate with an inspector's number affixed to the cover.[24] He added that the Papagos were armed with these rifles. According to the version of this affair by James R. Hastings, Mrs. Hughes denied this.[25] Oury's account mentions the use of "clubs and guns" by the Papagos. After the raid, the rifles were cleaned, oiled, and returned to A. P. K. Safford, governor of the territory.

As they waited at Pantano Wash, Bill and Elías talked. "Don Guillermo, your countrymen are grand on resoluting and speechifying, but when it comes to action they show up thin."[26] There was little Bill could say. Eighty-two Americans had pledged to make the assault on the ranchería; six showed up.[27]

Oury and Elías talked for awhile with Francisco, the Papago Chief, and soon the expedition was formed into two companies, ready to move out. Elías was elected captain of the expedition by the unanimous vote of all present. The column moved down the Pantano Wash to the Rillito, and there made a brief halt. Oury, reasoning that the absence of fifty-four Mexican and American males from Tucson might act as a tip-off to the authorities, scribbled a hasty note and gave it to Bailey, directing him to give it to the driver of the provision wagon to take to Tucson. It was to be delivered to Hiram Stevens. It read:

H. S. Stevens, Esq. Tucson.

Send a party to the Canada del Oro, on the main road from Tucson to Camp Grant, with orders to stop any and all persons going toward Camp Grant until 7 o'clock, A.M., April 30, 1871.

W. S. Oury

Bailey handed the note to the driver, saying: "Don't forget the note, and drive like hell until you get to Steven's place."[29] The driver did as he was told, and none too soon. Captain Dunn, the commanding officer at Camp Lowell, did think it odd that so many of the town's men were missing. He sent two couriers to Whitman to warn him of possible trouble. The couriers were unable to reach Camp Grant; they were detained by the two men Stevens had sent to Cañada del Oro at Oury's request.

The column resumed its march then, up towards Cabadilla Pass, crossing over the mountains to the San Pedro side. Halting for occasional rests, it came down the east side of the mountain and into the San Pedro Valley at daybreak on the twenty-ninth. Elías and Oury conferred, deciding to rest there throughout the day, so as not to disclose their position by raising clouds of dust. As darkness fell, Elías gave orders to resume the march. Some six or eight miles further on, he halted again to send out a scouting party to determine the distance between the column and the objective. Three men were chosen to ride out; a Mexican, a Papago, and William Bailey.

Elías had estimated his position to be fifteen or sixteen miles from the Apache ranchería. As it turned out, it was nearer thirty miles. By the time the column reached the head of the canyon, it was almost dawn and Camp Grant was in sight. If the raiders were seen by the sentries there, the expedition would be a failure, broken up and dispersed before ever reaching the Apache camp. Elías acted swiftly, dividing his outfit into two companies, Indians in one, Mexicans and Americans in the other. The Mexican-American group would "skirmish up the creek" until it could see the Apache camp; the Papagos would then charge it upon signal. Soon the village came in sight, and all was quiet.

On the Brink of Massacre

Bill sat there looking down on the sleeping camp, hoping that his horse wouldn't nicker, or that some one of Francisco's men wouldn't kick a rock over the bluff. Quietly he motioned to a Papago tracker to come to his side. Sitting by a small fire in the distance were two figures, a man and a woman, placed as lookouts for the ranchería. Bill whispered to the tracker and he padded softly off into the clump of greasewood. He carried a heavy stick he had picked up along the trail. So ghostly quiet was his approach that the poor sentries never knew what hit them. There was not even a muffled cry as he hit the two in swift succession. Now the coast was clear; Bill signalled to Elías to give the charge order.

The charge was swift and sure. The Papagos (whether with clubs or guns, or both) hurtled down the hill into the village, shouting. The Apaches came tumbling out of their wickiups, confused and sleepy, and were felled at once.

There was no checking the infuriated Papagos now. They killed every Apache in sight, and these were squaws, children, and a few old men. To the Papagos, it made no difference; an Apache was an Apache, male or female, large or small. To the Mexicans it made little or no difference either. Too long the Apaches had raided the little towns in Sonora, lifting Mexican scalps, and leaving whole families of dead Mexicans for the vultures to pull at. Side by side, the Papagos and Mexicans killed, hard-faced, vengeful, resolute.

But what of the six Americans? Did they kill? No one knows, really. Bill never said that he did or did not. Nor did Sidney de Long, or Bailey, or James Lee. They were there. They did nothing to stop the slaughter. But they had come to wipe out an Apache nest, and were in no mood to differentiate, to pick and choose. It is doubtful whether their shouts might have been heard (or heeded) above the general din anyway.

Oury says: "All who escaped them (the Papagos) took to the bluffs and were . . . despatched by the other wing. The attack was so swift and fierce that within a half hour the whole work was ended, and not an adult Indian left to tell the tale. Some 28 or 30 small papooses were spared and brought to Tucson as captives. Not a single man of our command was seriously hurt. . . ."[30] He then concludes: "By eight o'clock, our tired troops were resting and breakfasting on the San Pedro, a few miles above the post in full satisfaction of a work well done."[31]

And so the killing ended, and the rays of the morning sun shone down upon the awful scene. And it became very quiet. The dogs drew fearfully away into the bushes and not a sound was heard. Each man stood for a moment alone with his thoughts, making a momentary peace between himself and whatever God he served. But this was no time for reflection. Soon the Camp Grant guard would know of the attack, and a new situation would be at hand. It was time to move on.

On the way back to Tucson, the column had a brief skirmish with some Apache stock-tenders in Cabadilla Pass. The column opened fire on them, killing several, and took the stock to the Orosco Ranch nearby. The party broke up at Pantano Wash, and in the words of William Bailey: "We scattered in the brush and silently rode home."[32]

The Apache camp was strewn with dead. Bailey says: "We counted thirty dead Apaches. The ones shot at a distance we did not count as dead, because we did not go to where they fell. There were eight or ten of these."[33] On this issue of Apache casualties, there is much disagreement. Whitman, in his report to the Commission of Indian Affairs (House Executive Document 1, 42d Congress, 2d Session 1871–72, p. 487) listed 125 Indians "killed or missing." In his testimony at the trial of the raiders later, however, he said he had seen "about thirty or forty dead bodies." D. A. Bennett, speaking with some of the raiders on their return estimated that some 150 Indians had "been killed or taken prisoner." Writing of the incident in 1936, Andrew Cargill listed 86 women and children, and one old man as casualties. Elliott Arnold (the author of *Broken Arrow,* a tale of Cochise) lists 108 casualties, while the San Carlos Indian Agent John P. Clum claimed that 118 were killed in the affair.[34] In its report of 6 May, 1871, the Tucson *Citizen* listed the number of casualties as 85. The casualty lists run from 30 on the low side to 150 on the high, a considerable disparity, but are conclusive enough in any case to establish the fact that many Apaches were put to death on that cool April dawn of 1871. James M. Barney writing of the affair in Phoenix in 1946 said:

It seems inconceivable that Americans and Mexicans could have clubbed to death such a large number of helpless women and children, no matter what the provocation. Let us rather think that the greater slaughter was done by the Papagos, hereditary enemies of the Apache, whose tribal laws, in force from time immemorial forbade them to show mercy to their foes. In the fierce warfare between those two tribes, no quarter was asked or expected, and neither the sex nor the age of their victims was considered.[35]

A Prescott paper of June 10, 1871, declared:

We have seen the action of Papago Indians and the men who accompanied them termed a cowardly slaughter of helpless women and children. . . . We should be as ready as any of our contemporaries to denounce a war upon women and children, but such this was not. It was the action of the people, aroused by government neglect, who took up arms and marched forward, prepared to encounter the enemy of double their number, and avenge their wrongs or perish in the attempt, and we say — God speed every such mission.[36]

Despite the support of the Phoenix paper, and that of the Tucson citizenry generally, the raid was the cause of angry and noisy reactions in the East. President Grant termed the expedition "purely murder," and moved to begin an investigation of the affair immediately.[37] On May 2, 1871, he relieved General Stoneman of his command, replacing him with General George Crook. Grant then ordered District Attorney C. W. C. Rowell to go from California to Tucson, to try the participants of the Camp Grant massacre. Also, he sent Vincent Colyer, Secretary of the Commission of Indian Affairs to Tucson, carrying extraordinary powers over the military there established.

Smarting under the attacks from "the effete East," the local citizenry began a campaign of its own, a campaign to justify the raid in whatever way possible. Much of this took on the air of a crusade against Lieutenant Royal Whitman, seen by many as the real cause of all the trouble. He had established the Apache ranchería on the Arivaipa on his own authority, and fed an increasing number of Indians with government provisions. He had kept sketchy records of their comings and goings, and had permitted them to move several miles away from the camp, altogether out of sight. After the raid, he had written a letter to Colonel Lee at Camp Lowell, in which he flatly rejected the charge that the Camp Grant Apaches had ever raided San Xavier — or anywhere else. To substantiate this claim, he obtained statements from several civilians residing at Camp Grant. This was too much for the people of Tucson. From then on, Whitman was the target for all of the abuse an outraged citizenry could pour on him.

In its June 10 issue, the weekly Arizona *Miner* said:

Lt. Royal E. Whitman . . . made no effort to acquaint himself with the movements of the Apaches under his charge. Whether or not they were out murdering or plundering seems to have concerned him very little. This officer is notoriously addicted to strong drink, and is under the influence the greater part of the time. He has outrageously negelected his official duties.[38]

In another contemporary but undated article the *Miner* said:

. . . Whitman is an adventurer who works solely for himself, a liar, poltroon, drunkard, robber, and miscegenationist of the worst stamp . . . a disgrace to the Army and should be drummed out of it. He has no doubt made money by swindling the Indians and the government. . . . It is well authenticated that whatever influence he may have with Indians has been earned by the prostitution of his white manhood . . . (by) living polygamously with the frail squaws of the tribe. Such is this low, base, demoralized white man, who says he feels a strong personal interest in showing them (the Indians) the way to a higher civilization.

Oury says of Whitman:

. . . being a sharp man, and of thrifty turn, he soon saw that there was money in the Apache and lost no time in practical application of that knowledge, to do which required outside partners who were found in Tucson.[39]

Oury does not elaborate on these partnerships nor establish collusion between Whitman and any of the townspeople of Tucson.

Charges are Made

On December 2, 1871, Whitman was summoned to appear before a courtmartial board. This trial was called off before it could begin. How valid the charges were will never be known, but somehow their contents were made available to the *Arizona Citizen* which listed Whitman's alleged misdemeanors. He was charged with being intoxicated at a San Diego hotel (the Horton House, November 5, 1870), with drunkenness at "Point of Mountain," A.T., on or about November 24, 1870, with failure to pay for a round of drinks ordered by him at James H. Toole's saloon in Tucson, 1870, with "lying drunk" there later on that same day, with lying drunk and indecently exposed on the premises of Lord and Williams (later on the same day), with attempting to seat himself in a woman's lap in the "feast grounds" of a Tucson park (to the "scandal of the service"), and with behaving in such an unbecoming manner that the officers and men of his regiment refused to associate with him.[40]

Clearly, his enemies were reaching way down into the bottom of the barrel to pin something on him. In any case, General Crook dismissed the board, stating: "Owing to the movement of troops, consequent upon the transfer of the Third Cavalry Regiment from the Department, it is impracticable to reassemble the court. Lt. Whitman will be released from arrest and restored to duty."

In March, 1872, Whitman was relieved of his duties and detained at Fort Crittenden. A second court was convened in May, but was dissolved before taking action. He was tried finally in October of 1872, and found guilty of using disgraceful language and conduct unbecoming an officer and gentleman. At this stage of the game, one might overlook the gravity of the disgraceful language charge. Right or wrong, the beleaguered man had suffered enough at the hands of Tucson's irate townsfolk to cuss a little. Whitman left Arizona finally, his appointment as Indian agent denied on several counts, not the least of which was the statement that his health was "poor, and the climate of Arizona was injuring him."

In sending Coyler to investigate, President Grant further irritated the people of Arizona. Colyer was a Quaker, opposed to violence, and particularly opposed to planned retaliations such as that carried out by Oury and company. He had made up his mind in the matter of the Camp Grant incident before leaving Washington.[41] His first two acts, creating an Indian reservation at Camp Grant and retaining the services of Whitman set the tone for his reception by the citizens. Colyer soon held a conference with several Apache leaders, to get their version of the massacre; he did not call upon Oury, Elías, de Long, or any of the participants of the raid.

Crook, a fighter, did not take to Colyer the pacifist. Nor could he stomach Whitman. For whatever good it would do, Crook aligned himself with the citizens of Tucson against the appeasing Colyer. Nothing happened until new Apache raids brought about a turn in the administration's policy for Indian Affairs. The President gave Crook leave to pursue a new and sharp campaign against the Apaches. In effect, this cancelled Colyer's usefulness in Arizona, and he headed for home. But not before appointing Whitman as acting Indian agent. He did not retain his position long; in March, he was arrested and sent under guard to Fort Crittenden.

Colyer's mission had accomplished little else than to agitate an already aroused citizenry.

With Colyer's failure to effect peace between the citizens and the military, and between the military and the Apaches, the President appointed General Oliver O. Howard as special agent to look into the management of Indian affairs in Arizona. A fair and courageous man, Howard leaned toward Crook's point of view. Still, he was willing to do what he could to effect peace. On April 26, 1872, he met with the Apache chiefs and listened to their demands. Twenty-seven children had been taken by the Mexicans and Papagos in the massacre raid; they wanted them back. They wanted a peace treaty with neighboring tribes (the Papagos and Pimas). They wanted the removal of the Indian Agency from Camp Grant to a better location. And they wanted Royal E. Whitman restored as their agent. Howard listened to them with courtesy and set up a conference to take place a month later (May 20). In this second meeting, the peace treaty was inaugurated, and the Camp Grant reservation abolished.

Not more than a handful of the captured children were ever returned. It is presumed that they were sold or traded into slavery in Mexico. The demand for Whitman's reinstatement was denied. There was a great deal of feeling against him, not only among the bemused citizens of Tucson, but with his superior, General Crook as well. Howard, in his meetings with the Apaches at Camp Grant, and with Cochise in the Chiricahuas, did as much as any man to pour oil on the troubled waters. Even so, his work was not conclusive. After the death of Cochise, Geronimo harassed the countryside for years. He was finally captured by Lieutenant Charles B. Gatewood in Skeleton Canyon in 1886.

The Camp Grant episode horrified Easterners generally and outraged President Grant. He wrote to Governor Safford remarking that if the perpetrators of the massacre were not brought to trial immediately he would declare martial law in Arizona. On learning of this correspondence, Bill Oury requested a formal trial before an Arizona court. Sidney de Long was selected by the court to stand trial for the entire lot of plaintiffs, 100 in all. By agreement between the prosecutor and attorneys for the defense, the decision rendered on de Long would establish the guilt or innocence of all those named as defendants. Grant Oury served as counsel for the defense along with James E. McCaffry.

The United States Grand Jury acting in the case ended its nine-day session on October 23, 1871, and issued a report signed by its foreman, Charles T. Hayden.[42] As a prelude to the trial, this report was a blessing to the defendants; it outlined the history of Apache depredations from the year 1860, and placed the Camp Grant raiders in as favorable a position as they might expect.

A Chief Indicted

The report began with a ringing indictment of Cochise for his activities in and around Apache Pass in 1860–61, charging that the Chiricahua chief and his band lived there by "theft, robbery, and murder," and had "used" benevolent authorities with treachery and deceit.[43] The paper went on to outline the stupidity of the camp commander at Fort Apache in selling guns and ammunition to Apaches, and charged that the rationing activities at Fort Apache, Camp Goodwin and Camp Grant were so loosely administered that trouble with the Indians was inevitable. According to the report, although the Indians were considered prisoners of war and were fed and provisioned at government expense, they were not controlled in any way, nor were they made to give up their weapons. In substantiation of this charge, the jury related the case of the shooting of Colonel Stone (Deputy Collector of Customs in the Territory) on October 6, 1869.[44] The colonel was ambushed by Apaches working out of the "feeding station" at Camp Goodwin; he and his five companions were killed by the Indians who proceeded then to Fort Apache to draw their government rations.

The report continued by relating the stories of the murders of L. B. Wooster and Alex McKenzie, pointing out that these atrocities had been committed while the perpetrators were using the government military installation at Camp Grant as a staging area. With reference to this point, the report used these words:

We find that the hostile bands of Indians in this territory are led by many different chiefs who have generally adopted the policy of Cochise, making the point where Indians are fed the base for their supply of ammunition, guns, and recruits for their raids, as each hostile chief usually draws warriors from other bands when he . . . raids the citizens or the neighboring state of Sonora, where they continually make their depredations.[45]

The paper then levelled its guns on the conditions at Camp Grant, stating that: "with few marked exceptions, the habit of beastly drunkenness has generally prevailed among the officers at Camp Grant."[46] It was charged too that the rations there were unjustly distributed, and that in one instance bones were offered to hungry Apaches in lieu of meat. Officers at Grant were charged with "using their official position to break the chastity of the Indian woman." The paper ends with these words:

In conclusion of the labors of this U. S. Grand Jury, we would say that 500 of our neighbors, friends, and fellow citizens have fallen by the murdering band of the Apache Indians, clothing in the garb of mourning the family circle in many of the hamlets, towns, and cities of all the states of our country. Their blood cries from the ground to the American people for justice — justice to all men.[47]

This was scarcely the language of indictment, and it was obvious that if Hayden and his fellow-jurors could have had their way there would have been no trial. The pressure of the federal government to indict was strong, however, and the threat of martial law hung over the entire community. The Grand Jury indicted, and a trial was set for December. At the arraignment before the trial, eight of the participants, Oury among them, appeared in person to plead not guilty. Each posted bond for $10,000 as a guarantee of appearance at the December trial. When the court convened, ninety-nine men of the raid were present to answer the charges; one man of the 100 indicted was for some reason absent.

The trial was remarkable from several points of view. First, no one in Tucson really seemed to want it. Second, although 146 men had participated, ninety-nine were now facing trial, and only one actually was on trial — in terms of testimony, cross-examination, and so on.

The verdict of the Grand Jury was a ringing denunciation of the government's Indian policy, and could in no way be interpreted as an objective study. And then there was the charge to the trial jury by Chief Justice Titus.

The testimony of witnesses was concluded on December 11. Arguments before the jury were heard on the twelfth and forenoon of the thirteenth. At its afternoon session, Justice Titus had these words for the jury before its deliberation:

... the law which constitutes our code, criminal as well as civil, has grown up in quiet, populous, and strongly policed communities very different from this ... in such cases as this, the administration of the law requires peculiar care and caution to avoid judicial murder. The circumstances which constitute and control human natures here, are far graver than those of old, quiet, communities with law supported by numerous population and adequate police. ... The government of the United States owes its Papago, Mexican, and American residents in Arizona protection from Apache spoliation and assault. If such spoliation and assault are persistently carried on and not prevented by the government, then the sufferers have a right to protect themselves, and to employ force enough for the purpose. ...[48]

The *Daily Alta California* carried an editorial eulogizing the fairness of Judge Titus' charge, saying that it was "very interesting, and presents the law points involved in a clear and impartial manner."[49]

In another portion of his charge, Titus indirectly told the jury that the Papago participants could not be convicted of murder inasmuch as their tribal relationship with the Apaches was "not bound by American laws."[50]

After only nineteen minutes of deliberation, the jury came in with a verdict of not guilty. Andrew Hays Cargill, the secretary of the Grand Jury, was hung in effigy for his remarks about the "farcical" nature of the trial. So was the prosecuting attorney. The camp commander at Lowell threatened military action if either of them should be molested physically for dissenting views.

And so Bill Oury and his friends went free. The papers of the Territory exulted:

The parties who were recently tried . . . for killing hostile Apaches . . . return their sincere thanks to Messrs. McCaffry and Oury (Granville) for their noble act in volunteering to defend them. The trial will long be remembered, and the gentlemen named can always refer to their part in it with feelings of honorable pride. In later years, another paper was to reminisce: "Camp Grant was soon afterward abandoned, for the Apaches in that vicinity were so nearly exterminated that the soldiers were left without a job."[52]

Residents throughout Arizona Territory generally defended the Camp Grant action. Although many of them might have stood aghast at the slaughter of women and children, criticisms and recriminations in this vein are missing from the newspapers of the day. The general tenor of editorial statements might be summed up in the words of the *Daily Alta California:*

When the first report of the massacre was published, the community was shocked at the idea of an attack on a party of prisoners of war . . . but we think any unprejudiced person who reads the report of the trial will see that much may be said on the other side. We do not believe that any civilized community, after suffering so much as the people of Arizona have suffered from the Apaches in the last four years, could find a jury to convict the assailants in a case like that of Camp Grant.[52]

Certainly there had been provocation enough for some sort of reprisal against the Apaches. For a decade, they had plundered and killed at will, leaving a bloody trail across the barren face of the territory. The army, restricted by administration policy to react only to individual Apache forays, could not warrant any sort of real punitive expeditions (or it would not). Sick of it all, the townspeople sought military aid, but were rejected. And so they acted. Tragically, the victims of the raiding party were almost exclusively women and children. And this brings up a point. Where were the Apache men? In a community of some 500, 100 or more would have been adult males. Where were they? Whitman had testified that they never left the ranchería without being accounted for, that he could, in effect, put his finger upon any of them at any given time. As they were absent on the morning of the 30th, might not they have been absent also in the days when San Xavier was raided, and when Wooster, McKenzie, Israel and Kennedy were slain?

With regard to the Papago participation and the relationship of the Papago and Apache tribes, the *Daily Alta California* said:

These two tribes are, and for centuries have been, at war with each other. Their mode of warfare includes sudden surprise, and the general massacre of captives . . . with the Papagos, the massacre was a legitimate act of hostility, and therefore not a proper matter for punishment by the civil courts.[54]

The *Alta California* continued by blaming official Washington for the affair.

. . . If Congress will reward the brave and punish the poltroons among our soldiers, feed the submissive Indians, and fight the hostile, the government will gain much more credit than it has for the last five years. The chief responsibility is in Washington. When the Apaches give more trouble, we shall demand the scalps of the incompetents there on the first step towards peace in Arizona.[55]

Of the 146 raiders, ninety-two were Papagos. It may be assumed then that much if not most of the killing was done by these ninety-two in keeping with tribal custom. Still, forty-eight Mexicans and six Americans were there. What of them? Probably the Mexicans were as indiscriminate as their Papago companions. For centuries the Apache had raided Mexican settlements in Sonora; the Mexican memory was long and bitter.

As for the Americans, not much is known about their activities at the ranchería.[56] Bailey has said: "I stopped some of the Apaches with my sabre. That was the only time I had use for a sabre, and I made good use of it then."[57] DeLong and Lee are not quoted in the matter. Sam Hughes was not there. Bill may have taken a shot or two at the Apaches as they ran from their tents. He did not remark upon it, one way or another. As Charles Morgan Wood has said:

Whatever the world might think meant nothing to Bill Oury. In his own mind he was thoroughly convinced that there would be no peace, that the Apache would still be raiding around Tucson if it had not been for the Camp Grant massacre.[58]

Indeed, Bill listed his own stock losses before a notary public on March 10, 1872, to show that he had been the victim of Apache thievery for the two years preceding the Camp Grant affair. His losses went back to February 1869, when seven head of cattle were driven off his ranch by Apaches. His ranch was hit twice again in 1869; in March, when nine head were stolen, again in September when he lost four beeves. He lost a horse and a cow to Apaches in January, 1870, and three more cattle in March of that year. In all, he estimated his losses at $2,000. The *Enterprise* sketch quotes him as saying that the roads leading to Tucson were unsafe, and that if the proposed scheme to abandon Camp Crittenden should be put into effect, the settlements of the Sonoita and along the Santa Cruz would have to be abandoned.[59] The Camp (Fort) was closed (but not until some fifteen months after Bill's warning) on June 1, 1873. There was no wholesale exodus from the settlements referred to above, but sporadic stock raids by the Apaches continued for a long time.

In his paper to the Society of Arizona Pioneers, Bill concludes with this question:

"In view of all these facts, I call on all Arizonians to answer on their own consciences — can you call the killing of the Apaches at Camp Grant on the morning of the thirtieth of April, 1871, a massacre?"[60]

Well, one must answer yes, regardless of the justification for reprisal against the Apache depredations. A massacre denotes promiscuous and wholesale slaughter of those who can make little or no resistance. Certainly these conditions fit the attack made on that sad little Arizona clearing so long ago. Still, one ought not to fall into the trap of judging yesterday's acts by today's moral standards. In our relatively safe and comfortable daily lives, it is difficult for us to appreciate the unbelievable hardships suffered by our ancestors. Let us be critical, but let us be just.

CHAPTER 24

Sheriff Days

IN 1873, BILL OURY WAS ELECTED to the post of sheriff of Pima County, a position he held until 1877. In the relatively lawless frontier town of Tucson, where gunplay on the streets was a common thing, and thievery constant, his work was cut out for him. A bold, courageous man, his very presence in the office was enough to subdue many of the town's toughs. But not for long. A few months after he pinned on his star, there occurred one of the most brutal killings in the annals of Tucson crime. As sheriff, Bill was right in the middle of it; it has come down in Arizona history as the "Piedras Negras" Affair.[1]

A Mexican named Vincente Hernández had a little general store and jewelry shop on the corner of Convent and Kennedy streets. A few yards away, a man named Santiago Pérez had a nondescript little hole-in-the-wall where he sold tequila and cordwood. He employed several wood-choppers from time to time, among them Clemente López and Jesús Sahuaripa. These men, along with others from the rougher element of the town, would hang out at the Pérez place, loafing and drinking, and generally passing the time of day in a rowdy manner. On occasion, an Opata Indian by the name of Córdoba would join the company.

Sometime in the night of August 6, 1873, Vincente Hernández and his wife were clubbed to death in their house as they slept.[2] In the morning, a Mexican neighbor called to get himself some groceries. Unable to rouse anyone, he went around to the back of the place and looked over the wall into the courtyard and rear of the store. He saw a bloody footprint on the door-sill, and sensed that something was terribly wrong. He ran off to tell somebody and get help.

William Zeckendorf was the first to learn of it, and made straight for the Hernández store at the head of a chattering group of followers.[3] Breaking into the place, the party found the murdered couple amidst a dreadful shambles. Blood was spattered all about the place — on walls, counter, shelves, even on the sad little money till — empty of its cash. Both Vincente and his wife had been clubbed with a stout piece of wood, which was still lying there on the floor, its knots smeared with coagulating blood. Also, the throats had been cut, garishly, from ear to ear. The valuables in the little place had disappeared — money, a few pieces of silver jewelry, and other items.

The Chase Begins

Someone in the crowd ran off to get Sheriff Oury, and he arrived on the scene soon after. Oury's first thought was that the woodcutter, Pérez, might have had a hand in it. He walked up the street to the Pérez place and gained entry. In reaching the premises, he found a gun which had been stolen from his own office just the day before. Pérez denied the theft, claiming that Clemente López had pawned the gun to him the night before. Bill could get nothing else out of Pérez except the admission that López, Sahuaripa, Cásculo Hernández, and the Indian Córdoba had been hanging around his place most of the day on the sixth. Bill took Pérez into custody.[4]

Judge C. H. Meyer got into the act, and the mystery began to unravel. Knowing that López had been seeing a lot of a servant girl employed by Leopoldo Carrillo, Meyer went off to Carrillo's house and questioned the girl. As it turned out, she had been with López on the night of the sixth, but he had excused himself late in the evening saying that some friends were waiting for him. At about dawn on the following morning, she was sitting in front of her house and saw López and his mother pass by with a load of soiled clothing to wash in a ditch nearby. She had spoken to them, and the old woman had said she wanted to get her washing done while it was still cool.

Meyer decided to find López and ask him some questions. López had an adobe house on Stone Avenue. When Meyer got there, he could raise no one with knocks upon the door, so he kicked the door in. The old woman, badly frightened, was crouching in a corner. There seemed to be no one else there, but then Meyer saw a straw mat, rolled up and leaning against another corner of the room. A blanket was draped carelessly over the top of the roll. Meyer pulled rudely at the mat's edging, and Clemente López tumbled from his hiding place.[5] Meyer took him to jail, at gun point.

Questioned there by Oury and Meyer, López became truculent and would admit nothing. He did attempt to shift suspicion from himself by putting the law on Cásculo's trail. Meyer, L. C. Hughes, and a colored man named Martin set off to find Hernández and put the pieces of the sordid story together. There was a house on Meyer street known as a meeting place for loafers; the three men made for it straight away. Arriving there, Meyer asked a child playing in the street if anyone was in the house. The little girl told him she had seen some men go in some time before. As Meyer talked with the child, a policeman, Esparza, joined the search party. Meyer posted him at the rear of the house and then tried the front door, pistol in hand. Martin, the colored man, kicked in the door while the judge held his pistol at the ready. The men inside bolted for the rear door, but were held by Esparza whose gun was levelled at them. They were then herded down to Bill Oury who put them behind bars, Cásculo Hernández among them. Now Bill had two prime suspects in Pérez and López, and maybe a third in Hernández. He was still without a confession or conclusive evidence.

By now, everyone was playing sleuth and asking questions. On that evening (August 7) at about 8 o'clock, the policeman Esparza asked a merchant, Mariano Molina, if he had heard anything new. Molina had not, but ventured the guess that the Opata Indian Córdoba might somehow be implicated. While Esparza and Molina were still talking, who should saunter in but Córdoba himself! He was whisked off to jail. There he was stripped for searching, and his pant leg found bloodstained. His bare footprint matched precisely the footprint found on the doorsill of the murdered couple's house. Bill Oury saw what he thought to be dried blood under the toenails of Córdoba's left foot.[6] Judge Meyer flaked if off with a penknife, while William Zeckendorf rummaged through the Indian's trousers and fished out two five-dollar bills, both stained with bloody fingerprints.

One more man was needed for questioning, Jesús Sahuaripa. He was found sleeping on the dirt floor of a house nearby and brought in. Three men confessed to participation in the grisly affair: Córdoba, Clemente López, and Jesús Sahuaripa. Cásculo Hernández had been in on the plot originally, but he backed off before the event. He got away with his life on the condition that he would leave Tucson forever. He did. Santiago Pérez, while not similarly implicated, left anyway. The loot of the robbery was found under a pile of brush on the road leading to Warner's Mill.

Vincente Hernández and his wife were buried on Sunday morning, August 8, 1873. The saloons and stores were closed, as a large crowd followed the funeral procession to the cemetery. There was no trial; the condemned men were hung in vigilante fashion on the open square of the plaza on that bright Sunday morning. Had either judge or sheriff been present to witness the proceedings, the miscarriage of justice would have been greater than it was. Judge Titus was prevailed upon by Sam Hughes to visit San Xavier Mission that morning to "study the architecture."[7] Bill Oury stayed home, sick from "indigestion."[8] It was a ruse, pure and simple, but Bill was a direct and forthright man, and wanted justice now, not later. Córdoba had killed in cold blood; he had confessed, and was guilty beyond all doubt. Why delay justice with a trial? Why let some jackleg lawyer come in and get Córdoba and his accomplices off, scot-free? And so Bill turned his back on the proceedings in the plaza.

Citizens' Justice

By 10 A.M., just about the entire population of Tucson had assembled in the plaza. A "Citizens Committee" had gathered together the paraphernalia of lynching — ropes and several wagons. With the three murderers in jail was one John Willis, a man who had killed several times, his latest victim being Robert Swope of Florence, Arizona. He had been tried and sentenced to hang, but his sentence had been suspended pending his appeal to the Supreme Court. Someone in the crowd suggested that he be stretched up along with the others.[9] An ex-U. S. marshal in the crowd, Major Duffield, strongly objected to this but was bound hand and foot and left to wriggle helplessly until after the lynching.

The four condemned men were taken from the jail and marched off to Charles Etchell's blacksmith shop for hanging. Etchell refused to have anything to do with it, so everybody trooped back to the plaza. Here an improvised gallows was made by placing a beam on the forked portions of two tree trunks hurriedly secured for the occasion. The gallows were placed squarely where several persons made inflammatory speeches, William Zeckendorf among them. He recounted the lawless nature of Tucson, the everpresent danger from desperadoes on the streets, the impunity with which crimes were committed, and then recited the grisly work of the men about to die.

Córdoba wanted to confess and proceeded to do so at great length. Someone warned then that the troops were coming from Fort Lowell, and that if the men were to be hung, the executioners should get on with it. The four were tied, blindfolded, and placed standing in the wagons under the gallows beam. The ropes were adjusted, and at a signal, the carts jerked rudely from under the feet of the four culprits.

An inquest was held on the afternoon of the hanging. The finding of the jury was to the effect that "the distrust of the people in the administration of justice by the courts" had become so general that they had taken matters into their own hands.[10] Probate Judge W. J. Osburn was foreman of the coroner's jury council on that afternoon, and it was assumed that the verdict was "doubtless still among the archives of the court."

Who can tell how heavy this lawless act weighed upon the consciences of its perpetrators? In a rough and tumble society like that of Tucson in the 1870's, forthrightness, decision, and action were generally preferred to the gentler arts of reflection, forbearance, and the refinements of legal theory. The people lived in a hard society and were hard on its errant members in return. They were stern, unbending, and at times grimly righteous to the point of fanaticism. Right or wrong, and they were both, they made a civilization where none had existed before.

It was inevitable that Bill Oury should make enemies. His service as sheriff of Pima County brought them forward. The elections of 1874, in which Bill stood for sheriff, were rough, as always. He had had a year in which to make mistakes in his office, as well as to run an effective and successful one. His enemies took minute note of his shortcomings and tried to lay him low with charges before the electorate. They failed, as he was re-elected, but the failure was not for lack of trying, as the statement offered below will show. The statement was made in 1874 (exact date undisclosed) by Col. James H. Toole, J. E. McCaffry, George Cooler, and L. W. Carr. It is titled "To the Citizens and Taxpayers of the County of Pima," and comes from the rare document files of the Arizona Pioneer Historical Society in Tucson.[11]

William S. Oury having announced himself as a people's candidate for re-election to the office of Sheriff of Pima County, it is well at this time to inquire on what grounds he claims a re-election, and if he has done his duty honestly, truly, and faithfully.

He presented to the Board of Equalization an Assessment Roll for this year amounting to $677,683.81; to this Roll the Board added $32,998; property assessed after the Roll was in, amounted to $33,786. Total subsequent additions, $66,784. Total amount of taxable property as adjusted $744,467.81. Had Mr. Oury made a fair, just, and legal assessment of the property, the Assessment Roll would have footed up nearly One Million Dollars, and the tax rate instead of being $2.45 would have been $1.75, or at most $2 on the $100.

The law requires that the Assessor shall demand from each person and firm a statement under oath or affirmation of all property owned or controlled by such person or firm, and gives authority to enforce such demand. In this respect Mr. Oury has wholly failed to perform his duty, consequently the whole assessment is certainly irregular and possibly illegal.

He has assessed Ranches belonging to his friends as low as $200 or $300 each, while they were held by their owners at $6,000 to $7,000 each; and there are a great number of lots and blocks in Tucson not found on the Assessment Roll. The mismanagement of his Assessment Roll for the year 1873 can be overlooked on account of his inexperience, but no excuse can be pleaded by him in extenuation of his gross negligence and culpable carelessness in making the assessment this year. His duties are of the most plain and positive character; they are also clearly defined by law and should have been performed without mistake.

It was a well known fact that Charles V. Moore's name was not on the Assessment Roll, although Mr. Oury was using one of his horses valued at $200 or $250; and he had other property valued at $1000 to $2000.

He has allowed by his carelessness more prisoners to escape from the County Jail than any of his predecessors, and has recaptured less. He has allowed the Chain-Gang to be worked on private property, building fences, grading lots, and digging ditches at an expense to the taxpayers of from $6 to $10 per day without a dollar being collected for their services. Having from 5 to 7 County prisoners in charge, he has allowed the Court-house to be kept in such a filthy condition that it has been unfit for Judge, Jury or Spectator to sit on the benches; he allowed his deputy, Van Alstine, to make a demand on Governor Safford for a reward for simply doing his duty in arresting Wm. Hall, charged with the crime of murder, and he himself has refused to execute a criminal warrant placed in his hands because he would be compelled to travel 18 miles to the Point of the Mountain, and said he would receive no pay for it.

There should have been at least eight hundred Poll Taxes of $3 each collected last year, for seven hundred and nineteen votes were cast in this county when Mr. Oury was elected, yet last year only 264 Poll Taxes were collected, leaving uncollected at least 536 — amounting to $1,340, or more than two thirds of the whole amount.

This year he has done still worse, for while he should have collected 1,000 Poll Taxes, he has collected but 175, and the time for collection has expired.

By this unpardonable negligence, this County has lost $2,063.50, and this, too, after he has been repeatedly admonished by the Board of Supervisors of his duty in that respect.

If Mr. Oury had attended to his official duties with half the energy he has shown in electioneering, this County would have been in a much better financial condition than it now is, and Mr. Oury would have been re-elected without opposition.

Disturbances of the peace have occurred many times in the presence of Mr. Oury and his deputies, yet neither he nor they have been known to make an arrest as Peace Officers without a warrant, and this is violation of their plain duties.

In the year 1864 there was placed in the hands of Mr. Oury 105 muskets and 18,000 rounds of ammunition belong to the Territory of Arizona, to be distributed amongst the inhabitants of this County for their protection against hostile Apache Indians. Regardless of the loss of life and destruction of

*property that might be occasioned by his act, he sold the arms in Sonora for
$2000 in gold and kept the money.*

*After repeated investigations by different Legislatures, and the passage
of laws to compel him to disgorge some portion of this money, $1050 in paper
was collected from him in 1869 by J. B. Allen, then Territorial Treasurer. The
then value of this sum was less than $800 in gold so that to-day Mr. Oury
should be fairly indebted to this Territory in the sum of $1200 gold, with ten
years interest, and interest on $800 gold for five years.*

*In view of the foregoing facts showing malfeasance, misfeasance and
nonfeasance in office by Mr. Oury, with a reckless disregard on his part of
the rights of others, the interest of justice and the credit of the County demand
that he be no longer allowed to hold an office he has shown himself so unworthy
to fill — even if he be allowed to go in other respects unwhipt of Justice.*

These charges are quite serious and demand an accounting. Oury
is charged not only with ineptitude and malfeasance, but with flagrant
dishonesty, collusion, and theft. Perhaps Bill looked upon the slurs as
inspired wholly by political jealousy, and decided to let it go at that. There
was no accounting. Files of the Tucson newspapers for 1874 show no
evidence to substantiate Toole's charges, nor do they contain any Oury
statement of explanation or rebuttal. Records in the County Assessor's
office show the assessments made by Oury on Tucson property, but it is
impossible to tell which of the low assessments were made on properties
belonging to his friends. Presumably he was "friendly" with just about
everyone, as almost all of the assessments in the book are low ones.

On the charge of permitting prisoners to escape, he later said: "Let
the bastards go — it saves the county money to get rid of them."[12] The
charge of theft of 105 muskets and 18,000 rounds of ammunition does
not appear in any other paper than this one made by Toole and his friends,
nor have I been able to substantiate it in the "repeated investigations by
different legislatures."

It is possible that the enmity displayed by Toole was brought about
solely by political differences. Bill was in every sense of the word a Southern Democrat, an "un-reconstructed" rebel. His possessions were confiscated by the invading Union Army in 1862. His horses were taken from
him to serve the troops of Carleton's California Column, and his "History
of Arizona" was so edited and cut up by Col. Joseph R. West as to be
rendered useless. Toole had come to Arizona as a second lieutenant in
"G" Company of the Fifth U. S. Volunteer Infantry. Later, he was
detached to serve in the Quartermaster Department in Tucson. On being
mustered out of the service after the war, he made Tucson his home. In
Bill's eyes, he was all "Yankee."

The two men never hit it off. Toole engaged in business with Hudson
and Company and prospered. He was considered as one of the most

successful and influential business men in the territory. Ultimately, Hudson and Company failed, and although Toole had nothing to do with the failure, much feeling against him was generated throughout the Territory. Blameless, the failure nonetheless preyed upon his mind. In a moment of tragic despondency he shot himself in a sleeping coach near Trinidad, Colorado, while enroute to Tucson. In the usual flowery (but appealing) language of the day, the eulogy in the Tucson *Daily Star* concluded:

Whatever may have been his faults, let the mantle of charity cover them, and his many virtues be only remembered, for he was a man among men, honored and beloved wherever known.[13]

Not only was Bill successful in his quest for re-election in 1874; in the same issue of the *Star* carrying the news of Toole's death, he was listed as a candidate for supervisor on the Democratic ticket. He was elected in that race too. In spite of diatribe and charge, he flourished like the green bay tree.

A few years later, one S. W. Carpenter took a crack at Bill in more indignant and colorful manner even than George Toole. Carpenter's salvo was continued in "a card," printed in the *Arizona Star* on October 3, 1878. It read:

"Whom the gods would destroy they first make mad" is an adage demonstrated in almost every act of retributive justice, & retribution is as sure to overtake the false traducer & maligner . . . as surely as there exists a just God above us.

For years Mr. W. S. Oury has enjoyed the political confidence of a number of our best citizens, both Mexican & American and might still continue to retain it, had not selfishness & ingratitude unmasked him.

That I may not be classed among traducers I am prepared to prove every assertion I make, & will also prove that it is with a sort of pity & contempt devoid of malice that I am compelled in self-defense *to* refute *the accusations of this slanderer.*

My record is open to criticism, & Mr. Oury has the right to criticize fairly, but not in the cutthroat manner he has adopted.

I am a poor critic myself, but for once I am compelled to give Uncle Wm *a lesson on criticism, taking himself for the subject, and confine myself to two simple propositions, viz: what Mr. Oury would have the people think him to be, & what Mr. Oury's acts prove him to be.*

In 1861, Mr. Oury would have the people think him a secessionist: It was popular.

In 1862, the federal troops were in possession. Secession was not popular & Mr. Oury disposed of all his confederate stock & would have the federal officers think him to be a Union man, & so far succeeded that he received a military appointment as recorder from Maj. D. Ferguson.

In 1869, Pima Co. had a very popular sheriff & the office was considered lucrative. Mr. Oury would have the people think that he loved this popular sheriff very much & would send him to Congress . . . that his real object was not to have the lucrative office for himself. In the fall of 1872, by traducing & vilifying this former friend, . . . Mr. Oury became sheriff.

In 1874, Mr. Oury would have the people think that the salvation of Arizona depended on sending Mr. Stevens to Congress . . . that he was acting disinterestedly and that his real motive was not to secure the support and money of Mr. Stevens' friends to keep him (Oury) in office. This was accomplished however, and Mr. Oury gave public expression of his gratitude & fidelity to his benefactor. But in the very next campaign, like the thoughtless bird, "pecked the hand that fed it."

In 1875, Mr. Oury would have the people think that "some are born great," others achieve greatness, but that he, in particular, would not have greatness thrust upon him. The people took him at his word and did not nominate him supervisor, & this shattered his hopes of future advancement.

He repented and began to demonstrate that the grapes were not so sour after all. He fawned, intrigued, preached political economy & petitioned himself finally into the Board of Supervisors which he seems to have absorbed into his own identity.

Clothed again with "brief authority," Mr. Oury would have the people think that he studies economy, that individuals have no rights whatever, that Pima Co. & the Democratic party are omnipotent, & that he is Pima Co. & the Democratic party.

His economy consists in driving to suicide an unfortunate Capt. of the Fed'l army who served with distinction during the war, Mr. Oury calling him a refugee from Sonora.

When more recently appealed to in behalf of poor George Esslinger, his reply was: "He is a worthless scoundrel, let him die in the gutter like a dog." Poor George was an industrious & harmless citizen, but unfortunately a periodic inebriate, who had no political influence outside of his individual vote. Poor George did die, but not in the gutter thanks to the magistrate, C. H. Meyers, who humanely sent him to the hospital the evening before his death.

Mr. Oury would have the people think that he is the Democratic messiah of Arizona, and in the most undemocratic style voted himself into an imaginable chair — the chair was too ethereal, & when Mr. Oury attempted to sit down, he hurt himself.

This is fair and impartial criticism supported by facts, without descending to the level of my traducer, who is now hurling Billingsgate broadcast throughout the country. Let the impartial public judge us!

S. W. Carpenter.[14]

The cause of Oury's quarrel with Carpenter is not known. The issues of the *Star* in the weeks preceding and following the appearance of the "card" carry no news of any bitterness between the two men. Obviously, Bill had raked Carpenter over the coals for some reason or other, and Carpenter was lashing back. Carpenter was wrong, however, in labelling Bill a turncoat. Oury was born, lived, and died a Southern rebel. It was true that he took Major Ferguson's appointment in 1862; he could do little else. The Union army had taken away his possessions, livestock, and left him standing as bare as a sundried bone. He had a family to support, and he did what he had to do; he took a temporary job from the conqueror, a thing done by many hundreds of thousands of people in similar circumstances since the beginning of time.

An Unfortunate Man

The Captain Ledyard whom Bill "drove to suicide" was an unfortunate man, although Bill's public censure of him was no more acrimonious that that of many others of the period. He had served with distinction in the Civil War, taking the sword of his own brother in surrender at Petersburg. He was related to General Irvin McDowell and detested him. At a McDowell dinner in San Francisco after the war, Ledyard was called upon to propose a toast. He said: "Here's to the hero of Bull Run!" This was in mocking derision of McDowell's rout at First Manassas by General P. G. T. Beauregard. Although McDowell had gone into the battle with some 35,000 men, as opposed to Beauregard's 16,000, his losses were almost a third again as many (2896 as against 1982), and he was sent reeling back in the direction of Washington, amidst panicked civilian onlookers who had come out to see a smashing Union victory. Ledyard had refused to salute a superior officer who he felt had cheated him out of a deserved command. As a consequence, he was sent to an isolated post in Arizona, and shortly thereafter resigned from the Army. He drifted to Sonora where he took one thing and then another, and married a Mexican woman.

There may be more than just a little truth in Carpenter's assessment of Oury's feelings as a Democrat. He almost always used the word "black" as the first portion of a hyphenated word in speaking of Republicans. He always ran for office on the Democratic ticket. When his son Frank was born in 1865, Bill ran down Calle Real shouting: "I have a son, a son! Another Democrat in the family, by God!" Later, in speaking of Frank's impending graduation from the University of California (in 1886), Bill said: "I have but one son and he is of age today, which means another Democrat; he will never flinch from the old party."[15]

A man of such strong and implacable will as Bill Oury would perhaps even manufacture enemies where none existed before, especially in the engagements of public life. Right or wrong, Bill believed in what he said and did, which is something more than many men can say, whatever the issue or whenever the times.

CHAPTER 25

A Walk Around Town

As WAS INEVITABLE, the tempo of life for Bill Oury had to slow down.
On a bright morning anytime in the late 1870's or early 1880's, he might
take a stroll about town for exercise or pleasure. According to his grandson he did this frequently, and was a well-known figure to the early-bird
shopkeepers of the neighborhood. He saw a Tucson which was a far different place then than now. Some of the old buildings still stand, although
most have disappeared long since.

Coming out of his house on South Main Street, Bill might see the
Mexican circus setting up for the afternoon and evening performance. It
usually performed in a vacant courtyard directly across the street from
his house just behind the Occidental Hotel. He might stand at the Jackson Street entrance to the courtyard and watch the acrobats warming
up, or see the puppeteers practising with Punch and Judy. Later, in the
evening, he might take some of the neighborhood children to see the
show, which was illuminated by stalks of burning cholla cactus placed in
rows near the stage.[1]

On the Streets of Tucson

If he turned north, as he usually did, he would pass by several stores on his way to Levin's Park at the foot of Pennington. He might stop and chat for awhile with Miguel Roca in Roca's store just across the street from the Tivoli Theatre, a site later occupied by Reuben Gold's Furniture Store.

After leaving Roca, Bill would go on past the White House (dry goods), Lord and Williams, the Tucson *Citizen* office, and perhaps stop for a few moments with William Zeckendorf at his general store on the corner of Pennington and Pearl, an establishment later occupied by the Tidmark Engineering Company, "specialists in heating and cooling," a specialty unknown in Bill's day.

Crossing the street, Bill might tarry awhile with Carlos Tully or Estevan Ochoa, and then go on over to the Cosmopolitan Hotel for a cup of coffee with Hiram Stevens. This hostelry was known at one time or another as Hodges House, Levin's Hotel, and the Orndorff Hotel.[2] In its day it served many famous people, among them General Sherman, General Crook, General Miles, Charles Poston, Leonard Wood, and other notables of the era. Later its site became the city employee's parking lot.

After coffee, Bill might swing west and check on his Chinatown property. Here, where Calle del Correo (later Pearl Street) met Calle de las Milpas, were an opium den and a gambling parlor. Both were located amidst a veritable warren of Chinese "rooms," many housing six or eight coolie laborers. Most of the Chinese seemed to gravitate to this northwestern section of town, although later, when the railroad was being built, they put up a cluster of clapboard shacks north of Levin's Gardens. In those days an opium den went relatively unnoticed; it was simply a fact of life and did not cause civic furor.

Nearby was the old Overland Stage building, on the corner of Pearl and Calle del Arroyo. Bill would pay it "the tribute of a passing sigh"; it had been his "home" from 1858 to 1861. He missed the excitement and tumult of the place.

Continuing west, Bill would enter Levin's Park, strolling leisurely past the octagonal bandstand, and the brewery. In 1880, the park afforded a vista of quiet greenery, later giving way to the clinical austerity of the Arizona State Employment Service Bureau.

Coming back on to Calle del Correo, he would cross the acequia at the footbridge at Calle de la Misión, or at the foot of Calle de la Alegría (Congress Street). Here he might see the Mexican and Indian *lavanderas* hard at work washing on the banks of the open ditch. Or if it happened

SOUTH MAIN STREET. Coming out of his house in Tucson, "Bill might see the Mexican circus setting up for afternoon and evening performance. The show was illuminated by stalks of burning cholla cactus placed near the stage."

to be on San Juan's Day (June 24th), the irrigation stream would be the center of great activity and merriment. Bands and small orchestras played along its banks then, children jumped into the cooling waters shouting and squealing. As the day wore on, all would engage in games and contests.

Re-crossing the *acequia,* Bill would pass by Charley Etchell's blacksmith shop, and continue on home past Davis' tin and metal shop, and the house of Joaquín Téllez. This stroll would have been a short one, punctuated with pleasant stops along the way. Had Bill wanted brisk exercise, he might have gone on along North Main to Washington, past the E. N. Fish house, the Stevens place, and over to La Plaza de las Armas. Here, a few feet from the jail, was the place where the vigilantes had strung up the killers of Vincente Hernández and his wife, just a few years before — while Bill was sheriff.

Changes With the Times

Bill would not recognize Plaza de las Armas in modern times, with the city hall there and only a memorial plaque to Father Kino to turn memory to the past.

Bill was always fond of Bob Leatherwood, the "Little Giant" from North Carolina, and although the two were over a quarter of a century apart in age they seemed to hit it off handsomely, both being persistently

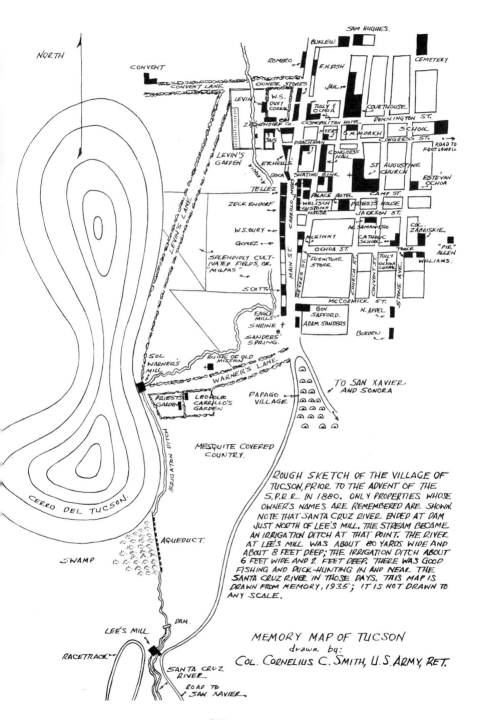

NORTH

SAM HUGHES.

BUKLEW

ROMERO

CONVENT

CONVENT LANE.

CHINESE STORES

LEVIN

W.S.
OURY
CORRAL

ZECKENDORF CO.

E.N.FISH

JAIL

TULLY &
OCHOA

COURTHOUSE

CEMETERY

PENNINGTON ST.

COSMOPOLITAN HOTEL

MYERS

SAIS

DRACHMAN

C.M.ALDRICH

CONGRESS ST.

SCHOOL

ROAD TO
FORT LOWELL

LEVIN'S
GARDEN

ETCHELLS

ROCA

CONGRESS
HALL

SKATING RINK

ST AUGUSTINE
CHURCH

TELLEZ

ZECKENDORF

PALACE HOTEL

CAMP ST.

ESTEVAN
OCHOA

WELISCH
CUSTOMS
HOUSE

PRIESTS HOUSE

JACKSON ST.

W.S.OURY

GOMEZ

McKINNY

M.SAMANIEGO

CATHOLIC
SCHOOL

COL.
ZABRISKIE

"PIE"
ALLEN

SPLENDIDLY CULT-
IVATED FIELDS, OR
"MILPAS"

OCHOA ST.

FURNITURE
STORE

TULLY
OCHOA
CORRAL

TOOLE

WILLIAMS.

SCOTT.

McCORMICK ST.

GOV.
SAFFORD.

N. APPEL

EAGLE
MILLS

SHRINE

SANDERS'
SPRING.

ADAM SANDERS

BORDEN

SOL
WARNER'S
MILL

RUINS OF OLD
MISSION

WARNER'S LANE.

PRIESTS
GARDEN

LEOPOLDO
CARRILLO'S
GARDEN

PAPAGO
VILLAGE

TO SAN XAVIER
AND SONORA

MESQUITE COVERED
COUNTRY.

CERRO DEL TUCSON.

AQUEDUCT.

SWAMP

ROUGH SKETCH OF THE VILLAGE OF
TUCSON, PRIOR TO THE ADVENT OF THE
S.P.R.R. IN 1880. ONLY PROPERTIES WHOSE
OWNER'S NAMES ARE REMEMBERED ARE SHOWN.
NOTE THAT SANTA CRUZ RIVER ENDED AT DAM
JUST NORTH OF LEE'S MILL. THE STREAM BECAME
AN IRRIGATION DITCH AT THAT POINT. THE RIVER
AT LEE'S MILL WAS ABOUT 80 YARDS WIDE AND
ABOUT 8 FEET DEEP; THE IRRIGATION DITCH ABOUT
6 FEET WIDE AND 2 FEET DEEP. THERE WAS GOOD
FISHING AND DUCK-HUNTING IN AND NEAR THE
SANTA CRUZ RIVER IN THOSE DAYS. THIS MAP IS
DRAWN FROM MEMORY, 1935; IT IS NOT DRAWN TO
ANY SCALE.

DAM.

LEE'S MILL

RACETRACK

SANTA CRUZ
RIVER

ROAD TO
SAN XAVIER.

MEMORY MAP OF TUCSON
drawn by:
COL. CORNELIUS C. SMITH, U.S.ARMY, RET.

217

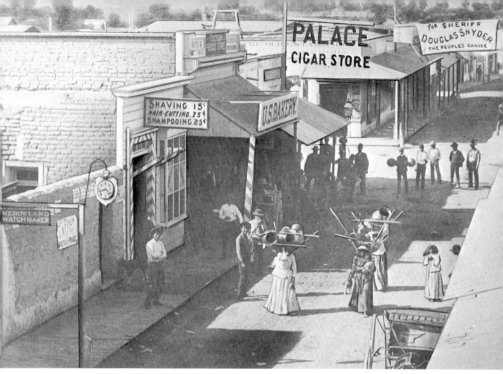

— Arizona Pioneers' Historical Society

CONGRESS STREET, Tucson. A stroll down the main thoroughfare, in the years before 1900, would lead to a center of services and supplies needed by the townspeople: fifteen-cent shaves, bakery goods, cigars, and the indispensable water-seller of a desert community.

Confederate. Bill liked to stop at Bob's corral, not only to talk about the war, but because he liked the manly cut of the place — the horses stamping in their stalls, the drovers herding teams in and out, the creak of ungreased axles, and the smell of mesquite fires. The Pima County Courthouse replaced the corral, and the exhaust fumes of cars the pungent wood smoke.

Leaving Bob's place, Bill would go on down to Meyer Street and head south. It would be too early to drop in at Hand and Foster's Saloon, but he might drop in at "Greek Alex's" for a haircut, and passing Mesilla Street, he might well see some of the town's more venal characters sneaking out of Big Carmel's place, or Apache Luisa's after an all-night debauch. There were a number of these houses in the Old Pueblo, some of them on Maiden Lane (Calle de la India Triste), and others sprinkled around here and there about the town. One easy-virtued proprietress was named Refugia Rivera, popularly known as "La Churea" — the roadrunner.

Among the most active crib districts was "Gay Alley," a short street running south from Ochoa, one block east of Meyer. A move was made in 1891 to place all of the houses here. This succeeded largely, although some of the madams refused to go along with the idea. In 1916, the county attorney, George O. Helzinger, tried to put the ladies out of business on grounds that there was a Catholic school not 400 feet away. The street was closed to "illicit traffic" in 1917.

Bill would continue down Meyer street past the little restaurant with the improbable name, "Maison Parée," past another brace of saloons, a gunsmith's shop, and an assayer's hole-in-the-wall before turning right on Jackson. He liked to drink and he liked to gamble, and there was no end of places where he might do both. The saloons run by Hand and Foster and by Charley Meyers were his favorites, although he would often drop in at any little hole-in-the-wall.

If he sauntered eastward from his home, Bill would come to Church Plaza within several minutes. Here was the lovely old San Augustine Church and the Sisters of St. Joseph School. Standing there in the square he could hear the piping voices of the children, droning like bees in an earnest recitation of the morning's lesson from the catechism.

He might walk across the street for a chat with Bishop Salpointe, or perhaps drop in on Dr. Handy for a political argument. On one such occasion, the two became so excited that they had to go into a saloon for a drink to cool down. There were a couple of pretty good saloons on the ground floor of the Arizona Daily Star building too. On occasion, Bill would drop in on L. C. Hughes at the paper and the two would go downstairs for a snort.

Bill might have had business at the Territorial Capitol Building on Ochoa Street at South Stone, later replaced by the Marist College and the Marian Youth Center.

Another time Bill might get behind a pair of his horses and take a buggy-ride around town, to Silver Lake or Elysian Grove, past the Wishing Shrine, Eagle Mills, and Adam Sanders Springs. Bill had a pet bear in Elysian Grove, although where and how he got it no one knows.

He might ride also out past the ruins of the old mission, out to Warner's Mill, stopping to reminisce for a while with Sol, or take the road to Lee's Mill where the Santa Cruz was dammed and the clear water was broad and deep. He could fish there, or try to shoot a duck or two in the marshes under El Cerro del Tucson ("A" Mountain).

In the News

Bill took many such walks and drives in the crisp morning air of Tucson in the late 1870's. It was a gay and fascinating town, not only in its physical layout, but in its lively character as daily expressed in the news items which ran the gamut from tragedy to pure comedy, and pulled

out stops all along the way. In reporting upon the formation of a cremation society in 1874, the Arizona *Citizen* said:

*... A meeting of those in favor of burning instead of burying the dead was
held at the rooms of the YMCA. About 25 persons were present. Like many
reforms, this one stops short of much good it might accomplish . . . . What a
purification of society it would be if on every occasion of burning a good
dead man, there could be thrown in a bad living one.*[4]

A three-line item in the same paper gives a tip-off on the casual construction of Tucson homes in 1874.

*Early this week was notable for heavy rains and leaky roofs in Tucson. Very
few drops fell last Saturday, and Sunday was misty with a drizzle now and
then. Monday night rain fell here in torrents, and nearly every roof in town
leaked, more or less.*[5]

For those interested in taking home fresh meat for the table, the
Citizen advised: "The Papago bucks are bringing in considerable veni-
son, and the squaws are daily on the streets with loads of new ollas."
Moderns concerned with water problems may ponder this little item:

*The people of Tucson are reminded that Martin Touhey delivers clear fresh,
spring water once or more a day at a very moderate price. He is punctual as
a clock, and delivers at house to suit customers. Call him for water and par-
ticulars.*[6]

Down in Tombstone, the weekly *Epitaph* was carrying this little gem
in the 80's. Dr. Salfield must have had a pretty good thing going, as his
home office was listed as being at 16 Kearney Street, San Francisco. Nothing like advertising across the country.

DR. SALFIELD'S REJUVENATOR

*This great strengthening remedy and nerve tonic is the legitimate result of
over 20 years of practical experience, and cures with unfailing certainity —
nerves and physical disability, seminal weakness, spermatorrhea, emissions,
impotency, exhausted vitality, premature decline, and loss of manhood —
from whatever cause produced . . . . Price $2.50 per bottle.*[7]

The good doctor stated his case admirably; one can just see him leer-
ing over the shining little bottles of snake oil.

In 1884, the Acme Restaurant at number 11 Mesilla Street (between
Meyer and Main) was advertising "good meals for twenty five cents —
better than any other place in Tucson; try us and be your own judge."[8]

In Yuma, Goldman and Company mixed business with politics in
a poetic outburst.

WILLIAM SANDERS OURY. "Born in one of the oldest states of the American Union, reared amid culture & Christianity with habits and inclinations eminently fitting one for social life, at the very dawn of manhood, as if impelled by the invisible hand of destiny, I was drawn by a force absolutely irresistible to the frontier . . . " (From the address by William Sanders Oury upon the arrival of the first Southern Pacific Railroad train in Tucson, March 20, 1880.)

Great excitment does prevail now
Over presidental contest
Lord, have mercy, and assist thou,
Democrats to gain conquest.
Many years they've been waiting
And great patience have they shown
Now good fortune, crown their efforts,

And send HANCOCK to Washington
Next in weight, comes our CLOTHING,
DRY GOODS, GROCERIES do we keep here.

Come to us before you're voting,
Our stock cannot be beat here,
Manifold is our selection
Patrons do not fail to call
All our good bear close inspention
Now is the time their price did fall,
Young ones, old ones, please come all![9]

Yours truly,
Goldman & Co.

For President   W. S. Hancock
For V. P.   Wm. H. English
For Congress   Granville H. Oury
                 (of Pinal County)

It is noted that Goldman and Company backed Grant Oury for Congress. One may wonder what the doggerel did for sales, or what finally became of Goldman and Company. As for Grant he was elected to Congress.

CHAPTER 26

The Later Years

BILL'S PARTICIPATION IN POLITICS continued as the new decade (1880's) began. During the first week in October, 1879, W. J. Osborn resigned as clerk of the Board of Supervisors in Tucson, and Bill was appointed in his place. The little notice in the *Daily Star* carrying the news of the appointment described the post as "the most important of any in the county, requiring the strictest integrity, and the best of good business and clerical qualifications — all of which Mr. Oury possesses."[1] The job was scarcely worth the praise. Actually, it consisted mainly in taking care of the correspondence of the board.

Bill was out of town when the appointment was made and, came home to find that he had literally "fallen" into the job. Of his trip, the *Star* said:

Uncle Billy Oury returned home yesterday from his San Francisco trip, twenty years younger than when he went away.

Bill made scome comments on the journey, causing the *Star* to report:

San Francisco is ablaze in enthusiasm over Ulysses. The general, however, took the whole business in his usual stoical way. . . . The washout of the railroad extended 37 miles, which when bolstered up, required seven hours to pass over. Uncle Billy thinks the road will not be completed for six months, and when it does come it will remain until the AT and SF reaches here. The Southern Pacific is short of iron. It is thought there is not more than 20 miles of rail at Casa Grande. Mr. Oury placed his son Frank in St. Mary's College, which is under the supervision of Father Justice, acknowledged as one of the greatest teachers in the country.[4]

Frank Oury went on from St. Mary's to the University of California at Berkeley, and was graduated three years later. Not so very many years later he lay dead of an assassin's bullet in the little border town of Arivaca near Tucson.

When the Southern Pacific Railroad did reach Tucson on March 20, 1880, the Honorable Estevan Ochoa presented the president, Charles Crocker, with a handmade silver spike, from silver bullion out of the Tough Nut mine in Tombstone. Bill Oury then gave the principal address to a large crowd. His exact words were these:

Gentlemen, I would that I were possessed of the control of language to properly, and as I would wish, respond to the toast which has just been given. It has been said that "out of the fullness of the heart, the mouth speaketh." To me this condition does not apply, for with a heart full to overflowing, the tongue fails to perform its office. The word pioneer brings to my recollection scenes & reminiscences spanning almost half a century inseparably linked with friendships dear and companionships so unselfish, and ties so binding that death only can sunder them.

Born in one of the oldest states of the American Union, reared amid culture & christianity with habits and inclinations eminently fitting one for social life, at the very dawn of manhood, as if impelled by the invisible hand of destiny, I was drawn by a force absolutely irresistible to the frontier; and the year 1835, and the 19th of my age, found me linked to the destinies of the Lone Star Republic. To her service in the companionship of such heroes as Crockett, Fannin, Milam, Bowie, Johnson, Houston, Travis, and a host such as the world has seldom known, the best years of my young life were freely given. For 13 years on the frontiers of Texas and ending with the termination of the Mexican War, my only associates and friends were frontiersmen, who carried their lives, as it were, in their hands ever ready to surrender them to their country's call.

In 1849 the marvelous tales of the golden weather of California reached the Atlantic Coast, and spread with lightning speed through the whole land, and again the services of the pioneer were called into requisition. Of the fidelity with which they performed their duty to the Golden State, many who now surround me are living witnesses. Again in 1856, after the purchase of this territory from Mexico, and when California no longer required their services, a noble band of pioneers disregarding every obstacle of sand, desert, alkali plain, and fiendish Apaches took up the line of march for Arizona.

Those who are now alive of that brave and generous host may be numbered without exhausting the fingers of both hands, and the history of those who have crossed over the dark river may be summed up in these sad words — their bones are scattered like milestones along the course of the Southern Pacific Railroad from the western to the eastern boundry of Arizona — peace to their ashes.

To me, as one of the oldest residents of this territory has been assigned the pleasant duty of welcoming to our midst the advent of the iron horse which has been today accomplished. I but reiterate the sentiment of all my old companions when I say thrice welcome to this so recently a terra incognita.

The men whose indomitable energy, pluck, and capital have pushed the iron wheels of progress to our door realizing today the anticipations of a quarter of a century, have placed us in direct communication with the whole civilized world. And permit me to assure you that we all desire that your brightest hopes of remuneration may be speedily realized, and that however great may be your reward for this apparently reckless expenditure of toil and money, no old Arizonan will ever begrudge it, for the boon you have now bestowed upon us cannot be measured by mere dollars and cents.

To all of us there remain some unbroken links in the chain of friendship, and blood, which binds us to the people of the Eastern states where most of us were born. Many of us have been for long years absent from the land of our birth, and the parental roof which covered and protected our helpless infancy. To you, gentlemen, we are indebted for the opportunity now afforded of speedily and cheaply visiting 'the old folks at home,' and the scenes of childhood's happiest hours, memories ever cherished and kept green in every manly heart, and only surrendered with life's last pulsation.

The pioneers of Arizona have spent the best years of their lives in preparing the way for that progress which we now see consummated, our life and death struggle with the ruthless Apache to retain a foothold upon the land of our adoption, running through many dark years is a thing of the past. Our mission is ended today. Here there arises the question, what are you to do with us? The enterprise of such men as now surround me has penetrated every corner of our broad land, and we now have no frontier to which the pioneer may flee to avoid the tramp of civilized progress. Moreover, the weight of years has fallen upon us, consequently the few remaining years which the Divine Master may have in store for us must be spent amongst you; and in the whirl of excitement incident to the race after the precious treasure embedded in our mountain ranges — our last request is that you kindly avoid trampling in the dust the few remaining moments of the first American settlement of Arizona.[3]

After the coming of the railroad, Bill continued in municipal and political affairs, and often appeared in print. He reminisced in the press on the political fortunes of his friend, C. D. Poston, the "Father of Arizona" and threw his weight in on the Tucson side in the dispute over location of the Territorial capital. He also signed his name to typically bombastic remarks appearing in the daily papers on Governor McCormick.

Bill liked Poston, but his low esteem of McCormick is evident in the acidulous remarks made in this statement. Before presenting these observations, it will be well to give a little background on the political picture of the era.

Politics of the Times

In July, 1864, Governor John C. Goodwin, residing at Fort Whipple, called for an election of legislative members and delegates to the federal congress. Poston was selected as the territory's delegate, and eighteen members were elected to the Territorial House, and nine to the Senate (called the "Council"). This new group comprised the First Territorial Legislature, and first met as a body in Prescott on September 26, 1864.

One of the first acts of the legislature was to pass the famous Howell Code of Laws, a code controlling the legislative granting of divorces within the newly created territory. To the chagrin of the large Catholic community in Tucson, several prominent persons availed themselves of the code's provisions at once; years later, Governor A. P. K. Safford himself obtained a divorce under the provisions of the code (during the incumbency of the Seventh Legislature). The Howell Code was "bad enough" for Arizonans. The famous Omnibus Divorce Bill passed by the Tenth Legislature was worse. In signing this bill, Governor John C. Frémont dissolved the marriages of fifteen couples.[4]

Bill, along with practically every other citizen of Tucson, wanted to see that city the Territorial capital. The clamor made by him and his friends was so insistent that after four sessions in Prescott, the legislature passed a bill removing the capital from Prescott to Tucson. A great cry arose, not over the move, but because the price for it was too high. It was charged that Governor McCormick had thrown in with the Tucson group only after its delegates had pledged to send him to Congress. The capital was moved to Tucson, then moved back to Prescott, and the Tucsonians were left "holding the bag." McCormick went to Congress, serving there from 1869 to 1875.

By Bill's standards, McCormick was a johnny-come-lately. He had been a newspaper correspondent with the Army of the Potomac in the early days of the Civil War. President Lincoln appointed him Secretary of Arizona Territory in 1863 — in the first Territorial Bill, which ironically had named Tucson as the Territorial capital. McCormick established two papers in the Territory: The Arizona *Miner* in Prescott in 1864; the Arizona *Citizen* in Tucson in 1870.[5]

In giving his reminiscences of the shenanigans in the capital-Congress proposition, Bill was answering an anonymous author who had written a piece entitled "Some Questions" (printed only a few days before on May 10th). In characteristic disdain for anyone ashamed to sign his name to a document of faith, and in his usual bombastic style, Bill wrote:

The *Daily* Citizen *of May 10th publishes an article headed "Some Questions," in which the writer, for lack of manliness . . . takes refuge behind the anonymous title of "Inquisitive" to relieve himself of a portion of the bile with which his frame is charged. . . . These (inquiries) are addressed to Hon. C. D. Poston, Arizona's first delegate to Congress. The first is: "Do you not remember that you were supported by nearly all the federal officers sent out to organize the Territorial government? To this . . . we answer emphatically, "No!" Mr. Poston was elected in spite of their combined efforts to defeat him.*

. . . Now we come to the McCormick trip in connection with the Howell Code, and schemes of private profit and aggrandizement. During his many trips to Washington for conferences with Poston, he (McCormick) learned that it was the intention of the latter to return to Arizona and stand for re-election to Congress. He at once interposed the objection that it was a long and painful journey and a useless expenditure of time and money; that Poston would be of more service by remaining in Washington and leaving him (McCormick) to attend to his interests in connection with the return to Congress. In an evil hour, Poston consented to this arrangement; not, as "Inquisitive" says, a few days before the election of '65, but in good time to influence that event by the following publication in his own personal sheet, the Arizona Miner: *"I am authorized to say that Col. C. D. Poston will not be candidate for re-election to Congress from this Territory." In order to understand how such perfidy could be accomplished without detection, it is necessary to understand that then there was no regular mail service in the Territory; communications were so slow and uncertain as to require three or four months to get news from Arizona in the East. The result was that Governor Goodwin was elected to Congress before Poston knew he had not been a candidate, the act having been accomplished by such treachery as would put Judas Iscariot to shame.*

In the ensuing election, Poston was a candidate, and came to the Territory to make canvass in person, to save himself from his whilom friends. But the people of the Territory were so much exasperated by his having entered into alliance with the vile crew of carpet-baggers that they would not support him. He was defeated by a carpet-bagger, Coles Bashford, in one of the most disgraceful elections ever held in this or any country. . . . At the Calabasas precinct where there were only seven legal votes, over 125 were polled, composed of soldiers and "Sonorians," affording ample reason for Poston's remark that they "voted like sheep."

. . . McCormick, by cheating Tucson out of the capital . . . had incurred the ill-will of this section of the Territory. As it contained a large portion of the voting population, all hope of accomplishing the most cherished desire of his heart (a seat in Congress) was impossible unless he might conciliate the people of this section. This could only be effected by one of those base acts of ingratitude and perfidy which characterized his whole career in Arizona, and was attained as follows:

He began by communicating with some of our prominent citizens, insinuating that upon certain conditions the removal of the capital from Tucson to Prescott could be accomplished. These conditions were . . . two; first, a pledge from our people to send him to Congress; second, the purchase of three members of the legislature necessary to give us a majority of that body. With shame, we confess that both propositions were accepted by our people.

. . . Upon the arrival of our delegation in Prescott, they at once waited upon his Excellency, Governor McCormick, and learned that the three necessary to make the majority had been seen, the specific amount in greenbacks agreed upon, and the conditions precedent to the vote would be placed where there would be no chance to go back on them (the three). This matter being satisfactorily arranged, it was necessary only to introduce the bill for removal of the capital from Prescott to Tucson. This was done, and everything was lovely . . . . One thing remained; the bill required the approval of McCormick. The people of Prescott had reason to believe that his interests were so identified with theirs that he would veto the bill; many anxious visits were paid to the gubernatorial mansion in that behalf.[6]

Here Bill veers off into a flight of fancy, putting his accusation in dialogue. It is possible, of course, that he was the "sage and venerable representative" alluded to, in which case the ensuing conversation would have to be counted authentic, even if partisan in nature. History does not record him as a member of the delegation to Prescott, however; the real participant was very likely a close associate of Oury's and hence the dialogue is second hand. In any case, Bill continues, saying:

During the night, when the excitement had subsided and most of the citizens of Prescott were reposing in peaceful slumber, one of Tucson's sage and venerable representatives was summoned to the mansion and the following conversation occurred between him and "Slippery Dick."

"Mr. —————, if I sign this bill I lose all my friends here and I must have positive assurance that you people will stand by me, as I must have friends somewhere."

"Well, Governor, what pledge do you ask? Our people stand ready to fulfill every obligation."

"I require the solemn pledge of your whole delegation that your entire people will vote for me for Congress; upon no other condition will I sign the bill."

Exit sage with great excitement and fear, rushing wildly to place:

"Hello, sage, what's the matter? You look as if you were frightened to death."

"We are ruined after all our trouble and expense: Mc won't sign the bill and all is lost."

"Calm yourself, sage, and let us know what is to be done."

"We must all go in a body and give a written pledge that Pima County will support Slippery Dick for Congress or else he will surely veto the bill, and we must lose no time in doing it."

The proposition of sage was promptly agreed to and the whole delegation solemnly took up the line of march at that still hour for the mansion. His Excellency, S. D., was seen, everything was satisfactorily adjusted, the bill was duly signed, the Capitol was removed to Tucson, S. D. sent to Congress, and here the curtain drops for the present.

W. S. O.[7]

P.S. — Should "Inquisitive" desire to make further INQUIRIES into the unwritten history of Arizona, we will be happy to accommodate him as our stock is inexhaustible.

Bill's Life in Politics

In any case Bill Oury remained lively on the political scene. An October 9, 1884, entry in the *Star* speaks of his holding many positions of honor and trust, among them the office of sheriff of Pima County from 1873 to 1877, clerk of the board of supervisors in 1879, and subsequently, the offices of councilman and county supervisor. The *Star* carried this note in 1885.

> *Hon. W. S. Oury has been appt'd Deputy Collector of Customs for this district by Collector Magoffin, of El Paso. Mr. Oury went to El Paso Sunday morning, at the request of the U.S. Collector. His bond which was made up last night has for his sureties Dr. J. C. Handy, A. Lazard & J. S. Wood.*
>
> *The appt. will give general satisfaction among the democracy and citizens of the territory, and especially Tucson. Mr. Oury's long residence gives him peculiar qualifiations to perform the duties of this office. He is very correct in the details of office work, is a good practical Spanish scholar, speaks the Mexican (!) language well, is acquainted with the people on both sides of the line. The* Star *congratulates Mr. Oury on his appointment and Major Magoffin on on his wise selection.*[8]

In June, 1886, Bill was called upon by one G. C. Wharton, Inspector of the General Land Office in Tucson to tell what he knew of the territory on the San Pedro River known as "Tres Alamos." By then, there were few people left who remembered anything about the area, but Bill was able to help Wharton with this statement: [9]

AFFIDAVIT OF W. S. OURY

TERRITORY OF ARIZONA, COUNTY OF PIMA

> *W. S. Oury, being duly sworn according to law, deposes and says: That he has been a resident of the city of Tucson, A. T., since the year 1856, and consequently familar with the situations, conditions, and traditions of the country; that he is well acquainted with the country bordering on the San Pedro River, particularly that portion known as the Tres Alamos section; that from the time of his arrival in Arizona there was no settlement on the San Pedro River in the neighborhood of Tres Alamos until the year 1861, which settlement was made by American citizens; that there was no wagon road or highway crossing the San Pedro near said Tres Alamos, except the one made by the Overland Mail Company in the year 1858, just below the present site of the town of Benson; that a great deal of the land about the place known as Tres Alamos was wet or marshy, caused by the beavers diverting the waters of the San Pedro River into dams; that he has since, learning that Tres Alamos was claimed under a Mexican grant, endeavored to ascertain from the old Mexican settlers of Tucson the specific point called Tres Alamos, and from all the information received from them he believes that the term "Tres Alamos" applied to a section of country and not to any definite point; that the three cottonwood trees which gave the distinctive name to the place have long since disappeared.*

William S. Oury

When the Arizona Pioneers' Historical Society was organized with Bill Oury as its first president, on January 31, 1884, not a man present could have envisioned the fine library, the rare documents collection, or the colorful and imaginative displays which eventually were to become integral parts of today's Arizona Pioneers' Historical Society. Bill remained heart and soul a member of the present Society until his death in 1887. And if he and his cronies could see the grand institution the society had become, they would be very proud indeed.

A giant of the past, Bill Oury was a figure dismissed by the present, a fate all too common with men of strong opinions and positive demeanor. His declining years were not happy ones, and yet, like all his kind, he never stopped trying. His dreams of recouping his fortune by raising and selling good beef stock never materialized. Rains were infrequent in the dry, sandy wastes of Arizona, and his herd languished rather than prospered. His political activities during the latter years were small and unrewarding. He had quarreled with his brother, and had quit Tucson in anger and frustration over the new order of things.

Hope, as it springs eternal in the human breast, springs with extra vigor in those breasts of passion and dedication. Had he lived to be one hundred, Bill would have kept his eyes on the distant horizon, and would have kept saying that somehow, by God's grace, things would turn out just fine.

Letters written to his daughter, Lola, in the years 1883–85, away with her soldier husband on an Eastern post, paint the picture of events as they were happening in the life of the Ourys. The first was written on Thanksgiving day, 1883 (November 29), and Bill says:

My darling child:

> *As this is Thanksgiving day and all the town is busy with schemes for passing the day pleasantly, I have thought that I could not devote it to a more useful or creditable purpose than dedicating it to converse with my own dear girl, especially as visions of roast turkey and plum pudding at my time of life do not intervene to excite the gastronomic propensities and divert ones ideas from the even tenor of common-place life. I shall say that your mama and I have concluded to give up city life, build a small but comfortable house at the Tanque Verde ranch, and give our entire attention to the raising of cows and calves. . . . With ordinary luck, at the end of four or five years, we will have accumulated a sufficiency of this world's stores to enable us to spend our declining years in California, or some other more hospitable clime. If I had arrived at this conclusion seven or eight years ago, when I left the Sheriff's office, we would not have now to wait longer. The trouble with me has been that until lately, I did not realize the importance of that branch of industry and left its care to those who did not faithfully discharge their trust. . . . Still,*

we have about 500 head of cattle left, most of them good, gentle, American stock. . . . With proper attention and no bad luck, they ought to increase in five years to 1500. At present rates this should produce some 35,000 dollars, more than enough to insure us against the poor house. . . . From the rents of our town property we will have enough to supply our necessities, and keep Frank in college until he will be prepared to carve out his own career in life. . . . I see nothing discouraging in the situation, as I have given up gambling for all time, *and there will be no leakage in that direction.*

Louise and the Dr. [Girard] with their little ones are still at Lowell, and will remain there until the early part of next summer, when they will go East (about the first of May). Where their lives may fall then it is impossible to say. One thing I do know, though; they will not want for anything. Aside from his position in the Army, the Dr. will carry with him some $25,000 in cash and leave here, some $5000 invested in cattle. They will be all right.

Frank is doing well at the University, and should complete his studies in a couple of years. He is a big, fine, manly fellow now, has the confidence of all who know him, and I expect will give a good account of himself in life. Your uncle (Granville) is in Washington. I know nothing of his doings for the past year, as he has not written me during the whole time. Probably his spite at the rest of the family extends even unto us. If so, I pity the poor devil, and will have a poorer opinion of his ability than I have heretofore had. With these few words, I shall consign the whole matter to the deep waters of oblivion. But I have not as yet answered your Aunt Senah's letter, and I confess that I feel loathe to do so. I may err in my judgment and instead of clearing up things make confusion more confounded. I had thought at one time to write a plain frank letter to Gran himself, but recollecting the delicacy of even an apparent interference between man and his better half, *I have been deterred from the undertaking. I have no patience with a poor,* hen-pecked husband, *especially when the operation is performed by so feeble a* pullet. *Tell Nell to keep her eyes skinned and not allow the glare of brass buttons to pull the wool over them; "all is not gold that glitters." . . . Your mama reminds me to say that Faustina is married — to a very worthy young fellow. With love to all, big and little.*

Yours affectionately,
Wm. S. Oury.[10]

Bill's move to the ranch at Tanque Verde had taken him to a wild and lonely place, far enough from town to offer him the solitude he desired, but placing him in real danger from attack by bands of marauding Apaches. The place was nestled in the foothills of the Catalinas, and was beautiful with the looming mountains on one side and the grand sweep of desert on the other. Unfortunately, he lost the place in the end, as he did so many of his other pieces of property.

No definitive reason ever has come to light for the apparent rift between Bill and Grant referred to in the letter. It is true that the two men had different natures. Where Bill was forceful, energetic, opinionated, and even pugnacious, Grant was inclined to be more deliberate, judicious, and temperate. Where Bill was completely "his own man," Grant was somewhat pliable, at least insofar as his relationship with Mina was concerned. The next letter was written some ten months later (September 8, 1884). In a sense, this one rather picks up where the other leaves off.

My darling child:

Besides my aversion to letter writing, so many difficulties have presented themselves that I have not been able until now to overcome them, and settle down to the task of addressing you. . . . We are now settled in our new country home, and have a comfortable house with all the concomitants in the way of conveniences — in the shape of outhouses, hen house, stable, carriage house — and what is of more value than all, a well of cool, pure mountain water. All things considered, we are as well situated and contented as one may be in a country like Arizona. I had entertained the hope all through the spring and summer that I would be able to attend the reunion of the Mexican War veterans to be held in St. Louis on October 8. But now the summer has passed, and we have had no rains to fatten the cattle, and hope has faded like the baseless fabric of a dream. A trip East is out of the question, at least for another year, and even then it will be attended with the same contingency. We have no other way of getting cash save through raising for sale our young steers. Without rain to make the grass grow, we can have no fat beef to sell. We were fortunate in having good rains last winter and spring, and sold enough steers to pay Frank's bills at the university, and to pay about 1200 dollars for building the new house. . . . I have had a narrow escape from malarial fever, occasioned by my own imprudence. . . . I have suffered less than I did last year, and shall in future be more careful. I realize that with 68 summers on my head I am no longer be the iron man I had until now considered myself to be. However, with reasonable care, I think I am still good for twenty years.

I am reminded that you have two boys fast approaching man's estate. Have you thought seriously what will be their positions in life? Corney I suppose is destined for military pursuits, but what of Gil? Before leaving this country he evidenced an inclination to pastoral pursuits. With the assistance I can give him (aside from the fact that he now has a cow and two heifers), if he comes to Arizona, and is wide awake and thrifty, his prosperity will be insured. Billy is yet too young to enter into much speculation as to his future. The girls — well they are girls, and life as everything in this world — for them is simply a lottery, the only way is to educate them as well as circumstances will permit, and trust to their own good bearing and luck for their standing and happiness in life.

About your friends in Tucson I can give you little or no information. I seldom visit the delightful burg, and then only on business, which as soon as I have done, I leave. I suppose you have already learned how the mighty of your day in Tucson have fallen, "like leaves in autumn weather," and others who cut no figure then, now occupy the places of the fallen. Mighty sick is life in the far west. Little remains to be said. Your mama enjoys excellent health — little Louise is as fat as a pig, and I am all right now. With love to all,

Yours afftly,[11]
W. S. O.

Bill's guess about his remaining years was not prophetic. In less than four years he was dead. Granville died four years after that in 1891.

A Military Family

Bill was right about "Corney," however. Fourteen years old at the time the letter was written, the lad went on to join the Army and to have an illustrious career. He won the nation's highest award, the Congressional Medal of Honor, in a fight with the Sioux at Little Grass Creek, South Dakota, on January 1, 1891. He went on to serve as a district governor in the Philippine Islands (Mindanao) under Generals Leonard Wood and John J. Pershing, as military attache in Venezuela and Colombia, and as a troop commander of the Fifth U.S. Cavalry at Fort Huachuca (near Tucson) in 1912–13. It was at Nogales that he took the surrender of Colonel Emilio Kosterlitzky, the colorful Mexican army officer sent north by the federal government to apprehend revolutionaries using the international boundary as a haven. Kosterlitzky had been chief of the famous "Rurales" under President Porfirio Díaz. He and Corney Smith became fast friends, last seeing each other in Los Angeles in 1928. "Corney," a lifelong Cavalryman, served as a colonel of infantry in World War I. He retired on April 9, 1920, after 30 years service, and died at his home in Riverside, California on January 10, 1936.

Bill was wrong about Gil, for he too chose the Army, rising to the rank of Major. Billy, "too young to enter into speculation about his future," followed his two older brothers into service life. He attended the West Texas Military Institute, graduating in 1896. Billy went on to Rice University in Houston, and entered the army in 1899. He rose to the rank of colonel, retiring in the 1930's.

The girls, chose their "lottery" in army circles. Inez married Henry Anson Barber, of a well-known family in Baltimore. Captain Barber died in 1917, after a brief but illustrious career. Inez lives quietly in Hollywood, California, and until a few years ago was living in Europe with her son, an army general officer serving in a diplomatic post in Spain. Emma married Pegram Whitworth of Louisiana. Whitworth had graduated from the U.S. Military Academy in 1889. He served in the famous "Pine Tree" Brigade (91st) in World War I, and rose to the rank of brigadier general. He died in Beverly Hills, California in 1961, in his 90's, with the same slim proud bearing he had shown as a cadet on the plains of West Point so long ago.

Little Louise who was "fat as a pig," married John Hemphill, who also rose to the rank of colonel in the United States Army. A charming and gracious lady, her home in Hollywood has been a storehouse of mementoes of the army years.

In another letter to Lola, written on Washington's birthday, 1885, Bill's continued state of financial distress is his main theme:

. . . I have been so completely occupied with the idea that I was to go East soon that I have neglected to write. I find now, much to my disgust, that I will have to forego that great pleasure; to obtain the means would require such an awful sacrifice that I do not feel justified in making it. We have had no rain for nearly two months . . . however, whilst I am writing, it is thundering, with the sky nearly as black as night, and everything indicates a heavy and prolonged rain. . . .

I suppose your Uncle Gran has told you that I was making an effort to get the appointment of Custom House Collector for the District of Arizona. If not, well, I shan't cry. I have placed the matter in the hands of the senators from Texas, Messrs. Maxey and Coke, who at the request of my old friend and fellow soldier, Gen. Walter P. Lane have promised to do all they can for me . . . .

I go to Tucson so seldom, and when I do am so anxious to get out out of it again that I know nothing of the doings of its people, and to be candid, I care less. I have taken a great dislike to its people and their ways, and am consequently indifferent to the town's fate — which from the many complaints I hear does not appear to be bright. There seems to be little business, less money, and the worst sign of all is that property is decreasing in value every day . . . the miserable management of the financial affairs of our county has increased our taxation to such an extent as to amount to confiscation, and the end is not yet, so you see that our prospect is not "color de rosa." Notwithstanding our drawbacks, we are all in full enjoyment of blessed health, and should not therefore complain at all. With love to you all,

Yours affetly,[12]
Wm. S. Oury

Bill's influence with the Senators Maxey and Coke turned out to be successful, if in a half-measured sort of way. He was not appointed Customs Collector for the Arizona District, but on September 2, 1885, was appointed as Deputy Customs Collector.

In a letter six months later, Bill reports to Lola on Grant's failure to be appointed governor, and again financial circumstances are plaguing him:

My dear girl:

. . . Your Uncle Gran failed to get the appointment of Governor of the Territory . . . the salary is so insignificant, only $2600, that he could not live in that position on it. He is living in Florence, practising his profession, and from his own accounts is doing much better financially than he could do in politics. . . . Frank is still at the University, this being his graduating year. He stands very high with the professors of the college, as well as with his fellow students. He thinks of going to the mining regions of South America, most likely to the

mining district of Copiapo, Chile, as soon as he leaves the University. He has a classmate, a young Englishman, whose father is very wealthy with large mining interests in Chile. He has invited Frank to go there with him as soon as they graduate. . . .

Your mama is living at the ranch looking after our cattle interests — at present in very bad condition. We have had no rain of any consequence for two years, and have been compelled to drive our cattle to the mountains to keep them from dying of starvation. . . . I am obliged on account of my office to live in town, and the confinement is very irksome to me, but the salary keeps us out of debt, and I must make the best of it for at least another year . . . .[13]

A word should be said here about Frank Oury. The delight of Bill's life, and a bright young man with a promising future, as was noted earlier he was cut down by an assassin's bullet in his twenty-ninth year. Both Bill and Inez Oury were dead when the tragedy occurred in Arivaca on September 19, 1893. According to the account given in the Arizona *Enterprise* on September 21, 1893, Frank had gone to Arivaca on mining business with General R. H. Manning, and was in a small store there in the company of two Mexicans; Pedro Miranda and one J. Ortiz. Three masked men entered the place and ordered everyone to throw up his hands. Frank chose to grapple with the bandit nearest to him, and seemed to be getting the better of the struggle when one of the others ran over to Frank, placed a gun against his ribs and pulled the trigger. Frank fell dead, and although a number of other shots were fired, no one else was hurt.

FRANK OURY. "Resolved that the universal sorrow manifested by the largest funeral cortège ever seen in this ancient pueblo but feebly expresses the cowardly assassination of this brave, generous, gifted, and heroic man." Bill Oury's son chose to grapple with a bandit in defense of himself and others, and was shot down in his twenty-ninth year.

The bandits made their escape. Frank's sister Louise came in for the funeral from Benecia Arsenal, California. Lola and Major Smith could not come in from the east.

On September 25, the federal Grand Jury passed the following resolution:

> *Resolved that the universal sorrow manifested by the largest funeral cortège ever seen in this ancient pueblo but feebly expresses the cowardly assassination of this brave, generous, gifted, and heroic man.*[14]

Bill's last letter to Lola was written on Christmas Eve in 1885, with an allusion to the "Rancheritos" and how to provide a merry Christmas for them.

> *... Your mama, Louise, Carlota, [a deaf-mute Apache girl who had been a servant in Bill's household for many years], the rancheros, their wives, and all the little "rancheritos" have arrived to spend Christmas in the city. As a matter of course, this knocks the poetry out of me, and brings me back to the stern realities of this matter-of-fact world, and sets me to devising means whereby all these little ones are to be supplied with toys, candies, and the various trifles so indispensible for the happy Christmas they so fondly look to through the whole year. ...*
>
> *Little is taking place in Tucson that is worthy of being chronicled. Sam Hughes oldest daughter was married a short time since to a young Mr. Corbett, brother of the one who was in the post office in your time. Mrs. Jacobs lost her only boy last week and is all broken up ....*
>
> *The event of the holidays will be the celebration of the anniversary of the Society of Arizona Pioneers, to take place on Dec. 29th. With few exceptions, it is to be confined to the members of the Society and their families. Everybody is anxious to be made the exception, and I fear that there will be a great deal of disappointment and bad blood over it. As it is impossible for us to invite everybody, I think that the best thing to be done is not to invite any, but confine it strictly to the families of Pioneers. I have written to your Uncle Gran to come with his wife and Genevieve, and I think they will probably do so, as a great many of the brotherhood from all parts of the Territory have expressed their intention of being present, and it promises to be a grand event. I will send you the* Star *which will contain an account of it. ... I will close with love, and a merry Christmas to you all.*[15]

On the last day of March, 1887, violent pains seized Bill Oury unaware, unheralded, and within minutes he was dead. The long trail from the green valley of Virginia came to an end. Behind were the lusty young years of Texas, the memory of Jim Bowie waiting quietly for the end, and of Colonel Travis telling the young boy to ride fast and tell General Houston how it was there at the Alamo. Gone were the days of shooting Comanches with Jack Hayes, and Big Foot Wallace, and the faraway dream world of the beans in the jar at Hacienda Salado. Gone were the fading thoughts of Palo Alto, Resaca de la Palma; of Monterrey, Ewing Cameron, Ampudia, and the Bishop's Palace on the hill. Vanished forever were the visions of great nuggets in the mountain streams of California, and the wagon trek from that golden land to the rocky wastes of Southern Arizona. Now the eyes were closed to the old Apache fires in the foothills of the Catalinas, and the butchered bodies trussed to wagonwheels, and the bewildered squaws running from the wickiups in the cold thin air of morning. Gone now the rumble of the stagecoach lurching into town, and the sound of whips cracking. Gone too the hurt of watching Yankee soldiers riding down Calle Real — and the Johnny Rebs disappearing in the distance over the rise for Texas. Gone now the joys and triumphs, the sorrows and the pain of seeing the old comrades cross over, one by one. Now it was all over; the old warrior, the tough and grizzled veteran of a lifetime of battle, lay dead — and life, as it always does — moved on. The *Citizen* told the story in these words:

> *The public was startled this morning at the announcement that Uncle Billy Oury was dead. The summons had come 'ere anyone was aware he was ill — indeed he had been but slightly indisposed last evening & it was not thought that anything serious troubled him. This morning he was seized by violent pains, apparently across the upper portion of his stomach, & in a paroxysm he fell forward from a chair to the floor . . . it was seen that the end had come. A physician was at once summoned, but when he arrived, Mr. Oury was dead. . . . He had passed away peacefully and quietly.*
>
> *In 1862, when the Calif. Column came to Tucson, Mr. Oury was about the only American that was not sent to Yuma for treason. His subsequent history has been the history of the growth & civilization of Pima Co., & in every measure of public welfare he has been foremost amongst the people. Although so prominently identified with current events, he did not seek office, but was content to help his friends. He was elected sheriff in 1872 & reelected in 1874, since which time, until he was appointed deputy collector of customs last year, he held no office.*
>
> *He was the Captain of the Papago expeditions in the old Camp Grant affair & these Indians still hold him in such high respect that a large delegation of them will be among the most sincere mourners at his funeral.*
>
> *Mrs. Oury was at their Tanque Verde ranch at the time of her husband's death, but arrived in the city shortly after noon today. She is completely crazed with grief & seems oblivious to the tender & tearful ministrations of the sympathetic friends that surround her.*
>
> *As a politician Mr. Oury was an uncompromising Democrat, ever ready to go to almost extreme measures to uphold the party's principles. In his private character he was above reproach & his integrity has never been assailed in the slightest degree. He was generous, hospitable & and cheerful to everyone & his benign countenance will be sadly missed from every public gathering and private walk of life.*
>
> *Peace to his ashes.*[16]

In the hour of parting, the Society of Arizona Pioneers came to do him honor. Bill had taken an unusually keen interest in the Society from its inception. He had spoken of it once as a "hobby." It was far more than that — it was a link with the West he had helped to make with his own hands. It was a way of life to him, and a bridge to the pioneer past now gone forever.

His old friend Sam Hughes called the membership into session immediately. The friends who carried Bill to his resting place all were pioneers like himself — Sam Hughes, Pete Kitchen, Sol Warner, Estevan Ochoa, Peter Brady, Bill Van Alstine, Charley Meyers, G. C. Wharton, and A. Lazard. Quiet in death, he was borne by eagles, men as passionately devoted to the spirit of the frontier as Bill had been in his hectic three score and ten.

Bill might have stayed in Texas after the Mexican War and prospered with the soldier's land grant he never took. He might have struck it rich in the California gold fields, or he might have become a political power in Arizona Territory. He might have — but he did not. Restless, impatient, quick-tempered, a man of action, he followed the sun across the mountains and deserts of the Southwest until it was too late for the attainment of wealth and glory. Yet his was a surging event-filled life, a life of vigorous living and bright memories of the past. He lived the only life he could have lived; all things considered, it wasn't a bad life at all.

Three-quarters of a century have passed since Bill died. He wouldn't know Tucson today, and he wouldn't want to. He would rather listen to the rumbling of an oxcart than the grinding of gears, or see a low adobe wall than a skyscraper. Or perhaps, from his place beside Inez in Holy Hope Cemetery, with the Angel of the Lord looking down upon them from the statued pedestal, he would simply repeat, if he could, these lines from an old poem:

> . . . How swift the merry days ran on
>   In old Tucson, in old Tucson,
> How soon the parting days came on.
>   But I oft turn back to my hallowed dreams,
> And the low adobe palace seems
>   Where her sad heart sighs, and her sweet voice sings,
> To the notes that throb from her viol strings.
>   O, those tear-dimmed eyes, and that soft brown hand!
> And her soul, that glows like the desert sand,
>   The golden fruit of a golden land!
> In old Tucson, in old Tucson,
>   The long, long days, oh time, speed on!

NOTES, SOURCES, CHRONOLOGY

Chapter Notes

CHAPTER I

1. *Pennsylvania Archives,* Fifth Series, Vol. III, pp. 314, 318, 319, 323, 327, 328. The last name is spelled variously also: Oury, Ourrey, Orey, Owry, Ourey, even Ourcy.

2. Letter, Senah Oury to Eunice Oury, Nov. 7, 1907. Original in possession of author.

3. Letter, John M. Oury to "Margaret" (last name not known), June 22, 1858. Original in possession of author.

4. Letter, Colonel William O. Smith, U.S.A., to Colonel Cornelius C. Smith, U.S.A., April 9, 1928. Original in possession of author.

5. Co-signers of Wendel Oury's petition to Governor John Penn in 1774 include such names as: Frantz Raupp, Nicholas Scheuer, Hannes Gunkel, Petter Uber, Peter Wannenmacher, Joseph Kleiss, and others equally Germanic. In fact, almost every name on the petition is of Germanic origin. On the other hand, given names like Elizabeth, Nancy, Melvina, William, and John, appear frequently in the Oury lineage.

6. Letter, William B. Foster (grandson of George Oury) to cousin Katie Mathews, July 3, 1909. Original in possession of author.

7. *Pennsylvania Archives,* Sixth Series, Vol. 14, "Early Petitions," p. 300.

8. *Ibid.,* p. 296.

9. *Ibid.,* p. 301. This location of Wendel Oury's farm is similarly listed by Thomas Lynch Montgomery in *Frontier Forts of Pennsylvania,* Vol. III, 373, 379.

10. Readers interested in the workings of the departments are referred to *Pennsylvania Archives,* and special studies by the Pennsylvania Historical and Museum Commission in Harrisburg, and an article by Walter Fee, "Colonel George Morgan at Fort Pitt," appearing in the *Western Pennsylvania Historical Magazine,* October, 1928.

11. *Pennsylvania Archives,* Fifth Series, Vol. III, p. 327. See appendix for copy of commission. Also, commission date is verified in Heitman's *Historical Register of Officers of the Continental Army, 1775–1783,* p. 422.

12. *Pennsylvania Archives,* Fifth Series, Vol. III, p. 375.

13. *Ibid.,* p. 305.

14. *Ibid.* Cited in the "day-book" (diary) of one Ephraim Douglas, entry of Dec. 5, 1776.

15. Information Bulletin Nr. 3, p. 2, The Pennsylvania Historical and Museum Commission, Pennsylvania Division of Public Records.

16. *Ibid.*

17. *Ibid.*

18. *Ibid.*

19. *Pennsylvania Archives,* Second Series, Vol. X, p. 660.

20. *Ibid.,* p. 375.

21. *Pennsylvania Archives,* Fifth Series, Vol. I, p. 355.

22. *Ibid.,* p. 310.

23. See Appendix for certified copy of land transaction involving Wendel Oury on April 4, 1780.

24. *Pennsylvania Archives,* Sixth Series, Vol. V, p. 720.

25. Letter, Senah Oury to William B. Foster, March 5, 1908. Copy in possession of author.

26. *Pennsylvania Archives,* Sixth Series, Vol. X, p. 46.

27. *Ibid.,* Third Series, Vol. XXII, p. 28.

28. *Ibid.,* p. 406.

29. *Ibid.*

CHAPTER 2

1. Lewis Preston Summers, "One Hundred Years of the History of Abingdon," address delivered before the Washington County Historical Society. Reprinted in *Publications of the Historical Society of Washington County, Virginia.* p. 30. (Each paper is dated; the published collection of papers is undated. Summers gave the above address on June 14, 1939.)

2. The exact spot is not known. Mrs. Fred Davis, an officer of the Washington County Historical Society told the author (in Feb. 1965) she believed the Oury cabin stood next to the first courthouse, and a short distance from the famous wolf den — that she had seen several papers and maps to that effect.

3. Summers, *Op. Cit.,* p. 33.

4. Marker on the tavern listing it as Abingdon's oldest building, and "probably" built by John Campbell.

5. The structure is partially rebuilt. It was fired by Union troops in December 1864 during the famous Stoneman Raid.

6. Summers, *Op. Cit.,* p. 33.

7. This Christopher Acklin was the grandfather of Kit Acklin who fought with Bill Oury at the Battle of Bandera Pass, Texas, in 1842.

8. George Oury sold land in Washington County to one Almerine Marshall in 1799, and Augustus Oury to William Trigg in 1823.

9. Lewis Preston Summers, *History of Southwest Virginia, 1746–1786; Washington County, 1777–1870,* J. C. Hill Printing Co., Richmond, 1903, p. 447.

10. *Ibid.*

11. *Ibid.*

12. *Ibid.,* p. 448.

13. *Ibid.*

14. Letter, Stephen X. Winters, S.J., Administrative Assistant to the President, Georgetown University, to Cornelius C. Smith, March 31, 1958.

15. Letter, J. Foley Snyder, Registrar, Georgetown College, Georgetown, Kentucky, to Cornelius C. Smith, June 14, 1958.

16. Summers, *Op. Cit.,* p. 447.

17. *Ibid.,* p. 664.

18. *Ibid.,* p. 662.

19. Summers, "One Hundred Years of the History of Abingdon," *op. cit.,* p. 34.

20. *Washington County Record Book* for 1833. Land transaction, Augustus Oury and James Sanders to Clark G. and Jeremiah Gardner, p. 143; Book 1823–1839, p. 224; Book 1834, multiple entries for Augustus Oury, p. 5, p. 149. Entry for George Oury (property exchange in November 1813), Record Book for 1811–1814; Fee Book for 1820–1824, entry for Christopher Oury, May 1823, p. 216.

21. Summers, "One Hundred Years of the History of Abingdon," *Op. Cit.,* p. 34.

22. The Preston mansion was purchased by the local Odd Fellows Lodge in 1853 and converted into Martha Washington College for women, which it remained until 1932. Since 1937, it has been the Martha Washington Inn, noted for old world charm and superb food.

CHAPTER 3

1. Henry Ryder-Taylor, *History of the Alamo.* San Antonio: Mic Tengg, undated, p. 18.

2. *Ibid.,* p. 19.

3. Cornelius C. Smith (Sr.), "A History of the Oury Family," (unpublished manuscript in possession of the author), p. 9. An early version of this manuscript was given by my father to the Arizona Pioneers' Historical Society in 1932, and forms a part of the library of that institution. My father had added considerable information to this early draft, and was still working on the manuscript at the time of his death in 1936. The study is almost wholly reminiscent in character, and reflects the author's memory of the stories related to him by his grandfather, William Sanders Oury. In those areas where documents are available to authenticate the manuscript, I have cited them, and in several instances reproduced them for inclusion in the Appendix. With but few minor exceptions all statements of fact have been verified, a factor which attests to the general soundness of the paper. It is an important source, and is quoted frequently in the chapters of this book.

4. A much disputed figure, listed variously from 182 to 187.

CHAPTER 4

1. Smith, "A History of the Oury Family," *op. cit.,* p. 4.

2. John Myers, *The Alamo,* (New York: Bantam Books, 1960), p. 124.

3. *Ibid.,* p. 126. Myers reports Travis as listing 150 men. Edward S. Ellis in *History of the United States,* 6 vols., (St. Paul, Western Books Syndicate, 1899), lists "182 Texans" in Vol. III, p. 776. Obviously he is speaking of the total number present at the fall, including Albert Martin and the men of Gonzales.

4. Smith, *op. cit.,* p. 7.

5. *Ibid.*

6. *Ibid.,* p. 9.

7. Lon Tinkle, *The Alamo, Thirteen Days to Glory.* New York: New American Library, 1960, p. 91.

8. Smith, *op. cit.,* p. 7.

9. Marquis James, *The Raven.* New York: Blue Ribbon Books Inc., 1929, p. 226.

10. *Ibid.*

11. Smith, "A History of the Oury Family," *op. cit.,* p. 12.

CHAPTER 5

1. Smith, *op. cit.*, p. 12.

2. The figure varies. Lord, in *A Time to Stand,* mentions "some 400 Texans" (p. 148). Myers, in *The Alamo,* lists "hundreds of them" (p. 158). Marquis James in *The Raven* says: ". . . 390 men had been executed in cold blood" (p. 239). F. T. Fields in *The Texas Sketchbook* (Houston, 1962) claims ". . . 350 men were caught . . . near Coleto creek," p. 62.

3. Tinkle, *op. cit.,* p. 149.

4. H. M. Henderson, "A Critical Analysis of the San Jacinto Campaign," *The Southwestern Historical Quarterly,* Vol. LIX, Nr. 3 (Jan., 1956), p. 344.

5. *Ibid.,* p. 345.

6. Smith, *op. cit.,* p. 14.

7. Henderson, *op. cit.,* p. 345.

8. James, *op. cit.,* p. 231.

9. Smith, *op. cit.,* p. 15.

10. F. T. Shields, "Retreat to Victory," *The Texas Sketchbook* (Houston, The Humble Oil Co., 1962), p. 65.

11. *Ibid.*

12. Henderson, *op. cit.,* p. 346. "From the time the army reached the Brazos, it appeared that Houston was almost daily threatened with being deposed and replaced by another commander."

13. Henderson Yoakum, *History of Texas* (New York: 1856), II, p. 115.

14. Shields, *op. cit.,* p. 65. Henderson, in his "A Critical Analysis of the San Jacinto Campaign," says ". . . the strength of Houston's army at Groce's reached 1500 men," p. 348. This is quoted from General Walter P. Lane in *The Adventures and Recollections of General Walter P. Lane, a San Jacinto Veteran,* (Marshall, 1887), p. 7.

15. Smith, *op. cit.,* p. 17.

16. Smith, *op. cit.,* p. 18.

17. Henderson, *op. cit.,* p. 357.

18. James, *op. cit.,* p. 246.

19. Lamar later became President of the Texas Republic. His signature, as Secretary of War, is affixed to one of Bill Oury's pay vouchers, dated January 1, 1838.

20. James, *op. cit.,* p. 248.

21. *Ibid.,* p. 250. Also mentioned in Henderson's "A Critical Analysis of the San Jacinto Campaign," p. 360.

22. Smith, *op. cit.,* p. 20.

23. James, *op. cit.,* p. 251.

24. Marquis James lists one Joel Robison as Santa Anna's captor (*The Raven,* pp. 253–254). Henderson credits the capture to Sgt. J. A. Sylvester, citing three sources: Brown, *History of Texas,* II, 21–30; Thrall, *A Pictorial History of Texas,* 91, 99–100; Yoakum, *History of Texas,* II, 141–146.

25. In a letter to Col. William O. Smith on Oct. 22, 1930, J. D. Newton, a civilian Quartermaster Corps clerk at Fort Clark, Texas, relates that his granduncle was in the scouting party which captured Santa Anna, and that the young soldier got a gold snuff-box from the general. Letter in possession of the author.

26. Henderson, *op. cit.,* p. 361.

CHAPTER 6

1. See Appendix.
2. See Appendix.
3. Smith, "A History of the Oury Family," *op. cit.,* p. 22.
4. *Ibid.*
5. James K. Greer, *Colonel Jack Hayes; Texas Frontier Leader and California Builder;* hereinafter cited as: Col. Jack Hays. (New York: E. P. Dutton and Co., 1952), p. 22.
6. *Ibid.*
7. Smith, *op. cit.,* p. 24.
   "Oury's companions from Texas to California were J. C. Hays and John McMullen, the former the famous Texas Ranger Commander, the latter a Texas patriot for whom McMullen County, Texas, is named. The friendship of these three men lasted through their lives. When beautiful Anna McMullen (daughter of John) married Hay's son Jack, in 1880, the young couple spent part of their honeymoon on a visit to Mr. Oury and family in Tucson.... I went to school with John McMullen, Jr., at St. Mathews Hall, San Mateo, California. Later, 1908 and 1909, as a captain of the 14th U. S. Cavalry, stationed at the Presidio of San Francisco, I saw much of the McMullen family socially. In 1909, I visited Jack and his charming wife in Visalia. ..."
   Note: My father is ambiguous at the beginning of this quote. Oury was not a "companion" of Hays and McMullen from Texas to California in the sense that the three made the journey together. They did not. They were friends and associates before and after the separate migrations to California. Oury went to the gold fields by way of Mexico as will be seen in a later chapter.
8. Greer, *op. cit.,* p. 33.
9. George P. Garrison (Ed.,), "Reminiscences of Judge Edwin Waller," *The Quarterly of the Texas State Historical Association,* (Austin: 1901), Vol. IV, p. 51.
10. Walter Prescott Webb and H. Bailey Carroll (Editors), *The Handbook of Texas,* (2 vols., Austin: Texas State Historical Association, 1952), I, 387.
11. Hubert Howe Bancroft, *History of the North Mexican States and Texas* (San Francisco: 1899), Vol. 16, p. 325.
12. Greer, *op. cit.,* pp. 39–40.
13. Garrison, *op. cit.,* p. 52.
14. Greer, *op. cit.,* p. 41.
15. Webb and Carroll, *op. cit.,* I, p. 105.
16. Greer, *op. cit.,* p. 48.
17. *Ibid.,* p. 49.
18. Smith, *op. cit.,* p. 25.

CHAPTER 7

1. Greer, *op. cit.,* p. 71. "... Caldwell's entire force totalled 225 men." W. W. Lastinger, in "The ill-fated Miér Expedition," *Frontier Times,* Vol. II, August 1934, gives a slightly higher figure. On page 500, he states: "Caldwell was joined by . . . Jack Hays, Lieutenant McCulloch, with additional men, making a total of 250 . . . ."
2. Greer, *op. cit.,* p. 70.
3. Lastinger, as cited, p. 500.

4. L. A. Duewall, *The Story of Monument Hill,* (Texas: The La Grange Journal, 1956), p. 12. "Having ridden all day Saturday (17th), and Sunday morning without stopping, men and horses were spent."

5. *Ibid.,* p. 13. "Several of the Texians, who expected no mercy from the enemy, continued to fire."

6. *Ibid.,* p. 14. Henry Gonzalvo Woods, Asley S. Miller, Thomas James.

7. Greer, *op. cit.,* p. 78. As quoted from the Telegraph and Texas Register of Jan. 15, 1843.

8. *Ibid.,* p. 80.

9. Smith, *op cit.,* p. 28.

10. Greer, *op. cit.,* p. 86.

11. John C. Duval, *The Adventures of Big Foot Wallace,* (Macon, Ga.: J. W. Burke and Co., 1871), p. 162.

12. *Ibid.,* p. 159. "A motley, mixed-up crowd were we . . . broken down politicians, renegades, refugees from justice . . . ."

13. *Ibid.,* p. 166.

14. Smith, *op. cit.,* p. 31.

15. Duval, *op. cit.,* p. 170.

16. *Ibid.,* p. 171.

17. Smith, *op. cit.,* p. 32.

18. Duval, *op. cit.,* p. 175.

19. Smith, *op. cit.,* p. 33.

20. *Ibid.,* p. 35.

21. Duval, *op. cit.,* p. 184.

22. *Ibid.,* p. 188.

23. Smith, *op. cit.,* p. 37. Always one of my father's favorite parts of the Oury saga. I remember, as a boy of 10 in San Diego, California (1923), my father telling me of when "your great grandfather killed and ate the rattlesnake."

24. Duval, *op. cit.,* p. 196.

25. Smith, *op. cit.,* p. 38. One thinks of the word "lousy" as of relatively recent origin. Bill Oury so described himself, while a prisoner of the Mexicans, showing that the word had some coinage at least as early as 1844.

26. There is no record that Oury was used as an interpreter in this instance. His Spanish was excellent, and he later served as interpreter for General Zachary Taylor after the battle of Monterrey in the Mexican War.

27. Lastinger, *op. cit.,* p. 502. According to Duewall, *The Story of Monument Hill,* p. 20, the figure is listed as 176 men.

28. Duewall, *op. cit.,* p. 21.

29. With the passing years, my father and I have met several people whose forebears participated in the bean-drawing episode: Mr. Thad Austin Thompson, U.S. Minister in Bogotá, Colombia in 1916 (nephew of J. M. Thompson who drew a black bean); Dr. W. Eastland, ship's surgeon of the S.S. San Juan, in 1922 (nephew of Capt. William Eastland who also drew a black bean); Jack Glover, owner of a western goods store in Sunset, Texas (great-grandson of Henry Journay, who drew a white bean).

30. This brave man said, just before death: "well, they don't make much off me anyhow, for I know I have killed 25 of them."

31. Duewall, *op. cit.,* p. 24.

CHAPTER 8

1. See Appendix for copy of this enlistment record.

2. Letter, William Sanders Oury to Alex M. Kenaday, reprinted in April 6, 1880 issue of Washington, D.C. *Vedette*. See Appendix. Oury's story of his foray through the Mexican lines to Point Isabel with Sam Walker is corroborated in most of its details by John Frost in his *History of Mexico and the Mexican War,* Philadelphia: Cowperthwait, 1849. "Walker volunteered to reattempt the communication . . . six (more) men immediately volunteered. . . . Walker and his little band started late on the 29th, and after passing many dangers, arrived safely at Taylor's position," p. 213.

3. Mathew Forney Steele, *American Campaigns,* (2 vols., Washington: Byron S. Adams, 1909), I, p. 86.

4. *Ibid.*

5. Major General John K. Herr in *The Story of the U. S. Cavalry,* (Boston: Little, Brown and Co., 1953), pp. 33–34, eulogizes May: "The cavalry has always produced colorful personalities, but May was a giant among men."

An enlisted soldier of the Mexican War, one Sam Chamberlain, held another view. "All the buglers hated Charley May for claiming the capture of General La Vega at the Battle of Resaca de la Palma, when it was actually a bugler, Winchell, of Company "H," 2nd Dragoons, who took the general prisoner." (Samuel E. Chamberlain, *My Confession,* New York: Harper and Brothers, 1956), p. 108.

6. Smith, *op. cit.,* p. 40.

7. Steele, *op. cit.,* p. 87.

8. Smith, *op. cit.,* p. 41.

9. Samuel C. Reid, *The Scouting Expeditions of McCulloch's Texas Rangers,* (Philadelphia: The Keystone Publishing Co., 1890), p. 41.

10. One of the finest works on U.S. Naval Forces participation in the Mexican War is Philip S. P. Conner's *The Home Squadron in the Mexican War,* (Philadelphia: 1896). Mr. Conner was the son of Commodore David Conner, and wrote his treatise from the wealth of his father's private papers.

11. Reid, *op. cit.,* p. 161. "He (Worth) saw at once that it would be necessary to carry by storm the battery on Federation Hill . . . as well as the fort on the ridge of the same height, called Soldada . . . ."

12. *Ibid.,* p. 164. "The brave Captain R. A. Gillespie of the Rangers was the first to gain and mount the enemy's works."

13. *Ibid.* "So close was the arrival of the separate units that Lt. Thomas G. Pitcher, of the 5th Infantry wrote with chalk on the first gun captured: 'Texas Rangers and Fifth Infantry.' "

14. *Ibid.,* p. 181.

15. *Ibid.*

16. *Ibid.,* p .183. ". . . He fell, mortally wounded, at the head of his company. As his men came up, they offered assistance to him, but he refused them, and cheered them on to combat."

Greer, in his *Col. Jack Hays,* p. 146, says: "The Rangers stood silent, Gillespie and Thomas had fought their last battles. Gillespie, educated, gallant, had pretended to be only slightly wounded, and waved his men on into the struggle when several sought to help him."

17. Reid, *op. cit.,* p. 186. Steele, in his *American Campaigns,* lists the total American strength at 6650 men, the Mexican force at about 10,000.

18. According to Sam Chamberlain, the name "doughboy" dates to the Battle of Monterrey, "when some of General J. Worth's infantry, who had captured the Bishop's Palace, baked a mixture of flour and rice in their campfire ashes, and boasted of their first hot meal after 48 hours of fighting."

19. Herr and Wallace, *op. cit.*, p. 35.

20. Smith, *op. cit.*, p. 44.

21. *Ibid.*, p. 45.

22. He was not alone in his sentiments. Sam Chamberlain said: "What a disgrace to American arms. . . . The Mexican Infantry retained their arms, the cavalry their horses, the artillery one field battery of six guns with 21 rounds to a gun!" Chamberlain, *My Confession, op. cit.*, p. 56.

23. Reid., *op. cit.*, p. 233.

24. See Frederick P. Todd, *Soldiers of the American Army, 1775–1954*, (Chicago: Henry Regnery Co., 1950). For colorful plates of the Spy Company uniforms (plates 12 and 14).

25. Herr and Wallace, *op. cit.*, p. 34.

26. This is the first instance in which official records substantiate family legend in the matter of Oury's San Antonio properties. Bill is thought to have acquired land after his release from Perote Prison in 1844, but I have been unable to produce records to prove it. However, records in the Bexar County clerk's office show that he did acquire land near Misión San José dé Aguayo in three separate transactions: on August 1, 1848, July 9, 1849, and September 28, 1849. The first purchase was "five lots 'suertes' of land, situated in the Misión San José, below the said mission building." It was bought in partnership with one Charles L. Pyron from Rafael C. Garza, his wife Maria Antonia Veramendi y Garza, and José Veramendi. The purchase price was $1100.00. Subsequently, Oury bought property from Marcos A. Veramendi, a lot in "El Barrio del Laredo" (July 9, 1849), and "one-half a suerte" for seventy-five dollars on September 28, 1849. On that same day, (September 28) he obtained another piece of land from Veramendi in "La Rincón de la Parra." It is seen, then, that in a period of some 14 months, Bill and his partner bought what amounted to eight separate lots for an aggregate sum of $1975.00.

27. Smith, *op. cit.*, p. 47.

CHAPTER 9

1. Smith, *A History of the Oury Family, op. cit.*, p. 49.

2. This appellation is reputedly a contraction of the two English words, "green-grow," used in the title of the song "Green Grow the Lilacs," sung by American soldiers in Mexico during the Mexican War.

3. Pastor Rouaix, *Diccionario Geográfico, Histórico y Biográfico del Estado da Durango,* Instituto Pan Americano de Geografía y Historia (Mexico, 1946), p. 138

4. The author's cousin, Oury Jackson, instructs in English at the University.

5. Named for Gines Vásquez De Mercado in 1552.

6. A pleasant pastime recalled by the author who made many such jaunts when living in Durango as a small boy in 1922.

7. Rouaix, *op. cit.*, p. 137.

8. *Ibid.*

9. The Indian legends of Sahuatoba, Tiopitzintli, Atlatzín, Tuitán (and others), and the Spanish legends of La Virgin del Valle, Doña Ana de Leyva, La Bruja del Tisonazo, and El Hechicero De San Juan Del Río.

10. Some ships were still making the trip around Cape Horn; other lines ran ships from New York and Boston to Central American ports on the Gulf of Mexico. There, passengers traveled overland to West Coast ports to continue the journey to San Francisco.

11. Frank Soulé, *The Annals of San Francisco* (D. Appleton and Co., New York, 1854), p. 553.

12. *Ibid.,* p. 557.

13. Well known to Senator Cornelius Cole, mentioned elsewhere in this book. Cole tells of Brannan's Mormon background and mercantile activities in *Memoirs of Cornelius Cole,* McLoughlin Bros. (New York: 1908), p. 74.

14. An excellent account of the incident is given in James Kimmins Greer's *Colonel Jack Hays,* E. P. Dutton Co., (New York, 1952), p. 276–278.

15. The first six "great fires" occurred in this sequence: December 24, 1849; May 4, 1850; June 14, 1850; September 17, 1850; May 4, 1851; June 22, 1851.

16. Smith, *op. cit.,* p. 49.

17. City Register, San Francisco, 1851.

CHAPTER 10

1. Cornelius C. Smith, Sr., "Some Unpublished History of the Southwest," *Arizona Historical Review,* Vol. VI, nr. 1, (January 1935), p.61.

2. John G. Bourke, *On the Border with Crook,* (New York: Charles Scribner's Sons, 1891), p. 63.

3. J. Ross Browne, *Adventures in Apache Country* (New York: Harper, 1869), p. 134.

4. John C. Cremony, *Life Among the Apaches,* (San Francisco: A. Roman and Co., 1868).

CHAPTER 11

1. Cornelius C. Smith, Sr., "A History of the Oury Family," *op. cit.,* p. 60.

2. Bernice Cosulich, *Tucson,* (Tucson: Arizona Silhouettes, 1953), p. 146.

3. San Antonio newspaper schedule for December, 1858. Unfortunately, the name of the paper has been cut away from this original clipping in the possession of the author.

4. The ads were printed in a short space of time. The *Arizonian* had a short life of five months, from March 3 to July 21, 1859. After Sylvester Mowry's duel with Col. Edward Cross (owner of the paper), William S. Oury and Sylvester Mowry purchased the paper for $2500.00 and moved the press to Tucson. The first Tucson issue was published on August 4, 1859.

5. *Tubac Arizonian,* May 18, 1859.

6. *Tubac Arizonian,* March 17, 1859.

7. *Tubac Arizonian,* April 28, 1859.

8. *New York Herald,* Nov. 11, 1858.

9. Cornelius C. Smith, Sr., "Some Unpublished History of the Southwest," *Arizona Historical Review,* Vol. VI, nr. 1, (January, 1935), p. 55.

10. Smith, "A History of the Oury Family," *op. cit.,* p. 64.

CHAPTER 12

1. Smith, "A History of the Oury Family," *op. cit.,* p. 66.

2. From biographical notes on Granville H. Oury in the library of the Arizona Pioneers' Historical Society, Tucson, Arizona (author not listed).

3. Smith, *op. cit.,* p. 67.

4. Biographical notes, Granville H. Oury, *op. cit.*

5. See Appendix for copy of company muster roll for Sept.–Oct. 1862.

6. *Ibid.*

7. Letter, Captain Granville H. Oury, C.S.A., to Brigadier General Sibley, C.S.A., February 22, 1863.

8. General Sibley's endorsement on Oury's letter.

9. *Ibid.,* Taylor's endorsement.

10. *Ibid.*

11. See appendix.

12. See appendix.

13. See appendix.

14. Hubert Howe Bancroft, *History of Arizona and New Mexico, 1530–1888,* (San Francisco: 1889), p. 537.

15. Arizona Daily Star (clipping) undated.

16. Bancroft, *op. cit.,* p. 525.

17. *Ibid.*

18. Smith, *op. cit.,* p. 71.

19. Reminiscences of Ed McGowan, *The Arizona Sentinel,* Yuma, Sept. 14, 1878.

20. Smith, *op. cit.,* p. 73.

21. Bert Fireman, "Notes on the History of the Goldwater Family," Manuscript, Chap. 14, p. 43.

22. *Ibid.,* p. 44.

23. Smith, *op. cit.,* p. 76.

CHAPTER 13

1. William A. Duffen in "Overland Via Jackass Mail," *Arizona and the West,* winter 1960, p. 354, edits the 1858 diary of Phocian R. Way. In footnote 2, p. 354, Duffen erroneously lists the date of this affair as April 27, 1857, and makes Grant (not Bill) a participant. Way's diary entry for July 4, 1858, would seem to clear the matter up, however. "Miles (Edward) had a brother shot and killed in a duel about two months ago. . . ."

2. *Ibid.* Duffen is right here. "Miles and Baker went to California and became active in Republican politics."

3. *Santa Cruz Sentinel,* July 5, 1858.

4. Smith, *op. cit.,* p. 78.

5. *Ibid.*

6. *Ibid.*

7. *Ibid.,* p. 79.

CHAPTER 14

1. Mowry was a close friend of Bill Oury's but was even closer to Grant with whom he had worked tirelessly to achieve territorial status for Arizona. Several of his letters to Grant are discussed elsewhere in this book. Mowry was born in Providence, Rhode Island, in 1832, and graduated from West Point in 1852. In 1858 he resigned his commission and started mining in Southern Arizona. His Patagonia mine was seized by General Carleton in 1862, and Mowry was packed off to Yuma prison. He was ultimately released, and died in England in 1871.

2. William Sanders Oury, "A Brief History of Early Journalism in Pima County," *Arizona Daily Star,* undated.

3. The Santa Rita Mining Company was organized in 1858 under the laws of the state of Ohio. Capital stock was issued in the amount of one million dollars. Thomas Wrightson was made secretary of the company, and William Wrightson director of the mines.

4. Not quite. The press did not arrive in Tubac until January 1859. The first issue of the Tubac *Arizonian* was on March 3, 1859. Another note on the paper comes from the St. John's Herald of November 7, 1889. "The first paper published in Arizona was named the *Arizonian* at Tubac. It survived only a short time, and on its collapse, 'Uncle Bill' Oury purchased the material and moved it to Tucson. . . ."

5. An excellent treatise on Sylvester Mowry's activities in behalf of territorial status for Arizona is that by Benjamin H. Sacks, running serially in *Arizona and the West* under the title: "The Creation of the Territory of Arizona," Vol. 5, nr. 1, spring 1963, and Vol. 5, nr. 2, summer 1963.

6. *Supra.* Sacks mentions this episode in the above-named article, Vol. 5, nr. 1, spring 1963, p. 54. "In the presence of a gathering at a place near Tubac on July 8, each of the duelists fired three shots in a high wind without reaching a target."

7. The paper put out 21 issues between March 3, and July 21, 1859. Bill, in his story, claims that the press was taken down on the same day as the duel. If the fight occurred on July 8, as claimed by Sacks, then it is difficult to reconcile the assertion with a July 21st edition — along with Bill's story about taking down the press right after the duel.

8. The statement is not exact. As the house organ for the occupying force of federal troops, the paper reflected pretty much what General Carleton and his staff (Republicans mostly) wanted it to reflect.

9. The November 7, 1899, issue of the St. John's Herald says: "In the spring of 1871, P. W. Dooner's Arizonian suspended, and "Uncle Bill" Oury again stored the material in his house on Main Street, Tucson." It will be noted that Oury's reminiscence and the *Herald* story offer different dates (1870 and 1871). As both were written years after the event, it is difficult to select the proper date. It is suggested that Oury's memory, after 20 years, might be slightly more accurate than the writer for the *Herald* after 40 years.

10. *Tubac Arizonian,* March 3, 1859.

11. *Tubac Arizonian,* March 17, 1859.

12. *Tubac Arizonian,* June 16, 1859.

13. There were only four more issues after this one: June 23 and 30; and July 7-21. For some reason, there was no July 14 issue. In his *History of Arizona,* p. 726, Joseph Fish gives several pieces of misinformation about the *Tubac Arizonian* — that its first issue was in February 1859; that Granville Oury seconded Mowry in his duel with editor Cross; that Mowry (alone) moved the paper to Tucson, and in 1860 instead of July 1859.

14. *Weekly Arizonian* (Tucson), Oct. 6, 1859.

15. John K. Herr and Edward J. Wallace, *The Story of the U. S. Cavalry,* (Boston: Little, Brown and Co., 1953), p. 116.

16. Herr and Wallace, *op. cit.,* p. 34.

CHAPTER 15

1. Roanna H. Winsor, "Arizona Territory, 1863–1963," *Arizona Highways,* March, 1963, p. 35.

2. Hubert Howe Bancroft, *History of Arizona and New Mexico, 1530–1888,* (San Francisco: 1889), p. 504.

3. Document is in the National Archives.

4. Winsor, *op. cit.,* p. 39, ". . . At the conclusion of his remarks (Secretary of State Richard C. McCormick) the flag was raised and the oath of office administered. Then the governor's proclamation was read. . . ."

5. Letter, Sylvester Mowry to Granville H. Oury, March 11, 1859. Copy in possession of author.

6. Charles Franklin Parker, "Arizona's Provisional Government of 1860," *Arizona Highways,* September 1962, p. 37.

7. *Ibid.*

8. Letter, Sylvester Mowry to Granville H. Oury, April 22, 1860. Original in possession of author. See appendix.

9. The man sent by President Polk as an emissary to Mexico in November, 1845. He was empowered to offer the Mexican government $30 million for California and New Mexico. The Mexican government refused to receive Slidell or listen to the American proposal.

10. A most interesting article on the subject is Bert Fireman's "What Comprises Treason?" *Arizoniana,* Vol. I, Winter 1960, p. 5.

11. Journal of the Congress of the Confederate States, I, 660–61, as cited in Benjamin H. Sacks, "The Creation of Arizona Territory," *Arizona and the West,* Vol. 5, nr. 2, Summer 1963, p. 118.

12. Letter, Granville H. Oury to President Jefferson Davis, C.S.A., Nov. 7, 1861. Copy in possession of author.

13. Letter, Granville H. Oury to President Jefferson Davis, C.S.A., Jan. 27, 1862. Copy in possession of author.

14. Document is in the National Archives.

15. Letter, Granville H. Oury to the members of the Provisional Congress from the State of Texas, February, 1862. Copy in possession of author.

CHAPTER 16

1. William S. Oury, "Cooks Canyon, scene of carnage enacted there in July, 1861," *Arizona Daily Star,* Tucson, July 27, 1879.

2. *Ibid.*

3. A disputed figure. Douglas D. Martin in "Battle at Cooke's Canyon," *True West,* Sept.–Oct. 1962, p. 17, states: "Although Oury made the claim that Cochise admitted 185 casualties dead and wounded, a more conservative estimate based on other studies indicates that less than 40 Apaches were slain and another 20 wounded — figures that without exaggeration are overwhelming in their own right. . . ." Martin does not list the other studies.

4. Oury, *op. cit.,* p. 3.

5. *Ibid.*

6. *Ibid.*, p. 4.

7. *Ibid.*, p. 5.

CHAPTER 17

1. Robert M. Utley, "The Bascom Affair: A Reconstruction," *Arizona and the West,* Vol. III, nr. 1, spring, 1961, p. 59. "That no two chroniclers agreed on what happened stems largely from the scarcity of original source material, and from the fact that the few participants who did leave testimony themselves disagreed."
   This is true, but it is of interest to note that Utley uses Oury frequently as a reference, and says, on page 63 of his article: "Oury gives the best and most complete account of this episode."

2. Benjamin H. Sacks, "New Evidence on the Bascom Affair," *Arizona and the West,* Vol. IV, nr. 3, autumn, 1962, p. 275.

3. *Ibid.*, pp. 266–267.

4. W. S. Oury, "A True History of the Outbreak of the Noted Apache Chieftain, Cochise, in the Year 1861." Article was serialized in the Arizona Star (Tucson), beginning June 28, 1877.

5. *Ibid.*, p. 1.

6. Mickey Free, who in later years became a scout and interpreter for General George Crook in the 1880s. He had a vicious disposition, and has been described as "half Irish, half Indian, and all son-of-a-bitch."

7. There is no conclusive proof as to which band of Indians kidnapped the boy. Some feel that Coyoteros not Chiricahuas made the abduction.

8. B. S. D. Irwin, "The Fight at Apache Pass," *Infantry Journal,* 32 (April 1928), pp. 3, 4: "Bascom was ordered to demand the immediate restoration of the stolen property, and in case Cochise should fail to make restitution, the officer was authorized to use the force under his orders to recover it."

9. Utley says "Monday, February 4th."

10. Oury, *op. cit.,* p. 2.

11. *Ibid.* The exact words used are in doubt. It is probable that either Bascom or Ward, telling Oury of the episode later, made some such remark in connection with this part of the story.

12. *Ibid.*, p. 3.

13. *Ibid.*

14. These grisly remains were apparently visible for several years afterward. Mina Oury in her diary speaks of seeing them enroute to Tucson in 1865.

15. No participant of the parley (other than Bernard himself) has mentioned Bernard's presence. Later writers, among them Frank C. Lockwood, have shown sympathy for Bernard's account of this incident.

16. Oury, *op. cit.,* p. 5.

17. *Ibid.*, p. 7. "... the same night a courier was despatched by Superintendent Buckley to the writer of this sketch relating what had occurred and asking him to send a messenger to old Camp Breckinridge ... calling for military assistance and to start himself immediately for the scene of war. The same night, I sent a messenger to Breckinridge with an account of what had occurred at Apache Pass, and requesting Lt. Lord and Lt. Moore to meet me as speedily as possible with their companies at Ewell Station. ..."

18. *Ibid.*

19. *Ibid.*, p. 8.

20. Some writers have condemned Bascom for not saving Wallace when he had the chance. He was of course concerned with Wallace, but could not sacrifice Jordan

and Lyons to save Wallace. On page 11 of his reminiscence of the Bascom affair, Oury says: "The reader who has followed me through this narrative will readily understand and commend the motive which prompted Lt. Bascom to refuse Cochise's proposition. What fair-minded man would fail to condemn him if he had made such unfair discrimination between his own countrymen? . . ."

21. *Ibid.*

22. Irwin, as cited, p. 6. An eight-page reprint of this article is available in the archives of the Arizona Pioneers' Historical Society in Tucson.

23. Sacks, *op. cit.,* p. 272.

CHAPTER 18

1. Ray C. Colton, *The Civil War in the Western Territories,* (Norman: The University of Oklahoma Press, 1959).

2. A Methodist church elder turned soldier. He had been offered the chaplaincy in the First Regiment of Colorado Volunteers, but turned it down for a majority.

3. Colton, *op. cit.,* p. 25. ". . . to establish a post at Tucson for the protection of western Arizona . . . and opening communication with southern California."

4. Calvin Horn and W. S. Wallace, *Union Army Operations in the Southwest,* (Albuquerque: Horn and Wallace, 1961), p. 39. Hereinafter cited as *Union Army Operations.*

5. Demonstrations or violence were not universal however. In speaking of electioneering talks before miners in California in 1860, Cornelius Cole said: "Our audiences were large, and, though made up in great part of our political opponents, we were accorded a respectful hearing on all occasions." Cornelius Cole, *Memoirs of Cornelius Cole,* New York: McLaughlin Bros., 1908, p. 135.

6. See appendix.

7. In the dedication ceremonies of a historical marker erected at the base of Picacho Peak in 1928, Gilbert Smith's son (my father), Col. Cornelius C. Smith, Sr., U. S. Army, made one of the principal addresses. "A strident bugle blast, a soft answering echo from the base of tooth-shaped Picacho, an airplane circling overhead, the strains of the national anthem, Old Glory lowered from the top of the rough-hewn shaft by a stalwart, silver-haired army officer — and then, christened with golden mid-April Arizona sunshine, Picacho Monument belonged to the ages."
   Gilbert Cosulich, "Soldier Dead of Picacho's Battle Honored by Living," Arizona Daily Star, Tucson, April 16, 1928.

8. Letter, Lt. Gilbert C. Smith to his aunt, Olive Cole, New San Diego Barracks, May 7, 1862. Original in possession of author.

9. A. L. Wagner and J. D. Jerrold Kelley, *The United States Army and Navy,* (Navy portion) Akron: The Werner Co., 1899, p. 236.

10. Letter, Lt. Gilbert C. Smith to Olive Cole, Fort Yuma, March 27, 1863. Original in possession of author.

11. James M. McNulty, surgeon, U. S. Volunteers, corroborates Smith's observations here. In his October 1863 report to Brigadier General W. A. Hammond, Surgeon General, U. S. Army, he said: ". . . the march from Fort Yuma to the Pima Villages was fatiguing in the extreme. The intense heat and alkali dust was almost unbearable; both men and animals suffered very much," from *Union Army Operations,* p. 85.

12. Letter, Lt. Gilbert C. Smith to Olive Cole, Gila Bend, June 6, 1863. Original in possession of author.

13. J. Ross Browne, *Adventures in Apache Country* (New York: Harper and Co., 1869), p. 100.

14. *Ibid.,* p. 102.

15. *Ibid.,* p. 134.

16. Letter, Lt. Gilbert C. Smith to Olive Cole, Tucson, June 24, 1863. Original in possession of author.

17. Letter, Lt. Gilbert C. Smith to Olive Cole, Pima Villages, July 20, 1863. Original in possession of author.

18. Letter, Lt. Gilbert C. Smith to his uncle, Cornelius Cole, Tucson, July 26, 1863. Original in possession of author.

19. *Union Army Operations,* p. 39. From a letter from Col. James H. Carleton to Major Richard C. Drum, assistant Adjutant General, U. S. Army, San Francisco, May 25, 1862.

20. *Ibid.,* p. 42. Quoted from General Order No. 11, July 21, 1862.

21. *Ibid.*

22. Proclamation setting aside a part of New Mexico now known as Territory of Arizona. From *Official Records,* I, 50: pp. 96–97 (part 1). Carleton was mistaken in calling Arizona an official territory. It did not become so until Feb. 24, 1863, under the Organic Act creating the Territory of Arizona.

23. *Ibid.,* Section I.

24. *Ibid.,* Section III.

25. Colton, *op. cit.,* p. 108.

26. Arizona Daily Star, Oct. 9, 1879, pp. 1–3.

27. *Union Army Operations,* p. 55. Letter, Brigadier General James H. Carleton to Lt. Col. Richard C. Drum, Santa Fe, New Mexico, September 20, 1862.

28. San Francisco Bulletin, Dec. 28, 1866.

CHAPTER 19

1. James M. Barney, "Early Days in Tucson," *Arizona Miner,* (undated).

2. Proclamation by John N. Goodwin, Governor of Arizona, appointing municipal officers for Arizona, May 11, 1864. Document in the National Archives.

3. *Ibid.*

4. *Arizona Miner,* May 25, 1864.

5. Barney, *op. cit.*

6. Bernice Cosulich, *Tucson,* (Tucson: Arizona Silhouettes, 1953), p. 122. "The humiliation of being seen by other citizens . . . did have a sobering effect."

7. General Order nr. 1, Section I, Headquarters, District of Western Arizona, August 5, 1862. Document in the National Archives.

8. *Ibid.,* Section II.

9. Index of Deeds, Real Property, Pima County, Arizona, Book 1, p. 37.

10. *Ibid.,* p. 38.

11. *Ibid.*

12. *Ibid.,* p. 39.

13. *Ibid.*

14. *Ibid.,* p. 40.

15. *Ibid.,* p. 52.

16. *Ibid.,* Book 2, pp. 140–141.

17. *Ibid.,* pp. 144–145.

18. *Ibid.,* Book 9, p. 379.

19. *Ibid.,* Book 12, p. 125.

20. *Ibid.,* p. 313.

21. *Ibid.,* Book 14, p. 703.

22. See appendix.

23. Cornelius C. Smith, Sr., "A History of the Oury Family," *op. cit.,* p. 94.

24. Letter, Lt. Col. Dan Showalter, Granville H. Oury, *et al,* to Lt. Gen. Kirby-Smith, C.S.A., San Antonio. Original in possession of author.

25. Letter, Senah Oury to William S. Oury, Louisiana, Missouri, May 17, 1864. Original in possession of author.

CHAPTER 20

1. Cornelius C. Smith, Sr., "Some Unpublished History of the Southwest," *Arizona Historical Review,* Vol. IV, nr. 3, Oct. 1931, p. 53. I have made a concerted effort to obtain Mina Oury's original diary. I recall looking at it, as a child, in Durango, Mexico, in 1922. It was then in the possession of a cousin, Genevieve Jackson (adopted daughter of Granville and Mina Oury), now deceased. Her heirs do not know the present whereabouts of the diary, or if it indeed still exists.

2. *Ibid.*

3. *Ibid.,* p. 54.

4. Irving Stone, *Men to Match My Mountains,* New York: (Doubleday and Co., 1956), p. 205. "Terry, A Texan, had Southern slavery antecedents. Broderick was a Northern free labor advocate.... Broderick was a goot shot; Terry was a Bowie knife expert." Cornelius Cole writes of the Terry-Broderick duel in his *Memoirs, op. cit.,* pp. 131–132. ". . . His last words tell the whole story. 'They have killed me because I was opposed to the extension of slavery and a corrupt administration.' "

5. Smith, *op. cit.,* p. 54.

6. *Ibid.,* p. 59.

7. *Ibid.,* p. 60.

8. *Ibid.,* p. 61.

9. *Ibid.,* p. 63.

10. *Ibid.,* Vol. IV, nr. 4, Jan., 1932, p. 47.

11. *Ibid.,* p. 49.

12. *Ibid.,* p. 51.

13. *Ibid.,* p. 57.

14. *Ibid.,* Vol. V, nr. 1, April, 1932, p. 62.

15. *Ibid.,* p. 63.

16. *Ibid.*

17. *Ibid.*

18. *Ibid.,* p. 64.

19. *Ibid.*

20. *Ibid.,* p. 66.

21. *Ibid.,* p. 69.

22. *Ibid.,* Vol. V, nr. 3, Oct., 1932, p. 235.

23. *Ibid.,* p. 237.

24. *Ibid.,* p. 239.

25. *Ibid.*

26. *Ibid.*, Vol. V, nr. 4, Jan., 1933, p. 333.

27. *Ibid.*, p. 337.

28. *Ibid.*, Vol. VI, nr. 1, Jan., 1935, p. 53.

29. *Ibid.*, p. 61.

30. *Ibid.*, p. 62.

31. See appendix.

CHAPTER 21

1. According to my father who lived at Lowell as a boy.

2. Ray Brandes, *Frontier Military Posts of Arizona,* Globe: (Dale Stuart King, 1960), p. 50.

3. *Ibid.*

4. Official U. S. Army Service Record of Service, Gilbert C. Smith, Office of the Adjutant General U. S. Army. Copy in possession of author.

5. *Ibid.*

6. Not a favorite of the young officer. In a letter to his aunt, Olive Cole, written from Gila Bend on June 1, 1863, Smith said: "Colonel Bowie is along with us. I do not think much of him as a military man. This march rather gets him. Everything he does is with an eye for politics, and you know those are not the men for the army. A good officer should be honest instead of a selfish, political trickster." Original letter in possession of the author.

7. Cornelius C. Smith, Sr., "Tucson and Fort Lowell." Unpublished manuscript in possession of the author.

8. *Ibid.*, p. 4.

9. *Ibid.*, p. 7.

10. *Ibid.*, p. 11.

11. See appendix for typical entries.

12. Weekly *Arizonian,* Nov. 5, 1870.

13. Letter, Capt. Gilbert C. Smith to Capt. W. Hughes, Sept. 5, 1868. From Quartermaster log-book of Capt. Smith in possession of author.

14. Smith, "Tucson and Fort Lowell," *op. cit.,* p. 17.

15. Smith, Cornelius C. Sr., "Water sold by the bucketful," Tucson Citizen, Oct. 15, 1920, p. 12.

16. Original certificate in possession of author. See appendix.

17. "Wedding in Tucson," Tucson Weekly Arizonian, July 4, 1868.

18. Later on, Captain Pegram Whitworth, husband of Gilbert Smith's daughter, Emma, became General Arthur MacArthur's aide in the Philippines.

19. Perhaps the most interesting (and popular) work on the travels of churchmen of that era is Willa Cather's *Death Comes for the Archbishop,* the story of Reverend J. P. Machebeuf.

20. I tried to verify this in 1959 while visiting San Xavier Mission. The Father in charge informed me that the records of baptism had been destroyed in a fire some time in the 1920s.

CHAPTER 22

All remarks and observations made in this chapter are taken verbatim from my father's diary, a paper beginning with his reminiscences of boyhood days in Tucson, and continuing on through his early years in the Army.

CHAPTER 23

1. There appears to be much speculation on the founding date. Listing 1859 are: H. H. Bancroft, *History of Arizona and New Mexico* (San Francisco: 1889), p. 497; Thomas Farish, *History of Arizona*, (Phoenix: 1915), Vol. I, p. 322; Averam B. Bender, "Military Posts in the Southwest," *New Mexico Historical Review*, 1941, Vol. 16, p. 135. Giving 1856 are: Rufus K. Wyllys, *Arizona, the History of a Frontier State*, (Phoenix: 1950), p. 124; Richard J. Hinton, *Handbook to Arizona*, (San Francisco: 1878), p. 311; Will C. Barnes, *Arizona Place Names*, University of Arizona Bulletin, Vol. 6, nr. 1, (Tucson: 1935), p. 61. Thomas Hamersley says May 8, 1860, in *Complete Regular Army Register of the United States for 100 Years*, (Washington: 1881), p. 123.

2. Ray C. Brandes, *Frontier Military Posts of Arizona*, Globe: (Dale Stuart King, 1960), p. 35.

3. *Ibid.*

4. *Ibid.*, p. 39.

5. James R. Hastings, "The Tragedy at Camp Grant in 1871," *Arizona and the West*, Vol. I, nr. 2, summer 1959, p. 149.

6. *Ibid.*, p. 150.

7. In Hasting's account the name is spelled "Aggera." Oury gives the usual spelling — Aguirre, undoubtedly one and the same person.

8. Arizona *Citizen* (Tucson), March 11, 1871.

9. Cornelius C. Smith, Sr., "Eskiminzin, Archfiend." Unpublished manuscript in possession of the author, p. 64.

10. *Ibid.*, p. 65 .

11. *Ibid.*

12. *Ibid.*, p. 66.

13. *Ibid.*, p. 67.

14. *Ibid.*, p. 69.

15. William S. Oury, "A Report on the Camp Grant Affair to the Members of the Arizona Pioneers Historical Society," delivered on March 20, 1880, p. 4. Hereinafter titled "Report on the Camp Grant Affair." Original manuscript in possession of the author. See appendix for reproduction of first and last pages.

16. *Ibid.*, p. 6.

17. *Ibid.*

18. According to a quote from the Arizona Citizen of April 1, 1871, given by Hastings, *Tragedy at Camp Grant, op. cit.*, p. 151.

19. Smith, "Eskiminzin, Archfiend," *op. cit.*, p. 70.

20. *Ibid.*

21. Arizona *Citizen* (Tucson), April 15, 1871.

22. Oury, "Report on the Camp Grant Affair," *op. cit.*, p. 15.

23. William Bailey, "The Camp Grant Massacre," manuscript in the files of the Arizona Pioneers' Historical Society. Bailey was one of the six American participants. Of Hughes, he said: "Some people claim Sam Hughes was in the party of avengers to go to Arivaipa, but he was not. He was heart and soul in it, for he furnished the arms to most of the men that took part in that execution," p. 1.

24. *Ibid.*, p. 2.

25. Hastings, *op. cit.*, p. 153. "Hughes wife later said, 'They tried to make out that he (Hughes) gave arms to the Indians, but he didn't. That was against the law. The arms and ammunition were given to the whites and the Mexicans, but not to the

Indians." This information comes from a manuscript by Atancia Hughes, published under the title "As Told by the Pioneers," in the *Arizona Historical Review,* Vol. 6, 1935, pp. 66–74. As the Papagos used guns, the question of who gave them the guns is academic. Probably Hughes gave the guns to Oury, Elias, or some of the Mexican members of the party, who in turn gave them to the Indians.

26. The Elias quote frequently given, and erroneously ascribed to Oury. Oury in his Report on the Camp Grant Affair actually quoted Elias as saying: "For months we have repeatedly held meetings at which many patriotic speeches have been made and glowing resolutions passed. . . . We cannot resolute the Apache out of existence. If that could have been done, every one of them would have been dead long since." p. 10.

27. Bailey, *op. cit.,* p. 3.

28. Oury, "Report on the Camp Grant Affair," *op. cit.,* p. 16.

29. Bailey, *op. cit.,* p. 4.

30. Oury, "Report on the Camp Grant Affair," *op. cit.,* p. 22.

31. *Ibid.*

32. Bailey, *op. cit.,* p. 9.

33. *Ibid.,* p. 7.

34. In telling of his experiences with the San Carlos Apaches in "Apache Years of the Man with the high Marble Dome," *Touring Topics,* Dec., 1931 (as told to John Edwin Hogg), John Clum eulogizes Eskiminzin, saying: "From what I had been able to learn of the Apaches before going to San Carlos, I was forced to the conclusion that much of their bad reputation was due to maladministration. That the conclusion was quite correct became evident to me very soon after my arrival at San Carlos," p. 15.

In a pencilled note to my father (Col. C. C. Smith), Anton Mazzonovitch wrote across the lead-sheet of the Clum piece: "Another brainstorm. I have read this story many times. In fact, I have it on file, sent to me by 'His Honor,' the first mayor of Tombstone."

35. James M. Barney, "Notes on the Camp Grant Massacre," Phoenix, Arizona, 1946. Manuscript in the files of Arizona Pioneers' Historical Society.

36. Weekly *Arizona Miner* (Prescott), June 10, 1871.

37. Arizona *Citizen* (Tucson), June 24, 1871.

38. Weekly Arizona Miner (Prescott), June 10, 1871.

39. Oury, "Report on the Camp Grant Affair," *op. cit.,* p. 3.

40. Arizona *Citizen* (Tucson), Jan. 13, 1872.

41. Hastings, *op. cit.,* p. 157.

42. The father of Senator Carl Hayden of Arizona.

43. "The Trial and Evidence Presented in Court," manuscript in the files of the Arizona Pioneers' Historical Society, p. 1.

44. *Ibid.,* p. 2.

45. *Ibid.*

46. *Ibid.*

47. *Ibid.,* p. 3.

48. Daily *Alta California,* Feb. 3, 1872. Taken from the complete transcript of the trial printed in this newspaper.

49. Daily *Alta California,* Feb. 4, 1872.

50. *Ibid.*

51. *Arizona Weekly Miner* (Prescott), Jan. 6, 1872.

52. Florence (Arizona) *Tribune,* Aug. 8, 1896.

53. Daily *Alta California,* Feb. 4, 1872.

54. *Ibid.*

55. *Ibid.*

56. Six Americans are generally listed as participants: William S. Oury, Sidney R. de Long, William Bailey, James Lee, and two unnamed men (Sam Hughes helped in staging the affair, but did not go to Camp Grant). In his report, "The Camp Grant Massacre," Bailey said: "Before we left the Indian village, Elías gave orders to march out in twos so as to have a check or count on his men. Oury and I led. There were 92 Papagos in our company as counted by Elías. Then he called for the Americans to form. There were only four. Some Mexican said, 'Bill Oury and the old soldier, Bill Bailey, make six. Yes, there are six Americans," said Elías." P. 8.

57. Bailey, "The Camp Grant Massacre," *op. cit.,* p. 7.

58. Wood, *op. cit.,* p. 18.

59. Weekly *Arizona Enterprise,* Oct. 3, 1872.

60. Oury, "Report on the Camp Grant Affair," *op. cit.,* p. 25.

CHAPTER 24

1. "Black Rocks," a nickname for Vicente Hernández, the owner of a small general store. The name Piernas Negras ("Black Legs") has been given erroneously by some writers. To confuse the issue even more, R. C. (Charley) Brown has referred to "Pedro Negras" in his reminiscenses.

2. The house and store were on the southeast corner of Meyer and Simpson streets. Several years ago, when I was researching in the area, a small confectionery "La Concha" occupied the site.

3. "Frontier Justice," Arizona *Weekly Enterprise,* Jan. 28, 1892. Reprint of the article is in files of the Arizona Pioneers' Historical Society, Tucson, p. 1.

4. *Ibid.* (Corroboration of this version of arrest by Oury was given by him to my father at Fort Lowell in 1885).

5. *Ibid.,* p. 3.

6. Charley Brown substantiates this statement in his "Reminiscences."(Manuscript on file in Arizona Pioneers' Historical Society, Tucson). "They had finished examining him and were about to let him go when Bill Oury said 'Wait a minute, look here!' — and pulling off the man's sandals he showed that the fellow's feet around the nails were all bloody. This man gave the other two away." P. 1.

7. "Frontier Justice," *op. cit.,* p. 6.

8. *Ibid.,* p. 8.

9. In his "Reminiscences," Charley Brown said: "An American named Willis fainted on the scaffold. The crowd was very quiet, there was not a word spoken and the tension was dreadful." P. 1.

10. "Frontier Justice," *op. cit.,* p. 8.

11. Colonel James H. Toole, J. E. McCaffrey *et al.* "To the Citizens and Taxpayers of the County of Pima." Document on file at the Arizona Pioneers' Historical Society.

12. Quote supplied by George J. Roskruge to my father, a slightly different variation than given in Roskruge's anecdote to Mrs. George F. Kitt in 1928.

13. Daily *Star* (Tucson), Oct. 17, 1884.

14. S. W. Carpenter, "A Card," (Tucson) Arizona Daily Star, Oct. 3, 1878.

15. *Daily Star,* Jan. 28, 1886.

CHAPTER 25

1. Bill told his grandson about the Mexican circus, saying: "It wasn't much, but the children liked it." A good description of the Mexican circus has been given by Hilario Gallego, whose reminiscences of old Tucson are on file in the Arizona Pioneers' Historical Society in Tucson.
2. The reception desk of the old Orndorff Hotel is now displayed in the Arizona Pioneers' Historical Society, complete with register, service bell, and other items.
3. Adam Sanders was related to Bill Oury, a cousin. He was the brother of Mina Sanders Oury (wife of Bill's brother Granville), and had made the trek into Mexico with her in June, 1865.
4. "Cremation Society," Arizona Citizen (Tucson), April 25, 1874.
5. Arizona *Citizen* (Tucson), Jan. 24, 1874.
6. Arizona *Citizen* (Tucson), March 15, 1873.
7. Tombstone *Epitaph,* July 15, 1882.
8. Tucson *Daily Star,* Oct. 14, 1884.
9. Yuma *Territorial Expositor* (date torn from clipping).

CHAPTER 26

1. Arizona *Daily Star* (Tucson), Oct. 9, 1879.
2. Arizona *Daily Star,* Oct. 12, 1879.
3. William S. Oury's address on the arrival of the Southern Pacific Railroad in Tucson, March 20, 1880. Copy of this speech is in the files of the Arizona Pioneers' Historical Society in Tucson. In his "Reminiscences," published in the Arizona *Daily Star,* Frank Lockwood said: "A supreme event in the history of Tucson was the arrival of the first railroad train in the Old Pueblo on March 20, 1880. To William S. Oury was given the honor of making the speech of welcome to the President of the S.P.R.R. and the high officers who had come on this first train to celebrate the event."
4. Bernice Cosulich, *Tucson,* (Tucson: Arizona Silhouettes, 1953), p. 179.
5. *Ibid.,* p. 181.
6. William S. Oury, "Scraps of Unwritten History in Arizona," Arizona Weekly Star, May 20, 1880.
7. *Ibid.*
8. *Arizona Daily Star,* Sept. 2, 1885.
9. Affidavit of W. S. Oury on "Tres Alamos," June 15, 1886. Original document in files of the Arizona Pioneers' Historical Society, Tucson.
   Each of the letters used as source material for this section is an original; all letters are in possession of the author.
10. Letter, William S. Oury to his daughter, Lola Smith, Nov. 29, 1883.
11. Letter, William S. Oury to Lola Smith, Sept. 8, 1884.
12. Letter, William S. Oury to Lola Smith, Feb. 22, 1885.
13. Letter, William S. Oury to Lola Smith, Nov. 20, 1885.
14. The resolution was signed by H. D. Underwood and S. B. Conley, foreman and secretary respectively of the Grand Jury. It was sent to members of Frank's family and to most of the Arizona papers.
15. Letter, William S. Oury to Lola Smith, Dec. 24, 1885.
16. *Arizona Daily Citizen,* March 31, 1887.

Sources

ACCOUNTS BY PARTICIPANTS

OURY, WILLIAM SANDERS: Letter to Alex M. Kenaday, reprinted in Washington, D.C., Vedette, April 6, 1880. Lengthy narrative on Oury's participation in the Mexican War, 1846–48. Original copy of Vedette in possession of author.

—————————: "A brief history of Early Journalism in Pima County," Arizona Daily Star (undated).

—————————: "A true history of the outbreak of the noted Apache Chieftain Cochise in the Year 1861," serialized in the Arizona Daily Star, beginning June 28, 1877.

OURY, MINA SANDERS: Diary kept on her journey into Mexico at the close of the Civil War. Diary begins in June, 1865, at San Antonio, Texas; the last trip entry is from Tucson, A.T., in November 1865.

OURY, WILLIAM SANDERS: "A Report on the Camp Grant Affair." This is a 25-page hand-written narrative by Oury on his part in the Camp Grant Massacre. (Original in possession of the author).

BAILEY, WILLIAM: "The Camp Grant Massacre." Bailey (along with W. S. Oury) was one of six American participants in the Camp Grant affair. This is his version of the story, in manuscript form, on file at the Arizona Pioneers' Historical Society, Tucson, Arizona.

OURY, WILLIAM SANDERS: "Scraps of Unwritten History of Arizona," Arizona Weekly Star, May 20, 1880.

SMITH, CORNELIUS C., SR.: Diary, 1890–1901. (Original in possession of the author).

CONTEMPORARY LETTERS

Originals in possession of the author

June 22, 1858.	John M. Oury to "Margaret."
April 22, 1860.	Sylvester Mowry to Granville H. Oury.
May 7, 1862.	Lt. Gilbert C. Smith to Olive Cole.
May 21, 1862.	Granville H. Oury to the People of Mesilla.
March 27, 1863.	Lt. Gilbert C. Smith to Olive Cole.
June 6, 1863.	Lt. Gilbert C. Smith to Olive Cole.
June 24, 1863.	Lt. Gilbert C. Smith to Olive Cole.
July 20, 1863.	Lt. Gilbert C. Smith to Olive Cole.
July 26, 1863.	Lt. Gilbert C. Smith to Cornelius Cole.
February 14, 1864.	Lt. Col. Dan Showalter *et al.* to Lt. Gen. Kirby-Smith, C.S.A.

May 17, 1864.   Senah Oury to William S. Oury.
November 29, 1883.   William S. Oury to Lola Smith.
September 8, 1884.   William S. Oury to Lola Smith.
October 18, 1884.   William S. Oury to Lola Smith.
November 15, 1884.   William S. Oury to Lola Smith.
February 22, 1885.   William S. Oury to Lola Smith.
May 13, 1885.   William S. Oury to Lola Smith.
November 20, 1885.   William S. Oury to Lola Smith.
December 24, 1885.   William S. Oury to Lola Smith.

Copies in possession of author
March 11, 1859.   Sylvester Mowry to Granville H. Oury.
November 7, 1861.   Granville H. Oury to President Jefferson Davis, C.S.A.
January 27, 1862.   Granville H. Oury to President Jefferson Davis, C.S.A.
February 1, 1862.   Granville H. Oury to Members of the Provisional
                     Congress from the State of Texas.
February 22, 1863.   Captain Granville H. Oury to
                     Brigadier General H. H. Sibley, C.S.A.

LATER LETTERS

All in possession of author
November 7, 1907.   Senah Oury to Eunice Oury. (copy)
March 5, 1908.   Senah Oury to William B. Foster. (copy)
July 3, 1909.   William B. Foster to Katie Mathews. (copy)
April 9, 1928.   William O. Smith to Cornelius C. Smith, Sr. (original)
October 22, 1930.   J. D. Newton to William O. Smith (copy)
July 10, 1931.   J. Marvin Hunter to Cornelius C. Smith (original)

OFFICIAL RECORDS

Pennsylvania Archives:
Second Series, Vol. 10.
Third Series, Vol. 22.
Fifth Series, Vols. 1, 3.
Sixth Series, Vol. 9.

Quartermaster log-book of Capt. Gilbert Cole Smith, U. S. Army, 1868–1870.
(Original log-book of 97 pages and 318 separate entries in possession of author).

MANUSCRIPT MATERIAL

All in possession of the author

SMITH, CORNELIUS C., SR. "A History of the Oury Family." This is an unpublished manuscript dealing with the entire Oury clan. While some of it is devoted to genealogy, much of it treats with the experiences of William Sanders Oury, held by the author to be "the most colorful of the lot." Much of it is reminiscent in character, as the author (William Oury's grandson) quotes Oury frequently. It must stand as a most important source on the doings of William Sanders Oury.

————————. "Tucson and Fort Lowell."

————————. "Eskiminzin, Archfiend."

NEWSPAPERS

Santa Cruz Sentinel, July 5, 1858.
New York Herald, Nov. 11, 1858.
Tubac Arizonian, March 3, 17, April 14, 28, May 18, June 16, 1859.

Weekly Arizonian (Tucson), Oct. 6, 1859; July 4, 1868; Nov. 5, 1870.
St. Louis Daily Missouri Republican, Jan. 1, 1860.
San Francisco Bulletin, Dec. 28, 1866.
Arizona Miner (Prescott), May 25, 1864; June 10, 1871; Jan. 6, 1872.
Arizona Citizen (Tucson), March 11, April 15, June 24, 1871; Jan. 13, June 1,
     Aug. 8, 1872; March 15, 1873; Jan. 24, April 25,
     May 2, 1874; March 31, 1887; Oct. 15, 1920.
Arizona Daily Star (Tucson), Oct. 13, 1878; July 27, Oct. 9, 1879; Dec. 15,
     1881; Oct. 14, 1884; Sept. 2, 1885.
Daily Alta California, Feb. 4, 1872.
Arizona Sentinel (Yuma), Sept. 14, 1878.
Tombstone Epitaph, June 17, July 15, 1882; Feb. 17, 1886; April 26,
     July 26, 1890.
Arizona Enterprise, June 2, 1888; Jan. 28, 1892.
St. Johns Herald, Nov. 7, 1889.
Florence Tribune, Aug. 8, 1896.
Kansas City Star, Dec. 24, 1928.

ARTICLES

BAKER, KARLE WILSON, "Trailing the New Orleans Greys,"
 Southwest Review, Vol. XXII, April, 1937.

BARKER, E. C., "The San Jacinto Campaign,"
 The Southwestern Historical Quarterly, Vol. IV, 1901.

——————————, "The Texan Revolutionary Army,"
 Texas Historical Association Quarterly, Vol. IX, 1906.

BARNEY, JAMES M., "Old Fort Bowie,"
 Sheriff's Magazine, Tucson, January, 1955.

BENDER, AVERAM B., "Military Posts of the Southwest, 1848–1860,"
 New Mexico Historical Review, Vol. 16, April, 1941.

BENTS, DORIS W., "The History of Tubac, 1752–1948,"
 Unpublished Master's Thesis, University of Arizona, 1949.

BLOOM, LANSING B., (Editor), "Bourke on the Southwest,"
 New Mexico Historical Review, Vol. 9, April, 1934.

BONHAM, MILLEDGE L., JR., "James Butler Bonham, a Consistent Rebel,"
 Southwestern Historical Quarterly, Vol. 35, 1931.

BOYLE, ANDREW A., "When Texas Fought for Independence,"
 Frontier Times, May, 1935.

BRANDES, RAY, "A Guide to the U. S. Army Installations in Arizona, 1849–1886,"
 Arizona and the West, Vol. I, nr. 1, Spring, 1959.

CASTAÑEDA, CARLOS E., "Silent Years in Texas History,"
 Southwestern Historical Quarterly, Vol. 38, October, 1934.

COFFMAN, EDWARD M., "Ben McCulloch Letters,"
 The Southwestern Historical Quarterly, Vol. LX, July, 1956.

CRIMMINS, MARTIN L., "The Alamo and Its History,"
 Frontier Times, Vol. XVIII, 1940.

DAVENPORT, HARBERT, "The Men of Goliad,"
 Southwestern Historical Quarterly, XLIII, 1939.

DAVIDGE, SARAH ELLEN, "Texas Rangers Were Rough and Ready Fighters,"
 Frontier Times, November, 1935, pp. 125–130.

DOBIE, J. FRANK, "The Alamo's Immortalization of Words,"
 Southwest Review, Vol. 27, 1942.

DUFFEN, WILLIAM A., (Editor), "Overland Via Jackass Mail,"
 Arizona and the West, Vol. II, nr. 3, Autumn, 1960.

EATON, CLEMENT W., "Frontier Life in Southern Arizona, 1858–1861,"
Southwestern Historical Quarterly, Vol. 36, Jan., 1933.

FAULK, ODIE B., "The Controversial Boundary Survey and the Gadsden Treaty,"
Arizona and the West, Vol. IV, nr. 3, Autumn, 1962.

FIREMAN, BERT W., "What Comprises Treason?"
Arizonian, Vol. 1, nr. 4, Winter, 1960.

GALLEGO, HILARIO, "Reminiscences of an Arizona Pioneer,"
Arizona Historical Review, Vol. VI, nr. 1, Jan., 1935.

HALL, MARTIN H., "The Skirmish at Mesilla,"
Arizona and the West, Vol. I, nr. 4, Winter, 1959.

HASTINGS, JAMES R., "The Tragedy at Camp Grant,"
Arizona and the West, Vol. I, nr. 2, Summer, 1959.

HENDERSON, H. M., "A Critical Analysis of the San Jacinto Campaign,"
The Southwestern Historical Quarterly, Vol. LIX, January, 1956.

HOUGHSTON, MARY, "Old Fort Lowell,"
Arizona Highways, April, 1948.

HUNT, AURORA, "California Volunteers on Border Patrol, Texas and New
Mexico, 1862–1866," *Southern California Historical Society Quarterly,*
Vol. 30, December, 1948.

————————, "California Volunteers,"
Southern California Historical Society Quarterly, Vol. 36, June, 1954.

HUNTER, J. MARVIN, "The Opening Campaign of the Texas Revolution,"
Frontier Times, September, 1935.

IRWIN, BERNARD J. D., "The Apache Pass Fight,"
The Infantry Journal, Vol. 32, nr. 4, April, 1928.

KING, ROBERT W., "Southern Pacific; Seventy-Five Years of Service to Arizona
and the West," *Arizona Highways,* May, 1955.

LOCKWOOD, FRANK D., "Early Military Posts in Arizona,"
Arizona Historical Review, Vol. II, Jan., 1930.

————————, "Tucson, the Old Pueblo,"
Arizona Historical Review, Vol. III, July, 1930.

McMILLEN, KATHRYN SMITH, "Descriptive Bibliography on the San Antonio-
San Diego Mail Line," *Southwestern Historical Quarterly,* Vol. 59, 1955–56.

McMURTRIE, DOUGLAS C., "The Beginnings of Printing in Arizona,"
The Arizona Historical Review, Vol. V, nr. 3, October, 1932.

MUIR, ANDREW F., "The Destiny of Buffalo Bayou,"
The Southwestern Historical Quarterly, Vol. XLVII, 1943.

————————, "The Mystery of San Jacinto,"
Southwest Review, Vol. 36, 1951.

MULLIGAN, RAYMOND A., "Down the Old Butterfield Trail,"
Arizona and the West, Vol. I, nr. 4, Winter, 1959.

OGLE, RALPH H., "Federal Control of the Western Apaches,"
New Mexico Historical Review, 1939.

OURY, WILLIAM S., "A True History of the Outbreak of the Noted Apache
Chieftain Cochise in the Year 1861," *The Arizona Star,* June 28, 1877.

OFFICER, JAMES E., "A Note on the Elías Family in Tucson,"
Arizona and the West, Vol. I, nr. 4, Winter, 1959.

PARK, JOSEPH F., "The Apaches in Mexican-American Relations, 1848–1861,"
Arizona and the West, Vol. III, nr. 2, Summer, 1961.

POSTON, CHARLES D., "Apache Land,"
Overland Monthly, Vol. 24, September, 1894.

RAMSDELL, CHARLES, "The Storming of the Alamo,"
  American Heritage Magazine, February, 1961.

SACKS, BENJAMIN H., "New Evidence on the Bascom Affair,"
  Arizona and the West, Vol. IV, nr. 3, Autumn, 1962.

—————————, "The Creation of Arizona Territory,"
  Arizona and the West, Vol. 5, No. 2, Summer, 1963.

SCHMIDT, LOUIS B., "Manifest Opportunity and the Gadsden Purchase,"
  Arizona and the West, Vol. III, nr. 2, Summer, 1961.

SLOAN, ELEANOR B., "Seventy-Five Years of the Arizona Pioneers' Historical
  Society," *Arizona and the West,* Vol. I, nr. 1, Spring, 1959.

SMITH, CORNELIUS C., "The Army and the Apache,"
  Arizona Historical Review, Vol. IV, January, 1932.

SMITH, RUBY C., "James W. Fannin Jr. in the Texas Revolution,"
  Southwestern Historical Quarterly, Vol. 23, 1919.

SUMMERS, LEWIS PRESTON, "One Hundred Years of the History of Abingdon,"
  Publications of the Historical Society of Washington County, Virginia.
  Society Publication, undated.

TAYLOR, MAUDE WALLIS, "Ben Franklin Highsmith,"
  Frontier Times, April, 1938.

TERRELL, A. W., "Recollections of General Sam Houston,"
  Southwestern Historical Quarterly, Vol. 16, 1912.

TOMPKINS, WALTER ALLISON, "Old Fort Bowie, Guardian of Apache Pass,"
  Arizona Highways, March, 1959.

TOULOUSE, JOSEPH, "Military Forts in 1869,"
  Arizona Historical Review, Vol. VI, July, 1935.

UTLEY, ROBERT M., "The Bascom Affair; A Reconstruction,"
  Arizona and the West, Vol. III, nr. 1, Spring, 1961.

WILLIAMS, AMELIA, "A Critical Study of the Siege of the Alamo,"
  The Southwestern Historical Quarterly, Austin, 1934.

WINTHER, OSCAR O., "The Southern Overland Mail and Stagecoach Line,
  1857–1861," *New Mexico Historical Review,* Vol. 32, 1957.

WOODWARD, ARTHUR, "Sidelights on Fifty Years of Apache Warfare,
  1836–1886," *Arizonian,* Vol. II, Fall, 1961.

BOOKS

ADAMS, WARD R., *History of Arizona,*
  Phoenix: The Record Publishing Co., 1930.

ANDERSON, ROBERT, *An Artillery Officer in the Mexican War, 1846–47,*
  New York: G. P. Putnam's Sons, 1911.

BANCROFT, GEORGE, *History of the United States of America,*
  New York: D. Appleton and Co., 1883.

BANCROFT, HUBERT HOWE, *History of the North Mexican States and Texas,*
  San Francisco: A. L. Bancroft and Co., 1884–1889, 2 Vols.

—————————, *History of Arizona and New Mexico,*
  San Francisco: The History Co., 1889.

BARKER, EUGENE C., *The Life of Stephen F. Austin,*
  Nashville: The Cokesbury Press, 1925.

BARNES, WILL C., *Arizona Place Names,*
  Tucson: University of Arizona Press, 1915.

BEALS, CARLTON, *Stephen F. Austin, Father of Texas,*
  New York: McGraw-Hill Co., 1953.

BINKLEY, WILLIAM C., *The Texas Revolution,*
Baton Rouge: Louisiana State University Press, 1952.
————. *The Expansionist Movement in Texas, 1836–1850,*
Berkeley: University of California Press, 1925.
BOLTON, HERBERT EUGENE, *Texas in the Middle of the Eighteenth Century,*
Berkeley: University of California Press, 1915.
————. *With the Makers of Texas,*
Austin: Texas University Press, 1904.
BOURKE, JOHN G., *On the Border With Crook,*
New York: Charles Scribners, Sons, 1892.
————, *An Apache Campaign in the Sierra Madre, 1883,*
New York: Charles Scribners, Sons, 1958.
BROWN, JOHN HENRY, *Early Days of San Francisco, California,*
Oakland: Biobooks, 1949.
BROWNE, J. ROSS, *Adventures in Apache Country,*
New York: Harper, 1869.
BUTTERFIELD, JACK C., *Men of the Alamo, Goliad and San Jacinto,*
San Antonio: The Naylor Publishing Co., 1936.
CASTAÑEDA, CARLOS E., *The Mexican Side of the Texas Revolution,*
Dallas: P. L. Turner, 1928.
CHABOT, FREDERICK C., *The Alamo as Mission, Fortress, and Shrine,*
San Antonio: The Naylor Publishing Co., 1941.
————. *The Alamo, Altar of Texas Liberty,*
San Antonio: The Naylor Publishing Co., 1931.
CHAMBERLAIN, SAMUEL E., *My Confession,*
New York: Harper and Brothers, 1956.
COLE, CORNELIUS, *Memoirs of Cornelius Cole,*
New York: McLaughlin Bros., 1908.
COLTON, RAY C., *The Civil War in the Western Territories,*
Norman: University of Oklahoma Press, 1959.
COSULICH, BERNICE, *Tucson,* Tucson, 1953.
CREMONY, JOHN C., *Life Among the Apaches,*
San Francisco: A. Roman and Co., 1868.
de LA BARCA, MADAME CALDERON, *Life in Mexico,*
New York: Dutton and Co., 1931 (Reprint)
de LONG, SIDNEY R., *The History of Arizona from the Earliest Times Known,*
San Francisco: Whitaker and Ray, 1905.
DE SHIELDS, JAMES T., *Tall Men and Long Rifles,*
San Antonio: The Naylor Publishing Co., 1935.
DOBIE, J. FRANK (ed.), *In the Shadow of History,*
Austin: Texas University Press, 1939.
DUVAL, JOHN C., *Adventures of Bigfoot Wallace,*
Macon, Ga.; J. W. Burke Co., 1871.
    *(Also printed in Philadelphia, 1871, by Claxton, Remsen, and Haffelfinger,
    under title: Bigfoot Wallace, Texas Ranger and Hunter).*
FORBES, ROBERT H., *The Penningtons, Pioneers of Early Arizona,*
Tucson: Arizona Archaeological and Historical Society, 1919.
FROST, JOHN, *History of Mexico and the Mexican War,*
Philadelphia: Thomas Cowperthwait Co., 1849.
GALLEGOS, JOSE IGNACIO, *Compendio De Historia De Durango, 1821–1910,*
Mexico: Editorial Jus, 1955.
GARRISON, GEORGE P., *Texas, A Contest of Civilization,*
Boston: Houghton, Mifflin Co., 1903.

GREEN, THOMAS J., *Journal of the Texian Expedition Against Miér*,
New York: Harper and Brothers, 1845.

GREER, JAMES KIMMINS, *Colonel Jack Hays, Texas Frontier Leader and California Builder*, New York, E. P. Dutton and Co., 1952.

HAFEN, LEROY R., *The Overland Mail, 1849–1869*,
Cleveland: A. H. Clark Co., 1926.

HALL, MARTIN H., *Sibley's New Mexico Campaign*,
Austin: University of Texas Press, 1960.

HANIGHEN, FRANK CLEARY, *Santa Anna, Napoleon of the West*,
New York: Coward McCann, 1934.

HEITMAN, FRANCIS B., *Historical Register of Officers of the Continental Army, 1775–1783*, Washington: Rare Book Shop Publishing Co., 1914.

HERR, JOHN K., and WALLACE, EDWARD S., *The Story of the U. S. Cavalry, 1775–1942*, Boston: Little, Brown, and Co., 1953.

HORN, CALVIN, and WALLACE, W. S. (Editors), *Union Army Operations in the Southwest*, Albuquerque: Horn and Wallace, 1961.

HUNT, AURORA, *Major Gen. James Henry Carleton, Western Frontier Dragoon*,
Glendale: Arthur H. Clarke Co., 1958.

HUNTER, J. MARVIN, *Pioneer History of Bandera County*,
Bandera, Texas: Frontier Times, 1922.

HUNTER, WILLIAM A., *Forts on the Pennsylvania Frontier, 1753–1758*,
Harrisburg: The Pennsylvania Historical and Museum Commission, 1960.

JAMES, MARQUIS, *The Raven*,
New York: Indianapolis: The Bobbs Merrill Co., 1929.

KENLY, JOHN R., *Memoirs of a Maryland Volunteer in the War With Mexico, 1846–48*, Philadelphia: J. B. Lippincott Co., 1873.

KETCHAM, RICHARD M. (ED) *et al.*, *The American Heritage Book of the Revolution*, New York: American Heritage Publishing Co., 1958.

KIRBY, ROBERT LEE, *The Confederate Invasion of New Mexico and Arizona, 1861–1862*, Los Angeles: Westmoreland Press, 1958.

LOCKWOOD, FRANK C., *Pioneer Days in Tucson*,
New York: The MacMillan Co., 1932.

——————, *Arizona Characters*,
Los Angeles: The Times-Mirror Press, 1928.

——————, *More About Arizona Characters*,
Tucson: University of Arizona Bulletin, Vol. 13, nr. 3, 1943.

——————, *The Apache Indians*,
New York: The MacMillan Co., 1938.

LORD, WALTER, *A Time to Stand*,
New York: Harper, 1961.

MORFI, JUAN AGUSTIN, *History of Texas* (translated by Carlos E. Castaneda),
Albuquerque: The Quivira Society, 1935.

MOWRY, SYLVESTER, *Arizona and Sonora*,
New York: Harper and Brothers, 1864.

MYERS, JOHN M., *The Alamo*, New York. E. P. Dutton and Co., 1948.

ORMSBY, WATERMAN L., *The Butterfield Overland Mail*, (Edited by Lyle H. Wright and Josephine M. Bynum), San Marino: Huntington Library, 1942.

OTERO, MIGUEL, *My Life on the Frontier*,
New York: Press of the Pioneers, 1935.

POSTON, CHARLES, *Building a State in Apache Land*,
San Francisco: A. L. Bancroft and Co., 1878.

PRESTON, JOHN HYDE, *A Short History of the American Revolution,*
New York: Pocket Books Inc., 1933.

PUMPELLY, RAPHAEL, *Across America and Asia,*
New York: Leypoldt and Holt, 1870.

REID, SAM C., *The Scouting Expedition of McCulloch's Texas Rangers,*
Philadelphia: The Keystone Co., 1890.

ROBINSON, WILL H., *The Story of Arizona,*
Phoenix: The Berryhill Co., 1919.

ROOT, FRANK A., and CONNELLY, WILLIAM E., *The Overland Stage to California,* Topeka: Published by the authors, 1901.

ROUAIX, PASTOR, *Diccionario Geográfico, Histórico, y Biográfico Del Estado De Durango,* México: Instituto Pan Americano de Geografía y Historia, 1946.

RYDER-TAYLOR, HENRY, *History of the Alamo,*
San Antonio: NIC TENGG, undated.

SCHMITT, MARTIN F. (ED), *General George Crook; His Autobiography,*
Norman: University of Oklahoma Press, 1946.

SHACKFORD, JAMES, *David Crockett, the Man and the Legend,*
Chapel Hill: University of North Carolina Press, 1956.

SINGLETARY, OTIS A., *The Mexican War,*
Chicago: University of Chicago Press, 1960.

SONNICHSEN, C. L., *The Mescalero Apaches,*
Norman: University of Oklahoma Press, 1958.

SOULÉ, FRANK, *The Annals of San Francisco,*
New York: D. Appleton and Co., 1854.

SOWELL, ANDREW JACKSON, *Early Settlers and Indian Fighters of Texas,*
Austin: Ben C. Jones and Co., 1900.

——————, *Life of Bigfoot Wallace*
Devine, Texas: Ben C. Jones and Co., 1899.

STAPP, W. PRESTON, *Prisoners of Perote,*
Philadelphia: La Grange Publishing Co. 1933 (first published in 1845).

STONE, IRVING, *Men to Match My Mountains,*
New York: Doubleday and Co., 1956.

SUMMERS, LEWIS PRESTON, *History of Southwest Virginia, 1746–1786; Washington County, 1777–1870,* Richmond: J. C. Hill, 1903.

——————, *Annals of Southwest Virginia, 1769–1800,*
Kingsport, Tennessee: Kingsport Press, 1929.

TEVIS, JAMES H., *Arizona in the Fifties,*
Albuquerque: University of New Mexico Press, 1954.

TINKLE, LON, *Thirteen Days to Glory,*
New York: McGraw-Hill, 1958.

TOLBERT, FRANK X., *The Day of San Jacinto,*
New York: McGraw-Hill, 1959.

VESTAL, STANLEY, *Bigfoot Wallace,*
Boston: Houghton Mifflin Co., 1942.

WEBB, WALTER PRESCOTT, *The Texas Rangers, A Century of Frontier Defense,*
Boston: Houghton Mifflin Co., 1935.

WELLMAN, PAUL I., *The Indian Wars of the West,*
New York: Doubleday, 1956.

WYLLYS, RUFUS K., *Arizona: The History of a Frontier State,*
Phoenix: Hobson and Herr, 1950.

YOAKUM, HENDERSON, *History of Texas from Its First Settlement in 1685 to Its Annexation to the United States in 1846,* New York: Redfield, 1856.

Chronology

1817	Aug. 13	William Sanders Oury born, Abingdon, Virginia
1825	Mar. 25	Granville H. Oury born, Abingdon, Virginia
1833	———	Augustus Oury moved family to Louisiana, Missouri
1834	———	W. S. Oury migrated to Texas
1836	Feb. 23	W. S. Oury moved into Alamo with Travis, Bowie, *et al.*
	Feb. 29	Travis sent Oury as courier to Gonzales, Texas
	Mar. 13	Oury left Gonzales with Gen. Sam Houston
	Apr. 21	Oury participated in Battle of San Jacinto
	Nov. 5	Oury rejoined Texas Army (First Regiment of Regular Infantry, "D" Co., Capt. Irvine)
1837	May 28	Oury furloughed (under Gen. Houston's order)
	Dec. 30	Oury discharged from Army
1839	Summer	Oury joined Texas Rangers
1840	Aug. 11	Oury with John Coffee Hays at Plum Creek
1842	———	Oury with Hays at Bandera Pass
	Sept. 14	Oury with Hays, scouting party vs. Gen. Adrian Woll
	Nov. 22	Oury started for Mexico with Somervell and Hays
	Dec. 25–6	Oury in fight at Miér, Tamaulipas, Mexico
	Dec. 28	Oury began long march for Mexico City as captive of General Ampudia
1843	Feb. 10	Miér captives arrived at Hacienda Salado
	Feb. 11	Miér captives made break for freedom
	Feb. 18	Oury and companions recaptured by Mexicans
	Mar. 25	Oury drew white bean from olla, Hacienda Salado
	May —	Oury imprisoned in Perote Prison, Mexico City
1844	Sept. 16	Oury released from Perote
1845	Sept. 28	Oury enrolled, First Regiment of Texas Mounted Volunteers, Capt. R. A. Gillespie

1846	May 8	Oury participated in Battle of Palo Alto
	May 9	Oury participated in Battle of Resaca de la Palma
	Sept. 22–4	Oury participated in Battle of Monterrey
	Sept. 29	Oury discharged "in camp at Monterrey"
1847	Jan.-Feb.	Oury with Ben McCulloch's Spy Company
1848	Aug. 1	Oury acquired land in San Antonio
1849	July 9	Oury acquired land in San Antonio
	Sept. 28	Oury acquired land in San Antonio
	———	Oury married Inez García, Durango, Mexico
	———	Oury and bride left for California goldfields
1856	Feb. —	Oury arrived in Tucson, Arizona
	Apr. —	Granville Oury arrived Tucson
	Aug. 29	G. Oury signed petition to the U. S. Congress seeking territorial status for Arizona
1857	Apr. —	G. Oury tried to rescue survivors of Crabb Expedition, Caborca, Sonora
	———	W. S. Oury named Tucson agent for Butterfield Overland Mail Company
1858	July —	W. S. Oury killed Benjamin H. Miles in a duel, Tucson
1859	———	The Reverend J. P. Machebeuf, Vicar General of New Mexico made his famous "Jornada de Muerte" from Santa Fe to Tucson. Willa Cather told the story in *Death Comes for the Archbishop*. Machebeuf and Oury were good friends.
	July 30	W. S. Oury purchased Tubac *Arizonian* (with Sylvester Mowry) from Col. Edward Cross, Tubac
1860	———	W. S. Oury killed Benito Fluornoy in a duel, Tucson
	Apr. 2–5	G. H. Oury appointed Chief Justice in Provisional Government, Tucson
1861	Feb. 4	Lt. George N. Bascom, Seventh Infantry, tried to arrest Cochise at Apache Pass Station
	Feb. 10	W. S. Oury (as Overland Mail agent) arrived at Apache Pass Station
	July 21–4	Cooke's Canyon fight
	July 29	Battle of Mesilla
	Aug. 1	Arizona Confederate Territory proclaimed
	Aug. 5	G. H. Oury elected as territorial delegate to the Confederate Congress, Richmond
1862	Feb. 28	Capt. Sherod Hunter, C.S.A., occupied Tucson
	Apr. 15	Battle of Picacho Peak
	May 20	Advance echelon of Carleton's California Column arrived in Tucson, raised American flag
	May 21	G. H. Oury issued letted to "People of Mesilla," and joined army, C.S.A., same day
	July 21	Col. Carleton appointed Major David Ferguson Commander, District of Western Arizona
	Aug. 5	Ferguson issued General Order Nr. 1
	Aug. 10	W. S. Oury named Recorder by Maj. Ferguson

1863	Feb. 22	G. H. Oury resigned from Confederate Army
	Feb. 24	Arizona attained territorial status upon President Lincoln's signature of bill
	June 1	Lt. Gilbert C. Smith, "B" Co., Fifth California Volunteer Infantry, arrived in Tucson
1864	May 8	City government convention held at Tucson; Gov. Goodwin proclaimed Tucson incorporated city
	May 11	W. S. Oury appointed as Tucson's first mayor
	June 28	W. S. Oury's Tucson property confiscated by the federal government
1865	June 20	G. H. Oury and wife, Mina, left San Antonio for Mexico
	June 26	Oury party met General Joe Shelby, ex-C.S.A.
	July 17	Oury party met sizable echelon of the French Army at Parras, Coahuila, Mexico
	Sept. 16	G. H. Oury and wife separated in Janos, Chihuahua, Mexico, to reunite in Tucson
	Sept. 24	Mina Oury and brother, Adam Sanders, reentered U. S. at El Paso, Texas
	Oct. 8	G. H. Oury swears allegiance to U. S.
	Nov. 6	Mina reunited with husband, G. H. Oury, Tucson
1866	June 11	Gilbert C. Smith appointed Chief Quartermaster, District of Arizona
	Aug. 29	Camp Lowell activated
1868	July 1	Gilbert C. Smith married Lola Oury, Tucson
	Sept. —	W. S. Oury introduced shorthorn cattle into Arizona Territory
1869	Apr. 7	Cornelius C. Smith (Sr.) born, Tucson
1871	Mar. 25	W. S. Oury, Sidney R. de Long and J. W. Hopkins called upon Gen. Stoneman to protest frequency of Apache raids around Tucson
	Apr. 10	Apache raiding party hit Papago settlement at San Xavier Mission
	Apr. 28	W. S. Oury, Jesús Maria Elías and large punitive party met at Pantano Wash near Tucson
	Apr. 30	W. S. Oury participated in Camp Grant Massacre
	May 2	General George Crook replaced Gen. Stoneman as Commander, Department of Arizona
	Dec. 13	W. S. Oury and all other Camp Grant Massacre participants acquitted in Tucson trial
1873	Mar. 19	Camp (now Fort) Lowell moved to permanent quarters on the Rillito
	———	W. S. Oury elected sheriff of Pima County (to serve until 1877)
	Aug. 6	Vincente Hernández ("Piedras Negras") and his wife murdered in their store, Tucson
	Aug. 8	Killers of Piedras Negras lynched in Plaza de las Armas, Tucson

1879	Oct.	9	W. S. Oury appointed clerk, Board of Supervisors, Tucson
1880	Mar.	20	W. S. Oury delivered key address on occasion of arrival of Southern Pacific Railroad in Tucson
	May	20	W. S. Oury scored Governor McCormick in Arizona Weekly *Star*
1883	Nov.	—	W. S. Oury moved to Tanque Verde Ranch
1884	Jan.	31	W. S. Oury elected first president, Arizona Pioneers' Historical Society, Tucson
	Feb.	9	First meeting of APHS held in Probate Court in Tucson
1885	Sept.	2	W. S. Oury appointed Deputy Collector of Customs, Tucson
1887	Mar.	31	William Sanders Oury died, Tucson
1891	Jan.	11	Granville H. Oury died
	Jan.	28	Inez G. Oury died

APPENDIX

COMMONWEALTH OF PENNSYLVANIA
PENNSYLVANIA HISTORICAL AND MUSEUM COMMISSION
BUREAU OF RESEARCH, PUBLICATIONS, AND RECORDS
STATE MUSEUM BUILDING
BOX 232
HARRISBURG, PENNSYLVANIA 17108

July 23, 1964

TO WHOM IT MAY CONCERN:

This is to certify that one   V E N D E L   O U R R Y   was commissioned

Captain of a Company in Colonel Daniel Brodhead's Eighth Pennsylvania

Regiment, according to the evidence of a General Return dated June 9,

1777.

Wm. H. Work
William H. Work
Chief
Division of Public Records

Authority: Military Returns
(Line), Records of the Supreme
Executive Council, at the
Division of Public Records.

Vendel Oury's commission as Captain in the Eighth Pennsylvania Regiment, 1777

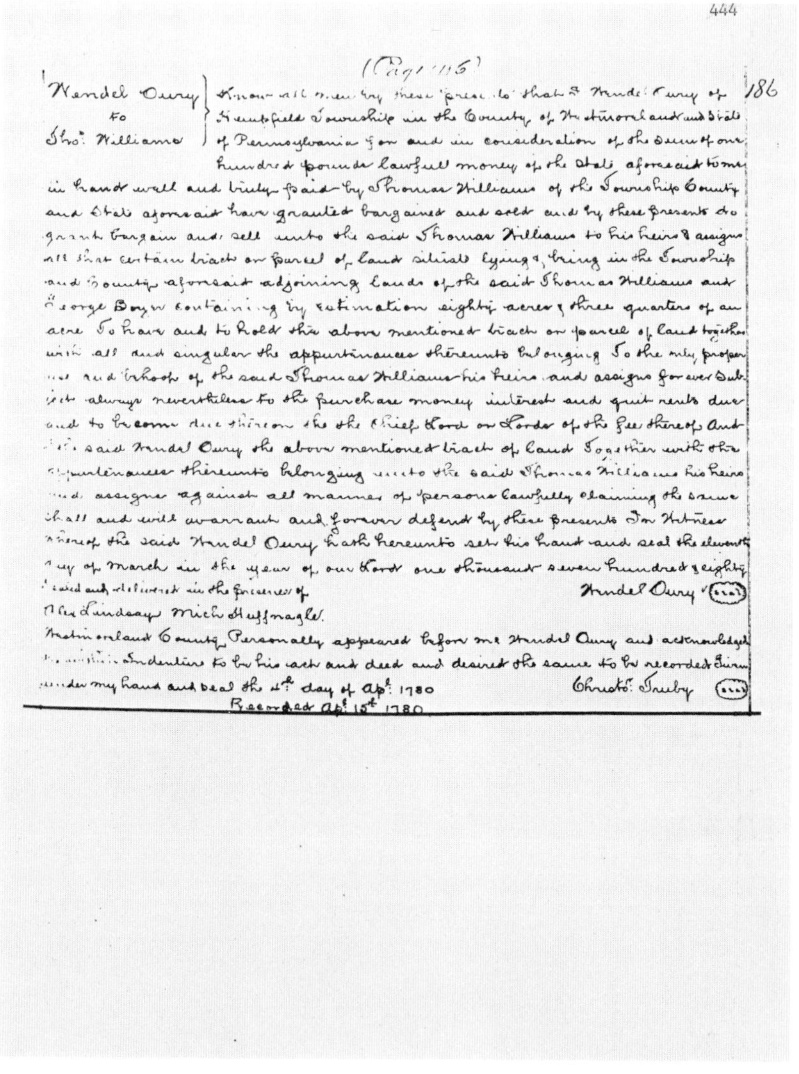

444

(Page 116)

Wendel Oury
to
Thos. Williams

186

Know all men by these presents that I Wendel Oury of Hempfield Township in the County of Westmoreland and State of Pennsylvania for and in consideration of the sum of one hundred pounds lawfull money of the State aforesaid to me in hand well and truly paid by Thomas Williams of the Township County and State aforesaid have granted bargained and sold and by these presents do grant bargain and sell unto the said Thomas Williams to his heirs & assigns all that certain tract or parcel of land situate lying & being in the Township and County aforesaid adjoining lands of the said Thomas Williams and George Boyer containing by estimation eighty acres & three quarters of an acre To have and to hold the above mentioned tract or parcel of land together with all and singular the appurtinances thereunto belonging To the only proper use and behoof of the said Thomas Williams his heirs and assigns forever Subject always nevertheless to the purchase money interest and quit rents due and to become due thereon to the Chief Lord or Lords of the fee thereof And the said Wendel Oury the above mentioned tract of land Together with the appurtenances thereunto belonging unto the said Thomas Williams his heirs and assigns against all manner of persons lawfully claiming the same shall and will warrant and forever defend by these presents In Witness whereof the said Wendel Oury hath hereunto set his hand and seal the eleventh day of March in the year of our Lord one thousand seven hundred & eighty

Sealed and delivered in the presence of

Wendel Oury (seal)

Alex Lindsay Mich Huffnagle

Westmoreland County Personally appeared before me Wendel Oury and acknowledged the within Indenture to be his act and deed and desired the same to be recorded Given under my hand and seal the 4th day of Apl. 1780

Christo. Truby (seal)

Recorded Apl. 15th 1780

Record of Wendel Oury's sale of land in Pennsylvania, in 1780

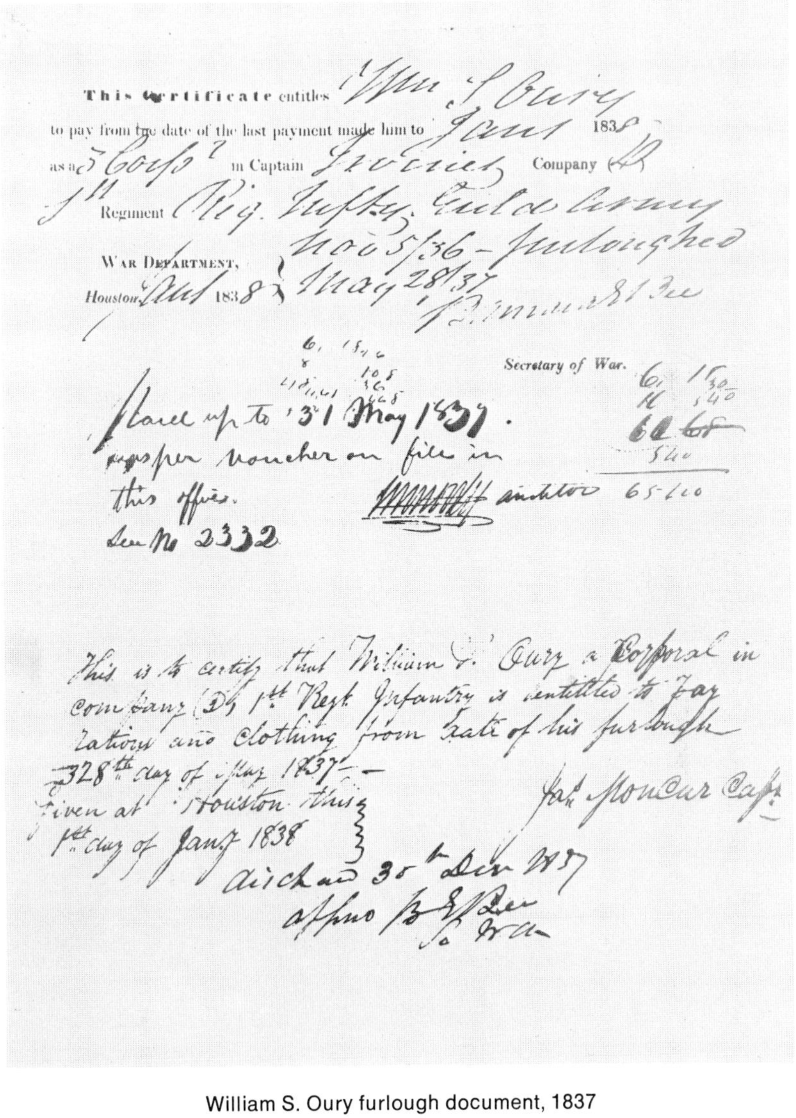

This Certificate entitles Wm. S. Oury
to pay from the date of the last payment made him to Jany 1838
as a Corpl in Captain [illegible] Company (D)
1st Regiment Reg. Infty. [illegible] Army
Nov 5/36 – furloughed
War Department,
Houston Dec 1838 May 28/37
[illegible]

Secretary of War.

Paid up to 31 May 1837
as per voucher on file in
this office.
See No 2332

[illegible] audited 65-60

This is to certify that William S. Oury a Corporal in
company (D) 1st Regt. Infantry is entitled to pay
rations and clothing from date of his furlough
28th day of May 1837 —
Given at Houston this
1st day of Jany 1838
Jas. Monroe Capt.
Audited 30th Dec 1837
Approved B. E. Bee
Se. War

William S. Oury furlough document, 1837

Pay voucher for William S. Oury from 1838

Wm. Oury

Pvt., { Capt. Gillespie's Co., Texas Mtd.
{ Rangers. (9 Months, 1845-6.)

(**Mexican War.**)

Age........years.

Appears on **Co. Muster-out Roll**, dated

San Antonio de Bexar Tex June 28 184 *6*.

Muster-out to date ...., 184 .

Last paid to *No payment* 184 .

When enrolled *Sept. 8*, 1845, for *9 mo.* *

Where enrolled *San Antonio* *

Mustered in .... *

Where ...., 184 . *

Clothing account: *

Last settled.........., 184 ; drawn since $........ 100

Due soldier $.........100; due U. S. $.........100

Am't for cloth'g in kind or money adv'd $........100

Due U. S. for arms, equipments, &c., $ 100

Bounty paid $.........100 ; due $.........100

Furnished himself subsistence and forage :

Subsistence, No. days *43*. Forage, No. days *43*.

Due N. Lewis, Sutler, $...*120* 00/100

Remarks : *Discharged Mch. 29 1846*
                                                    Oury

* The only roll of this organization as of 2d service which also
covers period of 1st service.

Book mark : ....

(361c)   *C. Chandler*
                                            Copyist.

William S. Oury's record on Texas Rangers' Muster-out Roll, 1846

[283]

Granville H. Oury's name on muster roll of Confederate Army, 1862

The Confederate States of America

To G. H. Oury Dr.

Pay at account	Commencement and expiration From	To	Term of service charged Months	Days	Pay per Mo. Dolls	Cts	Amount Dolls	Cts	Remarks
Pay for myself as Captain	July 21st 1862	February 28 1863	7	9	140	00	1022	00	
for Appointment of A.A.G.M.		January 28 1863	5	29	20	00	119	33	
							1141	33	

I hereby certify that the foregoing account is accurate and just, that I have not been absent, without leave, during any part of the time charged for, that I have not received pay, forage or received money in lieu thereof for any part of the time charged for, that the horses were actually kept in service and were mustered for the whole time charged, that for the whole of the time charged for my staff appointment, I actually and legally held the appointment and did duty in the department, that I have been a commissioned Officer for the number of years stated in the charge for every additional five years service, that I am not in arrears with the Confederate States on any account whatever and that the last payment I received was from Capt. Magoffin A.Q.M and to the 21st day of July 1862.

I, at the same time acknowledge that I have received of Capt. Jos. Magoffin A.Q.M. the sum of Eleven Hundred and Forty and One 33/100 Dollars being the amount in full of said account. this the 8th day of March 1863

Grs. Oury
Capt. Arizona Battalion

Signed Duplicate.

Severance Pay Voucher for Granville Oury

[285]

Oath of Allegiance
to the
Government of the United States

I, Granville H. Oury, do solemnly swear, that I will not voluntarily bear arms against the United States, that I will not voluntarily give aid, countenance, counsel or encouragement to persons engaged in armed hostility thereto, that I will neither seek nor accept, nor attempt to exercise the functions of any office whatever, under any authority or pretended authority in hostility to the United States; that I will not yield a voluntary support to any pretended government, authority, power or constitution within the United States hostile or inimical thereto. And I do further swear, that to the best of my knowledge and ability I will support and defend the constitution of the United States, against all enemies, foreign and domestic, that I will bear true faith and allegiance to the United States, that I take this obligation freely, without any mental reservation or purpose of evasion: So help me God.

Granville H. Oury

Sworn to before me, this eighth day of October 1865, at Fort Mason, Arizona Ty.

W. H. H. Fellows
2nd Lieut, 7th Inf. Cal. Vols
Provost Marshal
Southern Sub Dist of Arizona.

Granville H. Oury's oath of allegiance to the United States

Discriptive List of G. H. Oury a Captain in the so called Confederate Army, serving in the Arizona Regiment under Phil Herbert a Colonel in Taylors Division, served in Texas since 1862 until the close of the war;

Age	Complexion	Eyes	Hair	Height
40 Years	Florid	Blue	Light	5 feet – 10 inches

Remarks

He reported at my Office at Fort Mason A.S. and has taken the required Oath of Allegiance. his residence and place of abod Tucson Arizona Territory

Lieut W. H. H. Fellows
Provost Marshal
S.S. District of A.S.

Fort Mason October 8th 1865.

Physical Description of Granville Oury

Gilbert C. Smith's Commission

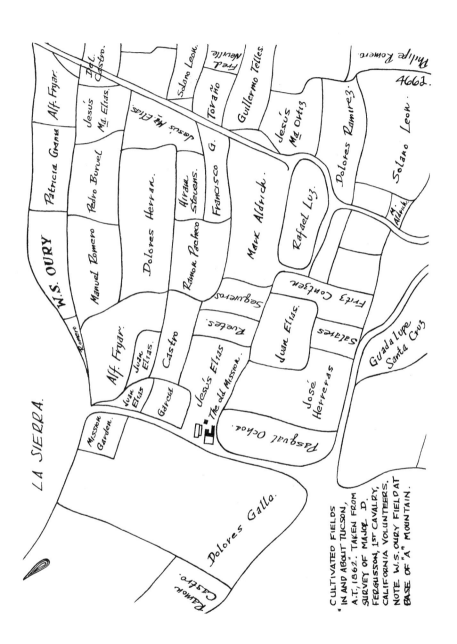

"CULTIVATED FIELDS
IN AND ABOUT TUCSON,
A.T., 1862." TAKEN FROM
SURVEY OF MAJOR D.
FERGUSSON, 1ST CAVALRY,
CALIFORNIA VOLUNTEERS.
NOTE W.S. OURY FIELD AT
BASE OF "A" MOUNTAIN.

LA SIERRA.

W.S. OURY

Alf. Fryar.
Patricia Grane
Manuel Romero
Romero
Alf. Fryar.
Mission Garden.
Juan Elias
Juan Elias.
Garcia
Castro
Jesus Elias.
The old Mission.
Dolores Galla.
Ramon Castro.
Pasqual Ochoa.
Jose Herreras.
Juan Elias.
Salares
Rieles.
Sequeres
Ramon Pachco
Dolores Herran.
Pedro Burvel
Jesus Ma. Elias.
Jesus Ma. Elias
Del. Castro.
Solano Leon.
Fred Neville
G. Toraño
Guillermo Telles.
Francisco
Hiram Stevens.
Mark Aldrich.
Rafael Luz.
Fritz Contzen
Jesus Ma. Ortiz
Dolores Ramirez.
Aldrich.
Solano Leon.
Philip Romero.
4662.
Guadalupe Santa Cruz

[289]

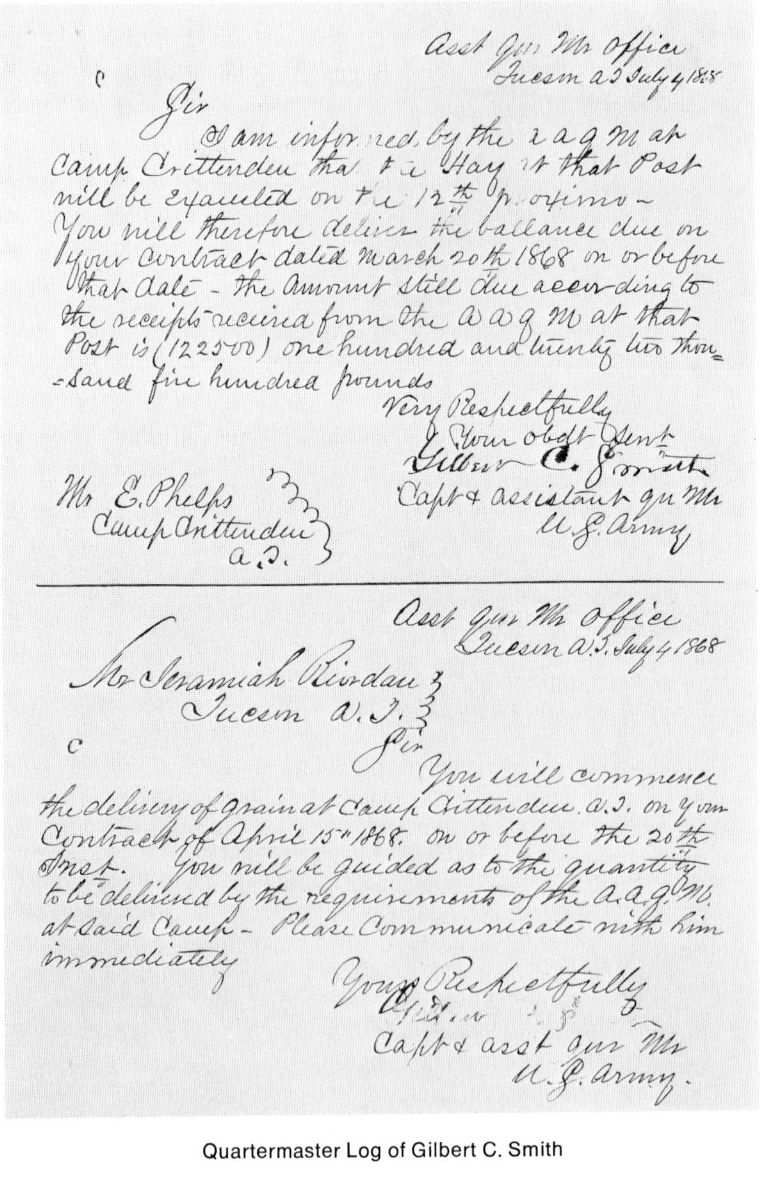

Asst Qur Mr Office
Tucson a.T. July 4 1868

Sir

I am informed by the A. A. Q. M. at
Camp Crittenden that the Hay at that Post
will be exausted on the 12th proximo –
You will therefore deliver the ballance due on
your contract dated March 20th 1868 on or before
that date – the Amount still due according to
the receipts received from the A. A. Q. M. at that
Post is (122,500) one hundred and twenty two thou_
_sand five hundred pounds

Very Respectfully
Your obdt Servt
Gilbert C. Smith
Capt & assistant Qur Mr
U. S. Army

Mr E. Phelps
Camp Crittenden
A. T.

Asst Qur Mr Office
Tucson a.T. July 4 1868

Mr Jeramiah Riordan
Tucson A. T.

Sir

You will commence
the delivery of grain at Camp Crittenden, A.T. on your
Contract of April 15th 1868. on or before the 20th
Inst. You will be guided as to the quantity
to be delivered by the requirements of the A. A. Q. M.
at said Camp – Please communicate with him
immediately

Your Respectfully
Gilbert C. Smith
Capt & asst Qur Mr
U. S. Army.

Quartermaster Log of Gilbert C. Smith

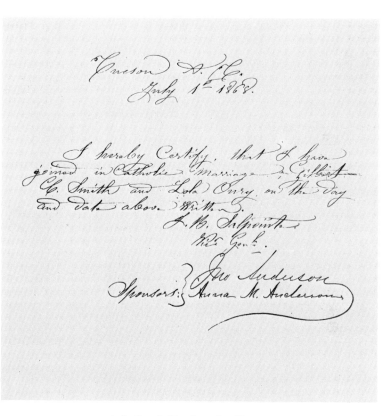

Lola Oury's Marriage Certificate

To the Society of Arizona Pioneers:

Having been chosen by our worthy President to give a paper upon some event connected with the early history of Arizona, the writer has selected as his theme, the so called Camp Grant massacre; believing it to have been one of the events most important—in its results to the peace and progress of our Apache cursed land. To give a mere recital of the act of killing a few, more or less, of blood-thirsty savages, without—a detail of the causes and provocations which drove a long-suffering and patient people to the adoption of remedial

little ones to Tucson for safety
of misery is complete up to that
now morning of April 30th, 1871,
ment was healt out to these
, and they were wiped from
Behold now the happy
following that episode: the
turn with their wives and
andoned crops on the
all other settlements
life springs up, confi
industry, bound forward

petus that has known no check in the whole fourteen years that have elapsed since that occurrence. In view of all these facts, I call on all Arizonians to answer on their consciences— can you call the killing of the Apaches at Camp Grant on the morning of the 30th of April 1871 a massacre?

Tucson Signed
April 6th 1885   Wm S Oury "

Bill Oury's Message to Pioneers' Society

[292]

INDEX

[*293*]